*Great Americana*

# The Navigator

Zadok Cramer

# The Navigator

## Eighth Edition

*by Zadok Cramer*

# Foreword

*The Navigator; Containing Directions For Navigating The Monongahela, Allegheny, Ohio and Mississippi Rivers* by Zadok Cramer, first printed in 1801, became the indispensable guide for travelers and settlers moving westward into the interior of the United States. At a dollar a copy, the book was an immediate best seller. Cramer constantly enlarged and corrected his original edition, adding material about the new territories acquired by the United States and expanding and bringing up-to-date earlier sections. In less than twenty-five years, *The Navigator* had run through twelve editions. Authors of similar guides plagiarized it freely.

The enormous popularity of *The Navigator* is easily explained. It contained the right blend of information a busy, practical people needed and wanted. Cramer told them where to obtain river boats, what to watch for in their purchase, how to load and how to pilot them. Detailed maps of the principal rivers, with textual descriptions of the towns and villages along the way, allowed the traveler to plan ahead. The individual bound for Pittsburgh knew he could expect to find the town "enveloped in thick clouds of smoke, which even affect respiration" because of the coal used in numerous manufactures there. He knew what articles Pittsburgh produced, the quantity, and the names of the persons engaged in their manufacture. If he desired to settle there, *The Navigator* told him cultivated land could not be had for under ten dollars an acre, forty if in the immediate vicinity of the town. Settlers headed farther west learned from *The Navigator* that in time of very low water Wheeling was a better starting point by boat than Pittsburgh. From the same source they knew that Cincinnati contained 400 dwellings, an elegant court house, jail, and other buildings. Perhaps they might find use for information that Mr. A. Chateau had erected a mill and distillery at St. Louis with excellent prospects for improvement. Doubtless they read with interest that planters around Natchez accumulated immense fortunes by raising cotton.

*The Navigator* also supplied historical background of the principal towns, evaluated the climate, and suggested projects for the improvement of the region. Throughout, Cramer exuded optimism about the development of the West and a pride in American accomplishment. "Prosperity smiles, must smile," he exclaimed, "on all governments equally mild, and equally just" as those of western Americans.

The present edition of 1814, the eighth, includes an appendix with material on the Louisiana Territory purchased in 1803 and an abridged account of the Lewis and Clark expedition. For more information about Cramer and his guide see Ethel C. Leahy, *Who's Who on the Ohio River and Its Tributaries* (Cincinnati, 1931), pp. 79-81, and Archer B. Hulbert, *Historic Highways of America* (Cleveland, 1903), IX, 73-99.

THE

# NAVIGATOR;

CONTAINING DIRECTIONS FOR NAVIGATING

## THE MONONGAHELA, ALLEGHENY, OHIO

## AND MISSISSIPPI RIVERS;

WITH AN AMPLE ACCOUNT

OF THESE MUCH ADMIRED WATERS,

FROM THE HEAD OF THE FORMER TO THE MOUTH
OF THE LATTER;

AND A CONCISE DESCRIPTION

OF THEIR

TOWNS, VILLAGES, HARBORS, SETTLEMENTS, &c.

WITH MAPS OF THE OHIO AND MISSISSIPPI.

———

TO WHICH IS ADDED

## AN APPENDIX,

CONTAINING AN ACCOUNT OF LOUISIANA,
AND OF THE MISSOURI AND COLUMBIA RIVERS, AS
DISCOVERED BY THE VOYAGE UNDER
CAPTS. LEWIS AND CLARK.

EIGHTH EDITION—IMPROVED AND ENLARGED.

———

## PITTSBURGH,

Published & Sold
BY CRAMER, SPEAR AND EICHBAUM,
FRANKLIN HEAD, MARKET
STREET.

—

Robert Ferguson & Co. Printers.
1814.

# DISTRICT OF PENNSYLVANIA, to wit:

# Advertisement.

---

THIS edition of the Navigator, being the eighth since the year 1801, is respectfully presented to the public.— It being designedly calculated as an useful and necessary guide to those who navigate or trade on the rivers of which it treats, much pains have been taken to revise, correct, and enlarge it throughout; to do this satisfactorily, we have had the assistance of several of the most eminent pilots and navigators, and the use of late manuscript journals of gentlemen of observation, to whom we present our compliments for their aid and politeness.

At a very considerable expense, the maps of the Ohio and Mississippi rivers have been added; and we flatter ourselves with the hope that they will be found as useful to the navigator as they have been troublesome to us.— These of the Ohio have been taken from actual survey— Those of the Mississippi partly from survey and partly from private charts, taken as accurately as the nature of that river will permit.

The account of the Missouri and Columbia rivers, as traversed by captains Lewis and Clark under the direction of the president of the United States, though but a brief view of that interesting voyage, we hope will be found entertaining. It has been collected from the letters of captain Clark and other publications since the return of the party.

The account of Louisiana is highly interesting; and it has been collected from documents published by the directions of the congress and executive of the United States, shortly after the acquisition of that country.

This edition is considerably enlarged by a more comprehensive description of the principal towns on and adjacent to the rivers; their commerce and manufactures; natural curiosities of the country, &c. The directions for navigating the Mississippi river from the mouth of the Illinois to that of the Ohio river; with the description of the District of Mobile, and geographical notice of Florida, will be found interesting.

Conscious of the imperfections of the Navigator, we depend much on the goodness of others to detect its errors and point them out to us, in order that they may be corrected in a future edition; observations, also, either of the rivers or the country through which they run, tending to enhance its value and make it more generally useful, will be thankfully acknowledged.

Upon the whole, we can assure the reader, that we have spared no pains to make this a useful book, and nothing is wanting but his aid as an encouragement to continue our labours to make it still more so.

THE EDITOR.

February, 1811.

# CONTENTS.

—

## APPENDIX.

## ADDENDA.

# References

# MAP OF PITTSBURGH.

———

O Episcopal church, situated on the angle formed by the junction of Liberty and Wood streets. 1 Court house, on the opposite side of the street is the Market house. 2 Presbyterian meeting house. 3 Dutch Lutheran church. 4 Office of discount and deposit, 5 Fort Fayette. 6 Covenanters' meeting house. 7 Ship-yard, immediately below which Suke's run empties in. 8 Jail. 9 Ruins of Fort Pitt. 10 Scite of Fort Du Quesne. 11 Glass works. 12 Academy. On the N. side of the Allegheny, are two ferry-houses, the uppermost belongs to major Craig and the next below to James Robinson, esq. On the S. side of the Monongahela the first house above the glass-works is Jones's ferry, the next above Black's or Beattie's, the next Bousman's, the next widow Craig's, the next Herd's, and about half a mile above this, though not mentioned in the map, is Emmet's, and opposite to it is Andrew Watson's, esq. On the right side of the Ohio, and opposite the entrance of the Allegheny, is a small island, about half a mile long. Some years since the state of Pennsylvania granted this to colonel Killbuck, an Indian chief of the Six Nations, by whom it is still held. It is now called Smoky island — the hill to the S. of the Monongahela is Coal-hill; that jutting out close to the ship-yard, is called Ayres-hill or Silver banks, belonging to Andrew Watson, esq.

The point of Grant's hill (not represented) enters the square formed by Fourth-street, Hammond alley, Cherry alley, and Grant street.

The streets running parallel to the Allegheny, are first, Penn, and next Liberty; the cross streets from Liberty to the Allegheny, are, beginning at the lowermost, Marbury and Hay streets, ——alley, Pitt street ——alley, St. Clair street, ——alley, Irwin's street, ——alley Hand street, ——alley, Wayne street. Those running parallel with the

Monongahela are, first, Water, Front, Second, Third and
Fourth streets, Hammond alley, Fifth street, Virgin alley,
Sixth street, Strawberry alley, Seventh street, Plumb alley,
Eighth street.  The streets and alleys intersecting these
are, beginning at the lowermost, West street, Short street,
Redoubt alley, Ferry street, Chancery lane, Market street,
Wood street, Smithfield street, Cherry alley, Grant street.

It may be noted that none of the streets cross each other
at right angles except those from Liberty street to the Allegheny.

☞ The top of the map is due north, the bottom south,
the right east, and the lower part west.

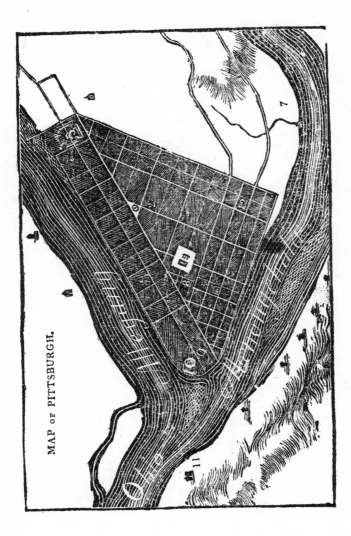

MAP OF PITTSBURGH.

# GENERAL DESCRIPTION

## OF

# *The Rivers.*

———◦❋◦———

## OF THE MONONGAHELA.*

NO country perhaps in the world is better watered with limpid streams and navigable rivers than the United States of America, and no people better deserve those advantages, or are better calculated to make a proper use of them than her industrious and adventurous citizens.

The Monongahela takes its rise at the foot of the Laurel mountain, in Virginia, thence meandering to a N. by E. direction, passes into Pennsylvania, and receives Cheat river from the S. S. E. thence winding to a N. by W. direction, separates Fayette and Westmoreland from Washington county, and passing into Allegheny county, receives the Youghiogheny river from the S. S. E. and unites with the Allegheny river at Pittsburgh, 13 miles below the mouth of the Yough, and about 55 by land, below the mouth of Cheat. The Monongahela is about 450 yards wide at its mouth, measuring from bank to bank, and in the fall and spring freshes, has water enough to carry ships of 400 tons burden; these freshes, however, subside quickly, and render the navigation of such vessels very precarious.

The Monongahela, after it enters Pennsylvania, runs through a rich and well settled country. Its waters, when high, are coloured with the washy disposition of clay-loam land, of which is borne down with its current a thick sed-

* This word is said to signify, in some of the Indian languages, *The Falling-in-Banks;* that is, the stream of the Falling-in, or Mouldering Banks.

B

iment.  Its banks are generally firm, bearing large and
stately trees of the buttonwood, hickory, white and black
oak, walnut, sugar-maple, beach, &c. and these afford a
good supply of logs for the numerous saw-mills erected
at and near the mouths of the creeks emptying into the
river.

This river, like most others in this country, is accompanied with considerable hills on each side, which sometimes approach close to the banks, and again recede, leaving spacious and rich bottoms, in which are generally
found large sugar camps, each sugar-tree producing, if
well managed during the season, four pounds of excellent
sugar, equal to Musquevado, especially if it has time to
ripen before used; and each pound is worth 13 cents;
thus, a sugar-camp containing 500 trees produces 2000
pounds of sugar, worth 260 dollars.  The sugar season
seldom lasts more than a month or six weeks, and a camp
of this size can be attended by one man and three or four
boys to carry the water—thus, leaving a handsome salary
for each during a season that very little else can be done
on a farm.  The sugar season sometimes however is precarious, owing to the irregularity of the breaking up of
winter, and the ushering in of spring.  But it certainly
would be provident in farmers to take special care of their
sugar trees, and rather than destroy a grove of 50 trees,
plant an orchard of 1000.  In order to give a spur to this
species of economy, our merchants ought not to receive
a pound of sugar from over the mountains, and by this
means give every encouragement for the use and consumption of sugar made at home.  This would stimulate
the farmer and reward the labourer.  The policy of such
a plan would be wise, and be the means of saving many
thousands of dollars in the country, which are now sent
out for sugars, of different kinds.  Indeed I do not see
why loaf and lump sugar could not be manufactured from
our maple sugar as good as that produced from the West
India sugar cane.

The land being generally rich on the Monongahela,
crops of wheat, rye, barley, oats, buckwheat, corn, potatoes, &c. are raised in great abundance; flax and hemp
are too much neglected.  The Monongahela flour is celebrated in foreign markets, for its superiority, and it gen-

erally sells for one dollar more per barrel in New Orleans than any other flour taken from this country to that market. The best and greatest quantity of rye whiskey is made on this river. Peach and apple brandy, cider and cider-royal, are also made in great abundance.

The mean velocity of the Monongahela is about two miles an hour, and from three to four miles when very high. The floods seldom rise above the common banks; when they do, it is noticed as remarkable, and much mischief is done by the sweeping waters, as was the case in May, 1807, when the floods rose at Brownsville about 40 feet above the common surface of the river. It is said that at least 15 grist mills, on and near the river, between Pittsburgh and Morgantown, were carried off and destroyed during this fresh, and with them, about 5,000 bushels of wheat, rye, and corn. Several mills were seen floating past Pittsburgh in one day, out of which skiff loads of wheat were taken by the citizens.

The navigation of the Monongahela is pretty good in its middling state of water, for periogues, keels, canoes and skiffs, from Pittsburgh to Brownsville, and from thence to Morgantown, a distance of about 100 miles above its mouth; above this the navigation is frequently interrupted by rapids, but small crafts may go up with difficulty as high as Clarksburgh, about 40 miles above Morgantown. The West branch of this river in high water is navigable for 15 miles, and communicates with a Southern branch of Little Kenhawa, by a portage of eight or ten miles.

It is matter of much importance that an easy and short portage could be had to connect the waters of the Potomack with those of the Monongahela. The head waters of Cheat and the Potomack, come together within about 30 miles, to which portage however, the navigation of both rivers is difficult, but might be rendered much better by clearing them out. Goods are at this time frequently boated up from Alexandria, Georgetown, &c. as high as Fort Cumberland, whence they are taken in wagons to Brownsville, a distance of about 80 miles.—By this route it costs about $2 50 per hundred pounds, from Alexandria to Brownsville, which is a saving of about $2 50 in the 100lbs. when brought all the way by land.

On the Monongahela old fortifications are frequently discovered, as vestiges of a people of whom time has kept no other record, and of whose character the present race of man can form but a feint idea; for like the mammoth, they have left nothing behind them but evident marks of their once having possession of the country, and having been well acquainted with the arts of war, and perhaps as well with those of peace, if we may judge from the quantity and quality of pottery, and many other articles of household convenience, found all through this country, as well as in many parts of the United States; all shewing the work of ingenious artists. Curious carving on rocks are to be seen on many parts of the Monongahela. At the mouth of Ten mile creek, above Redstone, there are many; some bearing the shape of a man's foot, a horse's foot, a hand, head, a turkey, a fish, birds, beasts, &c. all apparently carved by a people having had more tools than our Indians can be supposed to have had in those early periods of time. Of the nation of people having left those curious traces behind them, some ingenious writers are strongly disposed to believe them to have been from Wales in Britain; but it is highly questionable whether their history does not go far beyond the history of England, or any other part of Europe, and I have sometimes thought the discoveries of time may yet prove them older than the earliest history we have of the world. How they became extinct, be they whom they might, is a question equally difficult of solution.

One of the principal branches of the Monongahela is the Youghiogheny river, whose sources are divided from those of the Potomack by the Allegheny mountain; from the falls, where it intersects the Laurel mountain, to fort Cumberland, the head of the navigation of the Potomack, is 40 miles of very mountainous road. On the Youghiogheny and the streams emptying into it, are a number of valuable forges, furnaces, saw and grist mills, some fine farms and villages, among which, Connelsville, 45 miles by land above Pittsburgh, is the principal one. It is a thriving little town of Fayette county, 11 miles north of Uniontown, and 20 south of Greensburgh; pleasantly situate on the east bank of the river, over which there is a good frame bridge—In the year 1810 it contained 500 inhabitants. On the opposite side of the river is the village of New Haven, containg about 160 inhabitants—This place has usually been considered as the head of the navigation of the Yough river, although boats have come down from the mouth of Indian creek, which empties in about 6 miles above. Near the mouth of this creek there is a forge erecting by Messrs. Mochbee & Werts, which is now nearly ready to work—These gentlemen are also boring for salt-water on an island in the river a little below. The salt-works owned by J. Meason & J. Meason, jun. esqrs. are situated on the river 4 or 5 miles above Connelsville, and make from 25 to 30 bushels of salt per day. A little below on the river is the fine paper mill owned by Messrs. D. and J. Rogers & Walker, now in complete operation. A mile above town is Mr. Meason's forge. In the towns of New Haven and Connelsville are 1 air foundery, 1 rolling and slitting mill, 2 grist mills, 1 fulling mill, and 4 carding machines. Messrs. Baldwin, Norton & Mears are now erecting a cotton factory in the vicinity of Connelsville. About $\frac{1}{4}$ mile below the town are Messrs. Gibsons' rolling and slitting mill, grist mill, and tilt-hammer; one mile below town are Gibson's forge, grist mill and saw mill; two miles further down are Stouffer's grist mill, saw mill, and fulling mill; and seven miles below Connelsville, on the river, at the Little Falls, are M. Gibson's forge, furnace, grist mill, saw mill, and tilt-hammer. In short, the durableness of the streams, added to their rapidity, afford numberless seats for water-works of every description. A Mr. Lauderburn has discovered an extensive bank of earth near Connelsville, which, when burnt, serves all the purposes of Spanish-brown in painting; and of which he supplied in 1810 Messrs. Skeltons of Pittsburgh with 60,000 lbs.

Messrs. Huston & Taylor are now erecting a rolling and slitting mill on Dunbar creek, which empties into Yough one mile above Connelsville. On Indian creek are Fountain furnace, built in 1809 by Trevor & Rodgers; Mount Hope furnace, built in 1813 by Trevor & Sheave, (which makes iron at the rate of 21 tons per week, and of a quality equal to Juniata) and St. John's furnace, built about the year 1808. Messrs. M'Clurg & Barnes are also building a furnace on Jacob's creek, which is a tributary stream to the Youghiogheny, emptying itself about 10 miles below Connelsville. The great number of factories,

particularly in the iron way, in the neighborhood of Connelsville, will always render it a flourishing and lively
place for business, and by the fine markets which they
create for country produce, will also rapidly increase the
wealth of the farmers in its vicinity.

---

## OF THE ALLEGHENY.*

THIS is a beautiful, large, and navigable river, taking
its rise in Lycoming county, Pennsylvania, within a few
miles of the head waters of Sinemahoning creek, a navigable stream that falls into the Susquehanna river, to
which there is a portage of 23 miles. Thence pursuing
a north course, passes into New York state, winding to
the N.W. about 20 miles, turns gradually to the S.W. enters Pennsylvania, and meandering in about that direction
180 miles, joins the Monongahela at Pittsburgh.

Few rivers and perhaps none excel the Allegheny for
the transparency of its water, or the beauty of its bottom,
having a fine gravelly bed, clear of rocks and uninterrupted by falls. Its surface is unbroken, and its mean velocity
is about $2\frac{1}{2}$ miles an hour; when high it runs at the rate
of four miles an hour, being a little more rapid in its
course than the Monongahela. Its waters in some instances have proved medicinal; and the fish caught in it
are allowed to be superior to those of the Monongahela.

The Allegheny in its windings receives many large and
tributary streams: among these are the Kiskiminetas,
which is navigable for batteaux 40 or 50 miles, and good
portages are found between it and the Juniata; it enters
the Allegheny about 14 miles below Kittanning, the county town of Armstrong county, Pa. lat. 40° 40'—45 miles

---

* The word *Allegheny* seems to have been derived from an ancient tribe of Indians, called the " *Tallegawe,*" who, though represented to have been a tall and stout race of men, were totally
routed and extirpated by the Delawares and those of their stock.
The Delaware Indians do not say, " Allegheny"—but " Allegawe," and again " Allegawenink," which signifies with them,
as much as to say, " in the country of the Tallegawe—or the
country inhabited by the Tallegawe, or Allegawe people."

                                    *Western Tour,* p. 455.

above Pittsburgh. The Kiskiminetas receives in its course Little Conemaugh and Stone creek, which forms its head waters; after their junction it is called Conemaugh river;* it then receives Black Lick from the N.E. and 17 miles from its mouth Loyalhanna creek enters from the S.S.E.—Muhulbuctitum, another branch ʳ the Allegheny, 20 miles above, is passable in small crafts to the settlements in Northumberland county; Wheeling is its northern branch. Toby's creek enters the Allegheny 20 miles below Fort Franklin, may be navigated in flat bottomed boats a considerable way up, thence by a short portage to the west branch of the Susquehanna, by which a valuable communication is formed between the Ohio country and the eastern parts of Pennsylvania. French creek is a N. Western branch of the Allegheny, and enters it at Fort Franklin, 80 miles N.E. of Pittsburgh; it is navigable to Le Bœuf, now called Waterford, from whence to Erie there is a portage of 15 miles, on which a turnpike is now erected.

The Allegheny affords another communication to Lake Erie by way of the Conewango creek, at whose head is a small lake called Chatauque, thence to Portland, a new town laid off by Mr. John M'Mahon, on the bank of lake Erie, there is a good portage of but 9 miles. A small creek, called Chatauque, enters lake Erie at Portland, which is about thirty miles below the town of Erie, in the state of New York.

The trade carried on between the lakes and the Ohio, by way of the Allegheny and its branches, is at this time [1810] very considerable, and must in a few years become of great importance. There are about 4000 or 5000 barrels, and sometimes more, of Onondago salt brought down to Pittsburgh annually, worth per barrel 9 dollars, making an average of about 40,000 dollars worth of traffic in this one article. Exclusive of the article salt, there are an immense number of boards, shingles, and lumber of different kinds, floated down to Pittsburgh and the country be-

Salt water lately discovered itself oozing through the bed of this river, about half a mile above its junction with the Loyalhanna, 17 miles from the Allegheny by the Kiskiminetas, and 7 miles from New Alexandria in Westmoreland county, Penn.—Works for making salt have been erected, and are successfully conducted.

low on the Ohio. The quantity of boards and lumber that arrive yearly at Pittsburgh from the Allegheny and French creek, is supposed to be about 3,000,000 feet,* averaging about 9 dollars per 1000 feet, amounting to 27,000 dollars ; this added to the amount of the salt, makes the handsome sum to domestic trade of 67,000 dollars.

In the fall and spring of 1809–10, the quantity of Onondaga salt had increased in our market to the amount of between 12, and 14,000 barrels averaging eight dollars per barrel, amounting to about 104,000 dollars. So great a quantity, however, may not again be expected from that quarter, since the owners of the Kenhawa salt works say they can deliver at this place any quantity at from five to six dollars per barrel, a price at which it is thought impossible to deliver Onondaga salt, owing to the great distance it has to come, and the frequent reshipments, storages, land carriage, &c.

In return, the keel boats ascend loaded with whiskey, iron and castings, cider, apples, bacon, and many other articles of home production—and merchandise of foreign importation.—As long as the water keeps good, that is, neither too high nor too low, boats are ascending and descending continually, making a trip up in 17 days, and down in 5 days.

It has been suggested that goods might be brought by water from New York to Pittsburgh by way of the lakes and this river, for three cents a pound, which is one half less than is generally given from Philadelphia to Pittsburgh  By this Northern route, which would certainly be a very long and tedious one, there would be a portage of 15 miles from Albany on the Hudson or North river to Schenectada on the Mohawk, thence up that river and through Wood creek into lake Ontario, thence up Niagara river to the falls, thence 10 miles around Niagara falls, thence by water up Erie lake to the town of Erie, thence 15 miles portage to Waterford or Le Bœuf, thence down French creek and Allegheny river, making in all a land

* Mr Lambden, one of our board inspectors for the borough, informs that for the year 1812, about seven million feet of boards and scantling passed inspection.  The average price of lumber this spring, 1814, is $15 per 1000 feet.

carriage of 40 miles from New York to Pittsburgh, a distance by this route of not less than 850 miles.

The brig Dean, Galley Ross, and several other vessels of burden, were built on the Allegheny, and we hope to see many more borne down by the current of this beautiful stream. A brig of 160 tons burden was put on the stocks at the mouth of Plumb creek, on the Allegheny river, 12 miles above Pittsburgh, in the fall of 1809, and launched in the uncommonly high freshet* of November 11, (Sunday) 1810. She was constructed and built by Nathan Jones, shipcarpenter, and is owned by Brintley Robbins, an enterprising farmer. The brig is calculated for a double-decker, and will serve either for peace or war. She is of handsome construction, and perhaps has not been exceeded for beauty or durability by any that have left the western waters.

The Allegheny river joins the Monongahela nearly at right angles, and its current being more rapid, it generally marks its course across the mouth of the latter river,

---

* The Allegheny and Monongahela rivers rose at this place at a most rapid rate from about sunset Saturday evening until Sunday 12 o'clock at night, when they appeared at a stand, and soon began to give signs of withdrawing their floods from the already injured and alarmed inhabitants of their banks. The waters rose about 37 feet above the common level of the rivers, and both streams seemed equally strong, for neither appeared detained by the other in their sweeping courses. The water of the Monongahela was within eight feet of the level of Market street, and ascended Wood street gutters to Front street, and measured four feet on the ground floor of Mr Graham's tavern, corner of Wood and Water streets, and about the same depth in Messrs. T. & J. Cromwell's warehouse. The public wharf on the Allegheny river, opposite Fort Fayette, was carried off. Penn and Liberty streets were inundated, and the first floor of James Robinson, Esq's house, which stands on a second bank on the west side of the Allegheny, is said to have been covered with water.

A curious circumstance took place at Marietta. The Ohio had backed up the Muskingum for 12 miles, and occasioned a considerable retrograde current, into which some New Orleans boats got, and being enveloped in a heavy fog they discovered their mistake by being hailed as ascending the Muskingum.

This flood appears to have been about five feet three inches higher at Pittsburgh than those of 1807-8, which were at that time considered to have been the highest known for 20 or 30 years.

and forces the current of the Monongahela on the opposite shore with great impetuosity. Though their streams are now united, the clear and transparent water of the one and the muddy appearance of the other, form a singular contrast, and this difference is plainly observable ten or fifteen miles below their junction.

The Allegheny is about 400 yards wide at its mouth, and when Smoky island, lying to the N. W. is washed away, it will be nearer eight.——It runs through an immense tract of country, much of it rough and hilly land, the greater part of which is yet to be settled.——This river as well as the Ohio, are known and called by the name of Allegheny river by the Seneca, and other tribes of the Six Nations of Indians, from its head waters until it enters the Mississippi.

Among the natural advantages of the waters of the Allegheny, is *Oil* creek, which empties into that river about 100 miles from Pittsburgh. This creek issues from a spring on the top of which floats an oil similar to that called Barbadoes tar, and is found in such quantities that a person may gather several gallons a day. The oil is said to be very efficacious in rheumatic pains, rubbed on the parts affected. The troops sent to guard the Western posts, halted at this spring, collected some of the oil and bathed their joints with it; this gave them great relief from the rheumatic complaints, with which they were afflicted. They also drank freely of the water, which operated on them as a gentle cathartic.

This oil is called *Seneca Oil* in Pittsburgh, probably from its first having been discovered and used, by a nation of Indians of that name.

It is wise plan in Nature, to generally place an antidote where she has planted a poison.——No climate perhaps is more subject to pains of the rheumatic kind than ours, arising from the sudden transitions of heat to cold, and vice versa——and if it be true that the qualities of this oil are so effectual in the cure of diseases to which we are more or less subject, from the nature of our climate——it is equally true that Nature in her wisdom, has not been unmindful of her general plan of providing a good for an evil in this particular instance.

On the Allegheny and French creek, there are large bodies of low lands, covered with fine white pine and hemlock. These are noble trees, measuring from three to five feet in diameter at the butt; are remarkably tall and straight, and without limbs to near the top. They are well calculated for masts of ships, and can be floated down in high water with ease to Pittsburgh, thence down the Ohio and Mississippi; the heavy sediment of the latter river however, would perhaps tend to sink them and make them troublesome to float.——These white pine swamps afford also an immense number of excellent boards, and shingles, and lumber of different kinds, for Pittsburgh, and towns on the Ohio. Boats go loaded with pine boards even to New Orleans, where they sell for about 3 dollars per 100 feet.

Among the numerous advantages of the Allegheny river, there is one which may have escaped general observation, and this of immense value. Pittsburgh is badly situated for water courses giving fall sufficient for millseats, and such as afford water all the year. The Allegheny presents a remedy for this deficiency. By taking the water out of the river ten or fifteen miles above the town, and conduct it in a canal along the side of the hill down to the point of Grant's Hill, there may be had a fall of from 12 to 15 feet, and water in abundance at all seasons to turn as many works and mills as could stand together in the distance of two miles or more. This to be sure would cost a handsome capital. But no matter, since there is a security of that capital being expended in a stock which would probably yield 15 or 20 per cent, and a stock too as permanent as the running of the waters of the Allegheny itself. The thing at present may be thought visionary, but I should not be surprised, were life to last, to see some of the children now shouting about the streets of Pittsburgh, engaged in this project some 20 or 30 years hence,

## OF THE OHIO.*

The junction of the Allegheny and Monongahela rivers form the Ohio, and this discharges itself into the Mississippi, (in N. lat. 36° 43′ Hutchins—37° 0′ 23″ and W. long. 5° 55′ 38″ according to Mr. Ellicot†) about 1188 computed miles from Pittsburgh. The Ohio in its passage to the Mississippi, glides through a pleasant, fruitful, and healthy country, and carries a great uniformity of breadth, from 400 to 600 yards, except at its confluence with the Mississippi and for 100 miles above it, where it is 1000 yards wide; about 100 miles above the falls, which are 705 miles below Pittsburgh, it is 700 yards wide.

The Ohio has been described, as "beyond all competition, the most beautiful river in the universe, whether we consider it for its meandering course through an immense region of forests, for its clean and elegant banks, which afford innumerable delightful situations for cities, villages, and improved farms: or for those many other advantages, which truly entitle it to the name originally given it by the French, of "*La Belle Riviere*," that is, "the Beautiful river." This description was penned several years since, and it has not generally been thought an exaggerated one. Now the immense forests recede,

* This name is said to signify in some of the Indian languages, Bloody; so that the Ohio may be translated the River of Blood.
  *Brackenridge's Gazette Publication.*

† Mr. Ellicot in his Journal down the Ohio, having arrived at the mouth of that river, observes, "On the top of the stump of a large tree, to which the zenith sector was fixed, a plate of lead was laid, containing the latitude and longitude of that place.— The stump was then covered by a mound of earth of considerable magnitude; but which will probably be demolished in a few years by the annual inundations" Mr Ellicot and his party were detained at the mouth of the Ohio, in consequence of the inclemency of the season, from the 18th Dec. 1796, to the 31st of Jan. following, during which period, he ascertained from accurate observations, the latitude and longitude of the junction of the Ohio and Mississippi rivers, as above stated. It may be proper to inform the reader that Mr And. Ellicot was appointed commissioner on the part of the U S. for determining the boundary between them and the possessions of his Catholic majesty, from the year 1796 till 1800.

cultivation smiles along its banks, towns every here and there decorate its shores, and it is not extravagant to suppose, that the day is not very far distant when its whole margin will form one continued village.

The reasons for this supposition are numerous—the principal ones are, the immense tracts of fine country that have communication with the Ohio by means of the great number of navigable waters that empty into it; the extraordinary fertility, extent, and beauty of the river bottoms, generally high, dry, and with few or no exceptions, remarkably healthy, and the superior excellence of its navigation, through means of which, the various productions of the most extensive and fertile parts of the United States must eventually be sent to market.

For 30 miles below Pittsburgh it takes a N. W. course, then turns gradually to the W. S. W. and pursuing that course for about 500 miles, turns to the S. W. for nearly 170 miles, then it turns westward 280 miles, thence S. W. 180 miles, and empties itself into the Mississippi, in a flat and swampy country, where there are no hills to variegate the scene, nor mountains to overtop the union of these two noble streams.

The numerous islands that are interspersed in this river, in many instances, add much to the grandeur of its appearance, but they embarrass the navigation considerably, particularly in low water, as they occasion a great many shoals and sandbars. The soil of the islands for the most part is rich, timber luxuriant, and the extent of many of them considerable. Fruit is raised to great perfection on them, and seldom fail of a crop, as is generally the case in all the river bottoms.

In low water the navigation of the Ohio is difficult to the old Mingo-town,* about 75 miles below Pittsburgh; from thence to the Mississippi it is good for keel boats or barges carrying from 100 to 200 tons burden; up from thence it may be navigated with smaller crafts. In times of high water, vessels of 400 tons burden can descend with ease, except the difficulty arising from managing so unwieldy a bulk at the points of islands and short turns in the channel

* This was the only Indian village in 1766 on the banks of the Ohio from that place to Fort Pitt; it contained at that time 60 families. *Hutchins.*

C

of the river. Vessels of this tonnage have descended from Pittsburgh to Orleans in safety, but the chance of good water renders the undertaking a little hazardous. The Falls, however, are much the greatest impediment, for, unless vessels happen to hit the time of the highest stage of water, they are either detained, perhaps till the next season, or, if they attempt a passage over them, a wreck in part or in whole may be the consequence, in either case, putting in jeopardy property to an amount that few individuals can bear the loss of. A lock-canal round the Falls would remove this difficulty, and be of an immense advantage to the Ohio trade, and to the people on or near the river from the Falls up to the head of the Allegheny and Monongahela rivers.—There has been some talk of attempting the commencement of this lock-canal. What jarring and clashing interests prevent the undertaking, are not easily to be found out. It can scarcely be supposed to be the want of a publick spirit in the Kentuckians or their legislature.

There are many smaller impediments, however, in the river from Pittsburgh to the Mingo-town, which may be as long getting removed as even the Falls themselves : these consist of rocks that might be blown to pieces, and ripples that might be easily cleared out in such a way as to make the channel good through them. This is certainly an important national concern, but the people must begin to act first, before their representatives will bring the thing forward in the house of general assembly. It must be done by grants of monies from the state, aided by subscriptions from the people ; both must be liberal and vigilant, or the object will never be accomplished.

The consideration for opening the navigation of the Ohio, has become a matter of greater importance and necessity for the interest of Pennsylvania now than ever before. The United States' road from Cumberland on the Potomack, to Wheeling on the Ohio, when completed, will naturally draw a great deal of the trade of the northern states to the states of Ohio, Kentucky, Tennessee, and to Louisiana, through that channel, thereby abridging very much the trade from those states through Pennsylvania. Therefore, if Pennsylvania looks closely to her own interests, she will find that the completing the turnpike road from Harrisburgh to Pittsburgh, and opening the navigation of the Ohio, are the two principal objects which will tend to secure to her, her usual commercial, foreign and domestick, advantages. Exclusive of the probability of the United States' road drawing the trade to the south of Pennsylvania, New York state, on the north, is pushing her inland navigation, and opening easy communications from one end of the state to the other, by way of turnpikes, canals, &c. to an extent unparalleled in any other state in the Union. The spirit of the people in the back part of the state of New York is peculiarly turned to this point, and no exertions seem to be lacking in the industry of the one class; or money wanting from the other. The purses of the one and the labour of the other seem to be happily united for the good of the whole. When this is the case, a state must flourish in her internal improvements, and of course advance to wealth and independence.

The Ohio river has on its left in descending, Pennsylvania as far as the mouth of Mill creek; Virginia to the mouth of Big Sandy river; and the state of Kentucky about 60 miles below the mouth of the Ohio. On the right, Pennsylvania to the line crossing just below the mouth of Little Beaver; the state of Ohio from thence to the mouth of the Great Miami; and below this the Indiana to the mouth of the Wabash; thence to the Mississippi, the Illinois territory.

It receives in its course many large and navigable streams, the principal of which are; on the right, Big and Little Beaver, Muskingum, Sciota, Little and Great Miami, and the Wabash. On the left, Little and Great Kanhawa, Sandy, Licking, Kentucky, Green, Cumberland, and Tennessee rivers:— These will be more particularly mentioned as we go on with directions for navigating the Ohio.

The fish of the Ohio are numerous and of various kinds: the black and yellow cat, weighing from 3 to 100 pounds; the buffaloe, from 5 to 30 pounds; the pike from 4 to 15 pounds; the sturgeon from 4 to 40; the perch from 3 to 12 pounds; the sucker from 1 to 6 pounds; a few herrings sometimes caught, and in the spring of 1805, several shad were caught and sold in the Pittsburgh market, weighing about two pounds; eels and soft shelled turtles are sometimes caught.—These ascend the Allegheny and Monongahela rivers, and their principal branches, and are caught in seines, baskets, pots, and with trot-lines, hooks and lines, &c. The different species of the wild duck are numerous, and a few geese, brant, &c. are seen on the river, and the swan has sometimes been seen stemming the current. Turkies, pheasant and partridges, are numerous on its banks ; these, with the opportunity of sometimes shooting bears and deer swimming across the river, afford much pleasure to the navigator, and form sumptuous meals to the boat's crew. Boats, to take advantage of this profitable amusement, are generally well provided with ammunition and fire-arms.

The principal articles constituting loading for the boats trading on the Ohio and Mississippi, are ; flour, whiskey, apples, cider, peach and apple brandy, bar iron and castings, tin and copper wares, glass, cabinet work, windsor chairs, mill stones, grind stones, nails, &c. &c. And the principal articles brought up the Ohio in keel boats, are, cotton, lead, furs and peltry, and hemp and tobacco from Kentucky. This traffick is carried on briskly at this time, and no doubt a few years will greatly increase it, and much to the advantage of the adventurers.

Exclusive of the trading boats, there are many loaded altogether with merchandise of foreign importation, destined to Kentucky, Tennessee, Ohio and the territories. Many others are family boats, seeking places of settlement in these new countries, where their posterity may rest in safety, having plenty of all the necessaries, and many of the luxuries of life, where their children's children may enjoy the rich and prolifick productions of the land, without an over degree of toil or labour, where the climate is mild and the air salubrious,* where each man is a prince in his own kingdom, and may without molestation, enjoy the frugal fare of his humble cot ; where the clashing and terrifick sounds of war are not heard ; where tyrants that desolate the earth dwell not ; where man, simple man, is left to the guidance of his own will, subject only to laws of his own making, fraught with mildness, operating equally just on all, and by all protected and willingly obeyed.

* The following observations on the soil and climate are taken from the Journal of a col. Gordon, who passed down the Ohio as early as 1760.—" The country on the Ohio, &c. is every where pleasant, with large level spots of rich land, remarkably healthy. One general remark of this nature may serve for the whole tract of the globe, comprehended between the western skirts of the

The hills on both sides of the Ohio, as low as Grave creek, below Wheeling, are filled with excellent coal.† Below this coal grows scarce, and what is found, is not of so good a quality. Coal has been boated down from Grave creek to Marietta, Limestone, falls of the Ohio, &c. where it sells for 12 cents per bushel. Even at this price, it is not a very advantageous article of trade. It is also boated to Natchez from mines above the falls, and sells in that market to the blacksmiths at from 25 to 37½ cents per bushel, and is preferred at that advanced price to the charcoal of that country. A mine of mineral coal has been observed lately at the Yellow banks on the Ohio. The hills of the Allegheny and Monongahela rivers, are also filled with good coal mines up to their head waters; and in some places valuable iron ores are found in them.

The lands of the Ohio, and its branches, are differently timbered according to their quality and situation. The high and dry lands are covered with red, white and black oak, hickory, walnut, red and white mulberry, ash, poplar, dogwood, some yellow pine, cucumber tree, sassafras, chesnut, and patches of grape vines are sometimes to be found on the south side of the hills. The low and bottom lands produce butter-nut, tulip tree, papaw, black willow, locust, honey-locust, buckeye, cherry, mulberry, beech, elm, aspen, maple or sugar-tree, plum tree, hickory, walnut, grape vine, remarkably large, spice wood, black alder, &c. And below or southwardly of the Falls, are several cedar and cypress swamps, where the cedar and cypress trees grow remarkably large, and where also are great abundance of canes, such as grow in South Carolina, and on the Mississippi.

Allegheny mountains, beginning at Fort Ligonier, thence bearing southwesterly to the distance of 500 miles opposite to the Ohio falls, then crossing them northerly to the heads of the rivers that empty themselves into the Ohio; then east along the ridge that separates the Lakes and Ohio streams to French-creek, which is opposite the above mentioned Fort Ligonier, northerly. This country may, from a proper knowledge, be affirmed to be the most healthy, the most pleasant, the most commodious, and most fertile spot of earth, known to European people."

*Hutchins.*

† A coal mine was opened in the year 1760, opposite to Fort Pitt on the Monongahela, for the use of that garrison. *Ibid.*

The *Sycamore* seems to be the king of the forest on the banks of the Ohio. Their monstrous growth, towering height, and extended branches really fill the beholder with awe and astonishment. Between Wheeling and Marietta I measured several from 10 to 16 feet over, four feet above ground, and this seems to be but their common size. A gentleman of Marietta told me he knew of one 60 feet in circumference, and that in the hollow of another he had turned himself around with a ten feet pole in his hands, sweeping it at right angles with himself. And there is one of these huge trees in Scioto county, Ohio, on the land of a Mr. Abraham Miller, into whose hollow thirteen men rode on horse back, June 6, 1808, the fourteenth did not enter, his horse being skittish and too fearful to advance into so curious an apartment, but there was room enough for two more.

In the fall of the leaf, and when the year's growth of bark begins to peal off these trees, the rays of the bright moon playing through their white branches, form a scene uncommonly brilliant, and quite cheering and amusing to the nightly traveller.

The growth of the grape vines on the banks of the Ohio astonish the beholder not less than that of the sycamores. It is not uncommon to find them measure from seven to eleven inches over, and so numerous, that in many places for 250 yards in circuit they form a complete canopy or covering of a great body and thickness, in which the tops of the trees are left in the entwining branches and umbrageous vine leaves. The number and manner of their hanging 60 or 80 feet from the tops of the tallest trees without touching the trunk, rather puzzles the spectator how they could thus fix themselves. A sailor might say they were first planted in the tops of the trees, as he first fastens his ropes to the mast head, and then grew downwards and fastened into the ground at their leisure ; they have this appearance, but the principle does not answer the order of nature.

There is now on foot a new mode of navigating our western waters, particularly the Ohio and Missississppi rivers. This is with boats propelled by the power of steam. This plan has been carried into successful operation on the Hudson river at New York, and on the Delaware between New Castle and Burlington.—It has been stated that the one on the Hudson goes at the rate of four miles an hour against wind and tide on her route between New York and Albany, and frequently with 500 passengers on board. From these successful experiments there can be but little doubt of the plan succeeding on our western waters, and proving of immense advantage to the commerce of our country. A Mr. Rosewalt, a gentleman of enterprise, and who is acting it is said in conjunction with Messrs. Fulton and Livingston of New York, has a boat of this kind now (1810) on the stocks at Pittsburgh, of 138 feet keel, calculated for 300 or 400 tons burden.* And

* This steam boat called the New Orleans, was launched in March and descended the Ohio and Mississippi, and landed at Natchez in December 1811, where she took in loading and passengers for the first time, and passed on to New Orleans, in which route she has been successfully employed ever since. Her accommodations are good, and her passengers generally numerous ; seldom less from Natchez than from 10 to 20, at 18 dollars per head, and when she starts from New Orleans, generally from 30 to 50, and sometimes as many as 80 passengers, at 25 dollars each to Natchez. According to the observations of captain Morris, of New Orleans, who attended her as pilot several trips, the boat's receipts for freight upwards, has averaged the last year 700 dollars, passage money $ 900—downwards $ 300 freight, $ 500 for passengers—That she performs 13 trips in the year, which at 2,400 per trip, amounts to $ 31,200. Her expenses are, 12 hands at 30 dollars per month, $ 4,320, captain, one thousand dollars ; 70 cord of wood each trip, at $ 1-75, which amounts to $ 1,586, in all $ 6,906. It is presumed that the boat's extra trips for pleasure or otherwise, out of her usual route, has paid for all the expenses of repairs, and with the profits of the bar-room, for the boat's provisions.—In which case, there will remain a nett gain of $24,294 for the first year. The owners estimate the boat's value at $40,000, which give an interest of $2,400, and by giving $1,894 more for furniture &c. we have the clear gain of 20,000 dollars for the first year's labour of the Steam Boat " New Orleans." A revenue superior to any other establishment in the United States, and what is equally gratifying, arising out of a capital whose application is of singular benefit to the whole community, and particularly so as it respects the navigation of the western waters, whose resources in wealth is unknown, and whose enterprising inhabitants, we doubt not, will soon see the advantage of steam power over that of the oars and poles, and ere long have steam boats of all sizes and fashions, running up and down our numerous rivers, with as much ease and facility as does the common canoe under the direction of its skilful, original masters, the Indians.

there is one building at Frankfort, Kentucky, by citizens who no doubt will push the enterprise. It will be a novel sight, and as pleasing as novel to see a huge boat working her way up the windings of the Ohio, without the appearance of sail, oar, pole, or any manual labour about her—moving within the secrets of her own wonderful mechanism, and propelled by power undiscoverable !—This plan if it succeeds, must open to view flattering prospects to an immense country, an interior of not less than two thousand miles of as fine a soil and climate, as the world can pro-

The steam boat goes up in about seven or eight days, and descends in two or three, stopping several times for freight, passengers, &c. She stays at the extreme of her journey, Natchez and New Orleans, about four or five days, to discharge and take in loading. By pushing her, it is thought she is capable and ought to make a trip in every three weeks throughout the year, in which case her nett gain would be considerbly more than stated, three weeks to each trip giving seventeen trips, four more than she performed the first year.

I have descended twice in the steam boat from Natchez to New-Orleans, the first time she ran it in thirty two hours, that is, throwing off the time she stopped for wood, freight, &c. the second time in thirty one hours, making about nine miles an hour. She passes floating wood on the river, as you pass objects on land when on a smart trotting horse.

When we consider that England has had in use the steam power for upwards of one hundred years, and that it was left to Americans to apply its force to the propelling of boats against wind, tide, and the most powerful currents in our rivers, we cannot but rejoice, and for a moment, believe America possesses that happy kind of superior genius, willing to embrace all the better parts of the old, and capacitated to invent new principles, and, by combining the experience of former ages, with the inventive genius of the present day, it is not wonderful that something extraordinary is produced, especially when genius from the cradle, has, perhaps, above any other country in the world, an uncurbed reign, an open expanse, to work in—where the mind is as free as the air of heaven—where oppression is unknown—and where the tyranny of the parent, and of the government, would be equally disposed, and equally guarded against—where in fact we are one people, equally free from the taunts of the one, or depraved duplicity of the other—where each man feels a pride in being the first to assist the oppressed, to reward merit, encourage genius, free of prejudice, or partiality, for name or nation—the whole united with *a love of country*, a glow of patriotism, that makes man brother to man in all countries and in all situations.

duce, and to a people worthy of all the advantages that nature and art can give them, a people the more meritorious, because they know how to sustain peace and live independent, among the crushing of empires, the falling of kings, the slaughter and bloodshed of millions, and the tumult, corruption and tyranny of all the world beside. The immensity of country we have yet to settle, the vast riches of the bowels of the earth, the unexampled advantages of our water courses, which wind without interruption for thousands of miles, the numerous sources of trade and wealth opening to the enterprising and industrious citizens, are reflections that must rouse the most dull and stupid. Indeed the very appearance of the placid and unbroken surface of the Ohio invite to trade and enterprise, and from the canoe, which the adventurer manages with a single pole or paddle, he advances to a small square ark boat, which he loads at the head waters with various wares, liquors, fruits, dry goods and small groceries, and starts his bark for the river traffic, stopping at every town and village to accommodate the inhabitants with the best of his cargo.—This voyage performed, which generally occupies three months, and the ark sold for half its first cost, the trader returns doubly invigorated, and enabled to enlarge his vessel and cargo, he sets out again; this is repeated, until perhaps getting tired of this mode of merchandising, he sets himself down in some town or village as a wholesale merchant, druggist or apothecary, practising physician or lawyer, or something else, that renders himself respectable in the eyes of his neighbors, where he lives amidst wealth and comforts the remainder of his days—nor is it by any known that his fortune was founded in the paddling of a canoe, or trafficking in apples, cider-royal and peach brandy, whiskey, &c. &c. &c. From the canoe, we now see ships of two or three hundred tons burden, masted and rigged, descending the same Ohio, laden with the products of the country, bound to New Orleans, thence to any part of the world.—Thus, the rise and progress of the trade and the trader on the western waters; thus, the progress of our country from infancy to manhood; and thus, the flattering prospects of its future greatness through the channels of the Ohio and Mississippi rivers.

INSTRUCTIONS AND PRECAUTIONS, NECESSARY TO BE
ATTENDED TO BY STRANGERS AND OTHERS ABOUT
DESCENDING THE OHIO RIVER.

THE first thing to be attended to by emigrants or traders wanting to descend the river, is to procure a boat, to be ready so as to take advantage of the times of flood, and to be careful that the boat be a good one: For many of the accidents that happen in navigating the Ohio, are owing to the unpardonable carelessness or penuriousness of the boat builders, who will frequently slight their work, or make their boats of injured plank;* in either case, putting the lives and properties of a great many people at manifest hazard. This egregious piece of misconduct, should long before this time have been rectified, by the appointment of boat inspectors at the different places, where boats are built. But as this has never been done, it behoves every purchaser of a Kentucky boat, which is the sort here alluded to, to get it narrowly examined before the embarkation, by persons who are well acquainted with the strength and form of a boat suitable for a voyage of this kind.

The principal places where families and merchants stop to prepare for embarkation, are Brownsville, (or Redstone) Pittsburgh, and Wheeling. There are people in each of those places that make it their business to accommodate strangers descending the river with every article they may

---

* We were in hopes that these observations were no longer necessary, but a recent circumstance proves their truth and applicability; Some time in the last of October or beginning of November, 1807, a Mr Winchester's boat struck a rock a few miles below Pittsburgh, and one of the bottom planks being stove in, the boat sunk immediately; and the loading, consisting of dry goods, was materially injured, to the amount of several thousand dollars. The proprietor, not being with the boat at the time, immediately, on his hearing of the accident, conceived that it must have arisen from the carelessness of the person to whom he had entrusted the care of the boat and cargo; and in consequence, brought suit against the man for damages. The man, however, to prove his innocence, produced before the justice of the peace, (Doctor Richardson, of Pittsburgh, since deceased,) the broken plank, which proved to be rotten in the part where it was broken; and the justice discharged him as not being culpable for damages in this case.

want, either in provisions, farming utensils, boats, or other crafts, &c. at a cheap and reasonable price. There are large boat-yards at each of these places, and their boats are generally well made and strong, the price of which varies according to their make, length, and strength; one convenient for a family, between 30 and 40 feet in length, costs from 1 dollar to 1 dollar and 25 cents per foot, making perhaps 35 dollars for a comfortable family boat, well boarded up on the sides, and roofed to within seven or eight feet of the bow; exclusive of this expense, is the price of a cable, pump, and fire place, perhaps ten dollars more. Boats may also be had sometimes at New Geneva, Williamsport, Elizabethtown, and M'Keesport, on the Monongahela; and at some places on the Youghiogheny river; also at the mouth of Big Beaver, and Charlestown, on the Ohio, and perhaps a few other places. The Allegheny is now beginning to furnish boats, which descend the river in high water loaded with salt, boards, and lumber, and sell at Pittsburgh generally at a reduced price.

The number of embarkations, and their conveniences, which take place at Brownsville, Pittsburgh, and Wheeling, depend much on the different stages of the water in the different seasons: The first place is about 10 miles the nearest to the western waters from the eastward; and when the waters will suit, it saves length of road to take water there;—but the waters must be pretty well up to make embarkation safe at Brownsville; therefore, stopping there when the waters are really low, is attended with much loss of time, and of course expense.—Boats can go from Pittsburgh at a much lower stage of the water than they can from Brownsville; yet there are periods, and these generally happen from about the middle of July until the beginning of October, when embarkation at either place would be attended with considerable detention. Wheeling, therefore, is the safest point to strike at in very low stages of the water, and from thence boats may go at all seasons of the year. It is about 58 miles by land from Brownsville. Pittsburgh is preferred as a place of embarkation to Wheeling, when boats can descend from it, for two reasons: first, it is about 45 miles nearer Philadelphia or Baltimore; and secondly, merchants and travellers say they are better accommodated here with storage for their goods, and all other conveniences they may stand in need of, than they could be at Wheeling; therefore, they seldom go there, except in cases of very low water, embarking either at Brownsville or Pittsburgh. But families wishing to cross the Ohio, with their wagons, generally cross at Wheeling, Charlestown, Georgetown, and Big Beaver, according to the direction of the country they are about to remove to. Those destined to the country N. W. of the Allegheny river, and on lake Erie, and bordering the boundary between Pennsylvania and Ohio, generally cross the Allegheny at Pittsburgh.

The best seasons for navigating the Ohio, are in spring and autumn. The spring season commences at the breaking up of the ice, which generally happens about the middle of February, and continues good for about three months and sometimes four. The fall season generally commences in October, and continues good until the first of December, and sometimes all through that month; when the ice begins to form and the river close. But the seasons of high water can scarcely be called periodical, as they vary considerably, according to the wetness or dryness of the season, or earliness or lateness of the setting in, or breaking up of winter.

But freshes in the rivers are not entirely confined to the spring and fall; heavy rains frequently happen, during the summer months, in the mountains, and at the sources of the Allegheny and Monongahela rivers, which give a sufficiency of water to render the navigation of the Ohio perfectly eligible. Those freshes however are not to be depended on, and when they occur, must be taken immediate advantage of, as the waters subside rapidly.

When provided with a good boat, and strong cable of at least 40 feet long, there is little danger in descending the Ohio in high freshes, when proper care is taken, unless at such times as when the river is full of floating ice. In this case it is safest to permit your boat to have pretty much her own way, as rowing may tend to throw you out of the current or on the points of islands, before you are aware of it; in which case, nothing but presence of mind and great exertions will save you. Therefore, prevent yourself being caught on the river among floating ice if possible, unless indeed, when it is very thin and thawing very fast; and even in this case, it would be better to detain until the river is clear of ice.

As frequent landing is attended with considerable loss of time and some hazard, you should contrive to land as seldom as possible ; you need not even lie by at night, provided you trust to the current, and keep a good look out : If you have moon light so much the better. When you come to, the strength of your cable is a great safe-guard. A quantity of fuel, and other necessaries should be laid in at once, and every boat ought to have a canoe or skiff along side, to send on shore, when necessary, or as a relief in case of accident.

Although the labour of navigating the Ohio in times of high water is very inconsiderable to what it is when it is low, when continual rowing is necessary, it is always best to keep a good look out, and be strong handed. The wind will sometimes drive you too near the points of islands, or on projecting parts of the main shore, or into a bend where there is but little current, in either case considerable ex-ertions are necessary to get you under way again, and keep you clear of danger either on the one side or the other. You will frequently meet with head winds, the river being so very crooked as that which is in your favour one hour, may be directly against you the next ; and when contrary winds contend with a strong current, it is attended with considerable inconvenience, and requires careful and cir-cumspect management, or you may be driven on shore in spite of all your efforts. One favorable circumstance is, that the wind commonly abates about sun-set, particularly in summer.

Boats, have frequently passed from Pittsburgh to the mouth of the Ohio in 15 days in high water ; but in gene-ral, 10 days to the falls is reckoned a quick passage ; but sometimes a boat will be 2 weeks in going to Limestone, and in a very low state of water, 20 days.

One other precaution perhaps is necessary in case you are on the river in time of ice, which above all other sea-sons is certainly the most perilous :—If at any time you are obliged to bring to, on account of ice, great circum-spection should be used in the choice of a place to lie in. There are many places where the shore, projecting to a point, throws off the cakes of ice towards the middle of the river, and forms a kind of harbour below. By bringing to, in such a situation, and fixing your canoe above the boat, with one end strongly tied to the shore, and the other out

D

in the stream, sloping downwards, so as to drive off the cakes of ice, which would otherwise accumulate, and tend to sink or drive your boat from her moorings, you may lie with a tolerable degree of safety.

This is a much better way than that of felling a tree above the boat so as to fall partly into the river; for if the tree does not strongly adhere to the stump, ten to one but the masses of ice carry it down against your boat, and put you in imminent danger, much worse than if the precaution had not been taken.

The reflection here naturally occurs, how easy it would be, and how trifling the expense, in different places on the river where boats are accustomed to land, to project a sort of pier into the river, inclining downwards, which would at all times ensure a safe mooring below. The expenses of such erections would soon be repaid by the place becoming famous for a safe and convenient stopping place for boats.

The best mode perhaps in descending the Ohio, in time of low water, is in keel boats. These seem to be more at immediate command in navigating the river; and as they are always strongly manned, they go with greater expedition. They draw little water and require but a narrow channel. Merchants are beginning to prefer this method for safety and expedition; and instead of purchasing boats and taking charge of them themselves, they get their goods freighted down from Pittsburgh in keel boats by the persons who make them, and who make it their business to be prepared, with good boats and experienced hands, for such engagements.

This method is the safest, if not the cheapest, for this special reason: the cargo is consigned to the care of an experienced and careful man, who perhaps descends and ascends the river twice or thrice in the course of one season, and of course must be well acquainted with all the difficulties in navigating it.—On the contrary, when merchants are young, and inexperienced, they do not, often enough, as the Scotch phrase goes, " *Look before they loup.*" They, being flushed with the idea of a fortune before them, hastily buy a boat, load, jump into it themselves, fly to the steering oar, and halloo to the hands to *pull out.* Now swimming in good water, and unapprehensive of the bad, they think themselves safe, until alarmed by the rumbling of the boat on a ripple, or shoving herself into the mud on a sandbar.——And until now they believed themselves from having gone down the river once or twice, to have been master navigators, and capable of conducting a ship of 400 tons with equal ease and safety as a common Indian canoe.——Such are the mistaken calculations of the extent of our own knowledge and abilities.——And in common life, it does not unfrequently happen, that we run our ship aground, when we think she has most water to ride in.

As the trimming your boat, that is, loading her in such a manner as to draw an equal depth of water all around, is of considerable consequence to her safety, you ought to be careful to have it done before departure with a circumspect eye. For though the construction of our boats does not render them liable to overset, yet when loaded irregularly, and one corner sunken more than another, a stroke on a rock, or a log on the diagonal corner, subjects her to fill in that quarter much sooner than if properly trimmed.

There is another precaution which ought not to be neglected; that is, to see that your boat is kept afloat while loading, and when you bring to over night; for if the cable corner should rest on the shore, and during the night, the river should fall much, ten to one but before morning your boat would be filled with water. From a neglect of this kind I have seen a valuable cargo of dry goods sunk and much injured, before the boat was completely loaded.

The caulking of a boat ought to be well attended to before embarkation; for if she has been long built, her timbers and plank may have shrunk, and the caulking got loose. Boats are seldom caulked above the gunnel joint. I think this a great error, and an unsafe finishing. The next joint at least ought to be well caulked all around. And for fear of accident, it would be well that every boat was furnished with a few pounds of oakum, together with a mallet and caulking iron. These precautionary provisions might sometimes be the means of saving in part, if not in whole, a loading worth many thousand dollars. For the greater part of the accidents that happen on the Ohio, arise from a want of a proper knowledge of the means that ought to be taken to prevent them.——Some, indeed, possessing the knowledge, unpardonably neglect their duty, until sad experience puts them in mind of it, by a loss which perhaps they are little able to bear.

HAVING given some general and preparatory instructions, which we presume will be found useful if attended to, and a cursory view of the rivers, we now commence the more particular directions how to navigate them. The distances from place to place, except those marked ( M. D. ) not having been ascertained from actual survey, may not in all cases be found absolutely correct, yet it is hoped they will not be found so materially erroneous, as to militate against the utility of the work.

## OF THE MONONGAHELA,

*ITS CHANNELS, SHOALS, RIPPLES, SANDBARS, TOWNS, &c.*

|  | Mil. | Tot. |
|---|---|---|
| **CLARKSBURGH,** | | |
| Stands on the E. side of the river, 40 miles S. E. of Morgantown, is the chief town of Harrison county, Virginia, and contains about 50 houses, a courthouse and jail. From this to Morgantown the navigation of the river is very difficult in low water, and can be gone only in small crafts. | | |
| **MORGANTOWN,** | 40 | 40 |
| Is situated on the E. side of the river, the capital of Monongalia county, Virginia, contains about 60 dwellings, a courthouse, and stone jail. It is 303 miles from Philadelphia, and about 63 by land above Pittsburgh. | | |
| Boundary between Penn. and Vir. | 4 | 44 |
| Cheat river enters on the east side, | 4 | 48 |
| Four miles below the boundary between Pennsylvania and Virginia. At the mouth of this river is a long and ugly shoal, and the channel somewhat difficult. Here a person can be got to pilot you past the danger. | | |
| This river rises in Randolph Co. Virginia, on the N. W. side of the Allegheny mountains, is about 200 yards wide at its mouth, and has some valuable mills and iron works on it. Dunkard's settlement is 60 miles up it, to which it is navigable for small crafts. There is a portage of 37 miles from Cheat to the Potomack at the mouth of Savage river. | | |
| Dunkard's Creek, west or left side, | 2 | 50 |
| Here is a shoal but not very difficult. | | |
| George's Creek, east or right hand side, | 10 | 60 |
| Just below the mouth of this creek lies | | |
| **NEW GENEVA,** | | |
| A small village, which had in its vicinity a valuable factory of glass, erected by Albert Gallatin, esq. It is now removed to the Greensburgh side, and carried on | | |

by Messrs. Nicholson & Co. This town is in Fayette Co.
14 miles S. W. of Uniontown, and a little below it on the
opposite side of the river, stands

## GREENSBURGH,

A small village in Green Co. Pa.

| | | |
|---|---|---|
| Big Whitley Creek, left hand side, | 4 | 64 |
| Little Whitley, same side, | 2 | 66 |
| Channel near the middle of the river. | | |
| Brown's run, E. side, ch. middle of the river, | 2 | 68 |
| Middle run, E. side, ch. near the W. shore, | 2 | 70 |
| Cat's run, channel middle of the river, | 2 | 72 |
| Muddy creek, west side, | 4 | 76 |

Here are two old fish dams, the channel of the first is
near the middle, and of the other near the east side.

| | | |
|---|---|---|
| Ten mile creek, west side, | 7 | 83 |

Channel, a chute in the middle of the river. On this
creek, are iron works, grist and saw mills, and it runs
through a well settled country of rich farmers, principally from New Jersey.

| | | |
|---|---|---|
| FREDERICKTOWN. | 1 | 84 |

This is a small village; stands on the west side of the
river, Washington Co. Pa. contains two mercantile
stores, and a publick library, instituted principally by
Quakers.—Within a few miles is a large brewery and
distillery, and tanyard.

"About a mile below Fredericktown is a curious cave
called the *Panther's Den.*—It enters the hill about half
way from its base, by a small fracture or rent in the rock.
After going a few yards through a narrow and descending passage, you enter a wide but low room, in which
you can walk nearly upright—To the roof of this room
we found bats hanging in a stupid kind of sleep. The
next room we got into by clambering up another fracture in the rock—this room we had to roll ourselves
through, and entered a third, by a narrow and descending passage, occasioned by another rent in the rock.—
This room was extensive, and high enough to walk upright in, and was nicely divided by a partition of petrifactions, formed by the drippings of the water through
the roof. The formation of these petrifactions, had a singular appearance, something similar in shape to two
hay stacks, with their conick tops put one on top of the
other —We had gone crouching, pushing and rolling
ourselves through this fractured hill about 40 yards—
feeling tired we returned with candles and cord to the
mouth again in safety.—The first room had sufficient
marks of the animal's bones to entitle it to the name it
bears."

| James Crawford's ripple, | 1 | 85 |
|---|---|---|
| Channel near the middle of the river. | | |
| Josiah Crawford's ripple, | 3 | 88 |
| Channel near the middle of the river. | | |
| Dunlap's Creek, east or right hand side, | 3 | 91 |

Here has been a fish dam—the chute is near the middle of the river. Immediately above the mouth of this creek stands BRIDGEPORT, a small village, divided from Brownsville by a chain bridge over the creek. In it are several mercantile stores, an earthen pottery, tanyard, a wire weaver, card maker, hatters, a boat yard, and a market house. It contains 56 dwellings.

### BROWNSVILLE, (or REDSTONE.)

Lies immediately below Dunlap's creek, on the east side of the river, finely situated on a first and high second bank. It contains (1810) about 120 houses, principally of wood, some handsomely built with stone and brick; a market house, an episcopal church, 18 mercantile stores, two tanyards, a rope walk, two boat yards, two tin and copper manufactories, two factories of nails, one printing office, which issues a weekly paper, a post office, a warehouse, one scythe and sickle maker, blacksmiths, silversmiths, (one of whom makes surveyors' compasses,) tailors, shoemakers, saddlers, &c. Within a few miles of the town are four Friends' meeting houses, 26 grist, saw, oil and fulling mills, and within four miles up Redstone creek, a valuable paper mill, owned by Samuel Jackson. Byrd's fort formerly stood here. In addition to the above, a manufactory of steel, established by Morris Truman & Co. was in full operation in 1811. A glass-works for making of green glass, commenced in Bridgeport in October of the same year. Mr. John Gregg, near Brownsville, has contrived a machine for planking hats, either by horse or water. It is calculated to save much labour in the hatting business. Cotton and wool cards are also made. A large cotton manufactory is erecting, in which the steam power will be used; and a foundery, on an extensive scale, has been erected, as also a manufactory for making mill-saws. A steam boat was commenced in 1813, and is expected to descend the Ohio this spring; the engine constructed by Mr. French. The Monongahela bank was established here in 1813 with a capital of $300,000.

There has been built lately in the town side, a valuable grist and saw mill, turned by the water of the river, in which are wool and cotton carding machines. The mills are owned by Messrs. Gillespie and Clark, who got an act of assembly passed to throw a dam across the river, by engaging to make a safe way for the passing and repassing of boats up and down the river. This was at first done by a chute in the dam, and since by a lock canal.

The inhabitants of Brownsville are remarkably industrious, and the settlement around the town, is the oldest and richest in the western country, and is principally settled by quakers. This being a place of considerable embarkation, individuals make it their business to supply travellers with boats and all other necessaries for descending the river. It is in Fayette Co. Pa. and 12 miles N. W. from Uniontown, the seat of justice for that county ; 33 miles S. E. of Pittsburgh, 290 west of Philadelphia, and 25 E. of Washington, Pa. in N. lat. 39. 58. W. long. 81. 12½.

Near this place are rocks containing curious carvings, the hills abound with excellent coal, the river with fish, and there has been lately erected several wool carding machines in its vicinity.

In digging a cellar lately for a necessary in the town, there was found in a kind of box coffin a human skeleton. The coffin was found standing nearly erect, the boards much decayed; no doubt deposited here during the wars between the Indians and the white people, at the early periods of the first settlement of the country.

| | | |
|---|---:|---:|
| **Redstone creek, right hand side,** | 1 | 92 |

Channel is near the middle of the river, there being a smart ripple near the mouth of the creek. On this creek are several valuable saw, grist, and oil mills, one paper mill, and a wool carding machine at its mouth.

Over the mouth of this creek there has been thrown a chain bridge.

| | | |
|---|---:|---:|
| **Pigeon creek, left or west side,** | 18 | 110 |

Channel in the middle of the river.

### WILLIAMSPORT,

Situated on the left bank of the river, just below Pigeon creek, is a growing village, in Washington Co. Pa. 20 miles east of Washington, and about 23 above Pittsburgh.—Works for making glass are now erecting. Kentucky, New Orleans boats, and keels are built at this place.

| | | |
|---|---:|---:|
| **Parkinson's mill, right side,** | 3 | 113 |

Channel in the middle of the river.

| | | |
|---|---:|---:|
| **M'Farland's ferry,** | 6 | 119 |

### ELIZABETHTOWN,

| | | |
|---|---:|---:|
| | 2 | 121 |

Is a small village on the right bank of the river, in Allegheny county. Here is a boat yard, out of which were launched, the " Monongahela Farmer," and the brig " Ann Jean." The town does not thrive much. Original

proprietor, col. Stephen Bayard. It is 18 miles above
Pittsburgh.

Peters creek, left bank,                                    3|124

Here is a small ripple, channel near the west or left
hand shore.

### M'KEESPORT,                                            5|129

A small and dull village on the right or east bank,
just below the mouth of the Youghiogheny river, in Allegheny county, 12 miles above Pittsburgh. Original proprietor, John M'Kee, who laid it out in 1794. Boats may
sometimes be procured here. It has a large brewery,
two mercantile stores, a tan and boat yard.

The Youghiogheny is a considerable river, and affords
pretty good navigation, except in very low water, for
fifty or sixty miles. Passing S. W. of the Laurel Hill, it
precipitates itself over the Ohiopyle falls, 20 feet perpendicular. It passes through a part of Westmoreland,
Fayette and Allegheny counties, and where it discharges
itself into the Monongahela, it is about 150 yards broad.
Jacob's creek, on which are Turnbull and Marmie's iron-
works, enters the Yough about 35 miles above Pittsburgh.

Turtle creek,                                              5|134

A town was laid out above the mouth of this creek a
few years ago—but it has not progressed. Just at the
mouth of this creek is a long and difficult ripple.—Channel, at the head of the ripple, near the right side for a
short distance, thence, about the middle of the ripple it
runs to the left shore, and returns to the right shore
near the foot of the ripple.

Braddock's fields, right bank,                             3|137

Here is a ripple, channel right side.

These fields are rendered famous on account of general Braddock's being defeated here in an engagement
with the French and Indians, in the year 1755. Braddock's army was cut all to pieces in a short time ; the Indians and French being completely covered by woods,
grass, &c. while the English army stood in an open road
thick set with grass to receive the continual firing of
the enemy, whom they could not even see. Braddock*
was mortally wounded, and the late General Washington, then acting volunteer aid de camp under him, was
the only aid de camp left alive and not wounded on the
field of battle, and he had two horses shot under him,
and four bullets passed through his coat.†

---

* He was conveyed to Dunbar's camp near Uniontown, where
he died.

† Ramsay's life of Washington.

These fields are nine miles above Pittsburgh, and the owner‡ frequently ploughs up the bones of those who fell in this dreadful carnage.—It is said that a valuable brass piece may sometimes be seen in a very deep hole in the river opposite the field of battle; and the trees on the side of the hill still bear the marks of the balls fired during the engagement.—Braddock's fields are also celebrated on account of their having been a place of general rendezvous for the Whiskey Boys, as they were called, during the Western Insurrection, in the year 1794.

| | | |
|---|---|---|
| Nine Mile Run, (M'Dowel's) | 1 | 138 |
| Gordon's (now Colhoun's) ferry, | 2 | 140 |

Channel in the middle of the river.

| | | |
|---|---|---|
| Four Mile Bar, mouth of Four Mile Run, | 3 | 143 |

Channel on the right hand side of the river, which from this place, ought to be kept down to

| | | |
|---|---|---|
| PITTSBURGH, | 4 | 147 |

Opposite to this town is a sandbar three quarters of a mile long, nearest the S. or left hand side; it sometimes remains bare for three months; it was ploughed and sowed with buckwheat in the year 1801-2; the grain flowered, but the floods came and swept the crop away before it had time to mature.—The channel is on the town side.

---

## OF THE ALLEGHENY,

### ITS CHANNELS, RIPPLES, ISLANDS, TOWNS, &c.

#### INCLUDING THE PORTAGE FROM ERIE, (OR PRESQU' ISLE.)

THIS town is handsomely situated on the south bank of lake Erie, opposite the Peninsula, which runs several miles into the lake, forming between it and the town, a handsome harbour for vessels, though it is somewhat difficult to enter. Erie was laid out a few years since (in 1797-8, I think,) by the state of Pennsylvania, and from its commanding situation, must in time become a place of considerable business. It is increasing in buildings and business, is the seat of justice for Erie county, in lat. N. 42° 21' about 120 miles N. of Pittsburgh. The old fort just below the town, which contains

‡ George Wallace, esq.

the venerable remains of the late general Anthony Wayne,* (who died here, Dec. 14, 1796, on his return from his campaign against the Indians,) is totally evacuated. The country in its vicinity is settling rapidly; and the trade in salt, of which there are about 7000 or 8000 barrels enter that port annually, is increasing. The convenience of the turnpike road erected between Erie and Waterford, a portage of 15 miles, is very considerable.

Erie has a post-office, several mercantile stores and public inns, and a number of the mechanical branches are carried on with spirit. The town is well supplied with fish from the lake, and cranberries from the peninsula, of which many barrels are sold at the Pittsburgh market yearly. The advantage that Erie has from the trade of Detroit, and the northern lakes, with that of the St. Lawrence and the Mohawk rivers, added to the easy communications to it from different points of the Ohio, are certainly very great, and must eventually add importance to the place, and riches to the country around it.

The following statement will shew the increase in the article of salt at the port of Erie from 1800 till 1809, as registered by Mr. Foster, collector of that port:

| In the year | 1800 | . . . | 723 | barrels of salt |
| | 1801 | . . . | 396 | were entered |
| | 1802 | . . . | 834 | at this port & |

distributed along the lake in the states of New York, Pennsylvania, and Ohio, and a few barrels sent to Pittsburgh.

| In the year | 1803 | . . . | 2736 | barrels of salt |
| | 1804 | . . . | 3778 | were entered at |
| | 1805 | . . . | 7589 | this port for the |
| | 1806 | . . . | 7261 | consumption of |
| | 1807 | . . . | 6774 | this neighbour- |
| | 1808 | . . . | 9349 | hood and Pitts- |
| | 1809 | . . . | 14346 | burgh market, |

not including the supplies to the states of New York and Ohio—Making 52,776 barrels, or 263,880 bushels of salt, besides other articles of merchandize, though of less importance, yet to a considerable extent.

District and port of Presqu'Isle,
collector's office, Dec. 25, 1809.

THOMAS FOSTER, *collector.*

---

* The bones of the hero were removed in Oct. 1809, and interred in the family burying-ground, near the Paoli, by Isaac Wayne, esq. The Pennsylvania Society of Cincinnati having appropriated 500 dollars, to erect a monument to his memory, the 4th of July preceding.

### WATERFORD (FORT LE BŒUF.)    15 | 15

This town is situated on the north side of French creek, and is the nearest and best point of communication between that creek and Erie; and it is here where goods are deposited to be ready for transportation either over the portage, or down the creek. A frontier post* was kept here till the peace with the Indians in 1796. It is now destroyed. It has a post office, several mercantile stores, warehouses, public inns, &c. and is 15 miles S. of Erie, in Erie county.

French creek through Le Bœuf lake,    4 | 19
Muddy creek,    12 | 31
Dead water, end of,    14 | 45

### MEADVILLE,    18 | 63

This town stands on the E. or left hand side of French creek, is the seat of justice for Crawford county, Penn. has several mercantile stores, publick inns, a post and printing office, which issues a weekly paper, and from its central situation, in the heart of a rich and fertile country, it will no doubt become a place of considerable business. It has a well regulated school, a fixed preacher, and a society for the encouragement of home manufactures. It is about 86 miles north of Pittsburgh.

Wilson's Bend,    6 | 69
Little Sugar creek,    8 | 77
Big Sugar creek,    12 | 89

From this creek there is a considerable rapid down to

### FRANKLIN.    4 | 93

This is the seat of justice for Venango county, Penn. situated on the right or W. side of French creek, a little above the junction of it with the Allegheny river. It is bounded by large and stony hills on both sides. It progresses but slowly, and the country around it is but thinly settled. The French formerly kept a garrison here, which is now destroyed, but is said to have a brass piece of ordnance of considerable value buried in its ruins. It is about 63 miles northward of Pittsburgh.

Sandy creek, west side,    10 | 103
Scrub grass creek, west side,    8 | 111

---

* The French had a fort erected here as early as 1751. The English growing jealous of their encroachments on the Ohio, and in order to check their further progress, Mr. Dinwiddie, then colonial governor of Virginia, despatched the late Gen. George Washington, then in the nineteenth year of his age, with a letter of remonstrance to the French commandant, Mons. Le Gardeur De St. Pierre, then at that garrison. On this embassy, Washington set out from Will's creek, now called Fort Cumberland

| | | |
|---|--:|--:|
| Falling springs, | 3 | 114 |
| Montgomery falls, | 4 | 118 |

 Channel on the left hand side of a large rock in the middle of the river.

| | | |
|---|--:|--:|
| Ewalt's defeat, | 3 | 121 |

 This is a very rocky place, channel east side.

| | | |
|---|--:|--:|
| Patterson's falls, | 4 | 125 |
| Nicholson's eddy, | 2 | 127 |

 Here is a strong ripple, channel west side.

| | | |
|---|--:|--:|
| Stump creek, east side, | 8 | 135 |

 Channel east side.

| | | |
|---|--:|--:|
| Parker's or Amberson's falls, | 3 | 138 |

 Channel on the east or left side.

| | | |
|---|--:|--:|
| Catfish falls, channel east side, | 8 | 146 |
| Redbank creek, channel east side, | 7 | 153 |
| Cumming's rock, channel west side, | 5 | 158 |
| Mahoning creek, east side, | 2 | 160 |

 Channel west side.

| | | |
|---|--:|--:|
| Sloan's ferry, | 14 | 174 |
| Crooked creek, east side, | 4 | 178 |
| Nicholson's falls, channel west side, | 3 | 181 |

KITTANNING,   7 188

 Is a small but thriving village, situated on the east bank of the Allegheny. It is the seat of justice for Armstrong county, Penn. about 36 miles N. E. of Pittsburgh.

FREEPORT,

 A small village on the west side of the river, at the mouth of Buffaloe creek.

| | | |
|---|--:|--:|
| Owing's island, channel west side, | 4 | 192 |
| Bull creek, west side, channel east side, | 3 | 195 |
| Logan's ferry, mouth of Puckety creek, | 4 | 199 |

 Channel on the east side.

| | | |
|---|--:|--:|
| Hullard's island, channel east side, | 4 | 203 |
| Plumb creek, east side, | 3 | 206 |
| Sandy creek, east side, | 2 | 208 |

 Here is an island, channel east side.

| | | |
|---|--:|--:|
| Pine creek, west side, | 5 | 213 |
| Wilson's island, channel east or left side, | 4 | 217 |

---

on the Potomack, on the 15th November, 1753. Having delivered his letters, he returned to Williamsburgh, in Virginia, on the 78th day after his departure, a route at that period at once hazardous and fatiguing in the extreme.

       *Ramsay's Life of Washington.*

Here you may land below the wharf on the Allegheny,
or turning the point, ascend the Monongahela, and land
at any of its wharves.   The shores of either river are dry
and gravelly, but in high water the Monongahela affords,
from the gentleness of its current, the safest harbour,
and is the most convenient to the centre of the town.

---

## THE OHIO.

*WE now commence the directions for navigating the Ohio
river, and as it commences at Pittsburgh, it will not be
amiss to preface the more particular account of it, by a
short description of that place.*

## PITTSBURGH,

IS delightfully situated at the head of the Ohio river, on
the plain or point of land formed by the junction of the
Allegheny and Monongahela rivers ; the former running
from the north-east, and the latter from the south-west,
making an angle where they unite of about 33 degrees.
Few towns in America have been more frequently or
minutely described, so that it is no easy matter to speak
of it, without merely repeating what has been said by
others.   It is a place of note and celebrity not only in
America, but even in Europe.   The traveller, however,
on entering it for the first time, meets with some disap-
pointment.  The town enveloped in thick clouds of smoke,
which even affect respiration; the appearance of the
houses is dark and gloomy, from the general use
of coal, particularly in the numerous manufacturies,
which send into the air immense columns of smoke : there
are few elegant buildings compared to other towns of the
same size, and the streets are narrow and unpleasant,
with the exception of Liberty and Penn, but which are
thinly built. - But the topography makes amends for all
these disadvantages.   All concur in the beauty of its position.   It is built on a plain, confined by the two rivers
just mentioned, and what may be denominated the SOURCE

OF THE OHIO; this plain is confined by romantic hills, which environ the town on all sides. The hills to the east of the town, gradually attain an amphitheatrical elevation, and become more varied, as the two rivers diverge, and the space between them grows wider; affording many pleasant positions for country seats. Over the Allegheny, there is a high and beautiful plain, with rude hills in the back ground; here the town of Allegheny has been laid out, and some handsome improvements have been already made; in case a bridge should be built across the river, as is at present contemplated, this place will soon flourish, as the ground upon which Pittsburgh stands, is nearly built up, except a narrow plain which extends up the Allegheny river. The Coal hill on the opposite side of the Monongahela, rises with a very steep ascent, more than three hundred feet above the level of the river, and almost from the water's edge, there being scarcely more than room for a road, and the ferry houses, taverns, and some manufactures, in a line under the hill. This hill abounds with coal, from which circumstance its name is derived, a number of coal-pits are opened in it, and considerable quantities are carried over to the town, though the chief supply is derived from the pits on that side of the river. The prospect from the top of the Coal hill is extremely beautiful and romantic. The distant view presents forest clad hills, sloping into narrow vales; the beautiful Allegheny with its clear and limpid waters, bright and shining, and holding a rapid course compared with that of the Monongahela, which, on the contrary, seems with his turbid waters to advance lazy and slow, as if to yield involuntary submission. Immediately at the junction, there is an expanse of water of nearly a mile wide; the Ohio then passes off to the right, though not with the magnificence and beauty, that persons are apt to imagine who have not been here, as it is confined on the left by high hills, on the right its stream is divided by islands, and from its course the river totally disappears in the distance of a mile and an half. The hill is avoided by a road which follows the bed of the Saw mill run, a handsome stream which makes a deep break in the hill, and discharges itself into the very source of the Ohio; the first tributary this mighty river receives: but the road most commonly travelled to Washington,

Wheeling, &c. ascends the hill in a winding manner just opposite the upper ferry of the Monongahela, along a torrent which has worn a deep ravine in the side of the hill. Just above this place the river on the Pittsburgh side washes a steep hill, studded with romantic rocks, and leaves on the other a handsome plain, where a town, named Birmingham,* has been laid out, which already contains thirty or forty houses, and some extensive manufactures. In looking down from Coal hill into Pittsburgh, one is reminded of Shakespear's description of the view from Dover cliff: and seems a giant compared to the busy Lilliputians below.

> ————————how fearful
> And dizzy 'tis to cast one's eyes so low!
> The fisher men that walk upon the beach
> Appear like mice; and yon tall anchoring bark,
> Diminished to her cock, her cock a buoy
> Almost too small for sight————

Before entering upon a view of the present state of this place, it will not be improper to give a short sketch of its history, and some outline of the progress of its improvements. This spot, long before any town was built, had in very early times been a noted rendezvous of the traders with the Indians, and was selected by the French as an important point in the scheme of uniting Canada with Louisiana, and a fort was built called Du Quesne.— The reduction of this fort was at an early period pointed

* On the plain of the Allegheny, near the Two-mile run, another town has been laid out, called the town of Manchester. Is it not strange that we must borrow even the very names of Britain, and at a period when we are at war with her? O habit, how inveterate thy sway!

This plain, which is of a rich sandy loam, is about a half a mile in width from the Allegheny to the point of Grant's hill, its widest part; thence up that river it becomes narrower, until about four miles where it closes to the river. But the town may extend as far as Two-mile run; the bottom that distance is generally about a quarter of a mile wide, and well calculated to build upon: a few years ago it was a lane passed through, with orchards, meadows and grain fields enclosed on each side; but this has now became a long straggling street.

out by Washington, as a step of great moment; but before this could be effected, much blood was shed, at the battle of the Little Meadows, where he gained his first laurel, at Braddock's fields, where at the age of twenty-six, after the fall of Braddock, by a masterly retreat he saved the remains of the unfortunate army, and finally, in the defeat of Grant and his eight hundred Caledonians, on the hill which bears his name.*    The fort was however blown up and evacuated, on the approach of general Forbes in the year 1758.   A short distance above fort Du Quesne, (which was situated immediately at the junction of the rivers) Fort Pitt, so called in honor of the then minister, was built, by Lord Stanwin, and is said to have cost the British government £ 60,000 sterling, but has been long in ruins; in fact little is now to be seen but the ditch and mound, with the salient angles and bastions on the land side.    On part of this ground now stands a large brewery appertaining to col. O'Hara, and several dwellings; on the Monongahela side there is a kind of ship yard, where keel boats, and several steam boats for the western trade are built.   The ground immediately at the

---

* *Grant's* hill comes to a handsome point within the limits of the borough, eastward of the town.   From it you have a beautiful view of the town and the three rivers.   On its summit is a mound or ancient burying place of the Indians, which is now enclosed in the middle of a fine garden, and has an elegant summer house on the top of it.   This seat, which is among the handsomest of the place, formerly belonged to, and was first improved by Mr. Marie, a French gentleman.   He sold it to James Ross, esq. its present proprietor.   This hill takes it name from gen. Grant, who met with a defeat here by the Indians and French, in the war which ended in 1763.   Grant thinking his conquest sure, imprudently beat the *reveille* to the French garrison at sunrise.   But before he was aware of it, the garrison dividing itself into two parties, cautiously sallied out under the banks of the two rivers, and joining on the back of Grant, came down upon him like a torrent, took Grant himself prisoner, and cut and tomahawked his troops, which consisted of 800 Caledonians, or Highland Scotch, all to pieces in a few minutes.   The hill was then covered with wood and thick bushes, which added to the confusion of Grant, and to his easy defeat, he not being accustomed to fight in the *Indian fashion*, that is, behind trees, old logs, rocks, &c.   It was the ignorance of this method of fighting, that occasioned the sudden defeat, and dreadful carnage of the troops of general Braddock.

point or junction is rather too low, and too much subject to crumbling in of the banks, to be safely built on; although it is said that on the bank of the Allegheny, the Indian traders had built shortly after the English took possession, an elegant row of brick houses, but they have gradually crumbled into the river, as no vestige of them remains.

About the year 1760 a small town called Pittsburgh, was built near fort Pitt, and which contained about 200 souls: but on the breaking out of the Indian war in May 1763, they retired into the fort. The British officers commanding the garrison, had on the bank of the Allegheny, very elegant gardens, called the king's and artillery gardens, and large orchards of the choicest fruits; the ground is now occupied with dwellings on each side of Penn street which passes through it. The present town of Pittsburgh was first laid out in the year 1765; it was afterwards laid out and surveyed on its present plan in May 1784, by col. George Woods, by order of Tench Francis, esq. attorney for John Penn Junr. and John Penn. Fort Pitt being included in one of the manors of the Penn family, was sold by the proprietors and now makes a part of the town of Pittsburgh, though its banks and ditches form a considerable obstruction to its being regularly built upon, and very much spoil the beauty of the view from the heads of Liberty and Penn streets,to the river. The increase of the town was not rapid until the year 1793, on account of the Indian depredations which prevented the settlements from extending. The western insurrection by putting in circulation a considerable sum of money, is thought to have given it a start. Since that time it has increased with greater rapidity, not even excepting Lexington and Cincinnati, than any inland town in America. Those places are now covered with houses, and resound with the din of business, where, when a boy, I was want to " pluck the thistle's beard."*

*Population*—In the year 1800, Pittsburgh contained about 2,400 souls. The census of 1810, according to the return of William B. Irish, esq. gives a population of 4,740 souls, particularized as follows, together with the number and kinds of dwelling houses.

* M. S. S. of H. M. Brackenridge, esq.

### RETURN OF THE No. OF INHABITANTS AND HOUSES IN PITTSBURGH.

*Houses.* {
Whole No. of stone.—Stables and kitchens excepted.          11
do. brick.          do.          do.          do.          283
do. frame and log.          do.          do.          do.          473
}

Total No. houses—767.

*Free white males.* {
Under 10 years of age.          .          .          .          .          751
Of 10 years and under 16.          .          .          .          .          333
Of 16 and under 26, including heads of families.          .          614
Of 26 and under 45,          do.          do.          do.          513
Of 45 and upwards,          do.          do.          do.          213
}

*Free white females.* {
Under 10 years of age.          .          .          .          .          699
Of 10 and under 16.          .          .          .          .          355
Of 16 and under 26, including heads of families.          .          501
Of 26 and under 45,          do.          do.          do.          421
Of 45 and upwards,          do.          do.          do.          156
}

All other free persons except Indians, not taxed.          .          184

Total No. Inhabitants—4,740.

From this statement it appears that the population of the town has about doubled in ten years. In 1813, there were reckoned 956 dwellings, and the population estimated at six thousand. The war has had an evident effect in increasing the number of its inhabitants, the state of things having turned a great deal of the capital of the sea board into manufactures, much of it was attracted by this town, from its peculiar advantages. The increase has consequently been more rapid than it otherwise would have been. During the year 1814 a great number of buildings have been erected, and the population can be little short of 8,000.

*Manufactures, &c.*—With respect to the state of its manufactures, trade, and its progress, this will best be derived from the details published at different periods in the Magazine Almanac, and in the last edition of the Navigator.

The following statement of the number of master workmen in each particular branch, with the manufacturies, was taken in the fall of 1807: 1 cotton manufactury, having a mule of 120 threads, and one spinning jenny of 40 threads, 4 looms, and a wool carding machine under the same roof; 1 glass works, on the opposite side of the

Monongahela, for green, and one on this side, for white glass; 2 breweries, 1 air-furnace, 4 nail facturies, one of which makes 100 tons of cut and hammered nails annually; 7 coppersmiths, tin-plate workers, and japanners; 1 wire weaving and riddle factury; 1 brass foundery, 6 saddlers and harness makers, 2 gunsmiths, 2 tobacconists, 1 bell maker, 3 tallow chandlers, 1 brush maker, 1 trunk maker, 5 coopers, 13 weavers, 10 blue dyers, 1 comb & 7 cabinet makers, 1 turner, 6 bakers, 8 butchers, 2 barbers, 6 hatters, 4 physicians, 2 potteries of earthen ware, 3 straw bonnet makers, 4 plane makers, 6 milliners, 12 mantua makers, 1 stocking weaver, 2 book-binders, 4 house and sign painters, 2 portrait painters, 1 mattress maker, 3 wheelwrights, 5 watch and clock makers and silversmiths, 5 bricklayers, 5 plasterers, 3 stone cutters, 8 boat, barge, and ship builders, 1 pump maker, 1 looking glass maker, 1 lock maker, 7 tanyards, 2 rope walks, 1 spinning wheel maker, 17 blacksmiths, 1 machinist and whitesmith, 1 cutler and tool maker, 32 house carpenters and joiners, 21 boot and shoe makers or cordwainers, 5 windsor chair makers, 13 tailors, 1 breeches maker and skin dresser, 12 schoolmasters, 4 schoolmistresses, 33 taverns or public inns, 51 mercantile stores, 4 printing offices, 6 brickyards, 3 stone masons, 2 bookstores, 4 lumber yards, 1 maker of machinery for cotton and wool manufacturies, one factury for clay smoking pipes, 1 copper-plate printing press.

In the year 1810 there was the following enumeration made by the marshall.

In Pittsburgh and the immediate vicinity the following establishments are enumerated, and the quantity manufactured or value in dollars yearly, set down, viz.

One grist mill, by steam, manufactures 60,000 bushels of grain. Three carding and spinning mills, two of cotton and one of wool, amount in dollars 14,248. One mill for grinding flat irons, 2000 dollars. Two distilleries, which make 600 barrels of whiskey. Three breweries make 6,435 barrels of porter, ale and beer. Four brick yards, 13,600 dollars. One rope walk, 2,500 dollars.— Two air furnaces, 400 tons, 40,000 dollars. Three red lead facturies estimated at 13,100 dollars. Six naileries 49,890 dollars. Three glass works, one green and two white glass, 62,000 dollars. Two potteries 3,400 dollars. Two gun smitheries 2,400 dollars. Three tobacconists

11,500 dollars. Sixteen looms 19,448 yards of cloth.— Six tanneries 15,500 dollars. Seventeen smitheries 34,400 dollars. Four cooperies 2,250 dollars. Eight chair and cabinet makers 17,424 dollars. —— Saddlers and shoe and boot makers, number not set down; the amount of their manufactures estimated at 65,878 dollars. Ten hatteries 24,507 dollars. Four silversmiths and watch makers 9,500 dollars. Six copper, brass and tin factories 25,500 dollars. Three stone cutters, 8,800 dollars.— Three boat and ship builders 43,000 dollars. Two wagon makers 2,872 dollars. Three chandlers 14,500 dollars. One button manufactury 3000 dollars. One stocking weaver. One cutlery 3000 dollars. One glass cutting 1000 dollars. One wire weaving, at which sieves, screens, riddles, &c. are made to considerable extent.— Three printing establishments and one book bindery.

Some of the estimates in the foregoing statement are too low for the time, especially in the saddlery line ; which was ascertained with some degree of accuracy in the year 1809, to amount to about forty thousand dollars. In the same year boots and shoes were made to about the amount of seventy thousand dollars.

There is now in complete operation one wire drawing mill, propelled by the power of steam, which in a short time will be enabled to supply to a considerable extent the demand for wire. This establishment has been made by Mr. William Eichbaum, sen.

The manufacture of coffee mills and locks by Mr. James Patterson, an English artist, has lately been commenced. Fire shovels, tongs, drawing knives, hatchets, two feet squares, augers, chissels, adzes, claw hammers, door hinges, chains, hackles, locks, door handles, spinning wheel irons, plough irons, flat irons, &c. are made in numbers and form a portion of the trade of the place.

An extension in the manufactury of stirrup irons and bridle bits, is contemplated. A paper mill is erecting, in which the steam power will be used.

The following general view may give some idea of the present state of manufactures, &c. in this place. But these are continually undergoing so many changes and improvements, that it is difficult to make a statement which will remain correct for any length of time.

*Glass houses.*—The manufacture of glass has succeeded as well as the most sanguine had expected, the situation of this place is peculiarly favorable, notwithstanding some disadvantages in procuring some of the materials. The first was established by col. O'Hara, about the year 1798. There are two glass works on the opposite side of the Monongahela, erected by Trevor and Ensel, and one in the new town of Birmingham, under the firm of Beltzhoover, Wendt & Co. These, with the three before erected, to wit: O'Hara's, Robinson's, and Bakewell's, will be able to manufacture to the amount of $ 160,000 annually. Both flint and green glass are now made here to great perfection. Messrs. Bakewell, Page and Bakewell, have lately built another flint glass works, in addition to their former one. There are now in the town and opposite, two white and three green glass houses. Glass cutting is likewise executed in this place, not inferior to the best cut glass in Europe. The furniture of the apothecaries' shops, is altogether of home manufactury.

*Air foundries.*—Of these we have two, M'Clurg's, and Beelen's; on plans which enable them to cast, shortly after their establishment, about 600 tons a year of all kinds of hollow wares, machinery, cannon balls, smiths' anvils, sad irons, &c. worth 54,000 dollars. Mr. Price has also a small air foundry for casting but hinges and buckles for saddlery; he casts brass also. Messrs. M'Clurg and Beelen, *cast iron boilers*, which answer as a valuable substitute for copper stills for distilleries.* Besides these foundries there are two others, one established by the " Pittsburgh Steam Engine Company," and the other in the town of Birmingham, owned by Peter Kimmel. Mr. M'Clurg is also building one on the Allegheny river immediately above the town. At Mr. Beelen's 400 tons of castings are now made annually. At the same establishment he has erected a mill for boring cylinders, air pumps, and pumps and pipes for steam engines, for turning sugar rollers, pivots and shafts, and for grinding sad irons, sithes, sickles, &c. " The Pittsburgh Steam Engine Company," likewise bore cylinders, turn sugar

---

* In these the operation is carried on by steam with half the expense and labor, and probably a more wholesome liquor produced.

rollers, &c. The castings executed in Pittsburgh are not excelled in point of clear casting and beauty by any in the United States.

*Ironmongery.*—This is becoming a manufacture of the greatest importance. To our former establishments there are several new and very extensive ones now erecting.— Messrs. Brown, Barker and Butler, have established an extensive hardware manufactury, where they already make nails, and intend to make edge tools and cutlery generally. Messrs. Foster and Murry have erected steam works for the purpose of setting in operation a tilt hammer. They make shovels, spades, sithes, sickles, &c. Mr. Cowan has erected a most powerful steam engine to reduce iron to various purposes. It is calculated for a *seventy horse power*, which puts into complete operation *a rolling mill, a slitting mill and a tilt hammer*, all under the same roof. This establishment furnishes sheet iron, nail and spike rods, shovels, tongs, spades, sithes, sickles, hoes, axes, frying pans, cutting knives, vices, scale beams, chissels, augers, &c. &c. This is one of the most important establishments in the western country; it has been transferred to Messrs. Stackpole and Whiting, under whom it is in complete operation. There are other man- ufactures which furnish locks, files, coffee mills, plane bits, door handles, kitchen furniture, squares, hackles, and a variety of edge tools, it would be endless to enumerate the various articles of their mongery, which are manufac- tured. The stranger is stunned by an incessant din of clattering hammers, and blowing of bellows es from morn- ing till night. The amount of this manufactury, was es- timated two years ago at 396 tons, or 871,200 lbs. includ- ing all articles made from iron, as it comes from the forge, from the nail or sprig to the plough iron; and this aver- aging at 20 cents per lb. will make 174,240 dollars.— This amount has since probably doubled.

*Woollen and Cotton.*—This business is progressing handsomely. Mr. James Cumming gave a statement for 1812, in which year he made 5 wool carding and 2 cotton carding machines, 6 wool pickers, 1 mule and a billy.— James Arthurs' woollen manufactury has two jennies, 40 spindles each, 2 carding machines, and 8 looms. He cards 80 lbs. of wool per day, for seven months in the year, and intends to make blankets, cassinets and flannels.

Hugh and James Jelly are erecting a cotton manufactury to go by steam power. Mr. Kerwin's and Mr. Armitage's cotton facturies are progressing very handsomely. George Cochran purposes to manufacture flannels and blankets in company with Mr. Dowling, to carry on the worsted business, carding and spinning yarn for pantaloons, serges, bazes and stockings. For the first, Mr. Cochran has employed two carding machines, a billy of 40, and a jenny of 50 spindles, but there is some difficulty in procuring wool. Thomas Davis has constructed a wool spinning billy with 30 spindles. Isaac Wickersham, makes *cylindrical cloth shearing machines*, one of which, he says, can be operated on by a boy of ten or twelve years old, and shear in 12 hours 400 yards of cloth. In the cylinder are fixed 32 spring shears, which work in such a regular manner as neither to cut or injure the cloth in the slightest degree. Mr. Wickersham also goes on well in his weaving business. In the Almanac of the present year, (1815) there is this further notice:—" Mr. James Arthurs carries on extensively the wool carding and spinning, and contemplates shortly to manufacture woollen cloths. His machinery is propelled by steam; the engine partly the invention of one of his sons, to whose ingenuity great merit is due, not perhaps so much for originality or inventing, as by a useful and ingenious combination of the inventions of others. For instance, he has affixed the valve of Mr. French's engine to the common cylinder, which renders the engine more simple, more efficacious and less subject to disorder, than any we have yet seen. It is more efficacious as by the adoption of Mr. French's valve a great deal of friction is removed, and less liable to disorder, as the only valves he uses are those which let the steam on and off the gole way; instead of letting the steam on as by the common valves, it is here simply a common stop cock, which having a cross piece of iron fastened to it, is turned with great nicety and ease. James Jelly has erected a large three story building for carrying on the cotton carding, spinning and weaving. The whole is carried on extensively, and is worked by a steam engine made by Mr. Copeland of this place.— George Cochran at his woollen manufactury, makes all kinds of woollen cloths, blanketing, vest, patterns, hosiery, paper makers' felting, &c.

60 THE NAVIGATOR.

*Pottery, &c.*—Messrs. Alexander Trotter & Co. are establishing a *pottery*, at which they intend making all kinds of earthen ware, in a superior style, to any thing which has yet been attempted in the western country.— Mr. Trotter experiences difficulty in procuring clay; this is a great *desideratum*, in the United States.—It is hoped that our fellow citizens throughout the country, who are friendly to the real interest of their country, where they find any clay they think might answer the purpose of making fine earthen ware, will send a specimen to Mr. Trotter for examination, the trouble can be but trifling, and must be far counterbalanced by the reflection that they may have contributed to the establishment of an important manufacture, of an article which, from its brittle nature, we shall always have to pay double price if imported.

*White Lead Factory.*—There are two red and white lead factories, which manufacture extensively. Another *chemical laboratory*, for the manufacture not only of this article, but also the various acids and chemical preparations, is now erecting under the superintendence of doctor B. Toost, chemist.

*Steam Engine.*—There are three extensive establishments for making steam engines in this place. " The Pittsburgh Steam Engine Company," construct them on Oliver Evans' plan—" The Mississippi Steam Engine Company," on Fulton's; and Bolton and Watt's plan improved, are made by Thomas Copeland.

*Rope-walks.*—Messrs. John Irwin & Co. have lately erected an extensive rope-walk, at which they make large quantities of rope and twine of all kinds. At two rope-walks in this place the principal part of the cordage for the fleet on lake Erie was made. Two cables weighed about 4000 lbs. each; and $4\frac{1}{2}$ inches diameter.

*Stirrup irons and bridle bits*—Are made in large quantities at manufacturies in this place; and they give constant employment to about twenty-four workmen. These articles can be manufactured to the extent of the demand for them in the western country.

*Wheel irons.*—Messrs. Stevenson & Youard, make one gross of wheel irons weekly, at $ 30 per gross, making a yearly amount of this very useful article of 1560 dolls.

*Wire-drawing.*—Messrs. Eichbaum and son, have got their *wire mill* into handsome operation, and make beautiful wire of different sizes. The only deficiency in this establishment is, that it is not sufficiently extensive to supply the demand. There is at present a little difficulty in getting iron of a quality sufficiently good for this purpose. Mr. Eichbaum also carries on the glass-cutting business.

We understand a company is formed in New York with 1,500,000 dollars capital, for the purpose of manufacturing wire, and woollen and cotton cards.

*Buttons.* Reuben Neal manufactures about 100 gross of metal buttons weekly, being 5,000 gross, or 60,000 dozen annually—averaging from 47 to 125 cents per gross—a yearly amount of $ 5000. He also makes Titannia spoons, tin wares, &c.

*Knitting needle* making has been commenced by Messrs. Frethy & Pratt. In New York, *pin making* is going on lively. It is hoped our females will be well supplied with these articles, especially with the first.

*Silver Plating.* Benjamin Kendrick has just commenced this business. He plates stirrup irons, bits, harness trimmings, buckles and slides, castors, clocks, jewelry, &c. Mr. Ayres also carries on this branch of business.

*Morocco leather.* A manufacture of Morocco skins has been commenced by Messrs. Scully & Graham, and succeeds well. It consumes many, and has created a considerable demand for sheep skins. Thus we go on with the luxuries as well as the necessaries of life.

*White lead Manufactury.* Here also excellent paints are prepared out of lead, and in quantities. Mr. Beelen, proprietor. Mr. J. J. Boudier, an ingenious French gentleman, manufacturer, and owner of the laboratory.

*Suspenders.* These are manufactured, of an excellent quality, by Wm. Gore, who weaves ten webs at once, either of silk, woollen or cotton. He also weaves boot web, and boot cord.

*Brass Foundery.* Thomas Cooper carries on this business extensively. Beyond what he casts for machineries for various kinds, he makes brass candlesticks, hand-irons, cocks for distilleries, &c.

*Trunks* are made smartly by J. M. Sloan, who wants for this purpose deer skins with the hair on.

*Stocking weaving,* for want of encouragement, perhaps, goes on but slowly. We see no reason why a stocking cannot be wove as cheap and as good here as in any other part of the world.     F

*Brush-making.* Mr. Blair conducts this business to great advantage, and manufactures vast quantities of brushes. Much more could be done were the farmers more careful of their hogs' bristles.

*Saddlery.* The manufacture of saddles, bridles, harness, &c. is carried on in this place very extensively. It is calculated that one of our saddlers, Mr. Little, makes to the amount of about 60,000 dollars annually.

*Boots and Shoes.* We have about 100 hands constantly engaged in this business, who make yearly about 100,000 dollars worth of boots and shoes, fine and coarse.

*Acids.* Dr. F. Aigster, an ingenious German chemist and mineralogist is industriously engaged in establishing a manufacture of acids in this place. This must be a highly useful establishment to our western physicians and druggists. Doctor Aigster has already discovered a sufficiency of the native materials in the neighborhood of Pittsburgh, and nothing is wanting to perfect the manufacture, but time and perseverance.

*Breweries.* Of these we have two extensive, and one on a small scale. They consume about 20,000 bushels of barley and manufacture not far short of 7,000 barrels of beer, porter and ale, annually, worth about 40,000 dollars.

*Steam flour-mill.* This mill proceeds handsomely, she drives three pair of stones nearly day and night, which grind about 60,000 bushels of wheat, corn, and rye, annually, worth 45,000 dollars, when made into flour.

*Tin and copper wares.* The manufacture of these are carried on extensively, together with *japanning*. Copper stills, will, most probably, be in less demand, since it is found that the cast-iron boilers answer every purpose, and the substitution of the latter for the former is fortunate, particularly at this time, and ought to be encouraged on principles of economy and independence.

*Carpenters' plains*, are made of an excellent quality, and in such quantities as to supply the demand of the country. Mr. Wm. Scott and Mr. Lithgow are the principal manufacturers of this article.

*Trade, &c.*—The ratio of business of the place has increased still more rapidly than the population, and has become on a more extended scale: arising from the large manufacturies established, and from the supplying western merchants by wholesale, and since the war by the transportation of southern produce across the mountains. The following table will shew the extent of the trade of this place in 1810.

A view of some of the items which form the mass of trade in and through Pittsburgh, may not be uninteresting : The manufacture of hemp into ropes, rope yarn, and bagging, is a business in itself which is enriching the state of Kentucky much faster than if the citizens had discovered a gold mine equal to some of those of Mexico and Peru. The quantity of spun yarn for ropes, and hemp which has passed through this place for the Baltimore and Philadelphia markets, for the past season (1810,) stands thus:—

| | lbs. |
|---|---|
| Through Messrs. T. & J. Cromwell's warehouse, from May 1, 1810, to November 14, of the same year, 6½ months— | 882,000 |
| 980 kreels yarn, averaging 900lbs. each Hemp, | 308,944 |
| C. Cowan's warehouse, 83 kreels of yarn, averaging 9000 lbs. each, | 74,000 |
| G. Anshutz's warehouse, 254 bales hemp, | 24,000 |
| James Adams s warehouse, spun yarn in two months, | 90,000 |

Total spun yarn, and hemp—lbs. 1,378,944 Which is worth in the Philadelphia and Baltimore markets 15 cents per pound at a low average, amounting to the sum of $ 206,841,60 cts.

The quantity of bar iron and castings which are sold in our market stands thus:—

| | tons |
|---|---|
| G. Anshutz, bar, rolled, and slit iron, for 1810, | 332 |
| Castings, | 75 |
| C. Cowan, castings, | 50 |
| Sundry iron, | 300 |
| T. & J. Cromwell, iron, | 150 |
| Castings, | 100 |
| Say for what passes through all other hands, | 300 |
| | 1,307 |

Total, one thousand three hundred tons bar iron and castings, worth per ton upon an average $ 140, amounting to 182,980 dollars.

The following articles also form a busy and extensive trade in and through this place:—

|  |  | tons. |
|---|---|---|
| Bacon and pork, principally from Kentucky, Anshutz, | | 15 |
| Sundry bacon, Cowan, | . . . . | 35 |
| | Total bacon, | 50 |

worth 10 cents per lb. amounting to 11,000 dollars.

|  | lbs. |
|---|---|
| Bales cotton 600, averaging 400 lbs. Cromwells, Cowan, Anshutz & others | 240,000 |

worth 19 cents per lb. amounting to $ 45,600.

|  |  |  | lbs. |  |
|---|---|---|---|---|
| Cut and wrought nails, Anshutz, of Juniata iron. | | | 50,000 | |
| do. | do. | Cowan, | . | 40,000 |
| do. | do. | others, say | . | 20,000 |
| | | | lbs. | 110,000 |

One hundred and ten thousand pounds cut and wrought nails, worth 17 cents per pound, amounting to $ 18,700.

|  | lbs. |
|---|---|
| Tobacco, Cromwells, Cowan and others, about | 20,000 |

worth 13 cents per lb. upon an average, amounting to $ 2,600.

|  |  |
|---|---|
| Glass, (Cromwells) Geneva, worth each year, | $ 10,000 |

All the above articles, the nails excepted, which are manufactured here, may be considered about half of what may be called the *passing domestic* trade of Pittsburgh, and which amounts to the round sum of $ 458,624,60 cts. If we include salt-petre, of which I have no just idea of the quantity, but which I know is very considerable, lead, the articles of salt, whiskey, country linen, paper and a few minor articles, which form items of trade and barter, but which are not manufactured in town, I think we may safely give to this species of our commerce, the sum of *one million of dollars annually*. And probably about the same sum to articles actually manufactured by our citizens from raw materials. Thus have we a trade in domestic articles, which are the *soul* of our country, upon a rough and hasty calculation, and which I feel confident is within the mark, *of two millions of dollars annually*, half of which amount is manufactured from the products and raw materials of the country.

When the line of steam boats can be put in operation, a very important inland trade will be carried on between this country and the countries lower down; sugars, cotton, lead, and hemp, will be exchanged for ironmongery, glass, paper, saddlery, boots and shoes, &c. It is calculated that the freight from New Orleans to this place will but little exceed three dollars, which is less than the transportation across the mountains. A great number of barges constantly ply between this and the country below; some idea may be formed of the extent of this trade from the following estimate of imports from New Orleans, by one house here, (Bosler & Co.) from the 1st April to the 1st Sept. 1814.

| | |
|---|---|
| 1403 blls. sugar . . . | 365,672 lbs. |
| 15 boxes white Havanna sugar | 4.769 |
| 129 blls. coffee . . . | 19,604 |
| 380 bales cotton . . . | 128,793 |
| 28 bales Spanish wool . . | 13,244 |
| 100 kegs quick-silver . . | 7,000 |
| 30 surroons } | |
| 30 blls. indigo } . . | 7,800 |
| logwood . . . | 7,840 |
| 6 blls. rum | |

It is difficult to form a correct estimate of the present amount of trade, but it is presumed it cannot be less than 4 millions. The number of wagons constantly plying between this place and the eastern seaports is immense.[*] The quantity of boards and scantling which passed inspection in the year 1812, exceeded seven millions of feet, all of which was consumed in the buildings of the town. The number of boats which annually touch at this place on their way down the Allegheny and Monongahela rivers, is very great, but no one has yet taken the pains to estimate the number; this is daily increasing, from the

* It appears from an accurate account, taken by a gentleman who lives about four miles from town, on the great road, that the number of foreign or road wagons laden with merchandise, which passed his farm for Pittsburgh, from the 1st Jan. 1813, to the 1st Jan. 1814, amount to the surprising number of 4055!

*Pittsburgh Gazette, Nov.* 1814.

extension of settlements, and the increase of population on those rivers. This place was by act of congress declared a port of clearance, and at one time ship building was carried on with considerable spirit; whether this has been relaxed in consequence of the war, or from its having been shewn by experience not to be profitable, is not well known. The following is a list of the vessels which have been built here, as published in our former edition.

From the year 1802 to 1805, the following vessels were launched at the ship yards: The ships, *Pittsburgh*, *Louisiana*, *General Butler*, and *Western Trader*; Brigs *Nanina*, *Dean*, and *Black Walnut*; schooners *Amity*, *Allegheny*, and *Conquest*. The *Monongahela Farmer*, and brig *Ann Jean* were built at Elizabethtown. Misfortunes and accidents, in getting these vessels down the Ohio, which most probably arose from bad management in the persons entrusted with them, has given a damp to ship building at present. Barges, keels, Kentucky boats, &c. are built in great numbers, to the amount of about 12,000 dollars annually.

For the purpose of carrying on the trade, the following steam boats have been built, and are on the way: The New Orleans, built in 1811–12; Vesuvius, 1812–13; Enterprise from Brownsville descended the river in the spring of 1814; the Etna and Buffalo, lately built, and now at this place, and a large one on the stocks.

*Public buildings*—These are a large brick court-house, and market house in the same square, with two others on the space of ground on the Monongahela, laid out into town lots by col. O'Hara. A handsome octagonal brick episcopal church, on Liberty and Wood streets, a large presbyterian, a German lutheran, a covenanter meeting house, besides a catholic chapel which has an excellant organ.

*Inhabitants*, *&c.*—A mixture of all nations, though principally Americans; there are Irish, Scotch, English, French, Dutch, Swiss, &c. The proportion of people of color is not great, and are chiefly in the quality of hired servants and day laborers. The character of the people is that of enterprising and persevering industry; every man to his business is the prevailing maxim, there is therefore little time devoted to amusements or to the cultivation of refined social pleasures. Strangers are not much pleased with the place in point of hospitality merely; but those who have business to transact, will meet with as many facilities as elsewhere. They are of all denominations of the christian religion; many of them attentive on the duties of their worship, and but few addicted to gross vices and dissipation. Luxury, pomp and parade are scarcely seen; there are perhaps, not more than one or two carriages in the place. There is a public academy, but not in a flourishing state, where the Latin and Greek classics are taught. There are besides, a number of English schools where children are taught to read, write, arithmetic, grammar, &c. There is a seminary for young ladies, which is said to be well conducted. The amusements of these industrious people are not numerous, a few balls during the winter season; there is also a small theatre where a company from the eastern cities sometimes performs. A society has been formed for the purpose of mutual improvement in the different departments of natural history, and is flourishing; it has attached to it a circulating library, a cabinet of curiosities and chemical laboratory.

*Markets*, have risen very considerably within the last two or three years; they are now in many articles nearly as high as in Philadelphia—Beef sells for 6 or 7 cents per lb.; flour $ 4 50 per cwt. or nine dollars per barrel; potatoes 75 cents per bushel, and cabbage 6 cents a head; butter from 25 to 50 per pound; fowls 50 cents a pair; ducks 50; geese 75 to 1 25; and turkies from 75 cents to 2 dolls. each: venison 5; pork 7; hog's lard 11; mutton 7; veal 6; and cheese from 18 to 25 cents per pound: eggs at 25 cts. per dozen; onions 1 25 per bushel; Indian meal one dollar per bushel—and soup beans one dollar per bushel: fish from 4 to 5 cents per pound; and a variety of other articles with which the markets are abundantly filled on Wednesdays and Saturdays, the stated market days.

*Banks*—are "The Office of Discount and Deposit," a branch of the Pennsylvania bank: "The Bank of Pittsburgh," lately chartered, with a capital of six hundred thousand dollars: and "The Farmers' and Mechanics' Bank," with a capital of four hundred and fifty thousand dollars.

*Latitude, &c.*—Pittsburgh is the county town of the county of Allegheny, situated in lat. 40° 35′ N. long. 80°

38' W. being about five degrees westward of Philadelphia, It is 300 miles W. by N. of Philadelphia, 252 from Washington city, about 335 from Lexington, K. and about 1100 from New Orleans by land, though 2000 by water. Our climate, though irregular, and subject to many changes in the different seasons, is healthy; any thing like epidemical diseases, fevers, &c. being unknown among us; except those that rage without bounds; such as the *Influenza*, in the summer and fall of 1807, whose contagion, though but in few instances mortal, flew to all parts of the United States.

*Coal Banks.*—This place has long been celebrated for its coal banks, and both as to quantity and quality it is not exceeded by any part of America, or perhaps of the world. It is in fact in general use in all private houses, and in the extensive manufacturies established through the town.— Coal is found in all the hills around this place for ten miles at least, and in such abundance that it may almost be considered the substratum of the whole country. The mines or pits which supply the town, are not further than from one to three miles distant, between the rivers; until within a few years, no coals were brought across the Monongahela, but since the price has been advanced from the increased demand, a considerable supply is now obtained from that quarter. Little short of a million of bushels are consumed annually; the price formerly six cents, has now risen to twelve cents, keeping pace with the increased price of provisions, labor, &c. Several of the manufacturies have coal pits at their very door, such as those under the Coal hill, which saves the expense of transportation. The coal pits on the side of the Coal hill are about one-third from the top, which is about on a level with the stratum on the opposite side of the river.— There are forty or fifty pits opened, including those on both sides of the river. They are worked into the hill horizontally, the coal is wheeled to the mouth of the pit in a wheelbarrow, thrown upon a platform, and from thence loaded into wagons. After digging in some distance, rooms are formed on each side, pillars being left at intervals to support the roof. The coal is in the first instance separated in solid masses, the veins being generally from six to eight feet in thickness, and is afterwards broken into smaller pieces for the purpose of transportation. A laborer is able to dig upwards of one hundred bushels per day. It is supposed, and perhaps with good reason, that the *main* or principal stratum, lies considerably deeper, as in the English collieries; but the quantity so near the surface of the earth, will for a long period of time render it unnecessary to look for it at a greater depth. Fuel, that indispensable necessary of life, is so cheap here, that the poorest rarely suffer from the want of it. We do not witness near Pittsburgh that pitiable spectacle, the feeble infancy and decrepid age, of the unfortunate poor, suffering in a cold winter day for a little fire to warm their meagre and chilly blood—we do not see them shivering over a few lighted splinters or pieces of bark, gleaned from the high ways, or torn from the fences, in the skirts of the town.

As every blessing has its attendant evil, the stone coal is productive of considerable inconvenience from the smoke which overhangs the town, and descends in fine dust which blackens every object; even snow can scarcely be called white in Pittsburgh. The persons and dress of the inhabitants, in the interior of the houses as well as the exterior, experience its effects. The tall steeple of the court house, was once painted white, but alas! how changed. Yet all this might be prevented by some additional expense on the construction of the chimnies. In the English manufacturing towns, a fine is imposed upon those who do not consume their smoke. Incalculable would be the advantage to this place, could such a regulation be adopted. The advantages of cleanliness, and even health, not to mention the improvement in the azure of the sky, and in the light of the sun and moon, ought surely to rouse the public spirit of the inhabitants.

To sum up the advantages of Pittsburgh—It is noted as a place of manufactures, already established and which will doubtless be established in the course of time. This place is in fact less liable to changes and to sudden relapse than almost any situation in America. The contingencies of peace or war cannot effect its prosperity. The western merchant procures from Pittsburgh a variety of articles he was formerly in the habit of bringing across the mountains. The cheapness of fuel, and of all the necessaries of life, the favorable position for distributing its manufactures over an extensive country, will probably make it at some period or other the first inland town in America. The wholesale business has wonderfully increased within the last few years. The towns that begin to rise on the Allegheny and Monongahela rivers, and those round the head of the Ohio, and for some distance below, are even now, in some measure supplied with merchandise from Pittsburgh. In time there will be reservoirs of this kind from whence the neighboring towns will be supplied; for the profits of the country shop-keepers will scarcely warrant the expense and loss of time, in every instance, for travelling to the Atlantic states, for the purpose of procuring an assortment—besides, the difficulty of obtaining a credit where he cannot be very well known. Pittsburgh will become a place of deposit for the produce of the Allegheny and Monongahela countries; it will be the mart for such articles of the produce of the states of Ohio, Kentucky and Tennessee, as may be in demand in the western parts of the state, and since the war, in a variety of articles, particularly sugar and cotton, to be transported across the mountains: it will thus be the centre of the western inland trade.

*Price of property and rents.*—The price of property has increased in the most surprising manner within the last ten years; it is now at least ten times as high as it was at that period. There are but few sales of lots in fee simple, the custom is to let on perpetual lease: the price in Market and Wood streets, varies from ten to twenty dollars per foot, and in the other streets from four to eight, and in particular situations still higher. The rents are equally high. In Market, Wood and Water streets, the principal places of business, it is difficult to procure a common room in an upper story, under one hundred dollars per annum; the rent of stores, vary from three to five hundred dollars; there is one ware house which rents for twelve hundred: the rent of tavern stands, is from five to twelve hundred dollars. The rent of dwelling houses varies much, according to the locality and kind of the tenement; a genteel private family can scarcely obtain a good dwelling under three or four hundred dollars.

Having given this succinct view of Pittsburgh, we shall endeavor to give a short account of the country around it.

The surface is rough and broken, to use the common expression, that is, the vales are narrow, and the hills abrupt. There is much of the picturesque in scenery, though but little of the sublime or magnificent. The Monongahela and Allegheny are bordered with high hills, though presenting but few bare rocky precipices, and the sides clothed with timber. The Coal hill rises, as it has been already said, with a steep ascent almost from the water's edge, the bare ledges of rocks, shewing themselves in places, but in general covered with soil, yet with an acclivity so great, that it would be dangerous, if not impossible to clamber up. In summer when clad with green, it has a very beautiful appearance, through the vistas of Market street or Wood street; and in winter when whitened with snow, and begemmed with icicles, its appearance is no less venerable and pleasing. Between the rivers the country is very much diversified; about two miles from town, a small rivulet discharges itself into the Monongahela, near a beautiful meadow, belonging to Mr. Beelen, who has made some handsome improvements on his estate here: this rivulet rises a few miles in the hills towards the Allegheny, and has a descent of some hundred feet in that distance through a deep glen, forming several very pretty cascades and basons.— The country watered by Chartiers creek, a considerable stream which enters the Ohio a few miles below Pittsburgh, is extremely beautiful; much of the soil is admirably adapted to cultivation, and from the picturesque variety of the surface, it is susceptible of all those improvements which men of fortune and taste might be disposed to bestow. On the other side of the Allegheny, Pine creek, four miles above Pittsburgh, affords a great deal of wild and romantic scenery, it is a beautiful clear stream, bordered in some places, with high rocky precipices, with a few pines growing on them, and in other places by handsome vallies. The Connoquenessing, about twenty-five miles north of the Allegheny, has already become celebrated for the important improvements on its banks, effected by some industrious Germans. There is a very fine soil on the borders of the stream, and the upland is well timbered.

The country round the head of the Ohio is improving very rapidly, and filling with inhabitants. It is perhaps,

one of the most healthy spots in the United States; free
from stagnant waters and marshes, fevers are but little
known.  Lands have augmented in price in the same
proportion with the town lots; it is difficult to purchase
a cultivated tract under ten or twenty dollars per acre,
and even as high as forty or fifty in the immediate vicinity of the town.

There are in this neighborhood some of those scenes
of historical reminiscence, highly gratifying to Americans.  Of these Braddock's field is the most remarkable.
It was here that Washington first displayed those talents
which afterwards entitled him to the name of FATHER OF
HIS COUNTRY.  Here by a masterly retreat, he saved the
remnant of the defeated army.  The battle ground, which
is immediately on the bank of the river, is often examined by the curious; the marks of balls are still visible in
many of the trees, and human bones are yet to be seen on
the ground.

## OF THE OHIO RIVER,

### *ITS CHANNEL, RIPPLES, ISLANDS, SANDBARS, TRIBUTARY WATERS, TOWNS, DISTANCE FROM PLACE TO PLACE, &c.*

ON shoving off at Pittsburgh, if the water should be high, your boat will require but little attention, otherwise than keeping her bow foremost and giving her headway by the application of the oars. But in low water, for which these directions are intended, it requires more circumspection, in the first place, to prevent the boat grounding on a large flat bar at the mouth of the Allegheny, nearly meeting the foot of the Monongahela bar. There is, however, a good passage between these two bars, in a direction a little above the Point or junction of the two rivers, towards O'Hara's glass-works. Before you get quite opposite the Point, incline to the left, and you will get into the chute, keeping the foot of the Monongahela bar on the left hand, and the head of that of the Allegheny on your right. From thence you will find the best water near the left shore, until you begin to approach

Hamilton's (now Brunot's) Island, No. 1,     2
which you must keep to your left, taking the chute at the head of the island bar, close to the right hand bank. This chute is narrow and rapid, but safe and easily made, providing you pull for it in time, otherwise there is a danger of being thrown on the sand bar which runs up a good way above the head of the island.

Near the foot of No. 1, a bar puts out from the island, and opposite it on the right shore is an extensive shoal—in order to avoid both these bars, keep about three-fourths of the river to your right, and within about 50 or 60 yards of the island, thence the channel runs pretty close to the foot of the island, then bears off to the right again, receiving the water of the left hand pass of the island, with the addition of *Chartiers creek,* which empties in on the left, opposite the middle of the island. On this creek, which extends through part of Washington county Pa. are some of the oldest and best settlements in the western country. It is crossed twice over handsome bridges on the stage route from Pittsburgh to Washington, and it is on this creek, near the forks, and two miles below Canonsburgh, where the late colonel George Morgan attempted an extensive settlement, to which he gave the name of MORGANZA.

On the left and immediately below the foot of No. 1, is a projecting cliff, called *M'Kees Rocks.* No. 1 is

G

about a mile long, and finely improved by its proprietor,
doctor Brunot, well known for his hospitality to strangers and friends, and his taste in horticulture.

Irwin's (now Neville's) island, No. 2, three
    miles below No. 1,                              4 | 6

At the head of this island, is a bar putting out towards
the right shore, therefore you must keep about one-third
of the river to your right, and at the *first ripple*, opposite Baldwin's stone mill, leave a breaker or rock a little to your right. Thence bear towards the island, to
avoid the *second, or Horse-tail ripple*, which is about half
way down the island, leaving a bar to the right, and
some breakers to the left.

No. 2 is a fine large island, about six miles long, possessing several good farms and other improvements. It
belongs to the family of general Neville of Pittsburgh.

Hog island, No. 3, just below and joined to No.
    2 by a bar.

This island, though very small, forms a considerable
impediment to this part of the river. The channel is uncommonly crooked, narrow, and difficult to hit, hence,
the greater care is required. At its head a bar extends
out, and obliges you to keep pretty close to the right
shore, thence pull for the island, keeping pretty close
to it, and take the chute which runs directly across to
the left shore towards Middletown, and close under
the foot of the island, leaving a broad flat bar to your
right, on the head of which there is a danger of grounding, without great circumspection, and hard pulling or
poling, for there is a great proportion of the river runs
over this bar, but not in sufficient depth to afford a boat
channel, unless in a rise of the river, notwithstanding a
channel through the bar has been attempted by artificial means, running in a direct line with the river above.

After you get through the Hog island chute and floating near the left shore a short distance, the channel
bears to the right considerably, and at the distance of
half or three quarters of a mile below Hog island, having about two-thirds of the river to your left, you pass
the *Third or Woolery's ripple, or trap.*

Dead-man's island, No. 4, and ripple,             9 | 15

This is a very small island, and in floods nothing is
seen of it but the willows growing on it. The channel
is somewhat difficult and serpentine in very low stages
of the water. A bar extends upwards from the head of
the island, which forms a ripple, and which you avoid
by pulling for the right shore as soon as you get near it,
leaving the head of the bar and island to the left   After this first chute to the right, bear towards the island,

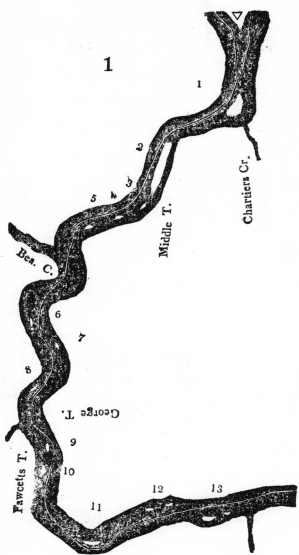

1

then again to the right shore, and then again incline to
the left, which puts you clear of Dead-man's ripple just
below the island, where the water, from a rocky bottom,
is rough, and looks formidable, but is not dangerous.

Big Seweekly creek, right side,                    2  17

Opposite the mouth of this creek is a sand bar, therefore, bear pretty close on the left shore.—Here used to
be an old French fishing basket.

Loggstown, right bank, Indian Loggstown, left
      side. (M. D.*)                             1½ 18½

Here is a large sand bar running up from the left
shore and approaches near the right, and between the
head of it and the right shore are large logs, the first of
which keep to the right, the second and third are opposite each other; you may go between these, and as soon
as you are past them, incline to the middle of the river.

Legionville is just below Loggstown, on the right side
of the river. General Wayne made an encampment
here in the year 1792, preparatory to his campaign
against the northern Indians, which terminated in the
total defeat of the latter, on the 20th August, 1794.—
Some of the old chimnies of the cabins built by general Wayne are still standing on the ground, which is an
extensive flat, high and timberless, except a thick
growth of young scrub oaks. On this flat there are considerable appearances of bog iron ore, as also in the banks
of the small stream above the encampment, which you
cross on the road from Pittsburgh to Beaver.

Crow's island, No. 5, divided by a gut,         5½ 24

Channel right side close to the island. A sand bar between the island and the right shore occasions a break
in the water, called *Walker's ripple.* Thence to Big Beaver you have deep and gentle water.

Duck run, left side,                              1 25
Big Beaver creek, right side, (M. D.)           4¼ 29¼

When about a mile above the mouth of Big Beaver incline towards the left shore, keeping about two-thirds of
the river on your right hand, in order to avoid two bars,
the one made by the entrance of the creek, which runs
down near the right side for a few rods below the lower warehouse, and the other, called Johnson's bar, a
quarter of a mile below the first, and also near the right
shore. Below this last bar and opposite the town of
Beaver, the right shore is shoal, and affords no land-

---

* (M. D.) Meaning measured distance, taken from col. Thomas Hutchin's "Table of Distances between Fort Pitt and the
mouth of the Ohio.

ing place until you get down to Carr's ferry, three miles below the creek. If you want to land at the town of Beaver, you must pull in just below the Beaver bar, where you will fall into an eddy, which will take you up a few rods to the Harmony warehouse, where is a good landing place. On coming out from the warehouse it requires care to clear Johnson's bar, which lies just below the Beaver bar; keep it well to your right and pull pretty well out into the river and there is no other impediment until you get down to Carr's ripple, which is made on the left side by the entrance of Rackoon creek, where the channel is nearest the right shore. Niblow's ferry is opposite Harmony warehouse, and Lawrence's ferry opposite Beavertown. Two-mile Run puts in on the right side two miles below the town.

Big Beaver is a large and valuable stream, 60 or 70 yards wide at its mouth, and three times that breadth at the falls, four miles from its junction with the Ohio, above which its navigation commences for keels and small crafts, which ascend to Youngstown, thence to Warren, seat of justice for Trumbull co. Ohio, 50 miles by land from its mouth.

The falls of Big Beaver are a singular, and at the same time a valuable construction of nature. The ground on the east side of the creek is so situated that a canal commencing at the head of the falls could be constructed, and convey water enough at all seasons, with sufficient fall, to drive as many mills, forges, furnaces, &c. as could stand crowded together for the distance of four miles, nay, 20 miles, if the canal was that long, and it could be carried up the Ohio that far and still have fall enough. The falls are three miles in length, and have on them at present 4 grist and two saw mills, a forge, a furnace, an oil and fulling mill, and a wool and cotton carding machines, and other works of utility. This place was purchased some years ago and settled by quakers, who had views of making extensive manufacturing establishments. It will require an immense capital, however, to do as much as ought to be done here. One million of dollars well applied at this spot, would yield an interest, superior, I am of opinion, to any banking institution in the United States, and much more to the general benefit of the community.

At Kishkuskes, 16 miles up, Big Beaver forks into two branches, one interlocks with French creek and Cherage, the other with Muskingum and Cuyahoga; on this last branch, 35 miles above the forks are several salt springs. On a north-eastern branch of Beaver 8 miles above the falls, is the town and settlement of Harmony and Zelienople. Harmony, from the rapid manner in

which it has sprung out of the forest, and from the singular union of its worthy inhabitants (all Germans) it
has become a very interesting place, and of much importance in manufactures and agriculture.

BEAVER (town of,)                                    ¾   30

Is situated three quarters of a mile below the mouth
of Big Beaver, on a high stony plain, where the old fort
M'Intosh stood, about 200 feet above the level of the
river.  The plain is amazingly full of pebble stones,
whose surfaces would lead to an opinion that they had
been rounded by the friction of the waters of the Ohio,
to have performed which, the bed of that river must
have been two hundred feet higher than it is at present.
Many other appearances in this quarter of the country,
go to justify this hypothesis.  Beaver was laid out on a
large scale, in 1797-8, and established the seat of justice
for Beaver county, Penn.  It has a court-house, a jail, a
market-house, a post and printing office, about 40 or 50
houses a good deal scattered, a number of mercantile
stores and public inns.  The inhabitants experienced
at first much inconvenience in getting a supply of water,
which, for several years was conveyed through pipes
from a spring at the base of a hill half a mile back of the
town.  After several unsuccessful attempts, a well at
length was sunk, which gives a supply.  It is upwards of
100 feet in depth, and the water is drawn by a windlass.
There has been lately established in Beaver, an extensive brewery, by Mr George Grier, whose beer is esteemed at Natchez and New Orleans.  Beaver has nothing in it to invite settlers, but a due attention to manufactures, as living is cheap, may increase the growth of
the town to some importance.

One mile below the town keep between some large
breakers and the left shore.

Rackoon creek, left side,                           2   32

This creek makes a ripple—channel nearest right
shore.

No. 6, first island below Beaver, ½ a mile long,   4   36

Channel left side, middle of the river. No. 6 lies near
the right side, and is very small.

No. 7, second island, about one mile long,          3   39

Channel right side, pretty close to the right bank, at
the head of No. 7, is a smart chute.

No. 8, Grape island, half a mile long,              2   41

Channel left side, close to the island—It lies rather
nearest the right shore.

GEORGETOWN,                                     1½  42⅔

A village of Beaver county, situated on the left bank
of the river, on a plain similar in height and formation to

the one at Beavertown. It contains one store, a post office, a tavern or two, and a few other scattered buildings, apparently on the decline. A few yards from the opposite shore, a little above the town, a spring rises from the bed of the river, throwing out a bituminous oil, similar to what is called seneca oil, supposed to proceed from a bed of mineral coal embowelled beneath the river. In a low state of the water the smell of the oil is sensibly felt on crossing at Georgetown.

Channel past the town is about the middle of the river.

Little Beaver creek, right side.     (M. D.)     $\frac{1}{4}$ 42$\frac{3}{4}$

This is a creek of Columbiana county, Ohio, and a valuable stream for water works, affording water at all seasons of the year, and a fine fall for seats   Near the mouth are two grist and one saw mill, and a mile above these is an extensive paper mill, erected in 1807–8, by Messrs. Coulter, Beaver & Bowman. Three miles above this last, is the Franklin paper mill, just got into operation, erected and owned by Cramer, Spear and Eichbaum & Co. Here also is a sawmill, tanyard, blacksmith shop, and the company purpose making several other useful manufacturing establishments, for which the seat and water is admirably calculated. Above this establishment are a number of saw and grist mills, furnaces and forges, and on the west fork, is a cotton carding, spinning and weaving establishment, by Mr. Corker, from Manchester, England, and others, for carding wool and cotton.

At the upper grist mill near the mouth of the creek, is a handsome arched bridge, substantially made, and well covered in, adding great facility to emigrants and travellers passing into the state of Ohio from this quarter.

New Lisbon, the seat of justice for Columbiana county, Ohio, a thriving village, is finely situated on the north-eastern branch of Little Beaver; and above it is the village of Salem, in the same county. On the eastern branch, near the head of the creek, Greersburgh is situated, in Beaver county, Pa. 12 miles north of the town of Beaver. This last town has a handsome stone academy, and is on the road from Beaver to Warren.

Mill creek, left side,                    $\frac{1}{4}$  43

Here the state line between Pennsylvania and Virginia on the one side, and Ohio and Pennsylvania on the other, crosses the river, running a due north and south direction.

No. 9, Mill creek island.

It is about a quarter of a mile long, and one mile below Little Beaver creek—channel on the left side—at the upper end of the island keep close to the left shore, leaving a small bar covered with grass to the right, then bear towards the island, until you are near the lower end of it, then keep about the middle of the river

No. 10, Custard's island, $\frac{1}{4}$ of a mile below No. 9.

Channel left side, close to the lower point of the island.

FAUCETSTOWN,                                          5|48

Is a small village on the right bank, half a mile below No. 10. About a mile below this town,

Little Yellow Creek puts in on the right side.

And about two miles below it, and two above Baker's island, is a

Sand bar in the middle of the river,

Channel right side.

Baker's Island, No. 11, (ending just above Big Yellow Creek)

Best channel right, close to the right shore at the upper end of the island.

Big Yellow Creek, right side,                     $6\frac{3}{4}$|$54\frac{3}{4}$

Channel pretty close to the left shore. Up this creek are several salt works, where has been made considerable quantities of salt.

No. 12, Neasley's Cluster of small islands,       $2\frac{1}{4}$|57

Channel right side, one-third over from the right shore at the upper end, then bear towards the island bar 300 or 400 yards down, leaving a small bar to the right, then turn short over towards the right shore.

No. 13, Tumbleston's Island, (and a small one below it)                                          2|59

Channel left side, between a snag near the shore and the island. Just below the island to the right is a sand bar, and a little below it to the left is another bar—there is no difficulty in going between these.

Crookston's Run and Mill, right side,

Black-horse Tavern, left side,                       3|62

Just below is White's tavern, a little below which are high broken cliffs on the left, and a short distance below these is

King's Creek, left side, and a tavern,

Brown's Island, No. 14,                              4|66

On the right of this island is a mill-dam, channel close to the left shore for 50 yards, thence towards the island keeping it to your right. On the left a steep and high hill presents itself to view. Below No. 14 is a *ripple*, keep close to the left shore.

*Island creek* comes in on the right side, opposite the middle of Brown's island, and on which are several valuable flour mills.

## Will's Creek, right side,

5 71

Channel close to the left shore, thence to Harman's creek keep near about the middle of the river, it being filled with logs and rocks.

Just above this creek on a rock under the hill there may be scraped up, especially after a shower and a warm sun, a fine white salt. And on the top of the same hill there is a spot where in winter the snow is observed to smoke as if occasioned by the internal heat of the earth. At the mouth of this creek is M'Causlin's flour mill.

## Harman's Creek, left side, (Holliday' Cove)

1 72

Here is warehouse, and is a principal place for the delivery of flour in this part of Virginia.

### STEUBENVILLE,

1 73

Is handsomely situated on a second bank, and occupies with its out-lots, a very fine bottom of the river, rich and extensive, and well formed. The penetrating eyes of James Ross esq. of Pittsburgh, and Bazil Wells esq. of this town, owning the land, and foreseeing the probable progress of settlements in the now state of Ohio, laid out a town on their ground in the year 1798–9, and in honor of the famous military character, Baron Steuben, called it STEUBENVILLE. The town having had a favorable beginning, with several favorable circumstances combined, it progressed rapidly and now contains about 150 dwellings, some of which are handsome brick buildings. It being the seat of justice for Jefferson county, Ohio, has a spacious brick court-house, which was built in 1807, and a stone jail. The presbyterians have a neat brick meeting-house; and the town is accommodated with a market-house, which, on market-days, affords a good supply of meat, fowls, vegetables, butter, cheese, fish, &c. A Land-office was early established here for the sale of Congress lands.

A bank was established in Steubenville in 1809, with a capital of 100,000 dollars, and a power to increase it to 500,000—Bazil Wells president. A newpaper is issued weekly. The town has about 12 stores, several well accommodated public inns; the schools of the town are under pretty good regulation. The citizens are industrious and hospitable, and they are beginning to turn their attention to the establishment of domestic manufactures, woollen and cotton particularly.

"The Steubenville Steam Mill Company," are erecting buildings in which it is intended to manufacture flour and cotton cloths, and to put up a tilt-hammer. And

Messrs. Ross and Baldwin of Pittsburgh, and Wells and Patterson of this place, have established a manufactory for woollens, with a capital of about $40,000. The steam power is used. A large paper mill is erecting by Messrs Scott and Bayless, in which they purpose to apply the steam power.

There are several valuable grist mills near Steubenville, which send a great deal of flour to New Orleans. The town has a post office receiving and discharging the public mail weekly. The fuel used is mineral coal and wood. Among the ingenious mechanics of Steubenville, is a Mr. Ross, who makes printing-presses of an excellent kind. From Pittsburgh to Steubenville by land it is only 38 miles, in a S. W. direction, by water it is 73 miles.

A run one mile below Steubenville, right side. A short distance below this run is a bad ripple, channel close to the right shore.

No. 15, Mingo bottom island,      2 | 75
Channel on the right side.

Indian Cross Creek, right side,

Virginia Cross Creek, left side, opposite each other, (M. D.)      $1\frac{1}{4}$ | $76\frac{1}{2}$

From a mile below these creeks to Charlestown, keep pretty close to the right hand shore.

About two miles below these creeks is a ripple, channel close to the right shore.

CHARLESTOWN,      $2\frac{3}{4}$ | 79

This is a town of Brook county Virginia, and has a handsome situation on a high bank of the Ohio. It contains about 80 dwellings, has a small court-house, a jail, a pillory,* a post office, an academy, public inns, several stores, and two or three large warehouses, from which are delivered annually, vast quantities of flour for the New Orleans market, there being a number of valuable merchant mills in the neighborhood, which deposite their flour here to wait the rising of the waters. Buffalo creek joins the Ohio just below the town, over which there was erected in 1812, a handsome chain bridge, on the plan of judge Finley's, of Fayette county, Penn.—Charlestown is a considerable place of embarkation, and boats can be had here generally, at a short notice. From Pittsburgh by land, on the stage route through Canonsburgh, Washington, and Middletown, it is 50 miles to

---

* What a pity that an enlightened people, in an enlightened age, should so far lose sight of the common principles of humanity, as to se- before the door, or public seat of justice, such a disgraceful, inhuman, and savage machinery of punishment.

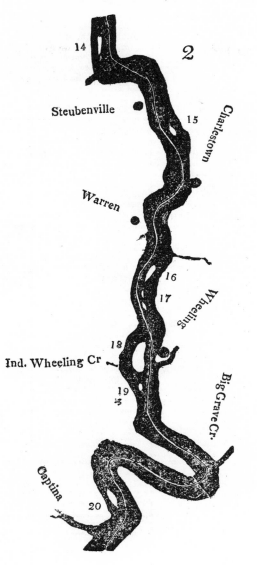

Charlestown, in a S. W. direction. Mr. William M'Cluney conducts a manufactory of delf ware in Charlestown; and Mr. Bakewell has an extensive stone ware manufactory at the upper end of the town; a large neat warehouse has been recently erected at the water's edge, four stories high from low water mark, from the upper story of which the flour is let down into the boats by pullies and windlasses, at the rate of from three to five barrels in a minute.

The channel past Charlestown is nearest the left shore.

Beach bottom bar, channel right side,                    3 82

WARREN,                    5 87

Is a small village just above the mouth of *Indian Short creek*, in Jefferson county, Ohio. At the mouth of the creek is a warehouse, for the deposite of flour. Boats are sometimes built here. Here, as well as at Charlestown, is a ferry for wagons and horsemen crossing into the state of Ohio.

Virginia Short creek comes in opposite Indian Short creek. At its mouth is a flour warehouse, and a good tavern kept by Mr. Simms. There is a bridge across this creek, at present out of repair.

There is a ripple just below these creeks—the best channel is rather nearest the left shore at the end of the bar made by Virginia Short creek, which shoots out a considerable distance into the river.

No. 16, Pike island, channel right side,                    4 91

No. 17, Twin islands, just below No. 16.

Channel right side, keeping close to the lower point of the uppermost one. Glenn's run, right side, two miles below Twin islands, channel opposite the run, close to the right shore.

No. 18, Wheeling island, about a mile long,                    5 96

Channel left side. At the upper end of the island, keep pretty close to the left shore, until you see the town, then bear towards the island to avoid some logs near the left shore. After passing the town, keep near the middle of the river. Across the river, on the right side of this island, there is a rope fixed from bank to bank to facilitate the passage of the ferry flats, but which prevents the descent of boats.

No. 18 is a fine large island, well farmed, and owned by col. Zanes, a very respectable old gentleman, and among the first adventurers to the country.

Indian Wheeling creek puts in on the right side opposite Wheeling island, just above whose mouth is a small village called Canton, containing a few scattered houses.

## WHEELING, (town of)

Fronts the Ohio on a high gravelly bank, opposite the middle of the island, and having immediately back of the town, Wheeling creek hill, which is steep and lofty, and so narrow at the top, that in some places there is scarcely room for a wagon to pass along, and nearly a perpendicular precipice to the bottom of the creek. This singularly formed backbone, as it were, between the Ohio and Wheeling creek, slopes off gradually into a fine bottom just below the town and above the mouth of the creek, but which is considerably lower than the ground on which Wheeling stands, and in some seasons has been known to be inundated by the floods. There are on this bottom an excellent public inn, a warehouse, a boat yard, and a rope walk, and some other buildings. Immediately above the mouth of the creek there used to stand a fort, serving as a frontier post during the wars with the Indians.

In consequence of the hill just mentioned, and which crowds the town close to the bank of the river, Wheeling has but one street, which is thickly built on for a quarter of a mile in length. The town has about 115 dwellings, 11 stores, two potteries of stone ware, a market-house, and it had in 1808-9, a printing office, a bookstore, and library; the two first quit the town for want of public patronage, the last is still upheld by the citizens. The mail stage from Philadelphia, Baltimore, &c. arrives here twice a week, by way of Pittsburgh, Washington and Charlestown; thence westward the mail is despatched once a week on horses.

The town has a court-house and jail, it being the seat of justice for Ohio county, Virginia. It is 58 miles S. W. of Pittsburgh, and 140 W. by N. of Cumberland. The hills about Wheeling contain a good mineral coal, which is used as fuel. The thoroughfare through Wheeling, of emigrants and travellers into the state of Ohio and down the river, is very great in the fall and spring seasons. Boats can descend from this place in all seasons of the year, and those going down the Ohio from Maryland and the lower parts of Virginia, if the water be too low at Brownsville, pass on to Wheeling for embarkation, where boats and other necessary provisions can be had at a short notice.

*St. Clairsville*, a thriving town, and seat of justice for Belmont county, Ohio, is handsomely seated on high hilly ground, in the midst of a fine rich settlement, eleven miles west from Wheeling, on the direct road to Chilicothe, Limestone, &c.

No. 19, M'Mahon's or Bogg's Island,

2

Channel at the upper end, near the left shore, at the lower end near the island.

| | | |
|---|---|---|
| M'Mahon's Creek, left side, | 2 | 100 |
| PULTREY, | 5 | 105 |

A small village on the right bank of the river, in Belmont county, Ohio.

| | | |
|---|---|---|
| Little Grave creek Bar, | $3\frac{1}{2}$ | $108\frac{1}{2}$ |

This bar lies in the middle, and occupies half the breadth of the river. The best and deepest channel is between it and the right shore—the left hand channel is narrow, shallow and difficult.

| | | |
|---|---|---|
| Tomlinson's ferry, at the mouth of Little Grave creek, left side, | $\frac{1}{2}$ | 109 |

This creek is so small, and so filled up with brush and logs, that it scarcely deserves the name of a creek, and will not be recognised as such by the passenger. [a]*

The hills of Grave creek furnish a good mineral coal and the ancient mounts and fortifications on Mr. Tomlinson's place are very interesting.†

* *See Appendix.*

† The appearances of ancient remains at this place are well worth a visit from every man of observation who may pass near them. The big mound, or grave, as it is called, is an object, which, on approaching it, I will venture to affirm, will surprise and astonish any man more than he is aware of. It is at present in the woods, and a quarter of a mile from Mr. Tomlinson's, in a S. W. direction. On coming close to this mound you are surprised at its mountain-like appearance, and the darkness occasioned by the height of the trees on its summit over those on the plain below. Its perpendicular elevation is about 75 feet, 180 yards in circumference around its base, and 40 around its flat on the top. It appears to be a very regular circle, and forms in its rising, an angle of about 80 degrees. The centre of its top is sunk in perhaps four feet, forming a basin of that depth and about eight or ten feet over. Its summit bears an aged white-oak of 4 feet in diameter, and its sides are richly clad with a luxuriant growth of all the different kinds of trees of the forest, and of the same size and appearance. It stands on an extensive plain, having neither ditch nor rising ground near it, nor can it be discovered where the earth, of which it is formed, has been taken from. East of the big mound, there are several small ones in the open fields, and a number of fortifications, whose particular dimensions I did not take. I have seen a number of these mounds in Pennsylvania, Ohio, Virginia and Kentucky, and have heard and read of others, but they all fall far short of the size and astonishing magnitude of the one at Grave creek. On this plain and immedi-

"The ' *Big Grave*,' as it is called, is a most astonishing mound. We measured the perpendicular height
and it was sixty-seven feet and a half. By the measurement of George Miller, esq of Wheeling, it is sixty-
eight feet. Its sides are quite steep. The diameter
of the top is fifty-five feet: but the apex seems to
have caved in; for the present summit forms a basin,
three or four feet in depth. Not having a surveyor's
chain, we could not take the circumference, but judged that its base covered more than half an acre. It is
overgrown with large trees on all sides. Near the top
is a white-oak of three feet diameter; one still larger
grows on the eastern side about half way down. The
mound sounds hollow Undoubtedly its contents will
be numerous, curious, and calculated to develop in a
farther degree the history of the antiquities which a-
bound in this part of our country."‡

Half a mile below Little Grave creek is

## Big Grave creek, left side.

Channel right shore—Just below Big Grave creek is
*Grave creek ripple*—channel half way over from the left
bank at the head of the ripple, thence close in to the
right shore.

## No. 20, Captina Island,     9  |  18

Channel left side in very low water, though it is narrow and difficult. At the lower end of the island it
runs hard around the point to the right, there being a
sand bar a little to the left, just below the foot of the
island. To the left of this sand bar there is another
channel, having a lodged log on the left hand—Both of
these channels are narrow and have very swift water.
There are indeed throughout a good many logs and
snags, which require care to avoid.

The right side of Captina is good when the river is
a little up, it is there the broadest and safest, though
there are some rocks in the bed.

## Captina creek, right side, $\frac{3}{4}$ of a mile below No. 20.

## Baker's Station, left bank, channel left shore, 2 |120

## No. 21, Wood's or Fish creek island.

ately amidst the smaller mounds and fortifications, Mr. Tomlinson
laid out a town about twenty-five years ago, which he calculated
would be chosen for the seat of justice for Ohio county, Virginia,
but Wheeling being fixed on for that purpose, Mr. Tomlinson's
town went to decay; an appearance, however, of an old town
still remains.

‡ *Harris's Tour.*

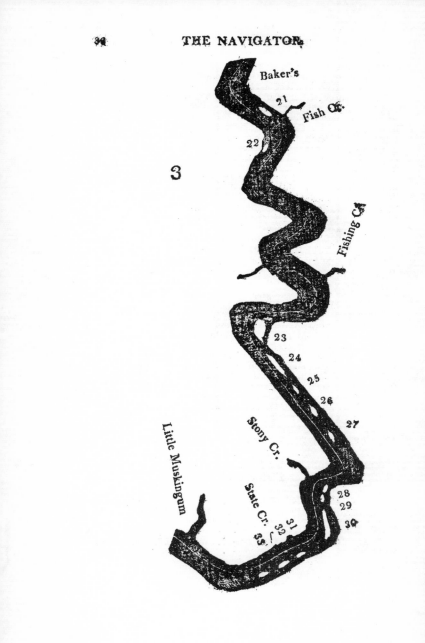

Channel on the right side of the island in low water.
*Cresap's* is just above No. 21, left side.

Fish creek, left side, just below No. 21,     3   123

At the mouth of this creek is a ferry and town—A little below it on the left side is a large tract of land called Butler's tract.

No. 22,

Is a large willow bar, about a mile below Fish creek —channel nearest the left shore.

Sunfish creek, right side,     5   128

Opossum creek, right side,     2   130

Proctor's run, left side, (Charles Wells, jun.
       just above it.     2   132

Just below this run is a sand bar—left channel close to the bar, leaving it a little to the left.

Fishing creek, left side, and Martin's Station, 5   137

Just below is a sand bar—best channel is on the right side of it. The river here winds considerably to the right, when you enter the head of

Long Reach and Peyton's Island, No. 23,     5   142

In this Reach, which is remarkably straight, and about 17 miles long, are five islands, first

Peyton's Island, No. 23.

Williamson's Island, No. 24.

Pursley's Island, No. 25.

Wilson's Island, No. 26.

John Williamson's Island, No. 27.

All of which keep to the left. Opposite Wilson's island, on the right side, Mill creek enters, having a bridge across its mouth.

Wells's tavern and fine farm, left side,     9 151

Here resides Mr. Charles Wells, sen. about half way down the reach, and between No. 25 and No. 26. After a youthful and vigorous life spent in toil, dangers, and fatigues incident to a new frontier country, to which Mr. Wells moved (in 1776) while yet a boy, he has now seated himself here on a fine farm, having a beautiful view of the Ohio, and where he enjoys all that plentitude and happiness, with his numerous family [b] which ought to be enjoyed by every man in the happy decline of life, when these blessings have been obtained by virtue and industry. Indeed the serenity and sage like physiognomy of Mr. Wells, justify the conclusion, that his wealth and happiness rests on no other foundation.—" Blessed are the fruits of a virtuous life —blessed he who holdeth out to the end, and soberly enjoyeth, in his old age, the good things procured by his youthful labors." Mr. Wells has also a fine garden in which is recognised the monthly strawberry, of which I ate excellent fruit in October.

**End of Long Reach,**                                           7 158

A little below the end of Long Reach is a large bar on the left—channel bears pretty close to the right shore, near which are some logs, deepest water inside of the logs, but may go on either side of them. Half a mile below this bar is Stoney creek, right side.

**Little island No. 28, Bat island No. 29,**          4 162

These islands stand abreast the smallest to the left, and are connected by a bar, channel right side. Opposite No. 28, a creek enters on the right side. No. 28 is ¾ of a mile long.

Middle island No. 30, lies close to the left shore, and begins about a quarter of a mile below No. 28 and No. 29. Middle island creek enters back of Middle island. No. 30 is about two miles long, and has but a small channel on its left side—channel right side—French creek puts in on the right side, a little below No. 30, just below which on the right bank is the newly commenced village of *Newport*, in Washington county Ohio.

First of the Three Brothers, No. 31, is small and lies partly abreast of the upper end of Second Brother, and near the left shore.

Second Brother, No. 32, lies in the middle of the river, and opposite it on the right side Stab creek enters.

Third Brother, No. 33, lies just below No. 32, and in range with it—channel past the Brothers on the right side.

**From Little island to Third Brother,**          8 170

Just below Third Brother near the left shore is a small willow island, and a sand bar—channel near the right shore.

**Buil creek, right side,**                                    4 174

From above this creek keep near the right shore for two miles.

**Little Muskingum river, right side,**          5 179

Has a handsome bridge over its mouth.

**No. 34, Duvall's island,**                              2 181

Best channel right shore.

Duck creek (opposite No. 34, right side) channel one-third over from the mouth of the creek, then bear over for the island a small distance, then again for the right shore, thence about the middle of the river until you are nearly opposite the entrance of the Muskin-

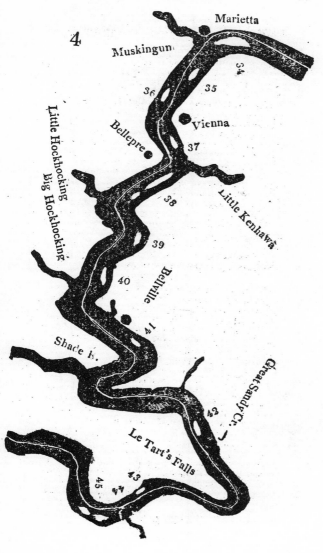

gum, when you must incline rapidly towards the left
shore to avoid a large ugly bar opposite the mouth of
that river.

Muskingum* river, right side,                    2|183

The floods of this river throw out logs and snags,
which are fastened on a bar opposite its mouth, consequently the channel is thrown over pretty close towards
the left bank of the Ohio.

The Muskingum is a fine gentle river, 250 yards
wide at its mouth, and navigable without any obstruc-
tions to the Three Legs, 110 miles up, with large batteaux, and to a little lake at its head 45 miles further,
with smaller ones; from thence by a portage of about
one mile, a communication is opened to lake Erie,
through Cuyahoga, which at its mouth is wide and deep
enough to receive large sloops from the lake. The
legislature of Ohio has passed a law to raise by way of
lottery the sum of 12,000 dollars for improving the navigation of these two rivers. The Big salt spring is
8 miles from the river and 50 from Marietta, it yields
water sufficient to keep 1000 gallons constantly boiling,
ten of which yield a quart of superior salt. At the
mouth of this river a ferry boat is carried rapidly
across by means of a rope extending from bank to bank,
and a windlass ingeniously worked at each end.

### MARIETTA,

Is finely situated at the mouth of Muskingum, having about 90 houses on the upper and 30 on the opposite bank, where Fort Harmar formerly stood. A bank
was established here in the summer of 1807, capital
100,000 dollars, of which Rufus Putnam is President.
Ship building is carried on here (1807) with spirit —It
has one printing office, a post office, two rope walks, a
court-house, a market house, an academy, two churches, and a steam flour mill, to which is attached a carding machine. The inhabitants are principally New
Englanders, whose industry is as proverbial as their
system of life is economical, moral and religious.—
About a mile above Marietta and on the bank of the
Muskingum are some curious remains of Antient fortifications.[c] Marietta is the seat of justice for Washington county, Ohio, Lat. 39° 34' N. Long. 82° 9' W.—
About 146 miles southwest of Pittsburgh by land.

Notwithstanding their high bold banks, Marietta is
subject to the inundations of the rivers, and sometimes
to loss and great inconvenience on this account. The
land a small distance up the Muskingum is considera-

---

An Indian name signifying " *The Elk's eye.*"

bly higher than where the present town stands, and the inhabitants, it is presumed, will not wait to be told of the propriety of seeking higher ground for their future buildings. What nature performs in one period, she may, and most probably will, perform in another.— There can be little doubt but that the site of Marietta has been made by the operation of the land and waters, and we have no reason to induce us to believe otherwise than the future floods of the rivers may be as great as those must have been which have made that and other bottoms along the river, and there is reason to believe that the season of high waters and hard winters are again returning to the western country, which for twenty years or more absented themselves to some other clime. The same thing is observed of the risings of the Mississippi, which depends for its floods altogether on those of the northern rivers. Forty or fifty years ago, it has been observed by an old inhabitant of Louisiana, the Mississippi began to decrease in its risings, and continued to decrease gradually for twenty years, and these last twenty years, it has been observed by a gentleman of accuracy, to increase yearly and by such gradual steps as not to be generally noticed, in consequence the banks have, within ten years back, got a considerable population, which now is obliged to retreat, half ruined, and abandon totally the fertile farms formed with much labor and difficulty. In the risings of the Mississippi in 1811, the inhabitants were much injured, but in 1813, all have been obliged to fly, except those protected by strong levees, and many of these suffered from the levees giving way.—In this year the river at Natchez was higher by about eighteen inches, than in 1811, and in consequence the losses of crops and stock have been beyond calculation One million of dollars worth of corn, cotton and stock are the estimated losses of the county of Corcordia, and this is not the greatest loss, for the whole of the inundated lands are now considered not worth possessing, which three or four years ago were thought to be invaluable, and selling at great prices.—I mention this circumstance of the south, as admonitors to the inhabitants bordering the northern rivers.

The first sea vessel on the western waters was a brig called the St. Clair, of 120 tons burden, built at Marietta by Commodore Preble in 1798 or '99, who descended the Ohio and Mississippi in her, went to the Havanna, and thence to Philadelphia, where he sold her.

*Zanesville*, the seat of justice for Muskingum county, is seated on the east side of the Muskingum river,

50 miles by land above Marietta. It contains (1807) 60 families. It is now (1810) made the seat of government of the state of Ohio, and in consequence has taken a rapid start in improvements, buildings and business. The falls of the Muskingum at this place are highly susceptible of great improvements, and the establishment of the various kinds of water-works for manufactures, would be made here to great advantage.— Licking, a valuable mill stream, puts in from the west side just above the town. Zanesville is well supplied with a fine mineral or stone coal from the adjacent hills, and the river affords excellent fish to every table. The great leading road from Pittsburgh to Kentucky, goes through Zanesville, which generally keeps it alive with movers and travellers. *Springfield,* opposite Zanesville, is also a thriving village.

Besides these towns, there are on the Muskingum above Zanesville, the villages of Wakatomaka, Tuskarowa, Newcomerstown, Salem, Gnadenhutten, Shoenbrun, Philadelphia, Gartentown, Bethlehem, Kingston, and Calcutta, near its head—and Fort Lawrence, a little below where Sandy creek joins the river.

| | | |
|---|---|---|
| Mill creek, right side, | 1 | 84 |
| Muskingum Island, No. 35, | 2 | 86 |

Channel right side—near the lower end is a bar, keep near the right shore. No. 35 is about 2½ miles long.

| | | |
|---|---|---|
| Second Island, No. 36, | 4 | 190 |

Channel left side. No. 36 is about half a mile long, and a mile below No. 35. Opposite the head of No. 36 a creek enters on the left side, with a bridge across its mouth; a little below which, is the settlement of *Vienna,* extending two miles on a fine rich and extensive bottom of the river.

| | | |
|---|---|---|
| Third, or James's Island, No. 37, | 3 | 193 |

Channel right side, in the middle of which is a large log. At the head of No. 37 on the right bank, is the farm and tavern of Mr. Coles, a New Englander. No 37 is about a mile and a half long, just below it Congress creek puts in on the right side.

| | | |
|---|---|---|
| Little Kenhawa river, left side, | 4 | 197 |

Is a long serpentine stream, heading in the first range of northern mountains, having Juneus's and several other creeks tributary.

### WOOD COUNTY COURT-HOUSE

Stands immediately above the mouth of the Little Kenhawa. The town is small and not of much business, but from its situation may rise to some importance—channel past the town is near the middle of the river.

### BELPRE SETTLEMENT

Is on the right side of the Ohio, opposite Little Kenhawa, extends several miles on the river, and ends about opposite the foot of Blannerhasset's island. This is a rich and pleasant settlement of Washington county, Ohio.

Blannerhasset's Island, No. 38,                2  199

Channel right side. In the channel opposite the head of the island are a number of logs and snags, easily avoided however, by care. It is about 2 miles long. Opposite it on the right is a beautiful high bluff bank of the Ohio, and at its foot two small islands.

This island was but lately celebrated for its elegant buildings, and other improvements of taste. Its former owner, Mr. Blannerhasset, an Irish gentleman, left it, and shortly after, its buildings were burnt to the ground, the stacks of chimnies only remaining as sorrowful monuments of their former greatness. The island is now owned by a Mr. Miller, of Lexington, K. who farms it with hemp, corn, &c. There is a fine apple orchard on it, and the soil is remarkably fertile.

Little Hockhocking river, right side,          5 204

Newbury settlement and island, No. 39,     2½ 206½

Channel right side, about half way between the bar and the right shore at the head of the island, there being a small bar to the right.—There is a cavern just above Newbury.

Mustaphy's island No. 40,                   1½ 208

Channel right side. At the lower end, keep well to the right shore to avoid a sand bar on the left.

Great Hockhocking river, right side,          2 210

This is a considerable river of Ohio State, navigable 70 miles. NEW LANCASTER* the seat of justice for Fairfield county, Ohio, is a new and thriving town, situated at its head  On this river are quarries of free stone, mines of iron ore, and one of lead is said to have been discovered, salt springs and coal also abound. On the Great Hockhocking 14 miles below New Lancaster a *paper mill* is now, [1810] erecting by the Messrs. Pitchers. About 25 miles up Hockhocking, *Athens*, a thriving village with an academy, is finely situated in a high, healthful country ; it is the seat of justice for Athens county, Ohio. *Troy*, a newly laid out town, is

* For an account of the " Standing Rock," near New Lancaster, see note [d] in the Appendix.

situated immediately above the mouth of Hockhocking, on the bank of Ohio.

### Lee's creek, left side,                    4 214

Belleville, a scattering village, left bank, just below Lee's creek; it occupies a fine high bluff, and an extensive rich bottom of the river.

Channel—Three quarters of a mile above Belleville, a bar puts out from the left shore; here keep pretty close to the right bank; thence the channel, in consequence of a bar on the right shore, bears hard over towards the town.

### Belleville island, No. 41,                 3 217

Channel right side—At the foot of No. 41, the channel runs pretty close to the right shore, though part of the water draws strongly across the foot of the bar to left, which you must be on your guard to avoid.

### Pond creek, left side,                     2 219

Channel left shore.

Devil's Hole, a remarkable cavern on the right side, just above Shade river; it is in the face of a rock, about half way up a steep hill close to the river.

### Shade river, right side,                   2 221

Channel—In high water hug the left hand point, or you may be thrown against rocks above and below the mouth of the river—One mile below Shade river, are two bars, opposite each other, channel goes between them, in the middle of the river, rather inclining to the right shore,

About three miles further on, are two other bars, one opposite a small creek on the left; the other just below it, channel to the right of both bars.

### Amberson's island, No. 42,                 6 227

Channel right side—It is rapid water and narrow, logs on each side and rocks in the bed of the river, therefore it requires attention to the boat's way, and hands at the oars, which, with care, will clear all with ease.—At the foot of the island the channel chutes out into the middle of the river. Half a mile above No. 42 is a flat ledge of rocks on the left shore—The channel there is in the middle of the river. This ledge of rocks continues on the same side below the island. No. 42 is about a mile long. [s]

Little Sandy creek puts in opposite No. 42, on the left side.

### Big Sandy creek, left side,                4 231

A mile above this creek a flat chain of rocks begin on the right shore, and continues near a mile below— Channel near the middle of the river, until you get below the creek, then it runs pretty rapidly and close to the left bank. Just as the first ledge of rocks quits you on the right, another ledge commences on the left as the river winds to the right. The river here is unusually narrow, channel about midway between this last ledge of rocks and the right shore.

## Large sand bar, with willows on it,      4 235

Channel right shore. Just below the foot of this bar, is a ledge of rocks on the right shore—channel pretty close to the rocks. *Old Town* creek comes in on the right side opposite this bar.

## Tanner's run, right side,      3 238

Just below this run on the left side of the river, is a sand bar, the channel runs to the right of the bar.

## George's or Goose Island, No. 43,      2 240

At the head of this island on the right shore, is a large sand bar—channel runs near the head of the island and on the right side of it. When you get one-third down bear towards the right shore through the bar, leaving two breakers on your left hand. At the foot of the island is another bar, which keep to the left. There is a pass between this last bar and the foot of the island, but not so good as the one to the right. No. 43 is about a mile long.

## Big and Little Mill creek, left side.

Two miles below these a large run enters on the right side.

## Island No. 44, below head of No. 43,      4 244

Channel past the head of this island is near the right shore, then it runs towards No. 45, which lies immediately below it, keeping No. 45 also on your left hand; from which the channel bears rather nearest the right shore to Letart's rapids, half a mile below the foot of No. 45. The river here winds much to the right.

## Letart's Rapids,      2 246

Channel—The chute through the rapids is rather nearest the right shore, and shews itself by a sheet of smooth water extending below the main ripple on either side, and which seems from above to come to a point below. Enter the centre of this sheet of water as near as may be, and keep your boat under good head way until you get through the rough water below the rapids, and there will be no difficulty in passing them.

At the Rapids, is a machinery for towing boats up them. Just below it is a grist mill.—Here, on the right side of the river, are fine extensive and fertile bottoms and some good farms ; on the left side are some farms, and a stupendous hill juts into the water's edge at the

rapids, the primary cause, most probably, of the river's
making so great a bend to the right, not having been
able to break through the barrier ere its arrival at this
spot, which evidently bears marks of some of nature's
greatest labors.

A mile and a half below these rapids is a harmless
sand bar on the right shore, with some snags on the
foot of it.   Channel on the left.

### Rock of Antiquity,                                    3,249

This is seen standing in the water's edge on the right
shore of the river, just as it begins to wind to the left.
I call it the *Rock of Antiquity*, because of its ancient
engravings, which conspicuously shew themselves on
its smooth, and almost perpendicular front.   Time, the
smoother of all roughnesses, has rendered all the engravings unintelligible, except one, which plainly repre-
sents the huge figure of a man with a pipe in his mouth
smoking.   He is sitting much in the style of our natives when at their ease in camp, with his elbows resting on his knees, which seem to meet his breast, his
shoulders and head leaning forwards, and holding the
pipe in his mouth with one hand.

The curious must land here, if at all, with small
crafts, as there are rocks and logs in the river just below, difficult to avoid with large boats.

### West creek, left, Dunham's run, right side,        5 254

Channel near the left shore—*Secrease's ferry* is about
a mile below these creeks.

### A ripple and bar, left side,                        3 257

Channel near the middle of the river—About one
mile below this ripple and bar, and where the river
turns to the left, is another ripple ; channel nearest the
left shore, a ledge of rocks on the right side.

### Sliding hill creek, left side,                      3 260
### Nailor's Branch, right side,                        3 263
### Leading creek, right side,                          4 267

There is a tavern at the mouth of Leading creek,
with Lombardy poplars before the door.   On the opposite side, mineral coal is said to abound in the river
hills.   Two miles above Leading creek on the right
side, a few hundred yards from the river, is a singular
rocky point, jutting out into a fertile field.   It ends in
an angular point, and is about two hundred feet perpendicular height, of a bare solid mass of rock, having a
fenced field with a few scattering trees on its summit.
Its appearance is novel and interesting, and helps to
vary the variegated scenery of the Ohio.

### Ten Mile creek, left side,                          3 270
### Eight mile Island, No. 46,                          3 278

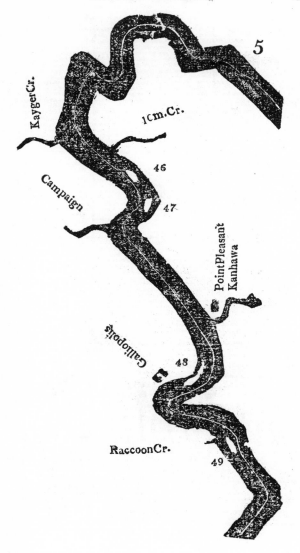

5

Kayger Cr.

1cm. Cr.

46

Campaign

47

PointPleasant
Kanhawa

Gallioplis

48

RaccoonCr.

49

Channel right side, pretty close to the right shore, there being a large bar extending out from the head of the island.   No. 46 is a small island, about half a mile long.

## Six Mile Island, No. 47,                    2 275

Channel right side.   No. 47 lies so close to the left side that it is scarcely discernible, having but a small channel around it.   It is about a mile long.—The river from Letart's falls to Little Guyundat, presents an interesting scene.   With the exception of the two ripples below Secrease's ferry, it is deep, with an unbroken surface of water, remarkably serpentine a part of that distance, and bounded alternately by stupendous hills and rocks on the one side, and farms and improvements on the other.

Just below No. 47, Kayger's creek puts in.—Here is said to be a stratum of slate coal.

## Campaign creek, right side,                 4 279

This creek is so called from gen. Lewis's campaign against the Indians, after the battle of Point Pleasant, in the year

## Great Kenhawa river, left side, (M. D.)     4 283

This is a considerable river of Virginia, 400 yards wide at its mouth.   By a portage of a few miles through the mountains, which occasions the falls, a communication may be had, by way of the Green Briar branch of the Kenhawa, with the head waters of the Monongahela river, and also with the waters of James's river, which falls into Hampton Roads, on the coast of Virginia, and which is navigable for ships of 40 guns to Jamestown, and those of 125 tons burden go as far as Rocket's, one mile below Richmond.   The head branches of the Great Kenhawa interlock with those of the Holstein river.   The newly commenced salt works on the Kenhawa, and the uncommon strength of the water, which is found in abundance, are of immense value to the western country.—For a more particular account of which see appendix, note [f.]

### POINT PLEASANT,

Is pleasantly situated immediately above the mouth of the Great Kenhawa, on an extensive and fertile bottom of the Ohio, of which it has a fine prospect up and down that river.   It is the seat of justice for Mason county, Virginia, contains about 15 or 20 families, a log court-house, log jail, and as usual, (but unfortunately,) in the Virginia towns, a pillory and whipping post [g] Point Pleasant seems rather on the stand in point of improvement, arising, it is said, from the difficulty in establishing the land titles.   It is, however, a considcrable place of embarkation for those descending the Ohio from the back and western parts of Virginia.— There is one merchant in Point Pleasant, Mr. William Langtry.

*Charlestown*, a post and county town for Kenhawa county, is situated 60 miles up the Kenhawa river on the east side. The salt works commence 2 miles above Charlestown, and continue up the river for twelve miles above it.

Fair Haven is a pleasantly situated village opposite Point Pleasant, right bank of the Ohio.

From Point Pleasant incline over to the right shore. The river here winds to the right.

Galliopolis Island, No. 48,     3 286

Channel left side and near the head of the island; when half way down, the channel runs towards the left shore, then towards the town of Galliopolis. No. 48 lies close to the right shore in the bend, is half a mile long, and three quarters above the town.

## GALLIOPOLIS,     1 287

Is finely situated on a high second bank of the Ohio, in a fertile and extensive bottom, commanding a handsome view of the river. About twenty-five years ago, Galliopolis was settled by 100 French families, who had been lured here from favorable representations of the country, and the cheapness of the land they had purchased for settlement. Their titles proving bad, the inhabitants, reduced and mortified, were obliged to abandon their establishment of an intended city. [h] Since which it has been settled by Americans, a few of the original families excepted, and is now in a thriving condition, being the seat of justice for Gallia county, Ohio. It possesses about fifty or sixty families, and several handsome buildings, a brick court-house, with cupola for a bell not yet hung (Oct. 1812.)—a log jail, a neat two story brick building, for the double purpose of an academy and church, 4 mercantile stores, two taverns, a baker, and a good proportion of industrious mechanicks. Several new brick buildings are on the way of completion. It is 63 miles from Galliopolis to Chilicothe. Five years ago, part of the first bank slipt into the river, which has very much injured the lower landing.

At and below Galliopolis, the river winds southwesterly to a south direction. At the lower end of the first right hand point below the town, on the right hand, are some snags extending half way across the river, keep them on the right hand.

First Island below Galliopolis, No. 49,     5 292

Channel past No. 49 begins in the middle of the river between it and the left shore, and then bears towards the foot of the island, opposite which, in the middle of the river, are some rocks and snags, which, keep to the left. *Raccoon* creek, right side, enters two miles below No. 49.

| | | |
|---|---:|---:|
| Meridian creek, left shore, a run below it, | 10 | 302 |
| Eighteen Mile creek, right side, | 2 | 304 |
| Swan creek, right side, a run above it, | 2 | 306 |
| Little Guyundat creek, left side, | 1 | 307 |

Green Bottom Ripple, six miles below Little Guyundat. Channel, one-third over from the left shore at the upper end of the ripple, then draw over for the right shore. This is a bad ripple.

Hanging Rock. Two miles above this rock is a sand bar on the left shore—Channel close to the right shore.

| | | |
|---|---:|---:|
| Federal creek, right side, | 7 | 314 |
| Nine Mile creek, left side, | 5 | 319 |
| Seven Mile creek, same side, | 2 | 321 |
| Bluff and Tavern, right side, | 1 | 322 |

The bank here is washing away, and leaves a very craggy shore.

| | | |
|---|---:|---:|
| Big Guyundat river, 80 yards wide, left side, | 5 | 327 |

Here is a long and difficult ripple—Channel, above the river, is near the left shore, when in full sight of its mouth, it crosses the river suddenly, until near the right shore, then it bears towards the middle of the river. This ripple continues to a creek one mile below Guyundat. *Indian Guyundat* puts in opposite Big Guyundat, right side.

At and below the mouth of this river, on a high bluff bank, stands the village of *Guyundat*, it is small, and seems rather on the decline, since the seat of justice for Kenhawa county, was removed from it. Above the mouth of this river are several houses, which seem to have the principal business of the place.

Just below Guyundat, the Ohio winds considerably to the S. S. W. and presents a smooth unbroken sheet of water for nine miles at one view, not exceeded in beauty of prospect by any place between Pittsburgh and Natchez. The settlements above and below Guyundat, are numerous and very fine on both sides of the Ohio,

| | | |
|---|---:|---:|
| Symm's, right side, | 4 | 331 |
| Buffaloe creek, right side, | 2 | 333 |
| Ten pole creek, left side, | 1 | 334 |

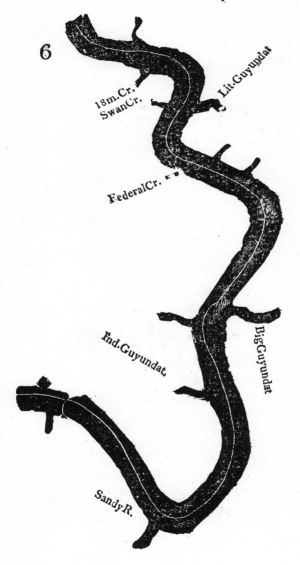

6

18 m. Cr.
Swan Cr.

Lit. Guyundat

Federal Cr.

Ind. Guyundat

Big Guyundat

Sandy R.

With a high bridge over its mouth.

| | | |
|---|---|---|
| Twelve pole, a fine creek, left side, | 1 | 335 |
| Great Sandy, or Tottery river, left side, (M. D.) | 6¼ | 341¼ |

Just above Sandy is a bar, channel in the middle of the river through the bar—half a mile below is a gut.

Great Sandy is the dividing line between Virginia and Kentucky. It is navigable with batteaux to the Ouasioto mountain. It passes through a range of the Cumberland mountains, and heads near a head branch of Clinch river.—The long reed or Carolina cane grows on this river in abundance; being an evergreen, it affords fine food for cattle during winter. The Great Rapids of Sandy are about 50 miles above its mouth.

From Great Sandy, the Ohio winds to the N. W. by N. thence S. W. thence N. W. by W. in which last direction, seven miles below Sandy, you have another beautiful view of the river six miles in extent, with an unbroken surface, and fine farms on both sides. The banks, however, along here, are much disposed to *slipping*, which injures their appearance, and in some cases renders it dangerous to build near their edges.

| | | |
|---|---|---|
| Hood's creek, left side, | 4¾ | 346 |
| Ice creek, right side, | 4 | 350 |
| Stoner's creek, right side, | 4 | 354 |

From Stoner's creek, W. N. W. to W. Immediately above and below the bluff or hanging rock, 2 miles below Stoner's creek, two runs enter, right side.

| | | |
|---|---|---|
| Ferguson's bar, | 4 | 358 |

A good channel on the right shore. The water from this bar to one mile below Little Sandy, is very shallow.

| | | |
|---|---|---|
| Little Sandy creek, left side, | 6 | 364 |

Channel in the middle of the river.

BURRSBURGH,

A town laid out by Mr. John Gabriel Gervais, on the right bank of the Ohio, included in the tract of 24,000 acres, granted by Congress to the French inhabitants of Galliopolis.* The town has not progressed.

| | | |
|---|---|---|
| Hale's or Pine creek right side, | 11 | 375 |

This is a long winding creek passing through the French Grant.

| | | |
|---|---|---|
| Little Sciota river, right side, | 6 | 380 |

* For particulars respecting this grant, called the *French Grant*, See note [h] Appendix.

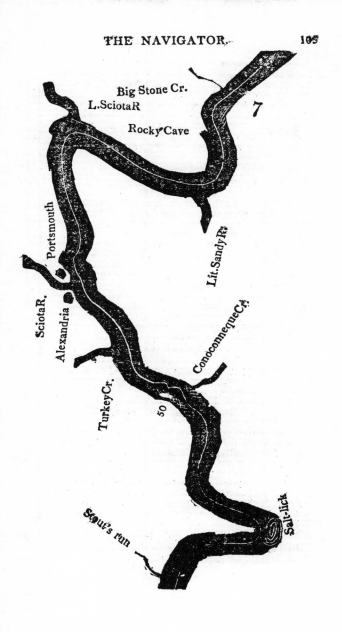

Big Stone Cr.
L. Sciota R
Rocky Cave
7
Lit. Sandy R.
Portsmouth
Conoconneque Cr.
Sciota R.
Alexandria
Turkey Cr.
50
Salt-lick
Stout's run

A ledge of rocks puts out here and extends half across the river—the channel at the upper end of the bar is near the left shore; at the lower end, close around the rocks.

Half a mile below Little Sciota is another bar extending also half way across the river; channel midway between the point of the bar and the left shore.—Just below this last bar on the right bank is *Stony Point ;* and a little above it is every appearance of a body of iron ore.

| | | |
|---|---|---|
| Tyger's creek, left side, | 6 | 386 |
| Big Sciota river, [i]    [M. D.] | 4 | 390 |

### PORTSMOUTH,

A village pleasantly situated three quarters of a mile above the mouth of the Big Sciota, on a high bank, and in a fine and extensive bottom of fertile land. It is in Sciota county, Ohio, and appears to be thriving, from the newness of several of its buildings, of which, it contains about 30, some neatly built with brick, 2 stores, 3 taverns, 1 commission ware-house. The land from the lower end of the town becomes low and continues so to the Sciota, in consequence, it is subject to the floods of the rivers. Goods intended for the Sciota country, are deposited here in ware-houses suited to their reception, thence they are shipped up that river in keel boats.—The *Sciota Salt-works* are about 20 miles N. E. from Portsmouth.

### ALEXANDRIA,

Stands on a fine high bank, just below the Sciota river. It is also in Sciota county, contains 15 or 20 houses, a stone house tavern, and several new buildings appear going up.

The situation of these villages, with the high and conic formed hills on the opposite side of the river, faced with towering perpendicular rocks, whose summits bear a thin growth of pine, hemlock, &c.—these, combined with the beauty of the Ohio, with its serpentine windings—altogether present a scene to the passing observer, at once sublime and highly interesting.

Channel past Portsmouth is near the middle of the river. On the left side of the Ohio opposite the Sciota, is a sand bar, and there are some logs and snags near the middle of the river opposite Alexandria. The river now winds to the S. then S. W. by S. thence nearly S. E.

| | | |
|---|---|---|
| Turkey creek, Coneck hills, left side, | 5 | 395 |

Half a mile above this creek resides major Belisle.

| | | |
|---|---|---|
| Conoconneque creek, left side, (Coglins) | 9 | 404 |

Island No. 50. This is a willow island and bar, ly-ing close to the right shore between Conoconneque and a small creek on the right side called *Pond* creek.—The channel begins half way between the island and left shore, then it bears off round a bar at the mouth of Conoconneque creek, thence it turns short to the left shore, to avoid the island bar which reaches near-ly across the river—thence it keeps that shore for a small distance, then runs to the middle of the river, the left shore below being full of rocks and sunken trees.

A bar five miles below Pond creek, channel near the left shore.

Twin creeks, close together, right side,                    8 412
Salt creek, left side, just below Twin creeks,

This creek empties in just below a short turn of the Ohio to the right; and near its mouth are some *salt furnaces*, in a little town called VANCEVILLE, at which are made large quantities of salt—From these salt works to Lexington it is 70 miles.

The best water here is in the middle of the river, both beaches being very rocky; but there is a good landing place in an eddy 400 yards above the creek, and also at the mouth of the creek.

In high water the rocks and eddy form a whirlpool.

Quick's run, left side,                                       3 415
Channel close to the left shore.

Pond run left, Stout's run, right side,                   3½ 418½
Graham's station, and Kennedy's bottom, left side.

Just above No. 51, above which for six miles you have it in sight, with a most charming view of the riv-er, which runs here about a N. W. by W. direction.—Kennedy's bottom is extensive and fine farmed, hav-ing a very fertile soil. The buildings on the bottom fronting the river appear on the decline. The river here is about half a mile wide.

Wilson's Island, No. 51,                                  3½ 422
Channel left side.—Approach towards the head of No. 51, thence the current draws to the left shore, and when half way down, pull over for the island, and pass pretty close to its foot, bearing towards the right shore, keeping a large log to the left, a small distance below which is a sawyer, which keep to the right. In a very low state of the river, the right side of No. 51, has the most water, but it is a crooked channel, nar-row and dangerous, being filled with logs and rocks, No. 51 is a small willow island. There is a small bar

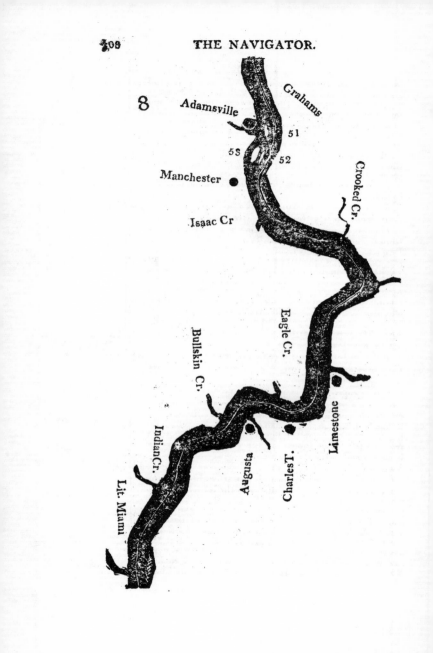

close to the left shore, opposite the bar attached to the head of Wilson's island ; you keep it of course on your left hand and the island bar on your right.

## ADAMSVILLE,

Is a small village of Adams county, Ohio, standing just below the mouth of *Brush* creek, and opposite Wilson's island. It was formerly the seat of justice for Adams county, but which has been removed to West Union, 18 miles N. W. from Adamsville. Its site is low, and in some seasons subject to inundation. Brush creek heads in Highland county, having at its source the village of *New Market*.

Sycamore creek, left side,

About two miles below No. 51—from it to the Two islands the channel is near the left shore. *Donaldson's* creek, two miles below Sycamore. Five miles below No 51, on the top of a high hill, on the left side, is seen a handsome dwelling, from which there is a most charming view of the river.

Two Islands, Nos. 52 and 53, nearly abreast, 17 439

Channel left of both these islands, about midway between the head of No. 52, the smallest, and the left shore. From No. 52 the current inclines toward the foot of Massey's, the largest island, No. 53, thence towards the town. It is a fine deep smooth channel; the left bank opposite No. 52 is giving way to the power of the current. Massey's island is about a mile long, has a fine farm on it, and lies near the right shore, No. 52 is quite small and occasions the river to belly considerably to the left. In lower water there is no passage between these islands, other than on a dry sand bar. The river past Manchester runs about a west direction, then W. S. W.

## MANCHESTER, 1 440

A village of Adams county, Ohio, pleasantly seated on the right bank of the river, stretching along above and below the foot of Massey's island. It contains about 25 houses, some neatly built with brick, all fronting the river, and thereby scattered. The bottom back and adjoining the town is extensive and fertile, with good farms on it

*Isaac's* creek puts in one mile below Manchester, on the right side, and opposite it on the left shore is a sand bar, therefore, the channel runs rather nearest the right side of the river.

Crooked creek, left side,                      4¾ 444¾
Cabin creek, left side,                         1½ 446
William Brooke's creek, left side,              3 449

K

A sand bar on the right shore; best channel is near but not close to the left bank.

Madison's and the town of LIBERTY, left side, about two miles below William Brooke's.

Limestone creek, and town of MAYSVILLE,                    3.452

This is the oldest and most accustomed *landing place* on the Ohio. The landing is good, and the mouth of the creek affords a safe harbor for boats. At the landing are several warehouses well accommodated for the storage of merchandise, wares, &c. these are kept by Messrs. January, Martin, and Chambers, whose obliging and accommodating dispositions, render the transaction of business with them safe and comfortable.— Their charges and commissions are considered moderate, and their attention strict and punctual.

Maysville is in Mason county, (K) situated on the south side of the Ohio, and on the west side of Limestone creek. It stands on a lofty and uneven bank, having the river hill close behind it, and is not seen from the river until you are within two miles of the own.— There is, however, a great deal of business done here; it has about 70 houses, a post office, several mercantile stores, and public inns. Vessels of considerable burden have been built here, launched and taken down the Mississippi with success. It is 4 miles northeast of Washington, the seat of justice for Mason county.[k] It has an extensive rope walk, owned by Mr. John Armstrong.

To give the reader some idea of the business of this little town, we inform him, that during the boating season of 1812, there were, according to Mr. Hart's account, shipped from Maysville landing, bound to Pittsburgh, Kentucky produce to the amount of 1000 tons, consisting of salt-petre, tobacco, hemp, spun yarn, cordage, gun powder, &c.

### CHARLESTOWN,                                         6.458

A small village standing on the left bank of the Ohio. Just below Charlestown there is a large sand bar— channel between the bar and the town, then crosses over towards the foot of the bar. The right side of the bar is good when the water is in tolerable navigable order. The bar heads at the lower end of the town.

Eagle creek, right side,                                   4.462

This is the first water of any consequence below Limestone. It runs through Adams and heads in Highland county, Ohio. It has East fork, Hill's fork, and Rattlesnake fork as tributaries. The village of *St Clairsville* is situated between the two last, in Adams county.

| | | |
|---|---|---|
| Straight creek, right side, | 6 | 468 |

Opposite this creek is a sand bar, channel left shore. *White Oak* creek, right side, is some distance below Straight creek, and is a pretty large creek.

| | | |
|---|---|---|
| Bracken creek, left side, | 4 | 472 |

Opposite this creek is a sand bar, channel left shore.

| | | |
|---|---|---|
| AUGUSTA, | 1 | 473 |

Is a handsome village very pleasantly situated on the left bank of the Ohio, with an extensive and rich bottom in its rear, and in its front, a fine view of the river, with a clean gravelly beach for its landing. It is the seat of justice for Bracken county, Kentucky, contains 40 houses, some handsomely built with brick, a court-house, jail, two stores, two taverns, and a handsome brick school house. On the opposite side of the Ohio are also some handsome brick buildings, and fine farms.

| | | |
|---|---|---|
| Bullskin creek, right side, | 6 | 479 |

Channel one-third over from the left shore.—Half a mile below this creek is a sand bar on the left shore, the channel is near the right shore.

| | | |
|---|---|---|
| Bear creek, right side, | 9 | 488 |
| Big Indian creek, right side, | 4 | 492 |
| Little Indian creek, | 2 | 494 |
| Cross creek, right side, | 4 | 498 |
| Muddy creek, right side, | 5 | 503 |
| Little Miami river [*l*] right side, (M. D.) | 13¼ | 516¼ |

Just below the mouth of this river a small sand bar puts out on the right shore.—The channel is on the left shore about half way to Columbia, one mile below the mouth of Little Miami, then it crosses the river about two-thirds over towards the right shore—thence to Cincinnati, the channel continues near the right shore.

| | | |
|---|---|---|
| Crawfish creek, right side, | 3 | 519¼ |

Between this and Deer creek, a large sand bar puts out from the left shore, which makes it necessary to keep well to the right shore below Columbia until you pass the bar.

| | | |
|---|---|---|
| Deer creek, right side, | 4 | 523¼ |
| Licking river, left side, (M. D.) | 1 | 524¼ |

This is a considerable river of Kentucky, navigable for 70 miles with small crafts. [*m*]

| | |
|---|---|
| NEWPORT, | |

Stands just above the mouth of Licking, having a fine view of the Ohio, and of Cincinnati, opposite it. It

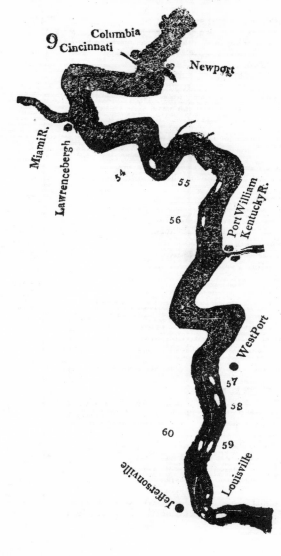

is a thriving village, with a number of handsome brick and other buildings, all fronting the Ohio. The United States' arsenal, or place of deposit for arms, and other munitions of war, fronts the river, and is a large brick building. There are also barracks for several companies within the public square. The town contains about one hundred and fifty souls, and is in Campbell county, Kentucky. The bottom above and below Newport, is extensive, fertile, and contains some fine farms on it. These, combined with the beauty of the river, and the two towns in view, give a very handsome prospect of the country.

## CINCINNATI. [n]

| | | |
|---|---|---|
| Mill creek, right side, | $2\frac{1}{4}$ | $526\frac{1}{2}$ |
| A large sand bar, | $3\frac{1}{2}$ | 530 |

The channel close to the right shore is safe, but it is very narrow.

North Bend,                                    15 545

There are some fine farms and improvements at the North Bend, and a town called *Cleves*, was laid out some years ago, but has not improved much in buildings. The ground here commands a handsome view of the Ohio, rising gently from the river to a considerable elevation, something in the form of half an amphitheatre. It is but a mile across from Cleves to the nearest part of the great Miami.

Great Miami river, [o]   (M. D.)         6 551

At the mouth of this river is a sand bar, channel on the left shore; about 300 yards below is another sand bar on the same side, channel midway between the bar and the right shore. Here ends the state of Ohio, the division line between that state and Indiana, strikes the mouth of the Great Miami, and thence runs a due North course to 41° 40' N. lat. thence a due east and west direction, striking lake Erie on the one hand, and touching the most southerly part of lake Michigan, passing on in the same direction to the Mississippi on the other, which line also forms the north boundary of Indiana and Illinois territories.

### LAWRENCEBURGH,                        3 554

Is situated in an extensive rich bottom, on the right bank of the Ohio, the seat of justice for Dearborn county, Indiana territory. It is at very high floods more or less subject to inundation, which may injure the progress of the town.

Laughrey's creek, right side,              8 562

Here is a great bar—channel close to the right shore.

Grape or Laughrey's island, No. 54,                    4|566
   Channel on the left shore, No. 54 is one mile long.

Chambers s bar,                                        4|570
   Here is a very large ripple—channel close into the
right shore, under a high bank.

Gunpowder creek, left side,
   At the mouth of this creek is a rocky ripple—channel close to the left shore until you are near the creek,
then it runs into the middle of the river.

Big Bone Lick creek, left side, [p] (M. D.)  13½|583½
   Here is a bar—channel close to the left shore—
Thence to the Nine mile island fine water.

Small willow island, No. 55,                         20½|604
   Channel on the left side.

Nine mile island, No. 56,                            12|616
   Here you must keep to the left shore, and immediately below bear over towards the right shore, and keep
close to the high bank until you are past the second
brick house, thence to the mouth of Kentucky, you have
good water. This is a small island lying near the
right shore. *Plumb* creek enters on the right side,
opposite the head of No. 56.

A large sand bar,                                     5|621
   Channel on the right shore.

THE VINEYARD AND NEW SWITZERLAND,
    right bank, six miles above the mouth of
    Kentucky river.

Kentucky river, [q] (M. D.)                          6¼|627¼
   This is a large river of the state of Kentucky, having at its mouth two villages, the one above and the o-
ther below it. The first is called PORT WILLIAM. It
commands a handsome view of the Ohio, and is situated on an extensive and rich plain or bottom of river
land. The difficulty of establishing the title, it is said,
is the principal cause of the dull progress of these
villages. The mouth of the river at Port William, affords a good and safe harbor for boats, particularly
when the waters are a little up. At the point opposite a counter current is formed by the two rivers,
which is hard to pull out of. John Filson's history of
Kentucky informs us, that James M'Bride marked the
initials of his name, on a tree at the mouth of this river, and the date, which was in the year 1754, when he
and others descended the Ohio, stopped at the mouth
of the Kentucky river, and having reconnoitered
the country, returned home with the news of their
discoveries of the finest country in the world. This
tree was, according to Mr. Filson, standing in the year

1784, whether now or not, I am not informed. If yet
living, it ought to stand as an item of the early attempts to settle the state to which the river gives
name.

## Little Kentucky river,                                    ¾ 628

This is a tolerable sized creek, also affording a good
harbor in its mouth for boats, at a middle state of the
river, particularly.

## A large sand bar,                                          5 633

This bar lies on the left shore, channel close to the
right shore. Opposite this bar, Locust creek puts in
on the left side.

### MADISON.                                                  7 640

This is a new county town of Indiana territory,
pleasantly seated on the right bank of the Ohio, 13
miles below Kentucky river. This village was begun
to be built in the fall of 1810. It is on a second bank,
two or three hundred yards from the edge of the
river.

Before you get to Madison, you have a view of a fine
farm on the top of a high hill on the left side of the river. The appearance of the buildings, which are handsome and large, and of brick, (I believe) at a great distance up the river, have a fine effect, and the stupendous rocky cliffs on the opposite side just above the
town of Madison, together with the singular slope of
the hills, altogether form a scene highly pleasant to
the imagination, and one that is mixed with something
of the romantic.

There are several fine new improvements on the
summits of the hills along this part of the Ohio, that
add variety and beauty to the scenery, while it betokens
the rapid progress the country is making in settlement, and the taste and wealth of the settlers.

From Kentucky river to West Port, you have fine
water, and a good settlement, and a view of a machine for carrying water up from the river to a house
on the bank.

### WEST PORT,                                               43 683

Is situated on the left side of the river, on a high
pleasant bank and looks more like a settlement than a
town. Just below it 18 mile creek enters on the same
side.

## Eighteen mile island, No. 57,                             3 686

Channel right side.

## Twelve mile island, No. 58,                               7 693

Channel right side.

## Six mile island, No. 59, and Goose island,
No. 60,                                                      6 699

Channel runs between these two islands. Goose creek enters on the right side, opposite Goose island.

A large *sand bar*, four miles below these two last islands, and two above Louisville. It lies nearest the left shore, and extends in breadth nearly one-third across the river. After you get past this bar, pull over for the left shore if you want to land at the mouth of *Bear Grass* creek ; if not, you can easily make a landing at *Jeffersonville*, on the right side, rather at the upper end of the town, where you will find good water, and a bold shore, and pilots to conduct you over the Rapids.

Bear Grass Creek, left side, (M. D )                6¼ 7 ℃ 5¼

This creek is in a bend of the river, just above the rapid descent of the falls, and half a mile below the commencement of the Indian schute. It affords, at its mouth, one of the best harbors for boats on the Ohio, having at the dryest season, 12 feet water from the creek, down to the middle of Corn island, No. 61, and extends out a considerable way into the river, vessels, therefore, of any burden may lie here in safety. Should they even get loose from their cables and fastenings, there is no danger of their being carried off by the current. It is also finely sheltered both from winds and the ice of the river. It is the landing always made by those who either live at; or want to stop at Louisville, therefore, it may properly be called the *Louisville Landing.* Boats descending further, and having landed here, are obliged to row up stream nearly half a mile, (in gentle water, however,) in order to take the *Indian* or *Northern schute*, the pass generally preferred in all stages of the water, except indeed when the river is very low, when it is not passable. Here you procure a pilot who resides at Louisville, for the boats safe conduct over the falls, for which he is allowed by a law of the state two dollars, paid by the owner of of the boat. The same regulation exists as to pilots at Jeffersonville.

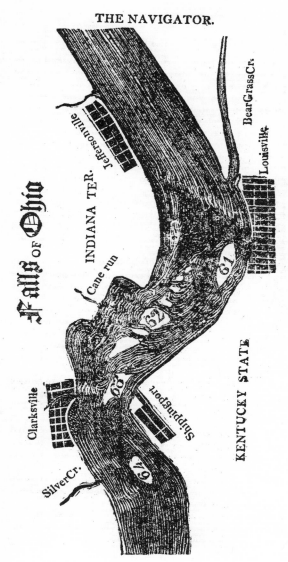

Falls of Ohio

## THE RAPIDS OF OHIO.

Are occasioned by a ledge of rocks which extend quite across the river, and are hardly to be perceived by the navigator in times of high freshes, unless by the superior velocity of the boat, which descends over them at the rate of from 10 to 13 miles an hour. When the water is low, the greater part of the rock becomes visible, and it is then that the passage becomes dangerous.

There are three channels or passes through the rapids : The course north or right of No. 62 or Goose island, called the *Indian schute*, is the main channel, but it is not passable in times of low water. The course between Nos. 62 and 63, Rock and Goose islands, called the *Middle schute*, is a safe and easy passage in all situations of the water above the middling stage. The pass between No. 63, Rock island, and the Kentucky shore, called the *Kentucky schute*, is lost in Rock harbor, and is passable only in time of high water.

Near the bottom on the left side of No. 63 is a fine mooring place for boats, called *Rock Harbor*. It is opposite the upper end of Shippingport, and has water enough at all seasons for vessels of any burthen.

No. 64, Sandy island, may be passed on the right in high water only. The left or south pass is the main channel. From No. 64, to No. 63, is excellent mooring ground, and water enough for vessels of any tonnage.

The pass south of Corn island No. 61, and the Kentucky shore, is passable only in time of high water.

From the great danger in passing the rapids, the courts of Louisville and Jeffersonville have been very careful to appoint experienced and trusty men as pilots, who can always be had at a moment's warning to conduct boats and vessels over them ; and from a little ambition shewn by the pilots of both places to excel in their occupation, accidents, arising from the want of either skill or care, very seldom happen.

In levelling the descent of the rapids, they have been found to be 22½ feet in two miles, the distance from Bear Grass creek to the foot of the falls.

Two miles above the rapids the river is deep, and three quarters of a mile broad ; and in low water the channel is contracted to the breadth of 250 yards.

## LOUISVILLE,

Is situated at the mouth of Bear Grass creek and extends down the Ohio to opposite the middle of Corn island, No. 61. It stands on an eminence of about 70 feet in height, which gently descends to a narrow plain along the river side in front of the town. From the lower end of the town the brow of the eminence takes its course to the Ohio, opposite Sandy island, No. 64, leaving a high plain between it and the river. It contains about 250 houses, a printing office, several mercantile stores and warehouses, a post office, is a port of entry, and the seat of justice for Jefferson county (Ken.) Lat. 38° 8' N.

Louisville has several rope walks extensively carried on. Messrs. Anderson and Gwathmoy had a valuable bagging manufactory, but which was burnt down by fire in December 1810, by design, it is suppposed. This is the second loss of the kind these gentlemen have experienced within eighteen months.

There have been a variety of circumstances which have operated against Louisville, and which have kept the improvements of the town constantly on the background, notwithstanding its superior and commanding situation, for a manufacturing and commercial town.— These circumstances, let them have arisen from what they might, are beginning to dispel, and like the sun after having been enveloped for a length of time in clouds and mists, and by degrees breaking through them, shines forth with redoubled vigor.—Such we believe and hope to be the situation of Louisville.

The river opposite Louisville is 1 mile and 25 poles wide, and commands a most charming view both above and below for a great distance, and the eye is carried over an extent of level country, terminated by the hills of Silver creek, which are five miles distant.

A canal has been proposed to be cut on the Kentucky side, to commence a little below Bear Grass creek, and open below Shippingport, a distance of 588 perches, or one mile and three quarters and twenty-eight perches.— The accomplishment of this object indeed would be a happy event to the trade of the Ohio. The highest ground through which the canal would have to be taken, would not exceed 29 feet, and its average depth would be

20 feet 6 inches. The route throughout is a stiff clay, lying upon a bed of rock not exceeding 40 inches higher than the floor of the canal. The canal is calculated sufficiently capacious for a ship of 400 tons, and this would afford a column of water greater than 3 feet by 24, during the lowest stages, and 24 feet fall.

From the known enterprising disposition of the Kentuckians, we have little doubt but this contemplated canal will be completed in a few years. If encouragement be wanting, we cannot see why the legislatures of Virginia, Ohio and Pennsylvania, should not throw in their strength to accomplish an object which would doubtless prove very advantageous to the citizens of each of those states, as well as to the state of Kentucky.

The first settlement we find made at the falls, was in the year 1774, when a number of surveyors, who were sent out by governor Dunmore of Virginia, to survey the interior of Kentucky, stopped here for some time, and erected temporary huts for their residence. About this time a small stockade fort was built at the falls, and commanded by general Clark. This fort, with col. Logan's, col. Harrod's, and col. Boon's, were the only forts in Kentucky at this time, and in them were all the white people in the country, a handful indeed, compared with the savage enemy, whose bloody tomahawk and scalping knife were eternally raised to kill and slaughter the inhabitants under the cover of every tree and old log in the vast wilderness. I cannot lay my hands on any thing at present giving date for the laying out and first building of Louisville. Our American publications are amazing deficient in point of dates and circumstances respecting the progress of settlement, extent, time, &c. of our own country. It is quite likely the beginning of Louisville is better known in London or Paris than it is by the inhabitants of that town themselves. Such is our carelessness in recording facts in such a manner that they will become generally known.

There have been lately added to Louisville, a banking company, a paper mill, a second printing office, a bookstore, a circulating library, a reading-room, an air foundary, for the casting all kinds of pot-metal, a glass house; and grist and sawmill by steam, and cotton manufactory by the same power were expected to be in operation this summer, 1814, and a number of handsome buildings, altogether having the appearance of its becoming a great commercial and manufacturing town. Nature herself has laid the plan of this place on a large scale. Its formation is as singular, as the prospect is grand and sublime. Man's mind is generally expanded or contracted in proportion to the objects around him, and shaped or moulded to the narrow or extended limits he has to move in.— I recollect, when a child, in the Pines of New Jersey, and going to a school, where Dillworth's spelling book and the testament and bible were the only books used, and crossing the Deleware into Pennsylvania while yet quite young, I was told as soon as we had crossed the river, by the person under whose charge I was, that " we were now out of New Jersey."—I stared him full in the face, amazed at the intelligence—I perfectly recollect of feeling too much surprise, and a certain kind of childish confused awkwardness at the moment to make any reply—" Out of New Jersey," muttered I to myself, for I had really been under an impression that all the world was New Jersey— the world across the big water excepted, where king George's refugees and tories came from, a circumstance impressed on my infantile mind during the troubles of the American revolution. I looked at the trees, the stones, the earth, with anxiety, in order to discover why or how it could be that we were out of New Jersey. I felt ashamed of my ignorance and was silent.—If the inhabitants of Louisville go on in the same generous and extended scale with the original plan, they must become a great people, and their town a great city.

## JEFFERSONVILLE,

*The following description of Jeffersonville, and the division of the territory in which it is situated, was written by some friends of that place and forwarded to us a few years since.*

By an act passed at the last session of Congress, the territory of Indiana is bounded by the Wabash as far as Vincennes, thence a due north course to the Michigan territory, by that territory on the north, the state of Ohio on the east, and the Ohio river on the south. The territory is divided into four counties, viz. Knox, which extends from the western boundary line to within a few

L

miles of Blue river ; Harrison, from thence to within 10 or 12 miles of the falls; Clark. from thence up the Ohio to opposite the mouth of the Kentucky river, and Dearborn, from thence to the Ohio line—Vincennes, the present seat of government of the territory, is the seat of justice of Knox county; Corydon, is the seat of justice of Harrison county, situated about 100 miles east of Vincennes, and 26 west of Jeffersonville—Jeffersonville is the seat of justice of Clark county, and Lawrenceburgh near the mouth of the Big Miama, is the seat of justice of Dearborn county ;—these are the only towns in the territory.

This county (Clark) was established in the year 1801 —the whole number of its inhabitants may be reckoned at present, at 3000 or 4000—the number of voters, who consist only of freeholders, are about 350.

Until the late purchases made by governor Harrison of the Indians, the grant made by the state of Virginia to gen. George R. Clark and the other officers and soldiers of the Illinois regiment, consisting of 150,000 acres, was the only tract of country in the county, belonging to the citizens of the U. States, the balance belonging to the Indians. As a tribute of respect to gen. G. R. Clark, to whom the acquisition of this territory to the U. S. may be ascribed, the legislature have named this county after him. The soil and productions of this country may be considered almost in every respect similar to that of Kentucky. Corn, pork, beef and Irish potatoes, form our principal articles of exportation.

Jeffersonville is situated on the north-west bank of the Ohio, nearly opposite to Louisville, and a little above the commencement of the great falls—the town was laid out in the year 1802, since which time it has grown in proportion to the surrounding country. It is the seat of justice of the county of Clark—a land office for the disposal of the United States' lands, and a post office are established here, there are also two pilots appointed by law for conducting boats across the falls, residing here; there are about 35 or 40 houses, which are principally of frame and log, except the court-house, which is of brick—and contains 175 inhabitants, of whom some are useful mechanicks. In point of natural advantages and beauty, there are few or no situations on the Ohio more eligible for a town. The bank is very high, and surrounded with a rich, level and fertile country. The current and channel of the Ohio for several miles above, are on the N. W. shore, and the depth of water being sufficiently great at any season of the year for boats or vessels of any burden, afford at all times an easy landing place, and good harbor for boats descending the Ohio. In descending the Ohio, the first place of landing is at Bloom's Eddy;—this eddy is just below the first and greatest obstacle in the rapids —it is a large and convenient landing place for boats at a low stage of the water, and from which, flat boats may pass the balance of the falls with their loading at a low stage of the water. The portage from the landing at Jeffersonville to the eddy, not being more than half the distance to the lower landing on either side of the river, it is thought it will become the principal landing place for boats having to unload above the falls.

In the vicinity of Jeffersonville, about half a mile to the north, is a medical spring, whose waters are supposed to be strongly impregnated with sulphur and iron. It has been much resorted to for several years, and thought to be beneficial in fevers that prevail in this country. There are several mills in the neighborhood, only one, however, of considerable consequence, that is built on a small stream called Mill Run, which empties into the Ohio at the foot of the falls, this is a very considerable merchant mill, and from the resources of the stream, although not more than 2 or 3 miles in length, continues to go during the whole year, except when stopped by back water from the Ohio. She is the property of Messrs. Cuthbert and Thomas Bullit, built about 100 yards from the river.

### CLARKSVILLE,

Is a small village situated at the foot of the falls on the N. W. bank opposite to Shippingport—this town was established as early as the year 1783 by the Virginia legislature, and attached to the grant made to the officers and soldiers of the Illinois regiment, from which time may be reckoned the first settlement of this country : soon after its establishment it contained a number of inhabitants who were encouraged to settle under promises of donations of lots by the trustees; and notwithstanding the imminent danger and great inconveniency, some of them continued to reside there to the end of the Indian war, and in a great measure contributed to the safety of the inhabitants of Kentucky in the neighborhood of the falls. There is a large and capacious eddy at this place for the landing of boats. The Knobs or Silver Hills, which commence on the Ohio about 10 miles below the falls and take their course through the country in a north-eastwardly direction, it is said by those who have taken some pains to examine, afford considerable quantities of ore of some kind or other, supposed to be iron. In the bank of Silver creek (a small stream that falls into the Ohio just below Clarksville) about two miles from its mouth, is found large quantities of copperas, a place well known by the name of Copperas Banks. The copperas taken from this bank is found to be equal (although not so clear in its present state) to any brought to this country.

## SHIPPINGPORT,

This town and landing is on the Kentucky side just below the foot of the falls. After passing the Rapids, boats put in here, and if they want, get a supply of bread, bacon, and other necessaries for their voyage. The landing has a bold shore and deep water. Mr. J. A. Tarrascon has an excellent flour mill at the foot of the falls on this side, in which he makes large quantities of flour for the New Orleans market, transported thence in barges and flat boats, under consignment to Messrs. Gilly and Pryor of that city. Mr. Tarrascon has also a store in Shippingport, and a rope walk, extensively conducted.— Mr. James Berthoud keeps a warehouse here, and does business on commission. Shippingport is also the landing place for all goods ascending the rivers to Kentucky, and for such as are obliged to be wagonned to the landing at Bear Grass creek, intended for the country above the rapids. Consequently, Shippingport is at present, and must become a very considerable place of business.— Were it not for the lowness of the ground the town would extend much faster. It however, contains several handsome buildings, and in the fall of 1812, I saw others progressing.

There is a small sand island with young willows on it, opposite this landing, about 100 yards from the shore, which requires some attention. The channel I believe is good on either side, but if you wish to land at Shippingport, you must keep it on your right hand.

| | | |
|---|---|---|
| Salt river, left side, | $24\frac{3}{4}$ | 730 |

This is a considerable stream of Kentucky, spreading out into four principal, besides a great number of smaller branches; Floyd's fork, its northern, and Rolling and Beach forks are its sou'hern branches.—*Bairdstown* is on Beach fork, *Bealsburgh* on Rolling fork. The heads of Rolling fork entwine with the waters of the Kentucky and Green rivers. There are a number of salt Licks on this river and its branches, from which it takes its name, Long Lick, Walton's Lick, May's Lick, Knob Lick, &c. Rrashah's is also a fine branch of Salt river  Salt river is about 150 yards wide at its mouth, and is navigable 60 miles.

| | | |
|---|---|---|
| Otter creek, left side, | 8 | 738 |
| Doe run, left side, | 8 | 746 |
| Falling spring, left side, | 5 | 751 |
| French creek, left side, | 8 | 759 |
| Buck creek, right side, | 10 | 769 |
| Indian or Wiandot creek, right side, | 6 | 775 |

Two Islands, No. 65 and No. 66,

Nearly opposite the mouth of Wiandot creek, (called in mistake in the former editions of the Navigator, Blue river)—Channel past the first is on the left side; past the second on the right side, keeping close to the lower point of it.

| | | |
|---|---|---|
| Big Blue river, right side, | 17 | 792 |

This is a pretty long and very crooked river of Indiana, heading near the waters of White river, a branch of the Wabash. Preston or Wood's creek puts in on the left side of the Ohio just above the mouth of Blue river.

| | | |
|---|---|---|
| Helm's creek, left side, | 10 | 3u2 |
| Little Yellow Bank creek, left side, | 10 | 812 |
| Harden's creek, left side, | 6 | 818 |

In a fork of this creek, near its head, stood Harden's fort, built during the first settlement of Kentucky. Sinking creek is a branch of Harden's, and what renders it singular, after heading in three springs and running several miles, it sinks, and runs about four or five miles under ground before it appears again.

| | | |
|---|---|---|
| Flint Island, No. 67, | 2 | 820 |

Here the channel is difficult. Keep the island on the left, hug it pretty close, and at its foot go as if you intended to make the left shore, after passing it in that direction, pull out quick towards the right shore, to avoid an ugly sand bar lying to the left be-

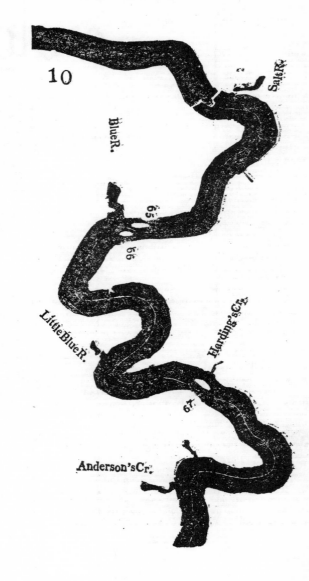

low the island. No. 67 lies close to the left shore, and is about three quarters of a mile long. It takes its name from a stone found on it, said to be excellent for gun flints.

The vessel Tuskarora grounded on this island in the spring of 1808. While here she was ungenerously stript of her bolts, bands, rings, &c. to the amount, it is said, of 2000 dollars worth. The general character of honesty of the inhabitants of the Ohio, ought to shield them from an accusation of this kind, but as there are exceptions to all general rules, so in the present instance, the neighborhood of Flint island, bears the burden of the charge at present, whether innocent or guilty of the robbery. The Tuskarora was built at Marietta, and was owned by Jones and Anderson.

Clover creek, left side,      10 830

Deer creek, right side,      6 836

In the lower part of the bend half a mile below Deer creek, is a pile of dangerous rocks 80 or 90 yards from the right shore, keep them well to your right hand at all times.

Anderson's river, right side,      15 851

Anderson's ferry, left side, a creek right side,      1 852

One mile below the ferry is a small island, lying close into the right hand shore, channel left shore.

About five miles below Anderson's ferry is a large sand bar called *Anderson's bar*, putting out from the left shore—Channel close to the right shore in low water.

Blackford creek, left side, Small creek, right side,      12 864

Here the cane begins to make its appearance on the banks of the Ohio, and from its ever-green foliage, it has a pleasant effect on the imagination, when all the surrounding vegetable matter is locked up in the winter's frost.

Hanging Rock, right side,      4 868

This rock is called by way of eminence THE LADY WASHINGTON. It shews a bare perpendicular front of solid rock of about 100 feet in height, commencing at the water's edge. It is the upper edge of a ridge of high ground, which ends here, extending half a mile on the river, having a flat country above and below it. A small distance above this rock a creek enters on the same side with it. Lady Washington would make a good site for a fort, having a fine com-

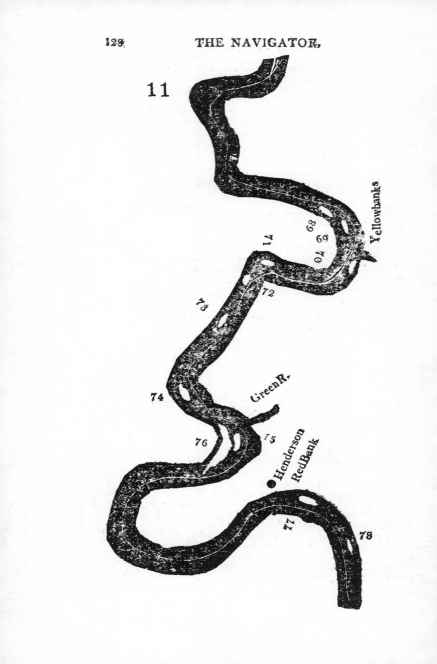

mand of the river above and below for several miles.
Now ends the river hills, a bluff now and then excepted, and the flat country commences.

### Islands No. 68, and No. 69,

7 875½

No. 68 lies close to the right shore, just below a
point as the river turns to the right, it is about half a
mile long. No. 69 lies half a mile below No. 68, also
close to the right shore, and is about 3 miles long—
Channel past both these islands is on the left side of
them.

### Yellow banks, left side,

5 880

Half a mile below No. 69, and five miles from the
head of No. 68. A frontier post was kept here until
Wayne's treaty at Greenville in 1794 A small creek
enters just below the buildings at the Yellow Banks.
This place takes its name from the yellow appearance
of the bank of the river.

### Island, No. 70,

3 883

Lies close to the left shore, about one mile and a
half long. Channel right side.

*Mistletoe* [r] begins to appear in bunches on the
top branches of the trees.

### Islands No. 71, and No. 72,

5 838

Lie pretty close to the right shore, No. 71 is a mile
and a half long, No. 72 is small, and lies to the left
and half way down No. 71—channel to the left of both
these islands. Below Nos. 71 and 72 you have a fine
view of the river for several miles.

### French Island, No. 73,

7 895

Channel left side. Not far from this island and
about seven miles above Green river, there is seen on
the right side, a high round knob of a hill, where formerly a Frenchman kept a trading house, it is now
called "French Camp."

### Three Mile Island, No. 74,

2( 915

It lies so close to the right shore that it can scarcely be distinguished. Channel left side.

### Green River. [s] left side, (M. D)

10½ 925½

### Green River Islands, No. 75 and No. 76,

You come to these islands immediately after you
get around the right hand point just below the
mouth of Green river The first is a fine large island,
pretty close to the right shore, about six miles long,
having several families settled on it. The second is
a small island lying to the left and along side of the
first, and near its lower end —Channel left side of
both. From these islands the river runs N. W. to

**Pidgeon Creek, right side,**                    9½ 935

Hence it forms a short bend to the left and runs
nearly S. E. to

**Hendersonville, or Red Banks,**                    15 950

Coming within five miles by land of the mouth of
Green river, though it is 25 by water. Ten miles above
Hendersonville there is a point of rocks on the right
shore, from which, however, there is no danger if you
keep in the middle of the river.

Hendersonville stands on a high left bank, and extends half a mile fronting the river, commanding a
handsome view up and down it for several miles. The
town contains 30 houses of brick and wood, 2 stores
indifferently supplied, 2 long tobacco warehouses, a
post office, a jail and court-house, it being the seat of
justice for Henderson county, Kentucky. This place
is included in Henderson's grant of 200,000 acres of
land, begining about 20 miles on the Ohio above Green
river, thence running about a south-west direction 20
miles to a corner near the mouth of Grove creek, 20
miles direct above the mouth of Green river, thence
27 miles in a N. W. direction until it strikes the Ohio,
about 4 miles above Highland creek. A short distance
above Hendersonville, and on the right side of the river is a large flat bar, which you must keep to your
right.

**Red Bank Island, No. 77,**                    3 953

Lies pretty close to the left shore, and is about a
mile and a half long. About half a mile below the
head of No. 77, keep pretty close to the island, to
avoid a sand bar which begins on the right shore and
extends ten miles down on the same side, enlarging
as it descends, thereby making it necessary to keep
pretty close to the left bank until you get below it.
At the head of No. 77, there is also a bar, which, with
the island itself, you keep on your left hand. From
Hendersonville the river makes another great bend
to the right, and after running about twelve miles in
almost a north direction, it comes again within a
mile and a quarter of the bend, 15 miles above Red
Banks, having travelled a distance of about 37 miles
below Green river, and only gained ten miles in a direct line.

**Diamond Island, No. 78,**                    12 965

Channel right side. As you approach this island it
has the appearance of making two great and formidable rivers, so suddenly and equally divided is the
current here, and so broad, that you scarcely know
which to take for the Ohio. No. 78, is a large and

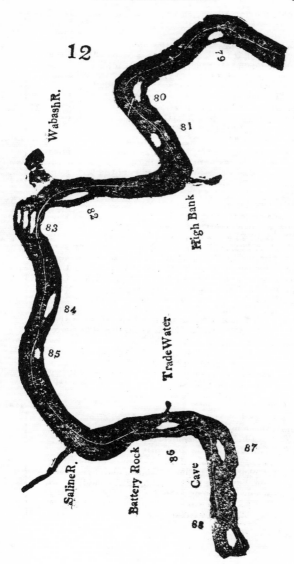

12

Wabash R.

79

80

81

High Bank

82

83

84

85

Trade Water

Saline R.

Battery Rock

86

Cave

87

88

noble looking island, and contains several thousand
acres of excellent land. It is about 4½ miles long,
broad at its head and comes to a point below, giving it the appearance of the shape of a diamond,
from which it is probable it takes its name. In the
left channel at its head is a small island, and another
immediately at its foot. A large bar, two miles below Diamond island, extends out around the first
right hand point.—Channel left shore.

Straight Island, No. 79,                                    10 975
    Lies close to the left shore, about a mile long.—
Channel right side.

Slim Island, No. 80,                                       10 985
    Channel right side, two miles long.—Two miles
below No. 80 is the first bend in the Ohio, similar in
shape and appearance to the bends of the Mississippi, hence we denominate it the *Mississippi Bend*, being about five miles long.

Willow Island and Bar, No. 81,                             3 988
    Lies close to the right shore, opposite the Missis-
sippi Bend, and terminates with it—channel left side.
It is about 2½ miles long. Just below the foot of this
island and bar, and as you turn the left hand point of
the Mississippi Bend, a ledge of rocks appear near
the right shore, from which there is no danger by
keeping near the left shore and pretty close round
the point. Two miles below this ledge of rocks,
another ledge puts out from the left shore, just below the first right hand point after leaving the first
ledge These last rocks are not seen except in very
low water, when the channel is near the right shore.

Highland Creek, left side,                                 5 993
    Five miles below the head of No. 81, and about one
mile below the Mississippi Bend. Good settlements
here on both sides of the Ohio, particularly below
the creek From Highland creek the Ohio runs W.
N W. to the Wabash river.

Wabash Island, No. 82,                                     7 1000
    This is a large island, five miles long, commencing
about three miles above the Wabash river, and ends
two miles below it—channel right side.

Wabash River, [t] right side,                              3 1003
    Here is seen a cabin above the mouth of the river,
the remnant of a trading establishment here some
years ago, but the waters proving detrimental, it was
abandoned.—Here ends the Indiana Territory, and
the Illinois commences, the divisional line between
these two territories striking the Ohio just above the

mouth of the Wabash, thence runs a due north course until it strikes the east and west line, which touches the most southerly point of lake Michigan, thence to lake Erie due east, and to the Mississippi due west, in the parallel of lat 42° 6′ north, making the division-al line 255 miles long, the mouth of the Wabash being in 37° 56′ north latitude.

## Brown's Island, No. 83,

3 | 1006

Lies close to the right shore—channel left side.

## Shawanee town, right side,

7 | 1013

This village formerly belonged to the Shawanee nation of Indians. It now possesses about 30 indifferent cabin-roofed houses, with the exception of one or two that are shingled. It has a post office, two or three indifferent taverns and several dram shops. The U. States' Saline saltworks being near this place, they give employment and afford a source of trade to such of the inhabitants as are industrious or enterprising. The town is subject to the inundations of the river, and during those of the winter and spring of 1813, the inhabitants were obliged to abandon their houses. The channel of the river is on the town side, there being a large bar opposite it on the left side.

## Stevenson's Island, No. 84,

4 | 1017

Channel right side.

## Island, No. 85, (a small island.)

3 | 1020

Lies close to the left shore—channel right side.

## Saline River, [n] right side,

1 | 1021

About two miles above the Saline there are three small willow islands or bars near the left shore—keep to the right of them, and this requires care, for if you approach too near their upper point the current draws rapidly to the left.

## Battery Rock bar,

3 | 1024

This bar commences about half a mile or three quarters above Battery Rock, and lies near the right shore, but flattens out a good way into the river It is a pretty high and broad sand bar and requires care to avoid it ; nearly opposite the upper end of it is a small house on the right bank. The channel at the lowest stage of the water is pretty close to the left bank, between it and the bar. This being a dangerous and conspicuous bar, it is a little strange how it escaped notice in the previous editions of the Navigator.

Battery Rock is just below the bar on the right side. Here is seen a formidable work of nature, a bare perpendicular front of rocks, jutting out from a tongue of lofty land, bounding the river for half a

M

mile, having level and cultivated farms above and below it. The Battery is about eighty or an hundred
feet high, of a circular form, and quarter of a mile in
length. About the middle it is handsomely turned,
and comes up to man's ingenious idea as a work formed for the purpose of the boldest and strongest defence. Its upper edge slopes gradually to the river's
edge, the lower end is broken, and huge rocks have
left their former bed and taken one in the river.

At the head of the Battery Rock an eddy is formed, the water deep, affording a good harbor, was it
not for the bar which ends just above it, and which
prevents boats going on that side of the river, except
in high water.

After you get three quarters of a mile below Battery Rock, draw over towards the right shore to avoid
sand bars on the left side of the river lying above
Trade water creek.

## Trade water Island, No. 86,                          2 | 1026

Lies pretty close to the left shore—just below
Trade water creek, is one mile long, and two miles
below Battery rock—Channel right side.

Two miles below No. 86, and three above Cave-in-
rock, is a bar pretty close to the right shore, as the
river winds to the right. Keep it to your right hand.

## Cave-in-rock Island, No. 87,                          7 | 1033

Stands near the middle of the river, is about a
mile long and ends opposite the Cave. Channel right
side.

## Cave-in-Rock or House of Nature.*                     1 | 1034

Here you are presented with a most stupendous,
curious and solid work of nature. For half a mile on
your right before you reach the cave, you have a front
view of a beautiful, perpendicular, smooth limestone
wall, a solid mass of rock, with regular horizontal
strata, of about 100 or 120 feet in height above low
water mark, and whose summit is handsomely clothed with a growth of small red cedars, the roots of
which springing through the close fissures, and apparently receiving their nourishment from the rocks.
The cedars on the top of these rocks appear to be
peculiarly the haunt of birds of prey, for what reason
I know not.

This Cave or House of Nature, opens to view fronting the river a little above high water mark, its
mouth is about 60 feet across at the base, narrow-
ing from both sides as it ascends, forming an arch

---

* The reader is here referred to note [p] Appendix.

of about 25 feet in its highest part, and running back to a point of about 120 feet deep. The top and sides of the cave bear the names of thousands who have visited it from time to time, and the dates of the year, &c. There are in the walls of this cave the same appearance of marine shells as those found in the rocks of Kentucky, and other parts of the western country. This cavern sometimes serves as a temporary abode for those wanting shelter, in case of a shipwreck, or other accident, which happen on the river near it. Families have been known to reside here tolerably comfortable from the northern blasts of winter. The mouth of this cave was formerly sheltered and nearly hid by some trees growing in front of it, but the rude axe has levelled them to the earth, and the cavern exposed to the open view of the passenger.

Emigrants from the states, 27 years ago, used to land here and waggon their goods across the Illinois country, it not being more than 120 miles from this place to Kaskaskia on the Mississippi.

Hurricane bars,

The first lies about a mile and a half below the Cave on the right shore, extending out, however, a good ways into the river, but being flat it is not seen unless the water is very low; it is about a mile and a half long, in shape something like a half moon, back outwards; it ends a little above *Tower rock*, a high point of rocks on the right bank, so called from their towering appearance and sugar-loaf form, coming to a point at top, and covered with lofty trees. This pile of rocks is a good land mark if the navigator will take notice of it. It stands opposite the most extended point of Walker's bar, which approaches the right shore within about 200 yards.

The Second, or *Walker's bar*, begins on the left shore, as the first quits on the right. It is a high, bold, and a difficult bar to get round. From the left side it runs out pretty suddenly, and approaches within 200 yards of the right shore, then turning suddenly it forms a pretty sharp point with a bluff bank, unless the water is very high when it is not seen.

The channel through these bars is thus: after you pass the cave incline gradually towards the left shore and keep pretty near it, which is bluff for about two miles, having the first bar on your right, then bear over pretty rapidly towards the right shore to within 150 yards of it, and when you get opposite the pile of rocks mentioned, called *Tower rock*, pull round the point of Walker's bar and make for the left shore, keeping the bar pretty close on the left hand, leaving the island on your right. In low water you cannot go to the right of Hurricane island, and it requires care to prevent your boat being thrown on the head of the island, or drawn into the right hand channel among snags, logs and shoals. The channel round Walker's bar has a swift current; is deep, and broad enough, but there are some logs opposite the head of the island that require care and vigilance to pass them in safety. The river above Hurricane island is about 1000 yards broad. When a boat, winding through this crooked channel, is seen from above, the beholder believes it impossible she could make the left of the island.

Just below the cave on the right bank there is a person who is sometimes employed to pilot boats through this serpentine channel, and it is better for a stranger to pay a dollar or two for this purpose, than run the risk of grounding on either one or the other of these bars in low water; when the water is high there is no occasion for a director, for either side of the island is good, but if you take the right side then keep near the right shore.

Hurricane Island, No. 88,                                    5 1039

Though you pass this island on the left side, it stands nearest the left shore, having but a narrow channel compared to that on the right of the island, but the water is deep and rapid, the greater part of the river passing through it. It is washing away at its head by the power and division of the current. It is pretty broad and about three miles long. The bars and island extend the river here to at least one-third more than its usual breadth.

Three miles below No. 88 is a large sand bar on the left side of the river—Channel right side of it, pretty close to the high bluff of rocks which overlook the right bank

Three miles further on is another long, broad, flat sand bar, near the middle of the river—Channel pretty close to the right shore, under a high bluff of iron colored rocks for a mile in extent. This bar has some snags on it, a mile or better below its head. The left shore opposite this bar is low.

Grand Pierre creek, right side,                              10 1049

This creek is a little way below the range of bluff rocks just mentioned, and immediately above a rocky point, under which stands some small houses with a farm adjoining them. Opposite the mouth of this creek stands a sturdy planter, channel good on either side of it.

**First of three Sisters, No. 89,**    2 1051

Channel right side. It is in the middle of the river, about a mile and a half long, and has a farm on it. Just below this island is Lusk's ferry, at the mouth of Lusk's creek, right side, where resides a Mr. Ferguson. There is a small creek and fine farm on the opposite side of the river, and a mile and a half below it is another creek and fine farm, also on the left. At Lusk's ferry the road from Kentucky crosses to Kaskaskia, St. Louis, &c.

**Second of three Sisters, No. 90,**    4 1055

At the head of this island is a large and very broad sand bar, which approaches very near the head of the island, and keeps you so near the right shore that you would think it impossible to go to the left of the island. But the channel shoots across suddenly from the right shore, and with application of the oars, keeping pretty near the sand bar on the left hand, you will take the chute with ease, having the head of the island on your right. This is a singular formed channel, crooked, deep, narrow, and rapid water, but with any thing like good management, not dangerous. The foot of the bar, and head of the island are bluff, and are washing away.

After you get through this narrow pass, the course the current takes your boat, with steerage, is perhaps the most correct channel. There are two bars to your right between the Second and Third Sisters, and two small islands and a bar on your left, close to the left shore, which do not interfere with the channel at present. The Second Sister is a small island lying nearest the left shore, and about half a mile or three quarters long. From its foot commence a chain of bars which run down to near the head of

**Third Sister, No. 91,**    2 1057

which you must keep on your left hand, having the foot of the bar, which is bluff, on your right. This is also a small island, lying nearest the left shore, not more than half a mile long. In appearance, there is nothing to prevent you from going to the right of all the sisters, but there must be some obstruction in the bed of the river between the Second Sister and the right shore, to occasion this sudden turn of the current, which now shoots you to the left of that island, and through the bar, which it would seem had formerly joined the island. Just below the Third Sister is a large willow bar, forming the right shore.

Three Sisters. After passing the last of these, keep close to the left shore, until opposite the left hand point.

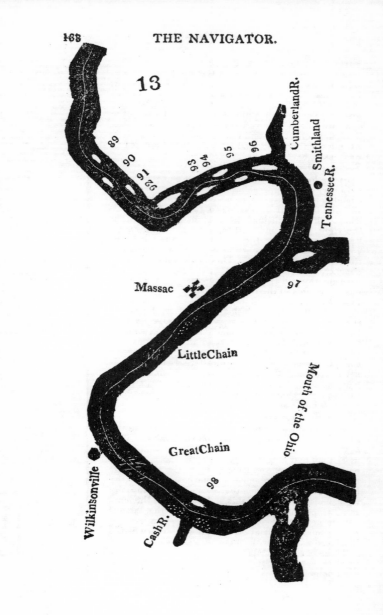

### Stewart's Island, No. 92,                           7  064

Channel right side.  No. 92 lies nearest the left
shore, and is about 2 miles long.  Two miles below
is a sand bar on the right shore—Channel on the left
side of it until about half way down, then bear over
towards the bar, leaving some large sawyers to the
left.

### First of the Cumberland Islands, No. 93,

Channel left side, it lying near the right shore,
about three miles below No. 92.  As you leave No.
93 on your right hand.

### Big Cumberland Island, No. 94,

Commences on your left, extending down about
three miles, and a mile and a half below Cumberland
river, which is hid from the view of the passenger,
together with the town at its mouth, unless the left
of this island is taken, which is not so safe only when
the water is in a good navigable order.  Burr, in his
flighty expedition to Mexico, encamped his party on
this island for some time in the winter of 1806-7.

Islands No. 95 and No. 96 are small, and so closely attached to the lower end of No. 94, that they can
scarcely be distinguished from that island.

### Cumberland river, [w]                               7 1071

At the mouth of this river is a small town, and a
warehouse owned by Joseph Woods, for the deposit
of goods destined up that river.  The town has a post
office, two stores, and about 15 or 20 houses, and may
from its commanding situation become a place of
considerable importance.

### Smithland, (settlement)                             3 1074

On your left three miles below Cumberland river,
and on a handsome rising ground, is Smithland, intended originally for a town, but now turned into a
farm.  A Mr. Coxe, about 20 years ago, laid out a
town here, with a zealous hope of its becoming the
seat of wealth and business, but he is not the first who
has got disappointed in the attempt to grow towns
in a forest.  This settlement is about a mile and a
half below the foot of the Big Cumberland island.

Five miles below Smithland is a broken willow bar
close to the left shore, with a bare bar running out to
the right at its lower end; keep pretty well on the
right side of the river opposite this bar.

Two miles further on, is a large flat sand bar on
the right shore, extending a good way out—channel
pretty close to the bluff bend on your left hand.  In
this bend, close to the bank of the river, grows a sturdy cypress, the first perhaps seen on the Ohio.

### Tennessee or Cherokee river, [x] (upper mouth,)          1 | 1084

A planter shews itself in the middle of the river just above the mouth of Tennessee. The current inclines you to the right of it, and bears hard against the right hand bank, where it is deep and rapid water, and requires pulling to keep off it. Opposite the upper mouth of Tennessee, and on the right bank of the Ohio, is a nuke occasioned by a slip of the bank, called *Dickey's Elbow*, from the circumstance of a boat getting into it in time to be saved from the driving ice in February 1811, when four or five other boats were stove at that place. After you pass the first right hand point below the upper mouth of the Tennessee, incline towards the left shore, to avoid a sand bar on the right, about two miles below the lower mouth of the Tennessee. At the first left hand point four miles below the lower mouth of the Tennessee is another bar which puts out a good way into the river. In the middle of the river about a mile below the foot of N 97, there appears, from the sounding, to be a bar also, but cannot be seen unless at a very low state of the water.

There are two islands immediately below the first mouth of the Tennessee, forming in fact three openings to that river, the second so trifling, however, that the boat passage through it is dangerous. Boats descending the Ohio sometimes pass into the first and come out at the third, which is the main or principal mouth, keeping the two islands on the right hand.— This can be done only when the Ohio is high and the Tennessee low, or when their currents are nearly equal in strength either high or low.

The first island is small, and is not numbered.— The second is a pretty large island, and is numbered 97.

No. 97, Tennessee island —There is a pretty large bar at the foot of this island, which you must keep on your left, going between it and the big bar near the middle of the river, and which is a small distance below to your right. About one-third of the river from the lower point of the island, is the proper channel.

### Fort Massac, right side,          11 | 1095

This fort stands on a high dry bank, and commands a delightful view of the Ohio, as far up as the Tennessee. The great breadth of the river, and the long easy bend it makes without any obstruction for 11 miles above and four or five below the fort, gives a most noble prospect to the eye, and a sentiment of admiration to the imagination, excelled only by a greater combination of nature's beauties. Fort Massac has, generally, a captain's command in it, and around it are a few cabins and several small fields cultivated. The place, however, is neither very elegible for a fort or settlement. As a station it is not of much importance to the United States, and the swamps, and ponds of stagnated water back of the fort, and for miles above and below it, render the country too unhealthy to invite settlers. These ponds are supplied with water by the annual high floods of the Ohio, and during the dry warm months of the fall season, they become putrid, sending forth by exhalation a swamp miasmata that creates intermittents, and renders the inhabitants unhealthy.

The earth on the bank of the river here, has a yellowish and iron like appearance, and from the love the cattle have in licking it, salt may also be an ingredient. On the shore above and below the fort the stones have a very rich appearance of possessing ferruginous matter, and indeed from their shape and color, they look as if they had been thrown out of an iron-ore bank.

The French had a fort here as early as the year 1757, and under the same name it bears at present. It is in lat 37° 12' north.

The channel past Massac is near the middle of the river, just above the fort near the right shore, is a sand bar, and the shore opposite the garrison is rocky and shallow.

## A large sand bar,        6 1101

This is a broad flat bar lying in the middle of the river—channel right side of it.

## Little Chain of rocks,        3 1104

Channel is near the middle of the river.

## Wilkinsonville, right side,        9 1113

In the year 1801, general Wilkinson established here a handsome station for the American troops under his command. Several large and well built frame and log houses were erected, and a number of smaller ones, and the place had for a season the appearance of a thriving village. It was abandoned soon after by the troops, and the houses have since been torn down and destroyed, and not a post or plank is there now to be seen to point out the spot where stood the city.

## Big Chain of rocks,        3 1116

The channel here runs about one-third of the breadth of the river from the left shore, until you are past the two last rocks in the middle of the river, then bear over towards the right shore, to avoid a sand bar just below, lying to your left hand.

Cash Island, No. 98, and two bars,                    9 1125

This island lies close to the left shore, and is about one mile long. Opposite this island and near the right shore, is a high sand bar. There is another bar adjoining the island—the channel is near the middle of the river between the island and the bar on the right shore. There is a narrow channel to the right of the bar last mentioned, which is sometimes gone in low water by keel boats ascending the Ohio.

Cash river, right side,                                 1½ 1126½

This is a considerable creek, having a small settlement at its mouth, and during ice or wind might be made to afford a good harbor for boats. The land is something higher here than at the mouth of the river

Mouth of the Ohio,                                     6 1132½

Here is a pretty good landing place on the right side, at the point of the highest ground, and immediately above the willow point, which runs down to the junction of the two rivers.

A temporary warehouse is kept here by col. Bird, who lives on the western bank of the Mississippi, opposite this place on a fine farm, from which he sometimes affords boats provisions at his warehouse.—Could a supply of bread, bacon, chickens, eggs, milk, butter, &c. be depended on here, it would be a matter of great convenience to those descending and ascending the rivers, and pay well the person keeping them.

The willow point at the junction of these two great waters, and which is nearly in form of a triangle, having sides from half to about three quarters of a mile in length, with a beautiful growth of young willows or cotton wood on it, was not to be seen eleven years ago, except as a bar of sand and mud; it is at this time about ten feet lower than the highest ground, but may in 10 or 12 years more be equally high with it, and form the main land. Such is the rapid growth of parts of the Mississippi, while other parts again are continually washing away and disappearing The right bank of the Ohio just above the landing place, appears to be washing away very fast.

From the high water mark on the trees at the junction of the Ohio and Mississippi rivers, it appears, the land is overflowed during the highest floods, from 8 to 16 feet deep. What a pity that the meeting of two of the greatest rivers in the world, so inundates the adjacent ground that not a town, settlement, nor even a warehouse of any importance, can be established with safety or profit.—But I anticipate the time with pleasure, when this place shall become the great DEPOSITE for the produce of the upper country on the Ohio and its branches, intended for the New Orleans market; and also for the return loads of the Mississippi sugar, cotton, rice, &c. consigned for the settlements on the Ohio as far up as Pittsburgh. A few years more the rapidly settling, and enterprising citizens of the western country, will point out the necessity of an establishment of this kind at this spot or somewhere near it. By leveeing it could now be rendered secure, but this would be attended with considerable expense, without a sure return. A little time, and a union of sentiment and interest, in those immediately concerned in the trade of the western waters, farmers, millers, merchants, and those engaged in boating, will overcome all difficulties, and they will, after what they have already experienced, soon be convinced, that without a place of deposit at a point, at all seasons navigable to market, there never will be any surety of getting a fair price for produce when taken to it. There are other reasons which point out the necessity of an establishment of this kind, affecting life, health, morality and religion, which will perhaps be spoken of hereafter.

On approaching the Mississippi the current naturally throws you over towards the Willow Point, from which, inclining downwards, without difficulty, (except the application of the oars and steerage, the better to keep the boat under head way, which ought to be done uniformly where two currents meet, there always being in such places more or less of a counter current) you enter the union of two of the most noble rivers in the universe. When the Ohio is the highest, your boat is taken half way across the Mississippi. When the latter is master, you will have to row pretty hard, to reach its current, the Ohio, in such cases being backed up for several miles.

The Ohio enters the Mississippi nearly in a S. E. direction, but the latter turns immediately to the S. W. and thence it moves on majestically to all points of the compass, and at a pace something more rapidly than the Ohio

Just above the mouth of the Ohio, an island in the Mississippi near the right shore, looking upwards, very much spoils the view up that river. The Mississippi is now particularly distinguished from the Ohio by the whitish muddy and turbid appearance of its water, it being, when any way raised, full of swells or whirls, thrown up by the fixed air, combined in, and set in motion, by the operation of the mass of descending water; these are increased in numbers and size in proportion to the depth and swiftness of the current. Sometimes these whirls, or swells, or boils, as they are sometimes called, are so large and strong that a boat is thrown half around in passing over them, and sometimes shot so rapidly out of them, either forwards, or towards the shore, that it takes strong rowing to get her under way again. I have seen a lightly loaded family boat shot out of one of these whirls so rapidly, that to the surprise of its owner, his boat nearly reached the shore across the current before he could understand the cause of her singular movement, or have time to call his men to the oars. Heavy boats are seldom affected by them, otherwise than turning them round a little, and this may be avoided generally by attention to the steering-oar, providing it be well handled by a stout, strong, active and an experienced man, and no other ought to have the command of the steerage, for in this depends very much the safety of the boat and cargo.

## THE MISSISSIPPI RIVER.*

———

THIS noble and celebrated stream, this Nile of North America, commands the wonder of the old world, while it attracts the admiration of the new. From its mouth to where it receives the Ohio, is 1000 miles by water, but only 500 by land, passing through the Chickasaw country. From the mouth of the Ohio to that of the Missouri, is 230 miles by water, and 140 by land, from thence to the mouth of the Illinois river is about 25 miles.

The Mississippi is said to take its rise in the White Bear lake, lat. 48° 16′ N. long. 23° 17′ W. But the natives of the country say that it loses its name at the falls of St. Anthony, lat. 45° N. and above them, it assumes the name of Blue river, which is navigable 300 miles, making a distance of about 2580 miles from the mouth of the Mississippi, taking its meanderings.

The following are the principal rivers which empty into the Mississippi on the eastern side, from below the falls of St. Anthony to the mouth of the Missouri, with the distances from river to river, and how far they are navigable, viz, River St. Croix, 90 miles below the falls, said to be navigable 200 miles; Sotoux, 60 miles further down, navigable 80 miles; Buffalo river, 15 miles, navigable 100; Black, 65 miles, navigable about 100; Ouiconsin river, 150 miles, navigable 200; Rivière à la Mine, 120 miles, navigable 50 miles; Rivière à la Roche, 210 miles; Illinois, 160, navigable about 450, and is 400 yards wide at its mouth.

Between a branch of the Illinois and the Chickago river, which empties into lake Michigan, there is a portage of two miles; from this portage to the lake is a batteau navigation of 16 miles. By this happy connexion of waters, there is a complete communication from New York to New Orleans, through that northern and extensive route, having only about 28 miles land carriage, in the

---

* The word *Mississippi*, in the language of the aborigines of the country, is called " *Messachipi*," which signifies the *Father of waters*.

distance of nearly 4000 miles, the greatest stretch of inland navigation, perhaps, known in the world.—This route from New York, is by the Hudson river to Albany, thence by land to Schenecktada, 16 miles, thence up the Mohawk river, and through a canal of 4 miles into Wood creek, thence into lake Ontario, and up that lake and Niagara river to Queenstown, 7 miles below the falls of Niagara; thence 10 miles land carriage round said falls to Chippaway, thence up the river into lake Erie, and through that lake into lake St. Clair, thence into lake Huron, through lake Michigan, and into the Chickago river, mentioned above, thence down the Illinois and Mississippi rivers. This route comprehends the most extensive channels, and gives a wide scope to trade in general, and may one day be made a very profitable use of to individual citizens, as well as highly advantageous to the trade and commerce of the United States, especially if they get possession of the northern fur trade now carried on by the British.

The country of the Illinois is perhaps not exceeded in beauty, levelness, richness, and fertility of soil, by any in the United States, nor perhaps in the world. Its appearance is truly delightful, and some are of opinion that this, is the spot that is called by some French writers "The Terrestrial Paradise." It yields great quantities of grapes, from which the inhabitants make a very good red wine for their own consumption. Coal mines, and salt ponds, 100 yards in circumference, are found on the Illinois river; and on a branch of it an alum hill has been discovered; there are also appearances of copper. It yields red and white cedar, pine and mulberry; indigo, tobacco, hemp and flax are raised to advantage; the sugar and fruit trees flourish admirably; and some dying and medicinal plants are found.

The French used to get their mill stones about 250 miles up the Illinois. There are several beautiful lakes near its borders; and one 210 miles from the Mississippi, called the Illinois lake, which is 19 miles and a half in length, and three in breadth, and contains great plenty of fish, particularly the Sturgeon and Picannau. The Illinois has a number of rivers emptying into it, and some of them large, and navigable for 150 miles. The river Michilimackinack which enters it about 190 miles from the Mississippi, is navigable 90 miles, and has at its mouth 30 or 40 islands, which at a distance, look like a small village. The banks of the Illinois are high and the water clear, and at the bottom of the river are white marle and sand. It has a number of islands in it, some of which are 10 miles long. The Prairies or extensive meadows abound much on and near the Illinois river; these yield fine large grass and small shrubbery. A Fleche or arrow stone is found on this river, from which the Indians make their gun flints and point their arrows.

Twenty-five miles below the Illinois, the Missouri joins the Mississippi on the W. side. It is in fact the principal river, contributing more to the common stream than does the Mississippi, even after its junction with the Illinois. It is remarkably cold, muddy and rapid. Its overflowings are considerable. They happen during the months of June and July; and on account of their commencing later than those of the Mississippi, it is thought that the sources of the Missouri are northward of those of the Mississippi.—Traders go up the Missouri 2000 miles, and for that distance its waters are unbroken with any considerable rapids.*

The Mississippi, below the mouth of the Missouri, is always muddy, and abounds with sand bars, which frequently change their places. It carries 15 feet water to the mouth of the Ohio, to which place it is about $\frac{3}{4}$ of a mile wide. The current is too powerful, and the river too crooked, to be stemmed by the force of the wind alone, acting upon sails. Barges and keel boats, however, may ascend by being rowed or poled: a sail is sometimes of considerable help, and gives ease to the hands. During the floods of the Mississippi, which are periodical like those of the Nile in Egypt, the largest vessels may descend if care be taken in the steerage, keeping them off the islands, which are numerous. These floods begin in April, and the river returns into its banks early in August. Its overflowings or inundations extend further on the western than on the eastern side, covering the lands in some places 50 miles from its banks. Above the mouth of the Missouri, it resembles the Ohio, like it, clear and gentle in its current, not quite so wide, the

* For a more particular account of the Missouri, See Appendix.

period of its floods nearly the same, but not rising to so great a height.—This river yields turtle of a peculiar kind, perch, trout, gar, pike, mullets, herrings, carp, spatula-fish of 50lb. weight, catfish of 100lb. weight, buffalo fish, and sturgeon.—Alligators or crocodiles have been seen as high up as the Arcansas. It also abounds in herons, cranes, ducks, brant, geese, and swans; and its margins are not wanting in musick, from a great variety of the "sweet songsters of the wood."

Fifteen miles below the mouth of the Missouri, St. Louis is handsomely situated on the western bank of the Mississippi, 215 miles by water, and 125 by land above the mouth of the Ohio. It stands on a high piece of ground, and is the most healthy and pleasant situation of any known in that part of the country.—St. Louis was first settled by a few French settlers from the east side of the river, about the year 1765. The country falling into the hands of the Spaniards by conquest from Britain, it remained in their possession until that government gave it up to France by the treaty of 1800 and 1801; from whom it passed by right of purchase dated 30th April 1803, into the hands of the government of the United States, and was regularly taken possession of on the 20th Dec. 1804. It is the seat of government for the territory of Missouri; the town contains about 200 dwellings, several mercantile stores, a post office, and is now fast increasing in population, buildings and business generally.—It has also a printing office issuing a weekly gazette. The fur and peltry trade of the Missouri and Mississippi rivers principally centres here. It is in lat. 38° 39' N. and the climate may be compared with that of Maryland and Virginia between 37° and 39° N. lat.

Cahokia, a small village, is situated 4 or 5 miles below St. Louis, on the east side of the Mississippi and one mile up a small river. About 45 miles lower down is the village of St. Philips. Fort Chartiers is 4 miles still further down. The village of Kaskaskia, 12 miles below Fort Chartiers, is situated 5 miles up a river of the same name which joins the Mississippi on the east side, about 90 miles above the mouth of the Ohio. The village of St. Genevieve or Missire, is situated on the western bank of the Mississippi, nearly opposite Kaskaskia village; in 1773, it contained 100 houses, and 460 inhabitants; this and St. Louis, were the only towns on the western side of the Mississippi at that period. Four miles below St. Genevieve, on the same side with it, at the mouth of a creek, is a Hamlet, called a Saline; where a vast quantity of salt is made, which can be afforded at about one dollar per bushel at the works.

A few miles westward of St. Genevieve are several lead furnaces, which make a large quantity of lead.— They sell it at the furnaces, from three to four cents a pound.—The lead mines in this part of the Mississippi country are very numerous, and when the settlements can afford them to be worked to their full extent, they must yield a vast revenue to the government of the United States.

The ridge which forms the eastern bank of the Mississippi above the Missouri, continues northerly to the Illinois river, whence from its summit, you have a most delightful prospect of the Mississippi river for 20 miles; and also of the beautiful meanderings of the Illinois for many leagues—Next presents itself to view, a level and fruitful meadow, of at least 100 miles in circuit on the western side of the Mississippi, watered by several lakes, and shaded by small groves or copses of trees, scattered in different parts of it, and then the eye, with rapture, surveys, as well the high lands bordering upon the river Missouri, as those at a greater distance up the Mississippi.

The fork or point of land formed by the junction of the Ohio with the Mississippi, is about 20 feet higher than the common surface of the river, yet the spring floods overflow it for several weeks. The point is remarkably rich, having the mud of the rivers deposited on it yearly; and it yields in its natural state peavines grass, &c. and in particular, the aspen tree, of an unusual height and thickness.

The current of the Mississippi runs at the rate of about $3\frac{1}{2}$ to about 4 miles an hour; when very high, something faster. From the mouth of the Ohio to the creek of the Fouche, which is twenty-five leagues above New Orleans, the Mississippi carries from 30 to 60 feet water; below this, to its mouth, from 30 to 40 fathoms, and is from three quarters to a mile in breadth. From the warmth and muddiness of the water, it is rendered a disagreeable

N 2

drink to navigators. By filling some jars with it over night, it becomes cool and clear, and is rendered more palatable. The waters of the Mississippi are said to contain medicinal qualities, having performed cures for most cutaneous diseases, operating on some as a powerful cathartick, and as a purifier of the blood. It is upon the whole, after filtration, and being kept cool in large jars sunk in the ground or shaded, the most agreeable water I ever drank, and I am led to believe the wholesomest. I have frequently drove off a slight stomach fever after eating, occasioning a head-ache and a quickened pulse, by drinking two, three, or four tumblers of this delightful water. And I have known those distressed with a sudden attack of a violent intermittent fever, whose pulse was very quick, and skin dry and hot, to get relief in a few minutes after drinking freely of this water; two or three tumblers full throwing the person into a fine and free perspiration.

The principal rivers which empty into the Mississippi below the mouth of the Ohio, are, Wolf and Yazooz rivers on the left side; rivers St. Francis, White, Arkansas, Red or Riviere Rouge, on the right. These will be more particularly noticed as we descend.

Among the fowls of this river, especially pretty low down, the Pelican are very numerous.*

After you enter the Mississippi you begin to wind con-

---

* The Pelican is a very large bird not unlike the swan in shape or color; but what renders it particularly singular among the feathered tribe, is its enormous bag or pouch which hangs under its long bill. This is large enough to hold four or five gallons of water; they use it principally, however, as a reservoir for the fish they catch, either for their own food, or that which they intend to carry to their young.—The pelican is said to have a melancholy countenance, is very torpid, and to a great degree inactive, so much so, that nothing can exceed its indolence but its gluttony, and that hunger is the only inducement it has to rouse from its stupid sleep It is asserted that they seem to be fond of musick. They are long-lived, and capable of being domesticated. History informs us that the emperor Maximilian had a tame pelican about 80 years. Their flesh is too coarse to be eaten. Their pouches are frequently dried and converted into bags or purses, for the use of the ladies. The pouch of this bird is said to have given rise to the fabulous story among the ancients, that it fed its young with blood from its breast.

siderably to the southward, and sometimes east of that point. The climate becomes mild and warm, and the winter gives but a trifling check to the growth of vegetation. The banks of the river, especially below Point Coupée, are lined with groves of orange trees, whose delightful fragrance, and the beautiful appearance of their flowers, added to the prospect of getting the fruit plentifully, has a charming effect on the feelings, and seem to form a temporary compensation to the wearied navigator, for many inconveniences he experiences, and the toils and the hazards he may have undergone since his embarkation.

The cotton wood tree also grows in great abundance on the banks of the Mississippi. This tree on examination has been found to be the same with the lombardy poplar, though some doubt its identity.

The waters of this river are kept in their proper channel, below Baton Rouge to New Orleans, by artificial banks, called the Levee, on which are erected a number of saw mills, which are turned by a sluice being cut through the bank or levee, and the water gushing forth and falling on the wheel, turns it with great velocity.— There being no tail-race, the water expends itself through the flat and swampy country below.

*We are indebted for the following interesting description of the river Mississippi and its Delta, with that of the adjacent parts of Louisiana, to Mr. William Dunbar, communicated by him to the American Philosophical Society, from whose work,* VOL. VI. *it is extracted:*

"THE multiplicity of the rivers which are tributary to the Mississippi, extending themselves over an immense tract, which comprehends nearly 20 deg. in lat. and 30 in long. must render this river, at all seasons, one of the most considerable on the globe. The annual inundation, being supplied from so great a variety of climates, must naturally be expected to be of long duration; and may generally be estimated at nearly half the year; beginning, (com. annis.) to rise in January, and fall in June; the two extremes being frequently extended by the early autumnal and winter rains in the southern latitudes, and by the protraction of the northern winters, which retards the dissolution of the immense accumulations of snow in those cold regions. At the landing of the Natchez (380 miles from the mouth of the river) the perpendicular ascent of the waters of the Mississippi, from the lowest ebb to the highest inundation, may be estimated at 50 feet. At Baton Rouge (200 miles distant) it was found to be 30 feet; at New-Orleans (80 miles above the mouth) it is about 12 feet; and at the mouth of the river scarcely any perceptible change is observed, excepting by a stronger current, charged with earthy matter, rolling into the ocean during the season of the inundation; at which time all the lakes and communications with the sea are replenished with the waters of the inundation, and the ocean itself is often repelled to such a degree that fresh water has been drawn up out of sight of land. This great difference in the perpendicular rise of the waters of the inundation is to be accounted for from the prodigious number of natural canals issuing from the Mississippi, and those immense sheets of water, often unbounded by a single horizon, flowing over the banks, and never to return, and inundating vast tracts of country, which owe their existence to the creative power of this grand river, and which finally discharge themselves into the Mexican Gulph by an infinite number of mouths, many of which are, in apparent magnitude, equal to the Mississippi itself; the space embraced by the Delta of this river, on the sea coast, being, from information, not less than three degrees of longitude.

"The waters of the Mississippi are not, at any time, perfectly transparent: during the absence of the inundation they are not much troubled, presenting a slight milky appearance, which is attributed to the Missouri; but during the time of the inundation, all the rivers which discharge their superabundant waters into the Mississippi are more or less charged with terrene matter, and during the decline of the inundation the turbidness is sometimes so great that a glass filled with its water appears to deposite, in a few minutes, a sediment equal to one-eighth of its bulk. This extreme impurity is not to be attributed entirely to the immediate effect of the Missouri, but principally to the falling in of the mud banks, either newly formed beneath the influence of the current of the river, or undermined by its rapidity, perpetually changing its bed, by enlarging the concavity of its bends, and projecting its points or head-lands. This operation has a natural tendency to lengthen the circuitous course of the river; but the effect is amply compensated by its own progress; for the enlargement of the bends frequently brings them so near each other, that the weight of the waters bursts at once through the solid soil, forming, in a few days, a new bed, capable of conveying the whole waters of this mighty river, and shortening thereby its course many leagues. The disruption which took place at Point Coupée cut off ten leagues, and within this territory, the cut-off at the Homochito, has thrown to the east of the Mississippi an island of seven leagues in circuit; and at the Yazooz a similar effect has been produced on the west side, by the formation of an island of five leagues in circumference. Those islands are now both converted into peninsulas, by the formation of new land across one of the mouths of the old channel, while the other is partially kept open by the discharge of the (comparatively) small rivers of the Yazooz and Homochito; the former of those, nevertheless, is not inferior in magnitude to that great commercial river the Thames. The consequence of those disruptions is the formation of lakes, which, in process of time, may be far removed from the actual channel of the river, and, in effect, are now found to be scattered in all situations over the immense valley of the Mississippi.

" When those lakes are first approached, they present so perfect a resemblance of the Mississippi, with regard to breadth, the appearance of the banks, and the natural serpentine form of its course, that many persons have been deceived thereby, and recognized their error only by the discovery of the stagnant state of the water, the appearance on its borders of the Nymphæa Nelumbo, and other aquatick plants. No person, therefore, doubts that those lakes have all, in their turn, served to convey the waters of this father of rivers, and now, during the season of the inundation, still flow with a full current, contributing their aid to the evacuation of the waters of a thousand rivers which precipitate themselves into the valley of the Mississippi. When we take a survey of this valley, upwards of thirty miles wide opposite to the Natchez, diverging very obtusely as we approach the sea-coast, where it is, perhaps, not less than three degrees in longitude, and that in no part of it do we discover any other soil than such as is now daily deposited by the waters of the Mississippi, it is impossible not to believe that this valley has, in the beginning, been a branch or inlet of the ocean, which received into its bosom this great river, similar to the river de la Plata, the gulph of St. Lawrence, Delaware bay, and many others not remarkable for the alluvial properties of their rivers. When, on the other hand, we contemplate the effects of the creative power of the Mississippi, which has filled up this prodigious space with soil, more or less solid, and which must, at Natchez, exceed 100 feet perpendicular above the level of the sea, sloping gradually, like an immense glacis, to the coast of the bay of Mexico, where, nevertheless, it does not terminate, but shelving off, by continual accumulation, frequently embarrasses vessels out of sight of land, along the coast, to the west of the Mississippi: I say, when we survey this immense work, performed by the hand of nature, we cannot accord with the opinions of certain visionary philosophers, who have been pleased to amuse themselves with the pretended infantile state of our continent, compared to their transatlantick world; but, on the contrary, we must grant to it an incalculable antiquity. When the inundation is at its height, the whole valley is replenished with water, every where in motion, making its progress towards the ocean; so that, at that season, the river may be said to be thirty miles or more in breadth at Natchez. The waters which pass over the west bank of the main channel never return. On the east, a chain of high land, which, at many points, is washed by the river, meandering along its valley, compels its waters to rejoin the primitive stream; but from Baton Rouge, the high land, which has hitherto held a southerly course, diverges suddenly to S. E. and is no more visited by the grand channel of the Mississippi. All the waters which escape to the eastward, between Baton Rouge and Manshae, (fifteen miles) are collected by the Iberville, which, passing through a breach in the high land of about sixty yards, delivers its contents to the river Amit, which empties itself into lake Maurepas, communicating with the ocean by the intervention of the more considerable lake Ponchartrain. The high land is continued in a very narrow tongue or promontory, in a south-easterly direction, along the island of New Orleans, which is disruptured in many places, thereby venting the waters of the inundation into the lakes, which otherwise would be collected into an oblong basin, formed by the high land on the one hand, and the bank of the river on the other. One half of the island of New Orleans would have thereby become so completely inundated as to be uninhabitable.

" The perpendicular height of the high lands above the level of the inundation is from 200 to 300 feet at Natchez; at Baton Rouge it does not exceed 25 ; and on the island of New Orleans it declines so rapidly as frequently to be lost under the accumulations of soil deposited by the waters of the inundation. In the sides of a canal from New Orleans to the river St. John's, communicating with lake Ponchartrain, I discovered the continuation of the high land cut through to the breadth of little more than 20 feet.

" To a stranger, the first view of the Mississippi conveys not that idea of grandeur which he may have pictured to himself: his first judgment will rest upon the appearance of its breadth, in which respect it is inferior to many rivers of much less note. Its principal channel is rarely a mile in width any where below the Ohio, unless where its stream is divided by islands or shallows : it is, not unfrequently less than half a mile. The magnitude of this river is not to be computed by its width, but by its depth ; in which it is, perhaps, equal to any on the globe; but it is so contracted at the place of its entrance into the ocean, as to be there less in width than it is found to be at a thousand miles from its mouth : the cause of this peculiarity is, perhaps, not difficult to develop. The natural effect of rivers is to increase continually the depth and breadth of their beds, by the perpetual abrasion of their waters. Such must be the consequence with regard to all rivers which do not supply by alluvion a sufficient quantity of matter to counteract this effect. Certain rivers, which, in the upper part of their course pass through fertile regions, whose rich and tender soil is easily broken down and carried away by the impetuosity of the current, not only supply this deficiency, but discharge such inconceivable quantities of earthy matter as to fill up in a great measure, those spacious bays and channels, scooped out by the hand of nature, in order to facilitate the mingling of their waters with those of the ocean. In such circumstances the breadth of the river will always be in proportion to the mean quantity of water discharged during the time it flows within its banks; for it is to be remarked, that during the time of the inundation the common channel of the river is in some measure lost in the immensity of waters which flow over its banks in all directions. The bottom and sides of the channel, during this time suffer no abrasion, but, on the contrary, from the diminution of the velocity of the inferior currents, gain rapidly upon the breadth of the river. The moment the current of the river is confined within its proper banks, it begins to exert its dominion over its own channel, and fashions its bed by the momentum of its waters, attacking sometimes one side, sometimes the other, according as the main filament of the stream is deflected from shore to shore; by which means large portions of the newly created soil are preserved, while in other situations the more compact earth is undermined and borne into the ocean, and thus an equilibrum is restored between the channel and its included waters. Hence, it comes to pass, that rivers which run through alluvial countries are much narrower, in proportion to the quantity of their waters, than those whose course are over rocks, gravel or sand; but, on the other hand, their depths are great, and they are consequently better fitted for the purpose of navigation. The Mississippi is supposed to be navigable (pursuing the western branch, or Missouri,) 3000 miles at least from the ocean. Those who have studied the theory of rivers inform us, that the stability of the bed of a river depends upon a due equilibrium between the velocity of the current and the tenacity of those matters which compose its bottom and sides. The velocity of rivers is greatest at the surface, gradually diminishing downwards. Hence, when the bottom is composed of matter of the most yielding nature, the channel will continue to deepen until the velocity at bottom is almost nothing, and the depth of the water will be regulated by those circumstances. The bottom of the bed of the Mississippi, within the alluvial country, being composed of the finest sand and lightest earth extremely comminuted, it is not surprising that its depth should be comparatively great. Its soundings have, it is believed, never been taken with minute attention; but from New Orleans to the mouth of the river, its depth is said to be from fifty to seventy fathoms, under the thread of the current, which follows the concave shore; diminishing gradually towards the elbows, where there are frequently considerable shallows. The sudden effect of the diminution of the velocity of water, is no where more remarkable than at the mouth of this river; for the rolling torrent no sooner arrives at the ocean, than, finding its bed indefinitely enlarged, it spreads on all hands; the thread of the current diverges into an infinite number of filaments, like radii from a centre; the velocity of the mass of water rapidly diminishes, until no longer able to propel the matter hitherto suspended and swept along by the swiftness of the stream, it is deposited in form of a crescent, opposing to the mouth of the river a bar, with from twelve to twenty feet water. The current being less, immediately to the right and left, than in front of the mouth of the river, the deposition and accumulation of matter will consequently proceed more rapidly on either side; and the velocity of the current being increased by the contraction of the channel, the bar will be protruded further into the ocean. Hence, it appears why the mouths of all alluvial rivers terminate in a promontory, projecting more or less into the ocean.— This last mentioned operation of nature points out the method of improving the navigation of the entrance of the Mississippi, which may be effected at no very considerable expense, by carrying out a pier on each side of the principal branch, composed of piles, so far as may be found sufficient to procure the desired depth. The bar will thereby be thrown into deeper water, and, in process of time, will accumulate and ascend to its former height, which will demand a new prolongation of the piers.— Every small rivulet passing through Lower Louisiana is a miniature of the Mississippi: what may be performed, upon a small scale, in respect to the latter, will certainly succeed (by well directed efforts) on the former. The river St. John's, sixty to eighty feet wide, entering lake Ponchartrain to the north of New Orleans, was found frequently so choaked up and impeded by a bar across its mouth, that canoes could sometimes with difficulty enter; sloops and batteaux being obliged, at such times, to remain in the lake, exposed to danger. The government directed two very simple piers, each composed of a double row of round rough piles, to be carried from the shore across the bar; and although the piers were pervious to the water, yet so much velocity was acquired, that the bar was very speedily swept off, and the river has always since remained navigable for small sloops and schooners, which proceed up to the city by the river and canal of Carondelet.

"The depth of the river diminishes considerably as we advance upwards; probably owing to the increased tenacity of the matter forming its bed. At Natchez, when the waters are low, it is about twelve fathoms; and there are situations below the Ohio, where the ordinary boats have been embarrassed to find a passage both upwards and downwards: a moderate fresh, nevertheless, renders the Mississippi navigable up to the Falls of St. Anthony, about 2000 miles from its mouth. The breadth of the river appears to be upon the increase upwards, in proportion as we get above the alluvial country, as high as the Missouri, notwithstanding the loss of a number of principal rivers which flow in below. In latitude 42 deg. it is said to be half a mile in breadth, which probably equals its mean breadth from Yazooz to its mouth.

"The margin of the river is the highest land to be found in the valley of the Mississippi. As the river overflows its banks, the waters immediately begin to deposit their grossest particles, which are chiefly sand and black marl; and in their progress backwards, this deposition is continued until, at length, a matter is deposited, so highly levigated that, upon the retiring of the waters, it assumes a compactness and solidity resembling pitch. When the river, by disruption, alters its course, and new accumulations of slime, sand and marl are laid upon this very compact earth, a false belief might be induced that this solid soil is not the offspring of the river, but the original parent earth coeval with the Mississippi itself, upon which this great river had afterwards deposited the rich spoils of the northern regions, borne down by its mighty tide.—This compact soil I have found at the depth of from ten to thirty feet; and in other situations no appearance is to be seen of any other than the common soil formed of the mud of the river. The soil near the river is sandy, particularly that which has been lately formed. From a quarter to half a mile from the margin of the river the sand is less apparent, and loses its name of "terre sablonneuse," acquiring that of "terre grasse," being the richest black marl, with a moderate admixture of sand. At greater distances, and frequently at some depth under the last mentioned soils, is found the above mentioned compact earth, called glaise (potter's earth :) it is no doubt eminently adapted to the use of the potter, though hitherto not much applied to the manufacture of earthen ware.—— Upon all lands long subject to culture, and defended from the inundation, although near to the margin, the appearance of sand is almost lost; but it is evident, from the friability of the soil, and the facility with which it is cultivated, that a large portion still remains intimately mixed with it; whereas the terre grasse (unmixed or pure marl) yields with difficulty to the plough: it exhibits proofs of the richest marl, a slight shower causing it to crumble into powder after being turned up: yet, as our climate is exposed to sudden and violent falls of rain, with hot sunshine, it frequently becomes so firm and unyielding, after the crop has been planted, that no mode of cultivation can be conveniently applied, but barely scratching the surface with the hoe; yet this became, with the French indigo planters, a favorite soil. Although less productive, it is more easily kept clear of weeds, the compacted soil refusing a passage to their tender fibrous roots, while the vigorous taproot of the indigo plant conquers the obstinacy of the subjacent stratum. From the river bank a natural glacis is formed, whose declivity at New-Orleans may be at the rate of six or eight inches in 100 feet, to the distance of 600 or 700 toises, diminishing; after which the descent becomes almost imperceptible, and is gradually lost in swamps, marshes and lakes, which finally communicate with the sea."

The following list of the indigenous plants, shrubbery and herbaceous, to be met with on the Mississippi, along the boundary, and in the Floridas, may not be uninteresting to many of our readers. To the popular names, those used by the botanists are added, in the manner practised by the ingenious and learned author of the " *Notes on Virginia.*" The botanical name constantly follows the popular one, and is included in a parenthesis.*

* Ellicott's Journal, p. 284.

" At the mouth of the Ohio, and down the Mississippi swamp, one of the prevailing species of timber is cotton-wood, (populus deltoides of Marshall,) it bears a very striking resemblance to the lombardy poplar, is equally quick in growth, open, soft, and porous. Black-willow, (salix nigra,) black-ash, (fraxinus nigra,) sugar maple, (acer saccharinum,) but not in great abundance, and becomes more scarce as you descend the river. I do not recollect of seeing but one tree of it south of the bounda-ry. Water maple, (acer negundo,) pecca, (juglans illi-noinensis,) this is met with as high as the Wabash, where it is not scarce, but becomes more abundant from thence down to the gulf of Mexico. Papaw, (annona triloba,) I have eat of the fruit in great perfection as early as the 17th of July, in the Mississippi territory. Button wood, or sycamore, (platanus occidentalis,) hickory, (juglans hickory of three species.) The cypress, (cupressus dis-ticha,) begins to make its appearance about the Arkansas, and becomes very abundant a little further south, and ap-pears to be inexhaustible before you reach the 31st deg. of north latitude. It occupies many parts of the swamp almost to the exclusion of any other timber. The cypress is a very useful wood, and generally used in that country for covering, flooring, and finishing buildings. It grows in swamps, marshes, and ponds, but not on high dry land. The stem, or body of the tree, generally rises from the apex of a large conical base, above which the workmen have frequently to erect scaffolds before they fall the tree. From the roots of the tree a number of conical excres-cences grow up, which are called cypress knees, some of them are eight or ten feet high, and being hollow are us-ed for bee-hives, and other purposes. The long moss, (tillandsia usneoides,) makes its appearance on the Mis-sissippi nearly in the same latitude with the cypress, and almost covers some of the trees to which it is appended before you reach the Walnut-hills. This is a very useful article, and answers almost as well for beds, and mattres-ses, as craped horse hair: it is nearly as elastick, and al-most as incorruptible. Although this moss, is not like the misletoe immediately connected with the trees on which it hangs, it will not live long on a dead tree. Sweet bay, (laurus borbonia,) magnolia grandiflora: this most splendid and beautiful tree, I do not recollect seeing above the Walnut-hills; but have no doubt of its growing much further north. It is common through all the rich lands of Natchez, and east to the Atlantic. The foregoing appear to be confined either to very wet, or very rich land, and will be met with in all such places along the boundary, and through the Floridas, with the exception of the peccan, sugar maple, and one or two others. The katalpa, (bignonia catalpa,) is not uncommon; but appeared the most abundant on the banks of the Coenecuh. The nyssa aquatica, is common on the Chattahocha below the boundary. Exclusive of those plants, which are generally confined to low or very rich grounds, the following will be met with in various parts of the country. Sassafras, (laurus sassafras,) which grows to a large size about the Natchez. Sweet gum, (liquid-amber,) common swamp gum, (nyssa integrifolia,) holly, (ilex opaca,) in great abundance in some parts of the Mississippi territory, and frequently becomes a large tree. Parsimon, (dyospyros virginiana,) very common. Locust, (robinia pseud-acacia,) honey locust, (gleditsia triacanthos,) black walnut, (juglans nigra,) elm, (ulmus americana,) dog wood, (cornus florida,) red bud, (cercis canadensis,) mulberry, (morus rubra,) wild plum, (prunus chickasaw,) tulip tree, (liriodendron tulipifera,) this is improperly called *poplar* in the middle states. White oak, (quercus alba,) black oak, (quercus nigra,) swamp oak, (quercus aquatica,) chesnut oak, (quercus prunus,) with several other species, or varieties. Live oak, (quercus virens,) this very useful timber is much confined to the coast, and a short distance from it. I do not recollect seeing it in any considerable quantity in West Florida, as far north as the boundary.— Red cedar, (juniperus virginiana,) this is likewise much confined to the coast, and in some places very abundant.— Pine, (pinus,) broom pine, (pinus palustris,) with several other species or varieties; the quantity inexhaustible.— Buck eye, (aesculus pavia,) this is sometimes confounded with the buck eye, (aesculus flava,) of the Ohio; they are not the same. Wild cherry, (prunus virginiana,) great palmetto, or cabbage tree, (corypha or palmitto of Walter,) cassina yapon, (ilex vomitoria,) the black-drink used by the Creeks, and some other Indian nations at their councils, and public meetings, is made by an infusion of the leaves of this shrub. Myrica inodora, (of Bartram,) from the berries of this shrub, the green wax, used in making candles is. collected : these two last are confined to the coast. Beech, (fagus ferruginea,) chesnut, (fagus americana,) chincopin, (fagus pumila,) some of them are sufficiently large in the Mississippi territory to be split into rails. Spice wood, (laurus benzoin,) Bermudian mulberry, (callicarpa americana,) cane, (arundo gigantea of Walter,) extends through all parts of the Mississippi swamp, and occupies equally the high, as well as low land, from the Walnut-hills down the river to Point Coupée, and easterly from fifteen to twenty miles or more. The whole of that high, rich, hilly and broken tract of country, except where the farms are opened, may be considered one solid cane-brake, and is almost impenetrable ; but will probably be destroyed in a few years by the cattle, hogs, and fires. Its general height is from twenty to thirty-six feet, though I have met with it on the tops of several hills forty-two feet high. The small cane, or reed, (arundo tecta of Walter,) begins to make its appearance on the boundary about twenty miles east of the Mississippi river, and with the arundo gigantea, or large cane, will be found on all the creeks and river bottoms, through to the Atlantic. The China root, (smilax China,) and passion flower, (passiflora incarnata,) are abundant in the rich grounds. The sensitive briar, (mimosa instia,) this beautiful and singular plant, is common to the poor sandy land. Several species of that beautiful plant, the saracinia, are frequently met with in the margins of swamps, and low grounds : and three or four handsome species of the water dock, (nymphea,) poke, (phytolacca decandra,) sumack, (rhus,) several species. Along the water courses, and in the swamps where the land is good, several species of well tasted grapes are found in great plenty. Many of the trees in the low grounds are loaded with a variety of vines, the most conspicuous of which are the creeper, or trumpet flower, (bignonia radicans,) and common poison vine, (rhus radicans,*) misletoe, (viscum,) is in great

* Mr Ellicott while ascertaining the boundary line between his catholick majesty and the United States, observes in his " journal," that while ascending the Chattahouche, (a river emptying into the Gulph of Mexico, and running through East Florida,) he was blistered by the rhus radicans (poison vine)from

abundance, and will be found attached to almost all kinds of trees. I have frequently observed it on peach and plum trees. In the middle states it is generally found on the common swamp gum, (nyssa integrifolia.)"

For a further botanical description of the plants, shrubs and trees of the Mississippi, and of the country east of that river, we must refer our readers to the interesting travels of William Bartram, whose account of that country and its natural productions is highly worthy of the perusal of every inquiring mind, and it may be a matter of no little surprise that " *Bartram's Travels*" are so seldom to be met with in the bookcases of gentlemen of taste and reading. We have under our eye a copy of the first edition, printed in 1776 in Philadelphia, by James and Johnson, and believe it to be the only edition ever published, which circumstance we esteem as a matter of unmerited neglect by the reading part of the community.

---

## INSTRUCTIONS AND PRECAUTIONS, NECESSARY TO BE ATTENDED TO IN NAVIGATING THE MISSISSIPPI RIVER.

THE hints we have already given respecting the precautions necessary to be observed in descending the Ohio, will in some particulars apply to the Mississippi.——But there being a considerable difference in the nature of these rivers, a difference of management, and a greater degree of circumspection, labor, and watchfulness, will be found absolutely necessary.

The boats intended for the Mississippi must be much stronger in their timbers, and more firmly built than those

head to feet. This aptitude, says he, to be disordered by this poisonous vegetable I have been subject to from my infancy, and have generally been confined in consequence of it, at least one week every summer since. The evaporation from the dew from this plant in the morning, falling upon me, is sufficient to produce the effect. The irritation and heat of this complaint was frequently so excessive, that I had to plunge into the river many times in the day, and lay whole hours in it during the night, which was the only relief I could find; medical aid had at all times proved ineffectual to relieve me.

for the Ohio only.—They ought also to be caulked better, and much higher all round, better roofed, and have longer and stronger cable, and it would be well, if proprietors can afford it, instead of taking along side a canoe, to procure a kind of long boat, that would carry, in case of a ship-wreck, a leak, or other accident, 20 or 30 barrels of flour or whiskey. This provision might sometimes perhaps be the means of saving a part of a cargo, and the boat would sell at Orleans, if well and neatly made, for as much as it might cost at Pittsburgh or any other place where they they could be purchased.

The following observations point out the principal impediments, and the most imminent dangers attending the navigation of the Mississippi:

These are 1st:—The instability of the banks.

2. Currents called bayous rushing out of the river in a state of its high waters; and,

3. Planters,¶ sawyers, and wooden islands.

We shall endeavor to instruct the unexperienced navigator how to avoid them. The instability of the banks proceed from their being composed of a loose sandy soil, and impetuosity of the current against their prominent parts (points,) which, by undermining them unceasingly, causes them to tumble into the river taking with them every thing that may be above. And if, when the event happens, boats should be moored there, they must necessarily be buried in the common ruin, which unfortunately has sometimes been the case. For which reason navigators have made it an invariable rule never to land at or near a point,

¶ PLANTERS, are large bodies of trees firmly fixed by their roots in the bottom of the river, in a perpendicular manner, and appearing no more than about a foot above the surface of the water in its middling state. So firmly are they rooted, that the largest boat running against them, will not move them, but they frequently injure the boat.

SAWYERS, are likewise bodies of trees fixed less perpendicularly in the river, and rather of a less size yielding to the pressure of the current, disappearing and appearing by turns above water, similar to the motion of a saw-mill saw, from which they have taken their name. They sometimes point up stream as well as down.

WOODEN-ISLANDS, are places where by some cause or other, large quantities of drift wood, has through time, been arrested and matted together in different parts of the river.

but always in the sinuosity or cove below it, which is generally lined with small willows of weeping kind, whence some call them, though improperly, willow points, and which being generally clear of logs and planters, the landing is easily effected, by running directly into them, the resistance of willows destroying a part of the boat's velocity, and the rest is overcome without much exertion by holding fast to the limbs which surround you. In those places the river generally deposits the surplus of soil, with which it is charged from the continual cavings of the points, and so forms new land on one side by destroying some on the other.

The banks of this river from where it receives the Missouri to its mouth, being with a few exceptions below high water mark, an immense country is inundated when the river is in its highest state, by which those extensive swamps are formed and supplied which prove the nurseries of myriads of musquitoes and other insects(to the no small inconvenience of the traveller)and the never failing source of grievous diseases to the inhabitants. There are also streams which at all times sally forth from the main river with astonishing rapidity, and his vortex extends some distance into the stream. Boats once sucked into such bayous are next to lost, it being almost impossible to force so unwieldy a machine as a flat bottomed boat against so powerful a current. It will therefore be safest for boats never to keep too close to shore, but keep some distance out in the river. To avoid planters and sawyers requires nothing more but attention for they always occasion a small breaker wherever they are, and if your boat seems to be hurried towards them pull from them quick, else if you are dilatory you must abide by the consequence.

WOODEN-ISLANDS, are more dangerous than real ones, the former being an obstacle lately thrown in the way of the current, and the bed of the river not having had sufficient time to form that bar or gradual ascent from the bottom of the river to the island, which divides the current at some distance from the point of the island above water, the current will hurry you against them, unless you use timely exertion. From all this it must be evident how imprudent it is attempting to go after night, even when assisted by a clear moon; but after you are once arrived at Natchez you may safely proceed day and night, the river from that place to its mouth being clear, and opposing nothing to to your progress but a few eddies into which you may occasionally be drawn and detained for a short time.

The islands of the Mississippi are numerous and many of them large, and from their being generally situated in the bends of the river, they become more difficult and dangerous to pass. We have been sedulous, however, in giving such descriptions of them and pointing out the method to avoid them, as we hope will be found very useful, and render the danger much less, thereby affording a considerable security to the cargo, and ease to the mind of the navigator.

The principal islands are numbered, together with such descriptions of their size and situation, as cannot easily be mistaken; and by recurring to the Maps you will find them represented by white spots, with their numbers opposite them. The sand bars are less white and cross-barred; and the channel is pointed out by a double white line, which in some few instances may be found contrary to the direction given in print, arising from the difference of opinion among navigators themselves:—where this is the case, we advise that the printed directions should be followed in preference to the line on the map.

The distances are taken from the head of one island or sand bar, to the head of those next below them, including the supposed length of each, which measurement, (being principally by the eye and running of the boat) is carried out to the column of totals, to make out the general distance as correct as possible.

*Directions for navigating the Mississippi from the Illinois to the Ohio, with a short description of the towns on its banks for that distance, and its islands.*

FROM the mouth of the Illinois [y] to Wood river a little below the Missouri, there is a beautiful settlement arpidly increasing, principally of Americans, and a few French. This settlement extends through an extensive rich prairie, affording strong vegetation, and is finely watered. The herds of cattle through this country are numerous, and their lively and sleek appearance, afford an evidence of the rich productions of the soil in which they pasture.

Island No. 1, opposite the mouth of the Illinois, channel right side.

Island No. 2,
Lies nearest the left shore, channel to the right. On the right shore opposite the head of this island is a sand bar.

Island No, 3,
Right side, channel to the left. From the head of this island, Portage Desieu strikes the Missouri in nearly a straight line, about six miles distant.

Island No. 4, channel to the right.

Island No. 5, right shore, channel to the left.

Island No. 6, immediately above the mouth of the Missouri,
Channel on either side.

Mouth of the Missouri.                                    18   18
St CHARLES, a handsome village, is situated about twenty miles up the Missouri on the left side. It contained in 1807, about 500 inhabitants, chiefly French; many Americans have settled here since the cession of Louisiana to the United States. It is 18 miles from St. Louis by land, over an excellent road, and through a rich country, principally prairie land. Three miles up this river is Belfont, the principal station for the troops of the United States in this territory.

Du Bois, or Wood river,                                    1   19

Islands Nos. 7 and 8, channel between them.

Sancere's house, right side,                               3   22
Opposite is a very large sand bar, channel good on either side. A small creek enters at the lower point of the bar, right side.

Island No. 9, left side, channel right side.
Mess river, right side,                                    3  25

Le Baum has a handsome situation on the right
side of the river.  Just above a small creek enters.

### Sr. Louis, [z]                                        8  33

Capital of Louisiana, is situated on the west side
of the Mississippi, in lat. 38° 39′ N long. 12° 51′ west
from the city of Washington.  It extends along the
river two miles, in three parallel streets, each rising
above the other, which has a very handsome appearance.  The bank of the river is high, and filled with
limestone, and most of the houses, are built of this
material, some of them in a grand style and surrounded with galleries.  Almost every house,has an extensive garden or park, around which high stone walls
are built.  The number of inhabitants is about fifteen hundred.  A mile from the town Mr. A. Cho-
teau has erected a mill and distillery; he has an excellent situation for improvement.

The country around and west of St. Louis for 15
miles is one extended prairie, in which vast herds of
cattle graze and fatten on the luxuriance of the soil.
Sixty miles southwest, the celebrated lead mines of
Louisiana are situated.  In the middle of the river
opposite the town, is a large sand bar island, No. 10,
channel on the town side.

On the opposite side of the river is Campbell's ferry, from hence the main road passing through the Il-
linios country, strikes Cahokia about 7 miles from St.
Louis.  This village is handsomely situated at the
edge of a prairie.  The inhabitants principally French.

The country on both sides of the river is exceedingly fertile, producing corn, wheat, rye, flax and
hemp, sweet and Irish potatoes, melons and fruit, as
apples, peaches, pears, cherries, &c.

A growing settlement called Turkey Hill Settlement, the settlers principally Americans, extends
from Wood river to opposite St. Louis.

Island No. 11, channel on either side,

There is a large and long sand bar at the upper
end of this island: in low water it is about a mile in
length.

### VITEPUSH,                                            8  41

This is a handsome French village on the right
side; it contains about 50 houses.  Opposite are two
large sand bars; there is a good channel between
them, but the best channel is on the right side.  Bi-
golua, a large creek, empties in on the left side nearly opposite the town.

About a mile distant from the river, left side, is lake Marrodizua, five miles in length, and from the lower end of which a small creek falls into the river. It is said to be well stored with fish, and is the resort of a variety of wild fowl. Some beautiful farms are situated in its neighborhood. Two miles below this is lake Bond, which is about two miles in length and two and a half from the river.

Island No. 12, best channel right side.

Island No. 13.

A bar at the upper and lower point; best channel right side.

| | | |
|---|---|---|
| Philip Fine's, an old settler, | 8 | 49 |
| Merrimack river, right side, | 3 | 52 |

This is a large stream of Missouri territory, and in high water is navigable a considerable distance.— There are a number of valuable salt springs on its banks; and in its neighborhood great abundance of lead is found. The Indians take quantities of it to St. Louis in flat pieces.

Islands No. 14 and No. 15, channel between them,

To the left of No. 15 is a large sand bar; opposite a small creek empties on the left side. Just below is a small bar, keep to the right.

Little Plateen, rock and creek, right side,     6   58

Island No. 16, near the left shore.

Opposite is a large sand bar, which joins the head of No. 18. A small creek from lake Bond enters opposite No. 16.

Island No. 17, channel right side.

Opposite the head of this island, Swashing creek enters on the right side.

Island No. 18, left side.

A large sand bar to the right of the lower point of this island, best channel on the right of the bar.

### HERCULANEUM,     8   66

A new town on the right side of the river; the proprietors are col. Samuel Hammond and major Moses Austin; it contains about 20 houses. Mr. Matlock has established a patent shot factory here; for which the situation is well fitted, the town standing high, on a rock. He has a fall for the shot of 200 feet perpendicular; and has been at but a trifling expense in preparing the place for his factory. In a due west direction about 50 miles from the town are situated

at a small village, called Mine a Burton, the lead
mines, which furnish vast quantities of this article.

Opposite Herculaneum is Legle creek, at the mouth
of which is a large store and tavern; from this place
the road leads to Kaskaskia.

## Islands Nos. 19 and 20, best channel to the right.

## Large Plateen, rock and creek,                    2    68

On the right side of the river. The bank of the
river from Little Plateen to this place, has a majestic appearance. It is a continued rock of limestone,
rising from the base, declining step by step to the
height of 2 or 300 feet; the steps or ledges not more
than 6 inches deep, and appear as if cut by the chis-
sel; and here and there springing forth are small cedars.

The soil on the top though somewhat broken is
very rich, affording every variety of grain and herbage.

## Island No. 21, left shore.

At the head of this island on the right is a sand
bar; channel between the bar and island. The island is in the form of a half circle.

## Fort Chartres,                                    10    78

Stands on the left bank of the river. It was formerly a place of considerable strength; built of stone
by the French, and sufficiently large to accommodate
1000 men. It is now falling to decay.

## Island No. 22, on the right, channel to the left.

## Island No. 23, good channel on either side.

Opposite this island Establishment creek enters
on the right. Prairie du Rochers is on the left
shore.

## Island No. 24, near the left shore, channel right side.

## Gabarre creek, right shore, .                     12    90

About three miles above the mouth of this creek lies
St. Genevieve, a town of about 200 houses, containing
12 or 1400 inhabitants. The first settlers were French,
but since the cession of Louisiana to the U. S. many
Americans have made this the place of their residence. There are about 20 stores; and it is the chief
mart for the lead brought from Mine a Burton, and
other lead mines in the territory. It has a handsome
church, in which the Rev. Mr. Maxwell officiates; he
is a hospitable man, and in him the stranger will find a

friend and adviser. Along the bank of the river extending about 5 miles lies the "Common Field," belonging to the inhabitants of the town, who are bound to keep the fences in repair.   It contains 7000 acres, perhaps the largest field in the United States; and its products are apportioned to the inhabitants, according to the property held by them in the town.   Corn is chiefly raised, but it will yield any other kind of grain.   Except in a small part near Gabarre, where the bank is broken and liable to cave, it is an even and permanent plain.

Islands, Nos. 25 & 26, left shore, channel to the right.

These islands are united in low water by a large sand bar.   A little below the point of the latter, on the right, is a bar—best channel to the left, in high water a good channel to the right.  Opposite the lower point of 26, is situated the

Public Ferry,                                                                 6 | 96

Three miles from this ferry and about seven from St. Genevieve, is situated in a beautiful plain, the town of Kaskaskia, on the Occoa or Kaskaskia river, and about five miles from its mouth.   It is the oldest French settlement in the Illinois country; for a considerable time it was declining rapidly, and the houses falling into ruin; but it is again reviving and promises to become a place of importance.

Islands, Nos. 27, 28 & 29, on the right side.

Channel to the left, about two miles lower down on the right bank, is

Camp Roudy,                                                              10 | 106

In the neighborhood of this place is a saline at which considerable quantities of salt are made.

River St. Lora, right side,                                            4 | 110

This a handsome stream of Louisiana.

Islands, Nos. 30 & 31, close to the right shore in a bend, channel left side.

Occoa or Kaskaskia river, left side,                          4 | 114

Flin's Ferry, right shore.

Islands, Nos. 32 & 33.

Opposite each other and nearest the left shore—channel to the right.

River St. Mary, left side,                                            4 | 118

Opposite this on the right shore is the fine settlement of Baubruly, extending 3 or 4 miles on the river, with some handsome improvements.

Island No. 34, near the left shore.

Island No. 35, nearer the left shore.

Islands Nos. 36 & 37.

Opposite the two last on the right, channel between the islands.

On the right of the lower point of the last island is an eddy, called the Great Eddy. A small stream, Cape St. Comb, enters on the same side. Miller's run enters on the opposite shore.

Island No. 38, channel to right and left.

Amite river, right shore,                                   14   132

Island No. 39, channel right side.

Island No. 40, channel to the right or left.

Three sand bars a little below, parallel to each other, channel left side of the one lying nearest the right shore.

Island No. 41, channel right side.

Calvin's creek, right shore,                               6   138

A little distance below this creek on the same side, Mr. Fenwick resides, a very hospitable man ; his improvements are extensive.

Obrazo river, right side,                                   4   142

On the left shore nearly opposite, in a bend of the river, is situated a rock, in which, about 100 feet from the surface of the water is a singular excavation, known by the name of the Devil's Oven.

The Grand Tower, near the right shore,          2   144

This is a rock standing in the river, of about 100 feet circumference and 150 feet high. There is a rapid current between the tower and the shore, and a narrow channel, but the main channel is to the left of the rock. The place appears to have been designed by nature for water works on a great scale.

Island No. 42 near the left shore.

On the right is a large sand bar, channel to the left of the island and right of the bar.

Riviere de la Pomme, right side,                      4   148

Muddy river, left side,                                        1   149

This is a considerable stream of the Illinois country. About 25 miles from its mouth, there is a large body of excellent stone coal, from which supplies for the smiths of the country are received ; and some is taken even to New Orleans.

Shawnee Town, right side,                                1   150

This is a large Indian village, which is the summer residence of a number of those people. They are very friendly and accommodating.

**Island No. 43, left side.**
A large sand bar projects from the head and one a little below the point of the island, channel right side.

| | | |
|---|---|---|
| Apple creek, right shore, | 2 | 152 |
| Island No. 44, channel right side, | 5 | 157 |

**Island No. 45, channel right side.**

**Island No. 46, channel right side.**

| | | |
|---|---|---|
| Devil's Island, | 6 | 163 |

Channel on the right. Just off the head of this island there is a large sand bar.

| | | |
|---|---|---|
| Cape Girardeau, right shore, | 3 | 166 |

The town of Girardeau is the capital of a district of Missouri territory. It was laid out by Mr. Low-rimee, who was formerly Spanish commandant; he is the principal proprietor. It is situated on a high bank, and is in a flourishing condition. The country is very fertile; and an extensive settlement stretching fifty miles back, strikes the settlement of New Madrid. A post road from this place to Fort Massac and the mouth of Cumberland river.

**Island No. 48.**
A bar projecting from the left shore nearly reaches this island.

**Island No. 49, a little below.**
Channel either between the two islands or to the right.

| | | |
|---|---|---|
| Island No. 50, channel to the right, | 3 | 169 |

A small creek enters on the left side.

| | | |
|---|---|---|
| Cape a la Bruche, right shore, | 1 | 170 |

A small creek enters on the right. Here is a vast ledge of rocks, which stretch across the river in a direct line. The best channel in the middle of the river, in which place in low water, there is not more than 6 feet over the rocks.

**Island No. 51, close to the right shore.**

**Island No. 52, just below.**
Channel good on either side.

| | | |
|---|---|---|
| Island No. 53, channel left side, | 4 | 174 |

Opposite this island is the growing settlement of Tyawapatia.

**Island No. 54, near the right shore.**

**Island No. 55, channel on either side.**
Lies opposite island 54. A small creek enters on the left side.

| | | |
|---|---|---|
| Tyawapatia creek, right shore, | 2 | 176 |

**Islands, Nos. 56, 57, 58, 59 & 60.**
A cluster of islands near the right shore. Best channel to the left.

**Island No. 61,**       12 | 188
Here the river makes a remarkable turn, called the Grand Turn. Channel on either side of No. 61.

**Islands, Nos. 62, 63 & 64.**
Do not pass between these islands; channel good on the outer sides.—63 and 64 lie opposite each other, a little below No. 62.

**Island No. 65,**       10 | 198
Island No. 66 lies opposite the lower point of 65 on on the right, and a mile below is island 67. Channel near the right and left shore.

**Island No. 68, channel right side,**       5 | 203
On the right bank of the river colonel Bird resides. In passing his house you have a beautiful view of the river Ohio.

**Junction of the Ohio,**       1 | 204

---

# OF THE MISSISSIPPI.*

*Directions for navigating the Mississippi from the Ohio to New Orleans, with a description of its islands, sand bars, bayous, rivers, creeks, towns, settlements, forts, &c. the distance from place to place being computed by the running of the current with a time piece, and is taken from the head of one island, bar, &c. to the head of another, including the supposed length of the island or bar.*

**ISLAND No. 1 below the Ohio,**       5 | 5
Lies close to the left shore; opposite it on the same side of the river, and just above Mayfield creek, stands fort Jefferson, now abandoned. No. 1 is about one mile long, and the channel cannot be mistaken, being at all times on the right side of the island.

* For Pike's account of the Mississipi from St. Louis to its source, see Appendix [a 2].

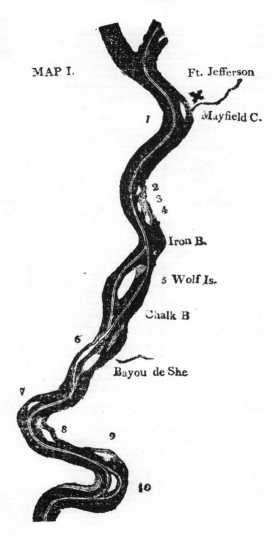

MAP I.

Ft. Jefferson

Mayfield C.

*1*

2
3
4

Iron B.

5 Wolf Is.

Chalk B

*6*

Bayou de She

*7*

*8*  *9*

*10*

Islands Nos. 2, 3 & 4,                              11|  16

Lie nearest the left shore, they are small and lie
just below one another—channel right side of them.

Iron Banks, (Mine au Fer) left side,               4|  20

Here is a bluff mixed with an iron colored earth of
a very fine sand and clay, constantly falling in, of the
height of 250 feet perpendicular, and extending a mile
on the river, and back from it in a ridge for five or
six miles, when it breaks into small hills, and declines gradually to the common level of the country,
which is there oak land.  There was a post here in
1773, near the south boundary of, then, Virginia.

Must not go too near the Iron Banks, there being
an eddy near the shore under them.  After passing
them, hug the left shore to clear a large sand bar putting out from the head of Wolf island, which you
must keep on your right hand.

Wolf Island, No. 5,                                4|  24

This is a large island lying to the right, though
when opposite its head, it seems to divide the current
equally, the right hand pass turning off suddenly to
the right around the island.

Wolf island sand bar begins at the head of the island, and spreads out so far as to occupy ¾ of the
breadth of the river, confining the channel to the left
bank, where at its narrowest point it is not more than
a quarter of a mile broad; the bar then declines towards the island, extending in length three miles,
and about one mile at its broadest part, the river being a mile and a quarter wide opposite the settlement,
and nearly two miles across at the head of the island.
When this bar is covered, there is no danger, it is
observed by boatmen, from any of the bars lower
down.  There are several clusters of willows on this
bar, particularly near the island, where there appears
to be a high water pass forming immediately under
Mr. Hunter's settlement.

This island is six miles long on its left side, while
the right is ten, and 5 miles broad, containing 15000
acres of the first rate land, well timbered, having near
its middle a beautiful prairie, high and dry, producing the finest grass for cattle.  Grapes grow on the
island in great abundance.  A Mr. James Hunter, the
only man I ever knew who seemed to take a pride in
letting it be known that he was a professed gambler,
is the only occupant of Wolf island at present.  He
says he has on it 1000 head of hogs, and a large stock
of cattle, with whose beef and pork he supplies boats,
barges, keels, &c. passing up and down the river, to-

gether with butter, milk, &c. I saw at his house a
pair of wild geese tamed, running with the common
geese, without any wish to leave them, I observed,
however, they always kept close together, and generally in the rear of the others ; they were caught when
goslins. This kind of wild and tame goose will not
breed beyond the first generation. [*b* 2]

A good landing can be made at the foot of the bar
near the island.

Chalk Banks, another high falling in bluff, begins
near the head of Wolf island, on the left side of the
river.

Sand bar, with some willows on it,                     7    31

It is two miles below No 5, about 300 yards from
the left shore, a mile long, and in high water it is covered—channel to the right of it.

Island No. 6,                                          3    34

Joins the above bar—channel right shore. Opposite this island on the left shore,

*Bayou De She* puts in, immediately above a point of
high land on the left, and which runs back from the
river a considerable distance into the country.

Island No. 7, four miles below No. 6,                  6    40

Lies close to the right shore in the upper part of a
bend; it is a large willow island, three miles long, at
its head there is a large willow bar—channel left
shore in all situations of the water.

Island No. 8, a mile below No. 7,                      4    44

Lies near the middle of the river, and opposite a
point of the left shore ; it is about 4 miles long. Best
channel on the right side of it, the left side is good
in high water, and is the nearest.

Island No. 9, three miles below No. 8,                 7    51

Is close to the left shore, and about three miles
long—the channel is on the right of the island in all
stages of the river.

Island No. 10, three miles below No. 9,                6    57

Lies nearest the left shore, river turns to the right.
At the head of No. 10 is an ugly sand bar covered with
willows. Best channel is to the right of both. First
left hand point below No. 10 there is a sand bar in
the middle of the river, channel to the right of it.—
In passing No. 10, especially in high water, keep
pretty close to the right hand point just above the
head of the island. No. 10 is about a mile in length.

This island and the right bank opposite it, shew
the first evident marks of the effects of the earthquake which commenced December 16, 1811. The

right bank for several miles above and below the island, appears to be several feet, about three or four, as near as I could judge from the adjoining land, lower than it formerly was. Many of the trees standing in all directions on the island, and particularly the willows on the willow point opposite it, clearly evince the concussions of the earth. This island is said to had cracked to that degree, that several large trees standing on the cracks, were split from the roots up to their tops.

Two miles above No. 10, a bayou runs out from the right side, and comes in again three miles below the island. A few years may make this a safe pass, and form another island. From the entrance or mouth of this pass or bayou, you have a fine view of New Madrid, six or seven miles ahead.

### New Madrid Bar,

Is of the first order in magnitude, beginning on the left shore four or five miles above the town, and extending down about three miles below it. It appears to be growing in width, and drives the current hard against the right bank, consequently that bank is falling in rapidly from three or four miles above New Madrid, to two or three below it.

### New Madrid, [c 2] right side,     13   70

There is a creek called Chepousa river, which heads in a lake 25 miles back of New Madrid, and puts in just above the town; it affords a good landing for boats at its mouth. To make it you must keep pretty near the right bank for some distance above the creek, and pull in so as to clear the counter current, and make the land just below the mouth of the creek. The nearer you land to the creek the better, for the bank opposite the town is almost constantly falling in.

### Island No. 11, (five miles below New Madrid.)     5   75

Lies near the right shore, close to the upper end of a small bend; it is about two miles long—Channel on the left side of it.

### Island No. 12,     4   79

Channel right side. No. 12 is close to the left shore, and is about three miles long.

### A sand bar two miles below No. 12.

It lies in the middle of the river, and opposite a right hand point—Channel right side of it. This bar was much convulsed during the Earthquake; it opened in places, throwing up blue clay, mineral coal, &c.

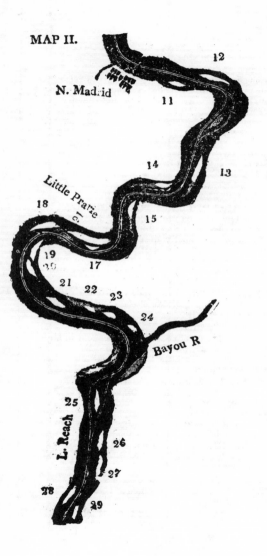

MAP II.

and is much larger than formerly. The river here winds to the right.

**Island No. 13,**                  9    88

Lies near the left shore, and is about three miles long—channel right side of it.

**Island No. 14,**                  4    92

Lies on the right of the river, and on the left of it are four or five willow islands; a sand bar adjoining them makes its appearance in low water—channel to the left of those islands in all stages of the water.— These islands have driftwood on their points, and are about three miles long.

**Island No. 15, two miles below No. 14,**    5    97

Is pretty large and lies close to the left shore.— Channel right side at all times. At the foot of this island is a long willow bar, which affords a good landing on the side of it in high water. No. 15 is about three miles long.

**Little Prairie, two miles below No. 15,**    5  102

This settlement is on the right bank. Having been much torn to pieces during the earthquake; the inhabitants have principally deserted it. The forest adjoining the town looks as if it had been in some desperate engagement, in which it had got much worsted in the battle, the trees standing in all directions and in great confusion.

**Island No. 16, one mile below Little Prairie,**  3  105

Lies close to the right side of the river, and opposite to it on the left, is

**Island No. 17, small.**

Take the left side of these islands, except in high water, when you may go between them. No. 16 is about 5 miles long. Here the banks appear lower than formerly, sunken and broken to pieces.

**Island No. 18, one mile below No. 16,**    6  111

Lies close to the right shore. Opposite the head of No. 18 is a bar, may go on either side of it. If you get between the island and the bar, keep close to the bar, for fear of being drawn on snags and sawyers on the side of the island. No. 18 is about 3 miles long.

**Island No. 19, opposite the middle of No. 18,**

And extends down one mile below it—channel on the right or between them.

**Island No. 20, just below No. 19,**    4  115

It lies on the right shore—channel right side. It is about 2 miles long.

**Island No. 21, opposite the foot of No. 20,**  2  117

It lies near the middle of the river—channel right side. In high water the left channel is good and the nearest. It is about two miles long.

## Islands, Nos. 22, 23 & 24,

Surround a left hand point above Bayou river—channel on the right side of all of them.

## Bayou river, just below No. 24,

Enters in on the left side. It is about 50 yards wide. Good landing between No. 24 and Bayou river.

7  124

## Willow Islands, three or four,

These are small and lie on a large sand bar adjoining the right shore—channel on the left hand of them. They are nearly two miles long. The river forms a half circle around these islands, and winds much to the right. Banks here much torn to pieces.

1  125

## A large sand bar,

About a mile below the willow islands. It is covered with willows and joins the left shore. It is about three miles long. Pass it on the right side.

3  128

## No. 25, two miles below the bar, [d 2]

Lies near the middle of the river—channel good on both sides. It is about one mile long. There is good landing two miles above No. 25 along a willow shore and eddy water, on the right side of the river. No. 25 has been severely handled by the earthquake.—From this island you have a fine view of

5  133

## The Long, called the *Canadian Reach.*

About 10 miles in length, at the lower end of which is a dangerous bar in the middle of the river, the pass is difficult, the river being filled here with snags.—The best channel is on the right side of the bar, two-thirds over from the right shore. This is one of the most dangerous places in low water between the Ohio and New Orleans.

It appears that a new sand bar has been formed between Nos. 25 and 26, to avoid which take the right hand side of No. 25, keeping the right side until you pass 26.

## No. 26, commences opposite the foot of No. 25,

And so close to the left shore you can scarcely discern the schute. It is about 3 miles long.—Channel on the right of it.

2  135

## N. 27, is joined to No. 26,

By a willow bar, and also lies near the left shore—channel right side. It is about three miles long.

Q

## No. 28, a narrow willow Island,                3 | 141

Lies close to the right shore, and begins opposite the foot of No. 27. It extends down about four miles—channel left side.

## No. 29, opposite No. 28.

Lies on the left side of the river, and ends with No. 28. It is about a mile long—channel right side.

## No. 30, one mile below No. 29,                5 | 146

And lies on the same side of the river with it.—At the lower point on the right side of the island is a large sand bar. No. 30 is about two miles long—channel right side.

## No. 31, two miles below No. 30,               4 | 150

This island is narrow and lies close to the right shore—channel left side at all times. At the lower end of No. 31 are a number of snags and sawyers; opposite, on the left side, is a sand bar of No. 32.

## No. 32, (destroyed by the earthquake.)
## Sand Bar of No. 32.

This large bar begins just below the left hand point, two miles above where used to stand No. 32, and extends three miles down on the left side. Keep in with the left shore passing No. 31, until you get near the left hand point, then strike over for the right hand shore, leaving the sand bar of No. 32 on your left. The river here is much filled with snags and sawyers.

## No. 33. Flo r Island,                        10 | 160

Is near the middle of the river—main channel now right side, (some prefer the left pass,) keeping as close to the right hand point as the water will admit of. It is about a mile and a half long. There is a good landing among the willows on the right side of the river opposite the foot of No. 33. This island takes its name from having had flour boats wrecked upon it.

## Upper Chickasaw Bluff,

Begins opposite the foot of No. 33 on the left bank, and continues down about a mile.

## No. 34, three miles below No. 33,            5 | 165

Stands about the middle of the river, and is nearly four miles long. There are two small islands close to No. 34, which may be considered a part of it, between which and the large one you must not venture a passage. There is an outlet on the left shore nearly opposite the middle of No. 34, and comes in again a mile above the second bluff—channel past No. 34, left side, some prefer the right.

**Second Chickasaw Bluff, three miles below No. 34,**    7 | 172

Here you see on the left hand a bluff bank of from 150 to 200 feet in height, singularly shaped, and variegated with different colors of the earth, of which the yellow is the most conspicuous. The river bearing hard against the bluff subjects it to an almost constant caving down, hence the face of the bluff is kept fresh in its appearance. The earth when first picked up at the bluff, and when it is wet, has a soapy feeling and would appear to be a good clay for potters, but on examination it is much mixed with a very fine sand, which, when dried, renders it friable. The yellow and the pink colored earths are sometimes collected, and when mixed with oil and ground, make a tolerable paint. These bluffs, with all the others on the Mississippi, are so irregular in their formation, the colored veins of earth running in such contrary directions, induces a suggestion of their volcanic origin. This bluff extends about two miles down.

The river here turns short to the right, and is very narrow. Close in to the bluff is an eddy, you may keep as near the outer edge of it as you please, and the channel is safe and good though very rapid.

**No. 35, three miles below second bluff,**    3 | 173

Is very broad at its head, the left pass turns pretty short to the right, and half way down is a large willow and sand bar on the left shore, must keep pretty close to the island past this bar. In low water the right side of No. 35 must be taken. This island is about five miles long. A mile below No. 35 is an outlet on the right side of the river.

**No. 36, three miles below No. 35,**    8 | 183

Lies near the middle of the river.—The right channel is now the best, and in fact the main one, though so bad a few years ago as to get the name of the *Devil's Race Ground.* The right hand point opposite the head of No. 36, is a high willow point or bar, reaching down for two miles; keep close to this point and then close round the sand bar, as the lower end of the schute is narrow and dangerous, there being snags and sawyers on the bar joining the foot of the island. On the left shore is a long sand and willow bar extending above and below the head of the island. The right pass is about three miles through, and the left six or seven.

**Third Chickasaw Bluffs.**

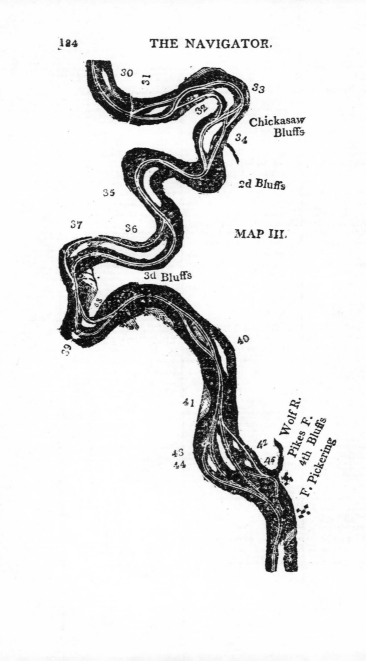

30 31 33
32
Chickasaw
Bluffs
34

2d Bluffs

35

MAP III.

37 36

3d Bluffs

38

40

39

41

Wolf R.
Pikes F.
4th Bluffs
F. Pickering
42
45
43
44

The left side and opposite No. 36. They are seen from a mile above the head of the island.

## No. 37, a willow Island.

Lies close along side and laps a little past the foot of No. 36, on its left side, therefore is scarcely observable when you take the right side of No. 36. Just below No. 37 on the left side of the river, are *three outlets*, within a quarter of a mile of each other, and joining, enter the river five miles below.

## A willow beach and bar,                          9 | 192

Three miles below No. 37, and on the left side of the river. Here the current sets hard against the right shore, and in floods rushes over the bank with great velocity. This bar is two miles long, and the river winds considerably to the left around it. A mile below this willow bar the three outlets enter in one handsome stream, forming an island of great magnitude, and by way of distinction, we will call it *Outlet Island*, the foot of it being about six miles below No. 37, and five miles in length.

## No. 38,                                          5 | 197

This island stands nearly in the middle of the river, which turns suddenly to the left, and forms a left hand point, so curious as to have obtained it the name of the *Devil's Elbow*. The head of the island is beset with snags—channel left side. In approaching this schute you must hug close round the left hand point until you come in sight of the sand bar, whose head has the appearance of an old field of trees, then pull over for the island to keep clear of the snags on your left, while you leave those along the head of the island on your right, taking care not to approach these last too near, for the current is so rapid that the striking one might so shock the boat as to endanger the cargo. The channel to the right of No. 38 is now too dangerous to be run, it being choked and filled with snags and sawyers. The left pass is about a mile through, the right three miles.

## Island No. 39, off to the right of No. 38,

And its pass is ten miles round, but never attempted to be run by boats, in fact the island is scarcely distinguishable from the main land. On the right side of the river before you get to No. 38 is a willow bar two miles in length.

## Twelve outlets nearly a mile below No. 38,       4 | 201

These are small and on the right shore.

## A sand and willow beach point,                   1 | 202

On this beach are large quantities of drift wood and

Q 2

rafts; it is about two miles long and joins the right shore. Here the river turns to the right.

## Island No. 40, 2 miles below the Beach point,    4 | 206

Is large, and lies nearest the left shore—channel right side at all times. One mile and a half below the head of No. 40 is a small island close to the right shore. A mile further down is a large willow and sand bar in the middle of the river, the willows on the bar are divided in several places, forming two small islands, with a third lower down, still smaller, but on the same bar. Low water passage is to the right of this bar, in high water the left may be gone. At the foot of No. 40 is a fine landing place, where there is gentle water and willows to make fast to.— This landing cannot be made well without taking the left of the bar. There is also a good landing on the right hand willow point below the foot of the island, which is easily made when you take the right of the bar. The right pass is about five or six miles long.

## Island No. 41, two miles below No. 40,    7 | 213

Lies near the right shore, and adjoining it is a bar —channel on the left of both. It is about a mile long.

## Nos. 42, 43, 44 & 45, three miles below No. 41,    4 | 217

By way of eminence, these islands have been dubbed with the name of "*Paddy's Hen and Chickens.*" They lie in a bend of the river, the two nearest the left shore, viz. 42 the upper, and the other 45, the one on the right of these is the largest, 43, and the one nearest the right shore is 44. On the right side of this last island is a sand bar.—The channel in low water is to the right of the bar as well as of all the islands. In high water any of the passes may be gone with safety. From the head of the first to the foot of the last is about six miles.

## Wolf, (called by Hutchins) Margot river,    7 | 224

This is a handsome little river on the left side.— The French had a fort here just below the mouth of the river, called Assumption-fort, built in the year 1736, during their wars with the Chickasaws, but in the year following a peace ensued, and the fort was demolished. A good landing may be had at Wolf river, by pulling over after you pass the four islands above.

*Fort Pike* formerly stood just below Wolf river, but a better situation was pitched upon and a fort built two miles lower down the bluff, called

## Fort Pickering.

It occupies the commanding ground of the *Fourth Chickasaw bluff*, on the left bank of the Mississippi. The United States have a military factor here, with a few soldiers. The settlement is thin and composed of what is called the *half breed*, that is, a mixture of the whites and Indians, a race of men too indolent to do any permanent good either for themselves or for society. A landing may be had a little above fort Pickering, but it is not a very good one.

The fourth Bluff affords a commanding, airy, pleasant and extensive situation for a settlement, and the soil is remarkably fertile. Opposite the Bluff or Wolf river, on the right bank of the Mississippi, there used to stand a Spanish fort, now demolished.

When this post was in possession of the Spaniards, the commandant had a road cut in a straight line from the mouth of Chickasaw creek, (a small creek two miles below fort Pickering) to Wolf river, for the purpose of taking exercise on horseback.

## No. 46, President Island, one mile below fort Pickering,     3, 227

This is a noble island, and lies nearest the left shore. Channel in all stages of low water on the right side of it—the left pass may be gone in high water with safety, and it is much the nearest, being but about six miles through, while the right is about 10 or 11 miles round.

## Island No. 47, is small, and lies opposite No. 46.

On the right side of it—channel right side. In low water a chain of rocks may be seen extending from the head of No. 46 to the left shore. A mile below No. 46 a willow beach begins and extends down four miles, along which is a good landing in high water.

## Islands Nos. 48 & 49, four miles below No. 46,     14, 241

Lie close to the left shore—channel on their right side at all times. On the right side of No. 49 is a large sand and willow bar, which, when viewed from below, looks like a cluster of small islands. There is a great quantity of drift wood at the head of this bar. The channel is on the right of it, which you cannot mistake. These islands are about 4½ miles long.

## Island No. 50, 1½ mile below No. 49,     6, 247

Is a wood and willow island lying close to the right shore, below a right hand point. It extends down three miles, and has a much larger opening below

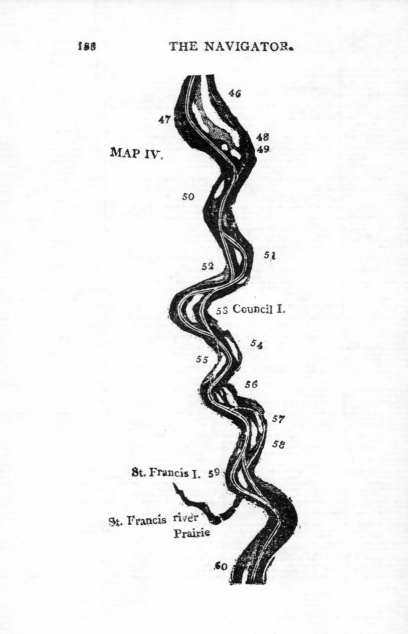

MAP IV.

46
47
48
49
50
51
52
53 Council I.
54
55
56
57
58
St. Francis I. 59
St. Francis river
Prairie
60

than above—channel left side at all times.  There is a good landing on the left side of the river a little below No. 50, where there are willows and quiet water.

When opposite the middle of No. 50, you have a fine view of the river for 10 or 12 miles.

**A sand and willow bar, 3 miles below No. 50,**                    6    253

Lies nearest the left shore—channel right side, and when the water is low keep pretty near the bar, so as to take the right side of No. 51.  This bar is about a mile long.

**Island No. 51, hardly a mile below the bar,**                    2    255

Lies near the middle of the river—channel left side. The right pass is the nearest, and safe in a middling state of the river.  It is about three miles long.  A handsome sized creek puts in opposite No. 51 on the right side.

**A willow island between Nos. 51 & 52,**

Close to the left shore, scarcely discernible.

**Island No. 52, four miles below No. 51,**                    7    262

Begins below a right hand point close to the right shore—channel left side at all times.  No. 52 is a willow island three miles long, and extends down to, and appears to be shutting up the right hand pass of Council Island.  There is a large bar at the head of No. 52, which, keep well to your right hand.

**No. 53, Council Island,**                    3    265

Seems to lie near the middle of the river, which turns suddenly to the left, and runs S. E. for several miles.—Channel left side at all times, the right pass being narrow, and appears to be closing up by the approach of the young willows at the foot of No. 52.

The left hand point here is a naked, desolate looking place, having, however, a few clumps of willows here and there, and a few straggling bushes growing on it.

From the lower end of No. 53 to No. 54. on the left side is a high willow beach.  Two miles below No. 53, after you get around the sand and willow point, is a good landing in quiet water along a handsome bold beach.

Four miles below No. 53, is a outlet, just below which is a good landing around a small point.  Half a mile below this point is a small sand bar a short distance from the right shore; the left side of the bar is the best channel.  No. 53 is above three miles long.

This island takes its name from a Council of Chickasaws, Chacktaws, and other Indians, and whites, having been held on the point opposite it some years ago, to settle a matter of national dispute.

### No. 54, (five miles below No. 53,)    8 | 273

Lies close to the right shore, having but a small passage on its left side, which takes out at right angles, with a slow current.—Channel right side. On the right side of No. 54 is a large, high sand bar, extending to the foot of the island, which keep also on your left This bar shoots past the head of No. 55. No. 54 is about 3 miles long.

### No. 55 (opposite the foot of No. 54,)    3 | 276

The right of this Island, called the *Grand Cut-off*, is now the best and most approved of, having more water and a deeper channel than the left pass, which was a few years ago altogether run. To take the Grand Cut-off, you must hug close to the right hand point at the head of the schute, for fear of being thrown on the island, to which the current sets powerfully, and on the side of which are sawyers and snags. With caution and expertness at the oars this pass is safe and rapid, and three miles the nearest, the left pass being five or six miles round. The Grand Cut-off makes so sudden a turn to the right, that it requires a good look-out to be prepared for it.

For some distance below No. 55, the river winds much to the right, and the current sets hard against the right hand bank, then it turns greatly to the left, round No. 56, forming nearly three-fourths of a circle.

### No. 56 (1½ miles below No. 55,)    5 | 281

Here are three islands pretty close to the left shore, but in low water they have more the appearance of one, therefore, we include them all in No. 56. Channel to the right of them at all times. In passing round this island, caution and some oar labor *is* requisite to keep out from among the newly felled trees along the right hand bank, against which the current sets so hard, as to occasion the timber to be almost constantly falling in during the high water season. About a quarter of a mile above the foot of the last of these islands in the bend on the right shore, around a small point, is a tolerable good landing. No. 56 is about three miles long, though the circle you are obliged to take is at least five.

### Nos. 57 [e 2] & 58, 3 miles below No. 56,    6 | 287

Lies immediately below a right hand point, beginning opposite each other, and pretty close to the right hand shore. No. 57 is a willow island one mile and a half long. No. 58 lies to the right of No. 57, is

a wood island and extends down two miles below it.
Main channel on the left side of both in all stages of
the water.

Opposite the heads of Nos. 57 & 58, in a bend on
the left side of the river, is a large sand and willow
bar, by the side of which is a pretty good landing.
The river between the head of No. 57 on the right,
and the willow bar on the left, is quite narrow, but
the channel good.

## No. 59, St. Francis Island,                          8 | 295

Lies near the middle of the river, 3 miles below
58—channel good on both sides. If you take the left,
which is the nearest, when about half way down the
island keep as close to the left shore as the water will
admit of, for fear of being drawn on a large raft of
sawyers on the side of the island. No. 59 is about
three miles long.

Just below the foot of No. 59, on the right side, enters

## St. Francis river.

A handsome stream of 200 yards broad at its mouth,
with a gentle current. It heads near the Osage river
of the Missouri—West river is a western branch of it.
On the right side of the St. Francis as you ascend, is
a considerable lake called Mitchegamas, running
parallel to, and joins the river just above its entrance
into the Mississippi, and again at its head. It seems
in fact to be the principal channel of the St. Francis.
The village or settlement at the mouth of the river,
forms a place of meeting of hunters and traders, and
a depository of their goods, furs, peltries, &c.

## Big Prairie, three miles below No. 59,              6 | 301

The settlement here was formerly considerable, but
it is principally abandoned. The site is on the right
side of the river, and is handsome, and beyond the
usual floods. One mile and a half back of the settlement is a lake two miles wide and five long, a place of
great resort for swans, geese, ducks, &c. The lake is
supported by streams flowing from the hills two miles
further back, and empties itself into the Mississippi
opposite No. 60.

## No. 60, three miles below Big Prairie,              6 | 307

Lies near the middle of the river—channel left side.
In a middling state of the water both sides are equally good. It is about one mile long, and the trees on
it are chiefly broken off and torn up by the hurricanes.
Opposite No. 60, on the right side a little back from
the river, are seen some hills and high land, said to

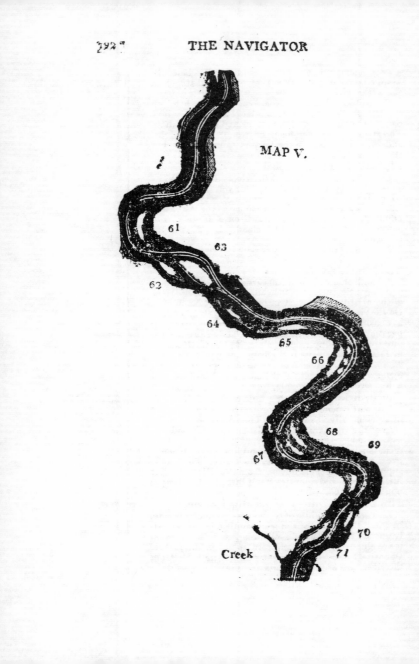

MAP V.

be good for tillage. This tract also is much torn to
pieces by hurricanes.

Three miles below No. 60, is a large sand bar and
willow beach on the left side of the river, extending
down two miles and a half.—Channel right side of it.
There is a settlement opposite the middle of the bar
on the right side, just below which a long willow
shore begins and continues two miles down, and where
it ends a new settlement is beginning, there being a
small new dwelling, but no land cleared.

There is a small sharp willow island near the left
side, a quarter of a mile long, and a large willow
beach and sand bar below it.—Channel right side.
On the right side opposite this island is a handsome
prairie bank. This island is about 9 miles below No.
60, and a mile below the last settlement. Here you
have a fine view of the river for about 10 miles.

Three miles below this willow island, on the right
side of the river, is a good landing near the end of a
willow shore, where there is deep water and a small
eddy, being in a right hand bend, a little below a left
hand point. Opposite this landing place, on the
left side, is a beautiful prairie bank.

| | | |
|---|---|---|
| **A small round willow Island (12 miles below No. 60,)** | 13 | 320 |

Near the left shore, with a large willow point on
its left, four miles below the last small island. There
is a small pass between this island and the willow
point, but the main river sweeps around a right hand
bend, therefore keep the island to your left.

One mile below the above round island, around a
right hand point, is a large bar, having an ugly appearance, being covered with drift wood, snags, willows and small cotton trees.—Channel left side.
There is a very rapid current from this bar to No.
61, and below it.

| | | |
|---|---|---|
| **No. 61, 7 miles below the small round Is-land,** | 8 | 328 |

Lies close to the left shore, having a small willow
island on its right and joined to it by a bar.—Channel
right side of both. No. 61 is about three miles long.

| | | |
|---|---|---|
| **No. 62, 3 miles below No. 61,** | 6 | 334 |

Lies close the right shore.—Channel on its left
side, also to the left of a large bar, lying between
and opposite the head of the two islands.

No. 63, lies in the great left hand bend, nearest the
left shore, and opposite No. 62, though extending a
little distance below it. The bar at, and extending
below the head of No. 63, and which is covered with

R

willows and drift wood at its head, must be kept on your right hand, the best channel in low water being between it and No. 63, on your left. In high water the pass is good to the right of the bar, between it and No. 62. No. 63 is about 3 miles long.

At the foot of No. 62 is a good landing, and also opposite its lower point on the right side there is good landing in an eddy, and beside a willow point just below a little bar, where the upper schute of No. 62 ends. Along this part of the Mississippi and below, the scrub grass is seen on the banks in great abundance. [f 2]

No. 64, 6 miles below No. 63,                                    6 | 340

Stands in the middle of the river, and has a willow bar joining it on the left side of the head of the island. The left hand channel is preferred in all stages of the water; the right is safe in floods. No. 46 is about three miles long.

T ere is a small outlet half way down the island, on the left side, running out at right angles.

There ia good landing on the left shore in a nuke opposite the foot of No. 64, where there is quiet water and a willow beach. There is also good landing on the right side, both above and below No. 64, along a willow shore.

No. 65, 3 miles below No. 64,                                    6 | 346

Is a small island, about three quarters of a mile long.—Channel left side at all times, there being but a small pass to the right of it.

No. 66, 4 miles below No. 65,                                    5 | 351

Lies pretty close to the right shore, a large sand bar and three small islands join it on the left side, the heads of which are covered with drift wood. The left hand channel must be taken at all times. This island is about 3 miles long.

No. 67 & 68, 5 miles below No. 66,                              8 | 359

These lie side by side and nearly in the middle of the river —Channel right of both. Never venture to the left of both, but in floods you may go between them. No. 68 is on the left of 67 extending down below it, and is about two miles long.

There is a bar between these islands with small willows on it, lying nearest No. 68; if you take the middle schute, keep the bar to your left. There is good landing at the foot of No. 67, and along the side of and near the foot of No. 68, along a willow shore.

No. 69, 3 miles below No. 68,                                    5 | 364

Lies close to the right shore, is small, and has on its left side a large willow and flat sand bar.—Channel on the left of both bar and island at all times. No. 69 is about one mile and a half long.

## No. 70, 1½ miles below No. 69,

Is small, lying close to the left shore, and is now no more than a willow and cotton wood beach, the young wood having approached and grown up close to the main land, leaving no passage around it — Channel of course on the right of it. It is about two miles long.

3 | 367

## No. 71, a mile below No. 70,

Lies on the right shore and is about five miles long.—Channel left side of it, and also of the bar. This is a large sand and willow bar, on the left side of No. 71, beginning a little below its head and continuing around the right hand point to near the foot of the island. In the left hand bend about half way down the bar is a curious outlet, rushing out and taking its course apparently up stream, tracing probably, an old bed of the river, having on its left a regular bank and large trees, and on its right a large circular willow beach of recent growth.

2 | 369

The suck of this outlet in high water is pretty strong, and requires a little care to keep out of its reach. You are advertised of its approach by a number of dead trees at the point through which the water rushes with great velocity, and by drift wood below its mouth.

## Scrubgrass creek, 2 miles below No. 71,

Is small and in a right hand bend. Two miles and a half below this creek, and on the same side with it, a settlement was began in April, 1809.

7 | 376

Opposite this creek, on the left side of the river is a willow point extending down a considerable distance.

## No. 72, 4 miles below Scrubgrass creek,

Lies very near the right shore, and is about two miles long.—Channel left side—In high water the right pass may be gone, but it is something longest. A little below the head of this island enters

4 | 380

## White river, right side,

Where is good landing if you take the right side of No. 72. About three miles up White river there is a water pass to the Arkansas, and which enters that river 20 miles above its mouth This is a nearer route to the post and village of Ozark, from above, than that of entering at the mouth of the Arkansas river, 50 miles up which the village is situated.

You can see the mouth of White river, when passing to the left of the island at the head.

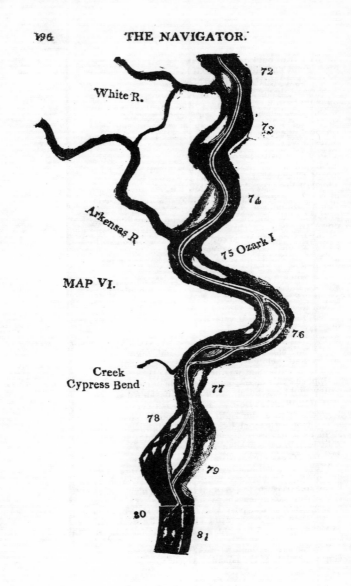

White R.

72

73

74

Arkensas R.

75 Ozark I

MAP VI.

76

Creek
Cypress Bend

77

78

79

80

81

There is good landing just below No. 72, on the left side of the river, along a willow beach.

Two miles below No. 72, is a large bar, lying under the first right hand point, extending out nearly two-thirds across the river; keep pretty well over to the left hand bank in passing this bar.

No. 73, 4 miles below No. 72,                          4 | 384

Lies very near the right shore, opposite the middle of this island on its left side is a bar.—Channel to the left of both island and bar. No. 73 is about two miles long.

No. 74, 4 miles below No. 73,                          6 | 390

Is a large flat willow and cotton wood island lying close to the right shore, in high water it is cut through in several places by the current which gives it the appearance of several small islands. At its head is much drift wood.—Channel always on the left side of it. No. 74 is about 3½ miles long.

The river here winds handsomely to the right, making a sweeping left hand bend past the mouth of the Ozark or Arkansas river, when it again winds to the left.

Arkansas river, [g 2] 1½ miles below No. 74,          5 | 395

This is a noble and a very long, navigable river of Louisiana, coming in from the west. About 50 miles up it is the post of Arkansas, and several Chactaw villages, where there is a good deal of trade carried on in furs, peltries, buffalo robes, &c. in exchange for goods, whiskey, &c.

There are several houses with small cleared enclosures just below the mouth of the Arkansas, where settlements have been attempted, but are now vacated, and probably totally abandoned, owing to the overflowings of the Mississippi, which unfortunate circumstance may oblige this noble river to wind its meanderings through an uncultivated forest for eight hundred, or a thousand miles in extent, for a century yet to come.

No. 75, Ozark island, 3 miles below the Arkansas,    3 | 398

Lies nearest the left shore—channel right side—the left is good in high water and is something the nearest. It is about 2½ miles long.

Island No. 76, 5½ miles below No. 75,                 8 | 406

Lies near the left shore, and is about three miles long—best channel right side in all stages of the wa-

ter.   Opposite the foot of No. 76, close to the right
shore, is a very small island, from which no danger
need be apprehended.

Good landing opposite No. 76, right shore, willows
and gentle water.   From the head of No. 76 the river winds to the right, making a very long left hand
bend.

A sand bar in the middle of the river three miles
below No. 76, where the Mississippi spreads itself to
a mile and a half in breadth.   In low water the left
side of this bar should be taken, where the principal
part of the current will be observed to draw.   The
right side is pretty good.   The bar is about a mile
long.

Island No. 77, 7 miles below No. 76,                    10   416

Lies close to the left shore, and the schute that runs
to the left of it is small and takes out at right angles
just below the left hand point—channel right side at
all times.   Opposite No. 77, in the right hand Cypress
Bend, a small creek empties in.   Great quantities of
timber is got here for the Natchez and New Orleans
market.   Whether it be strictly right that the most
valuable timber, to the amount of millions of dollars,
should be thus moulded to the use of private purses,
where in fact it is public property, may be a question
to be taken into consideration by those concerned in
this business.   Louisiana cost the United States
14,000,000 dollars, and the cypress trees were all included in the purchase, and are in fact in many cases worth ten times more than the land they grow on.

There is good landing on the left along a willow
shore below No. 77.   This island is about 3 miles
long ; the river begins to widen and turns gradually
to the left for seven or eight miles.

Nos. 78 & 79, 4 miles below No. 77,                    7   423

Lies nearest the right hand shore—main channel
on the left of both in all stages of the water.   These
islands are about three and a half miles long.

Island No. 80, 3½ miles below No. 79,                  7   430

Lies close to the right shore, and on the left side
of it is

Island No. 81, a very small island.

Pass both these on the left side.   No. 80 is about
two miles long.   The river below Nos. 80 and 81
bends to the right round a long willow point and bar.

Island No. 82, 7 miles below No. 80,                   9   439

Lies just below a right hand point—channel left
side.   In high water the right hand pass is pretty
good and much the nearest.   The river here sweeps

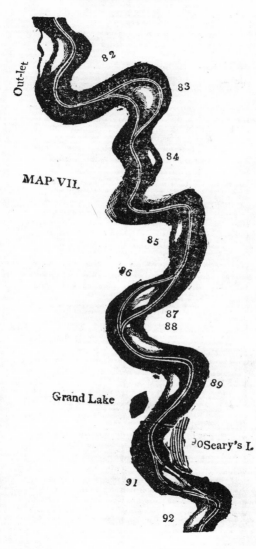

Out-let

82

83

84

MAP VII.

85

86

87
88

89

Grand Lake

90 Seary's L.

91

92

to the right, making a large left hand bend round No. 82. This is a large island, about five miles long.—Just below the foot of No. 82, is a very small island handsomely dividing the right hand pass of that island.

## Spanish Moss [h 2] bend just below No. 82.

This is a beautiful right hand bend forming three-fourths of a regular circle of about eight miles in length.

The left hand shore around this bend is clothed with willows and sand bars. Near the lower end of the bend the river in its highest state becomes much crowded together, not being more than one-third of a mile in breadth, consequently very deep and rapid, and full of boils or swells, but no way dangerous.

## Illechecko settlement.

This settlement, of four small cabins, occupied by one Indian, one French, and two American families, having as many corn patches of three or four acres to each house, is at the right hand point immediately below the Spanish Moss bend, and a little above the head of No. 83. The bank here is pretty high, but I fear the overflowings of 1813 have destroyed all present attempts to continue the settlement. The peach tree leaves were green here on the 21st December 1812, though the fall had been unusually cold and early, and the winter afterwards more severe than had been witnessed for 20 years.

Just above the settlement you run nearly east, and three miles below it as nearly west.

## Island No. 83, 9 miles below No. 82,          14  453

Lies nearest the left shore—channel right side, main schute and the nearest, keeping pretty near the right hand point to avoid a bar that runs out from the head of the island towards the right hand shore. At the foot of No. 83 is a small island. No. 83 is about two miles long, the river turns here much to the right. On the right shore opposite No. 83, is pretty good landing along a willow beach.

## A large sand bar,

Three miles below No. 83, and one-third over from the right shore—channel left side in low water.

## Island No. 84, 5 miles below No. 83,          7  460

Lies close to the left shore—channel right hand side at all times. The left hand pass which is small, takes out suddenly below a left hand point. A sand and broken willow bar lies along side of the island, filled with logs and snags, all of which keep pretty well to your left. Opposite the foot of No. 84, just below the right hand point, is a good landing place. This island is about 2½ miles long.

## Island No. 85, 6½ miles below No. 84,    9 | 469

Is pretty close to the right shore, and is covered with willows and cotton wood—channel left side at all times. Here is good landing by hauling to under the points or below the island. No. 85 is about two miles long.

## Nos. 86 & 87, 6 miles below No. 85,    8 | 77

Are nearly in the middle of the river and opposite each other, No. 86 beginning first and extends below No. 87, which lies a little to the left of No. 86.

No. 87 has a handsome grass prairie on it, with young cotton wood, and a sand and willow bar on its lower point—channel left side of both in low water; in floods the right pass is safe and something nearest —never venture between them, for they are joined by a bar. There is good landing on the side of No. 87, and opposite it on the left shore is a raft growing to the bank. At the head of No. 87 is drift wood and a willow bar. These two islands occupy a short left hand bend, and below them the river winds to the left.— They are about 2½ miles long.

## No. 88, 1½ miles below No. 87,    4 | 481

Lies so close to the left side that you don't observe it until you get opposite the pass that runs around it, and which takes out at right angles with the river; it is but a small pass and is never navigated with large boats—channel right side, which is the main body of the river.

At the head of this island is a settlement, and opposite it on the right side of the river are four others, two of which are newly made. No. 88 is about 3½ miles long.

Here and lower down are to be seen pelican, swan, geese, sandhill cranes and ducks, in millions. The sand bars for miles are covered with them, and at night their noise is so great that you can scarcely sleep for them. They sometimes rise from the small lakes adjoining the river, in such immense numbers, as almost to form a cloud over your head, the sandhill cranes particularly, whose noise you hear when you can no longer see them, their flight being very high.

## Island No. 89, 4½ miles below No. 88,    8 | 489

Is a small wood and willow island lying close to the right shore—channel left side at all times. It is about two miles long.

## Grand Lake, just below No. 89.

Though this is called a lake there is no appearance of one here at present, but is now grown up with willows, from the size of which the old bed of the river must have began near the head of No. 89, thence bearing off to the right, sweeping around and forming a great right hand bend, and crossing the present channel diagonally a mile below the foot of No. 89, thence bearing to the left, making as large a willow and cotton wood point to your left hand as the bend is on the right. At the lower end of this left hand point and enveloped among the young willow a considerable distance from the present channel, is Seary's Island, No. 90.

Distinguished by the tall trees with a growth of willows all round it. The lower point of the island approaches pretty near the river, and here it is easy distinguishing where the old bed of the river came in again, there being a young growth of timber to the left of the island broad enough for its former channel. It is about five miles from the foot of No. 89 to the foot of Seary's island. Near the foot of No. 90 is good landing, in quiet water and beside willows.

At the right hand point just below Seary's island is a large scraggy sand bar, to which has been given by some wag, the name of

## General Hull's left leg.

It was formerly a dangerous and deceptive enemy; it is now harmless, providing you bear well to the left and keep a good look out. The Mississippi used to flow over this bank of sand deep and smooth; its snaggy head latterly gets brushed by every log that passes; every wind that blows ruffles its prominent features; and every Kentuckian and Ohioan as they pass it by, 'shake their heads with a sentiment of regret and vexation.' Indeed the Pennsylvanians do not much like it, for though their losses have not been so severe, the mortification it has occasioned have been very galling to their feelings.

Island No. 91, 4 miles below No. 90,                    11 | 500

Is a small willow and cotton wood island in the middle of the river. In low water you must take the right side of it. In floods the left is good and the nearest. It is about a mile long. On the right side just above No 91, is a settlement.

Island No. 92, 6 miles below No. 91,                    7 | 507

Is near the middle of the river—channel left side in low water, in a tolerable state of the water the right is preferred. It is about three miles long.

On the right side of this island, and opposite its head, a sand bar begins and extends down a mile;

the foot of the bar is covered with willows, having a la ge raft of drift wood at their upper point. When you take the right hand pass of No 92, hug the right hand point to avoid being thrown on this bar.

Good landing just below the right hand point and opposite the head of No. 92, also at the foot of the island. Good landing along a handsome willow shore on the left side between Nos. 92 and 93.

### Island No. 93, 3 miles below No. 92,   6 | 513

Is in the middle of the river. At the head of this island two bars run out from each side of it. Best channel in low water left side, and pretty near the left bank. If you take the right pass, which is good in floods, keep near the right hand bank, avoiding the island in either case as much as possible. At the foot of No. 93 is a considerable eddy. No. 93 is about three miles long. Here commences the

### Nine Mile Reach.

Where you have a beautiful view of the river.

### No. 94, Stack or Crow's nest Island, 6 miles below No. 93,   9 | 522

Has been sunk by the earthquake or swept off by the floods; but just below where it stood, is a high sand bar, covered with young willows, and is about the middle of the river. This bar may grow into another Crow's, but it is to be hoped, not into another *Rogue's* nest [i 2]. The river here bears hard against the head of the bar, and also against the right hand bank—channel right side, near to the island, thence draws towards the right hand shore.

A creek empties in on the right side just above the two settlements. The Washita heads not far from this place, on which is a considerable settlement, 40 miles distant, and to which from hence is a cut road. It is thirty miles to Moorehouse's settlement on that river.

Crow's nest or Stack island was very small, and stood in about the middle of the Nine-mile Reach. A large bar had formed just below where the island stood, but it also has given way to the current, and is no more.

Four miles below this island (No. 94) is a sand bar in a right hand bend—channel on the left of it.

### No. 95, 7 miles below Stack Island,   7 | 529

Is close to the right shore, and on the left of it is a pretty long willow island—channel left side of both. No. 95 is about two miles long. The river here winds to the right.

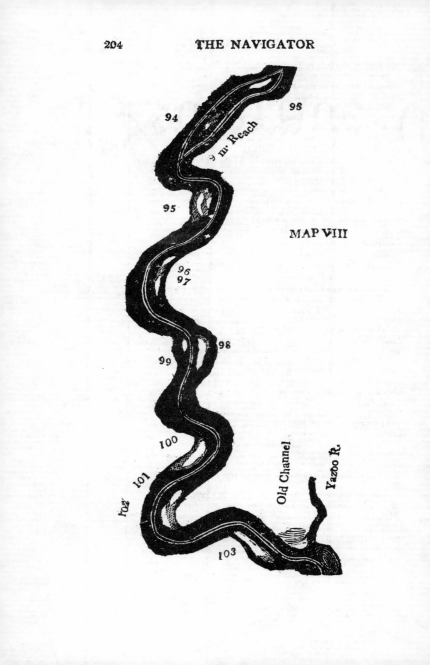

94

98

9 m. Reach

95

MAP VIII

96
97

98

99

100

102 101

Old Channel

Yazoo R.

103

The main shore in the left hand bend round this island is filled with snags and sawyers from the slipping in of the bank; keep pretty well out, as the current sets hard in among them. This left hand bend is about nine miles long. The right hand pass of No. 95 is narrow, and takes out suddenly below a right hand point.

### Nos. 96 & 97, 8 miles below No. 95,          10  539

Lie pretty close to the left shore, beginning just below a left hand point, and immediately above one another, having a small passage between them, and joined by a bar in dry seasons. No. 96 is much smaller than No. 97, they are about two miles long. —Channel to the right of both in all stages of the water.—Five miles below No. 96 is a sand bar on the right hand side of the river—channel on the left of it.

Opposite and below these islands on the right side are several small settlements.

### No. 98, 5 miles below No. 97,          546

Is pretty close to the shore in a left hand bend, and is about three miles long—channel on the right side of it in all stages of the water, and when the river is low keep pretty close to the island, leaving a bar at its head on your left hand. At the right hand point opposite the head of No. 98 is also a bar, which keep to your right hand.

### No. 99, a right hand point opposite No. 98,

Was once an island, but it is now joined to the main shore, and the channel which formerly run on the right side of it, is now grown up with willow and cotton wood. This is particularly distinguished from below the foot of the island, by an observable difference between the island timber, and that of a more recent growth in the former channel.

### No. 100, 9 miles below No. 98,          12  558

Lies below a right hand point and nearest the right side of the river, having on its right, and beginning a little above it, a long, slim willow island, between which and No. 100 there is a narrow but a tolerable safe pass in high water, but in low water it is nearly dry, as well as the small pass to the right of the slim willow island.—Main channel to the left of both islands, sweeping around the left hand bend. At the head of these islands are large rafts of drift wood, particularly at the head of No. 100, where a large sand and willow bar joins the island. No. 100 is about 4 miles long.

The slim island begins first and ends with No. 100, and a little below its foot is a very small island.

**Nos. 101 & 102, 2 miles below No. 100,**                6  5<s>6</s>4

Lie just below a left hand point, divided only by a small water pass.—Main channel to the right of both islands, round the right hand bend. The left schute of both is pretty good in high water, and if you take it, you must hug the left hand point, as it takes off pretty suddenly. No. 101 lies close to the left shore, 102 to the right of it and extending down a little below it. The river here bends to the left. From the head of No. 101 to the foot of No. 102, it is about 3 miles.

**No. 103, " *My Wife's*" Island, 9 miles below No. 102,**                                    12  576

Lies below a right hand point—channel left side. The right pass may be gone in floods, it is much the nearest, but not so safe

Good landing on the left side opposite 103, along a willow shore. The river bends to the right. This island is about 3 miles long.

Opposite the head of No. 103 on the left shore, the old bed of the river formerly ran across to the Yazoo, and entered that river two miles above its present mouth. This tract is marked by the young willows with which it is now filled.

Just below No 103, on the right side and in a right hand bend, is a considerable settlement, called SPAR-TA, on which resides judge Lindsey, below whose farm the river bears hard against the right hand bank, and it requires some pulling to keep out from among the fallen trees and snags near the shore. The bank having given way considerably in one place, an eddy is formed, but it presents no danger if you ply the oars well and keep pretty well out.

There are several small settlements on the right side between the Yazoo and the Walnut Hills.

**Yazoo river, [k 2] 3 miles below 103,**                6  582

Above and below the mouth of this river is a large willow beach, that very much spoils the appearance of its entrance, and gives it several mouths. In passing it, keep rather nearest the right hand shore to avoid eddies on both sides of the river.

**Walnut Hills, [l 2] 9 miles below the Yazoo,**                9  591

Here is a large eddy near the left hand shore which you must avoid in passing the Hills by keeping pretty well out. There is a good landing just below the eddy, and about opposite Mr. Turnbull's house. The river here makes a great left hand bend, bearing hard against the Hills, of which you have a very fine view before you get within two miles of them.

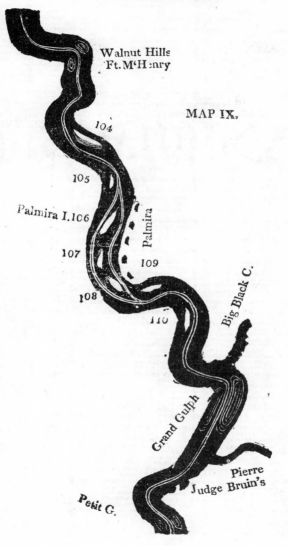

Walnut Hills
Ft. M'Henry

MAP IX.

104

105

Palmira I. 106

Palmira

107

109

108

Big Black C.

110

Grand Gulph

Pierre
Judge Bruin's

Petit G.

As you pass the Hills you have in view the river
for seven or eight miles below, and on the right hand
side several settlements.   Such is the crookedness of
the river here, that from seven miles below the Walnut Hills it is but four miles and a half across to the
Yazoo, while by water it is 16.

A sand bar,

Nine miles below the Walnut Hills, and a small
distance above Warrington, lying on the left side of
the river—channel past it close to the right shore.

WARRINGTON, 10 miles below Walnut Hills,   10   601

This is a small new village of the Mississippi territory, on the left bank of the river.   It has about 20 or
30 frame and log dwellings, and is the seat of justice
for Warren county.   Its subjection in high floods to
the inundations of the river operates against its progress and stability.   It was laid out in 1808-9 on lands
of Mr. Griffith.   Some distance back of the town
the land is high and possesses some good farms.
Half a mile above the town a small creek empties itself into the river.   Here, as all along the Mississippi, the water oozing out at the base of the bluff or
high land, contains so much mineral, part of which is
probably copper, that if drank by the cattle it frequently proves poisonous.   The inhabitants dare not drink
it.   It sickens, vomits, and sometimes purges.

A water possessing similar qualities oozes from the
banks of the Ohio, in many places towards its mouth.
I drank, with others, some issuing out in a small
clear stream opposite the mouth of the Tennessee.
It had a copperish and alumish taste, and the ground
over which it ran had the appearance of rusty iron,
but rather of a yellowish cast.   The quantity I drank
was small, and I could perceive no particular effect.
I was told at the time, that it had sickened several
who had drank of it.

At the first right hand point below Warrington and
a little above No. 104, is a large sand and willow bar,
which you keep to your right.   Here the river bears
hard against the left bank, and is washing away the
front of the farms.

No. 104, 3 miles below Warrington,          3   604

Lies close to the left side below a left hand point,
having a very small pass to its left, and which is
nearly blocked up with drift wood.   On the side of
No. 104 is a large sand and willow bar, reaching
down about two miles, below which is a handsome
willow beach, and good landing near the foot of the
island.

You keep the island and bar without difficulty on your left hand, taking the sweep around the right hand bend. Below the foot of No. 104, is a handsome settlement on the left side, and an abandoned one on the right. No. 104 is about three miles and a half long.

No. 105, Sand island, 1½ miles below No. 104,                                                    5 | 609

Lies close to the right shore, having but a small water pass on its right side—channel left side at all times. It is a small willow island one mile long. Opposite it on the right side is a settlement.

Palmira settlement.

This is a handsome settlement of about fifteen farms, closely adjoining. It was begun by the present settlers in 1801, but it was first improved about 35 years ago under British claims which are now put in by the original claimants, but in consequence of the beginning of their surveys being lost by the cavings of the river bank (it is supposed) their lines cannot be established, the board of commissioners therefore, had to consider their titles null and void, and the pre-emption rights of the territory (Miss.) to stand good.

The river round this settlement forms a singular tongue of land, it being but two miles lacking three chains from the upper settlement opposite the head of Palmira island across in a line with the tracts to where they strike the river again, although around by water it is seventeen measured miles.

Opposite this settlement, on the right side there is a lake within 100 yards of the river, which empties into the Tensaw, thence into the Washita, affording a good keel boat navigation from the head of the lake through the rivers just mentioned, into Red river, thence into the Mississippi. Such is the very singular manner the country on the right side of the Mississippi is cut up with lakes, bayous and rivers, all communicating their waters, and forming in every direction navigable streams from one end of the Mississippi valley to the other, which, to generations to come will be of immense value in facilitating settlements and commerce.

Palmira Island, No. 106, 3 miles below No. 105,                                                    4 | 613

Lies nearest the left side—channel right side. It is 4½ miles long. A settlement at the head of it.

No. 107, 2½ miles below No. 106,                          7 | 620

Channel good on either side. Two miles long.

A very large bar puts out from the left hand point, just below Palmira settlement, and nearly closes up half the channel, therefore, if you take the left side of Nos. 106 & 107, you must keep this bar well to your left hand, passing pretty close to the foot of 106 and to the head of 107. In very low water the left pass of 106 goes nearly dry. The right side of these as well as 108 is the main and proper channel in all stages of the water.

## No. 108, 1 mile below No. 107,  3  623

Lies pretty near the left shore—channel right side. It is two and a half miles long. No 109 lies close to the left shore just below No. 108—channel right side.

## Point Pleasant, 3½ miles below No. 108,  6  629

This is a handsome settlement on the right hand point 3½ miles below No. 108, and opposite Palmira Neck.

From opposite Point Pleasant to the upper settlement of Palmira, it is two miles less three chains across by land, and 17 miles by water, measured distance.

## Big Black Island, No. 110, 7 miles below No. 108 and about 4 below Point Pleasant,  4  633

Lies near the middle of the river in a left hand bend. Low water channel is on the left side; the right pass is safe in floods. It is three miles long.

There is a large sand bar at the head of No. 110, therefore keep pretty close to the left shore as you approach the head of the island.

## Big Black river, [m 2] 5 miles below No. 110,  8  641

## The Grand Gulf (Grand Goufre,) at the Big Black river.

Here is presented to your view a scene mixed with the singular and sublime. The river at a sudden turns to the right, rushes itself against a high point of land on the left, at whose base are some large rocks, which beat off the current, and, together with the suddenness of the turn, a large eddy is formed immediately below the bluff point, which extends down half a mile. On your right the land juts out to a very sharp and narrow point, and just below it and near the right shore, another eddy is formed, of less magnitude than the one on the left side. There is no danger in passing this place if you keep nearest the right hand point in high water, and thence nearly in the middle of the river, there being a broad channel, smooth and good between the two eddies, and if you should happen to get into either of these, you would only be detained a little while, and have some hard rowing to get out again. The prominent danger is in permitting your boat to get so far into the bend that she might get a stroke from the rocks at the foot of the bluff point. This however is easily avoided by a good lookout and timely rowing.

In low water you naturally sweep round near the left hand bank, and not far from the big rock at the base of the bluff point, then bearing out to the right to avoid the eddy on the left, and keeping a large bar, in the middle of the river and about a mile below the point of rocks, to your right.

At the sharp right hand point is a settlement, and another handsome one a little way below the Gulf on the left side.

A mile and a half back from the river on the left, is lake St. Joseph, 12 miles in length and a quarter or half a mile in breadth. It is fine for fish and fowl.

| | | |
|---|---|---|
| Bayou Pierre or Stony creek, | 10 | 651 |

From the mouth to what is called the fork of this river, is about 21 miles. In this distance there are several quarries of stone, the land of a clay soil with gravel on the surface. On the north side of this river the land in general is low and rich; that on the south is higher, but much broken.

Thirty miles up this creek is the village of Gibsonport, the seat of justice for Claiborne county, Miss. Ter. to which boats ascend when the waters are high in the Mississippi.

| | | |
|---|---|---|
| Petit Gulf, (Goufre) | 5 | 656 |

Here are eddies on both sides—keep near the middle of the river.

| | | |
|---|---|---|
| Island No. 111, 2 miles below Petit Gulf, | 2 | 658 |

Lies some distance below the first right hand point below the Petit Gulf and near the right shore. Opposite the head of this island is a bar in the middle of the river—the channel is near the left shore all the way around. It is about three miles long.

| | | |
|---|---|---|
| Island No. 112, 5 miles below No. 111, | 8 | 666 |

Lies in a bend pretty close to the right shore, and about half way down it, commences

Island No. 113, much larger than No. 112,

And lies also nearest the right shore. There is a good channel to the left of both these islands, the channel between them is good also. From the head

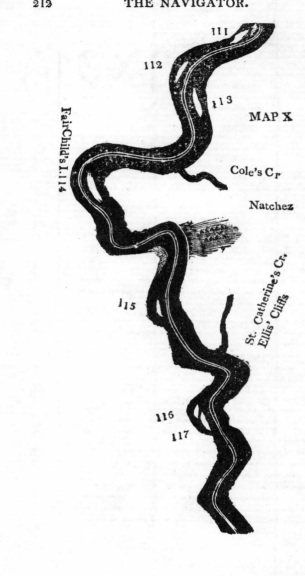

111

112

113

MAP X

Cole's Cr.

Natchez

Fair Child's I. 114

115

St. Catherine's Cr.
Ellis' Cliffs

116

117

of No. 112 to the foot of No. 113, it is computed to be about three miles.

The left hand bend is so great from the foot of No. 113 to a plantation five miles below Cole's creek, that it is 10 miles by water, and only 1¼ mile across by land. This bend may be called *Cole's creek Bend.*

A Bayou half a mile above Cole's creek, left side.

## Cole's creek, 5 miles below No. 113,      8 | 674

This is a considerable creek, spreading out into several branches, all well known for their great and sudden risings and fallings in times of rains. Some of the best settlements in the Miss. Ter. are on this creek and its branches.

Below this creek the bank of the river is tumbling in rapidly, and the shore, in consequence, is full of snags and sawyers, and it requires attention and not a little labor to keep out from among them. The right hand side is clothed with a handsome growth of young willows for several miles. Five miles below Cole's creek are good settlements on both sides.

Coles creek Bend is about 17 miles long, beginning at the head of No. 113 and ending at the head of No. 114, where the river again turns to the left.

## Fair Child's Island No. 114,      6 | 680

Lies near the left shore—channel in low water, right side, and pretty near the right hand shore, to avoid a large bar making out from the head of the island. In high water the left pass may be navigated with safety. The river opposite this island spreads out to a mile and a half in breadth. It is about four miles long, and has a pass through it near the lower end. Farms at and below the head of the island on the left side.

Nearly opposite the head of No. 114, the Bayou Teche goes out and empties itself by way of numerous small lakes, into the Tensaw, and the Tensaw by the same means, joins the Washita, thence by way of Black river you enter Red river and the Mississippi again. The settlers on the Tensaw and Washita take the route upwards, and entering the Mississippi by the Teche, descend to Natchez.

Fair Child's creek comes in on the left side a mile above the foot of the island.

At the foot of No. 114, you begin to see high bluff broken hills on your left, a small distance back from the river, and topped with pine trees, here also, for the first time, you are regaled with the sight of the deep green small leafed magnolia, which grow in numbers on the sides of those hills and in the bottoms along the river from this place to Natchez.

**Steam Saw mill, 5 miles below No. 114,**     9   689

On the right side of the river. It belongs to Messrs. Foster and Whethers of Natchez, who have done much business with it to advantage.

**Natchez Landing,**     6   695

Here you must incline towards the left hand bank from the right hand point two or three miles above Natchez, in order the easier to drop into the eddy at the landing. There is a small point with two or three big trees on it, just above the landing and at the head of the eddy, which shoots the current out with great velocity. Keep pretty near this point, and with smart rowing for a few minutes you will pass from the very rapid descending stream into the counter-current, where you will feel immediate ease, and be enabled to land your boat any where in the eddy, which is about a quarter of a mile long, and from 50 to 150 yards broad in a middling state of the water, and in the highest stages of the river as large again, when the waters reach the base of the bluff.

The Natchez landing affords a pretty safe harbor for boats, it being in the shape of a half moon. The winds seldom disturb it unless indeed very high, and not then to any damage if care be taken to fasten well and keep the boat easy and evenly afloat. Sometimes by unloading from one side and not to an equal amount on the other, and the boat being thus left untrimmed over night, the morning may find her filled, even without a storm, and what might have been prevented in half an hour by fulfilling the old maxim, "*leave nothing for the morrow that ought to be done to-day,*" now occupies twenty hours, and perhaps with the loss of much property.

### THE CITY OF NATCHEZ

Occupies a very handsome situation and one that is uncommon on the Mississippi. It is built on a hill nearly perpendicular, of about 200 feet in height from the surface of the river. This hill, called Bluff, affords a fine prospect up and down the river for two or three miles each way. The houses in Natchez are mostly frame with a great many doors and windows for the admission of the cool breezes in the hot months; they are low, being generally but one story high, and constructed principally for the convenience of business. The city contains about 300 houses. The bluff on which the town stands is about 200 yards from the river, and the intermediate space, called the Landing, is covered with a number of dwellings, taverns, dram shops, and trading houses. The bank being composed of a rich loose sand, the river is constantly making encroachments into the plain or bottom, and will in a few years, most probably, run close to the foot of the Bluff, and entire-annihilate this part of the city.

There is but one road from the Landing up the hill, along which are several Orange and Liquor shops, situated on the brink of the precipice. Though these shops might be undermined by a heavy rain, and precipitated down a steep of 100 feet, yet such is the temerity of their holders that they do not seem to think of the danger they are in.

In the year 1805, a large portion of the Bluff on the lower border of the town sunk in to a considerable depth; some houses were destroyed and others moved off with the earth without sustaining any injury.

Here are established several large mercantile houses which are much engaged in the cotton business, and many others less extensive; and a warehouse has been lately established for the storage of goods by James C. Wilkins & Co. who also do business on commission. The city has two printing offices, issuing weekly gazettes, a number of public inns, and many of the mechanic branches are carried on.

The staple commodity of this country is cotton, which is raised to great perfection, and with large profits to the planters, who accumulate immense fortunes by following it for a few years. Vast quantities of it are exported from Natchez, yearly, to the different seaport towns in the United States, and to many in Europe; England particularly, whose manufactories of cotton indeed depend very much on the American cotton planters for their supply of that article

Indigo, rice, flax, tobacco, hemp, and peas, are cultivated here with great success, and some sugar is made. Black cattle and sheep thrive well.—The Natchez country produces maize or Indian corn, equal if not superior to any other part of the United States; the time of planting it is from the beginning of March until the beginning of July. The cotton is generally planted in the latter end of

February and the beginning of March. Wheat does not succeed well; rye has been raised in some places with success. Plumbs, peaches and figs, are abundant; apples and cherries are scarce. The same kinds of vegetables raised in the middle states succeed here generally.

The same kind of mounds or tumuli found in different parts of the western country bordering the Ohio, and indeed throughout the United States, are also discovered in the Natchez settlements. In all parts where new plantations are opened, broken earthen ware is to be met with; some pieces are in tolerable preservation, and retain destinctly the original ornaments; but none of it appears to have ever been glazed.*

From the circumstance of the *Indian ware*, as it is called, being found, it would appear that this coutry must have been thickly settled centuries ago, perhaps with a people much better acquainted with the arts than any of the Aborigines of N. America ever did or do now pretend to boast. —This is a subject often touched upon by historians and speculative writers: But both early and late writers seem to be equally in the dark as to the period at which those settlements might have been made, how long they continued, by whom, or what nation or language of people made them, the cause of the total extinction or banishment of the settlers—and finally, they are equally confounded in the great chain of human events.—Not unlike the sea, whose waves are bounded by a Divine order, is man's mind— the same thing may be said of both, "so far shalt thou go and no farther."

Pope on the limitation of man's researches, has the following judicious observations:

> " Say first, of God above, or Man below,
> " What can we reason, but from what we know!
> " Of man, what see we but his station here,
> " From which to reason, or to which refer?
> " Through worlds unnumber'd tho' the God be known,
> " 'Tis ours to trace him only in our own."

Natchez is a port of entry, and vessels of 300 or 400 tons burden come up the river to the city, meeting with no other difficulty than the strength of the current and head

* Ellicott's Journal

winds. It is in lat. 31° 33′ N. long. 16° 15′ W. and is about 300 miles above New Orleans. It has a post office which receives and discharges the Mail regularly once a week—It is said that a line of stages is soon to be established from Lexington to New Orleans for the purpose of carrying the United States' mail.

It is observed that the wool of the sheep in the Natchez district is more hairy and less valuable than it is in the middle states; but that the mutton is well tasted—It is also observed that domestic animals generally are less tame and docile, owing perhaps to their being more able to get their living in the woods and swamps through the year, than is afforded them in the middle and northern states; and to their feeling less dependant on man for protection and subsistence.

The tract of good upland in the Natchez district is not very extensive, being about 130 miles in length along the Mississippi river, and not more than 23 in breadth. This tract is remarkably fertile, but the country being high and much broken with hills, a few years washing will render the soil of the cultivated parts less productive.

The making of sugar from the cane does not succeed very well in the neighborbood of Natchez; but from Point Coupee down to the Gulf of Mexico, it is manufactured to advantage and is the staple commodity of that part of the Mississippi—Sweet and sour lemons grow in great plenty on that part of the river.

The climate of Natchez is very changeable in winter, but the summers are regularly hot, being about 14° of permanent heat beyond that of Pennsylvania and New Jersey.

The accumulation of wealth being the grand polar star to which all the pursuits of the inhabitants are directed at present, the acquirements of taste and education perhaps are too much neglected in and about Natchez; but the valuable principle of hospitality generally prevails, especially among the rich planters; and it is this that affords true enjoyment and comfort to the stranger and the traveller, and never fails to leave lively impressions of gratitude on the mind of him who thus finds a friend, where, from the peculiar situation of the country, he is or may be most needed.

Island No, 115, 6 miles below Natchez,    6  701

Lies near the middle of the river, both sides are equally safe in a tolerable state of the water, the left being the nearest, in low water you must take the right passage. No. 115 is about 3 miles long, the river turns a little to the left.

St. Catharine's creek, ten miles below No. 115,    13  714

Enters in at a bend on the left shore.

Ellis's, or White Cliffs, one mile below,    1  715

These cliffs are on the left bank of the river, which bends short to the right.

Islands Nos. 116 & 117, 7 miles below,    7  722

The left of both is the best channel and the nearest, may go between them in high water; No. 116 lies nearest the left shore and projects a little above the head of No. 117; the river bends to the left; these islands are about three miles long.

Island No. 118, 14 miles below No. 116,    17  739

Lies in a bend on the right side, take the left passage at all times. No. 118 is about one mile long.

Homochitto river, 2 miles below 118,    3  742

Enters in on the left side, through a willow shore in a bend; it is a small river.

Buffalo creek, 6 miles below Homochitto,    6  748

This is a small creek, entering in on the left side.

Loftus' Heights, 2 miles below Buffalo,    2  750

Are on the left bank, and on which is situated Fort Adams.

Here is a large eddy on the left side immediately above the fort; in order to land near the fort, you must run near the lower end of the eddy before you touch it, then pull in and it will carry you up to the landing place. Pinkneyville, a small village, lies about 7 miles eastward of Fort Adams.

Line of Demarkation, below the fort,    6  756

This line was agreed upon between Spain and the United States several years prior to the latter government taking possession of Louisiana as ceded to it by France. It crosses the river in 31 degrees north latitude.

About one mile below the line is what is called the *Great Cut-off*, which is only five miles across, and it is reckoned as the river runs fifty-four miles round.

Red river, 9 miles below the line,    9  765

This is a very considerable river entering in at a large bend on the right shore. [n 2]

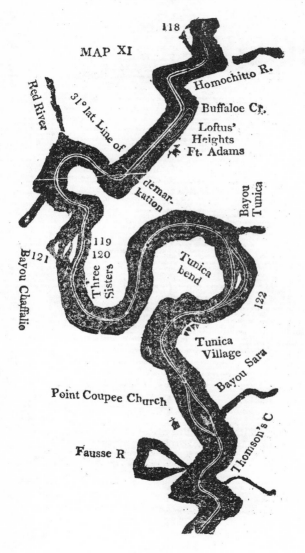

MAP XI

| | | |
|---|---|---|
| **Bayou Chaffalio, 3 miles below Red river,** | 3 | 768 |

Be careful that you keep pretty close to the left shore from Red river below this place, to avoid being drawn into this current, which runs out on the right shore with great rapidity. This is the first large body of water which leaves the Mississippi, and falls by a regular and separate channel into the Gulf of Mexico. Notwithstanding the magnitude of this river, it is not navigable to the Gulf Mexico, owing to an immense floating bridge, or raft across it, of many leagues in length, and so firm and compact in some places that cattle and horses are driven over it. This astonishing bridge is constantly augmented by the trees and rubbish which the Chaffalio draws out of the Mississippi, which it leaves in the westernmost part of that remarkable bend just below the boundary, and has every appearance of having been formerly a continuation of the Red river, when the Mississippi washed the high lands from Clarksville to the Bayou Tunica, (or Willings creek,) the traces of which are yet visible by the lakes through which a large current passes when the river is high. The distance on a straight line from Clarksville to the Bayou Tunica is not more than eight miles, but by the present course of the river, it is about fifty.

| | | |
|---|---|---|
| **Three Sisters, Islands Nos. 119, 120 & 121,** | 11 | 779 |

No. 119 is nearest the left shore, 120 lies to the right of it, and 121 still further to the right, close in a bend on the right shore; channel past these is always on the left in low water, may go between 119 and 120 in high floods; the river here is straight for several miles. No. 119 is about three miles long.

| | | |
|---|---|---|
| **Bayou Tunica, below the Three Sisters,** | 35 | 814 |

Is a small creek emptying in on the left side, on which are considerable settlements, cotton farms, &c.

| | | |
|---|---|---|
| **Island No. 122, 6 miles below Bayou Tunica,** | 6 | 820 |

Lies in the middle of the river, may pass on either side.

| | | |
|---|---|---|
| **Tunica Village, 4 miles below No. 122,** | 4 | 824 |

Is situated on the left bank of the river, which for about 30 miles above has been forming nearly a complete circle, and now comes within one mile and a half of the current where it runs nearly in an opposite direction. This is called the *Tunica Bend.*

| | | |
|---|---|---|
| **Point Coupée Church,** | 12 | 836 |

Stands on the right bank, and opposite on the left side,

**Bayou Sara empties in.**

About 9 miles up this creek is a beautiful settlement, cotton grows here in great perfection; David Bradford, Esq. formerly of Pennsylvania, resided here.

**A sand bar opposite Bayou Sara,**

Pass on either side, it is not seen in high water.

**Fausse Riviere, or Point Coupée,**     5 | 841

This is the old bed of the river, and is something like the Tunica bend, but not so large; it was cut through a few years ago by some Canadian Traders, by which a distance of about twenty miles is saved; it is on the right side of the present channel. Here is a beautiful settlement called

**Point Coupée Settlement.**

Here commences the embankment or Levee on the right side of the river, and continues down to New Orleans, and it is here where the beauty of the Mississippi and the delightful prospect of the country open to view. The banks of the river from below Point Coupée on the right, and from Baton Rouge on the left side down to the city of Orleans, have the appearance of one continued village of handsome and neatly built houses. They are frame buildings of one story high, and stand considerably elevated on piles or pickets from the ground, are well painted and nicely surrounded with orange trees, whose fragrance add much delight to the scenery.

**Thompson's creek, left shore,**     2 | 843

Up this creek also are some fine cotton plantations, the soil is remarkably rich and produces great crops.

**Cliffs on the left bank, one mile long,**     2 | 845

**Islands Nos. 123 & 124, 3 miles below,**     4 | 849

Lie in the middle of the river, the one immediately below the other, channel good on either side. They are about five miles long. Thence a fine river to

**Baton Rouge, 19 miles below No. 124,**     24 | 873

Is on the left bank of the river. Here commences the high lands contiguous to the river, and are thirty or forty feet above its greatest rise. Here also is a fine settlement, called

**Baton Rouge Settlement.**

The Levee on the left side of the river commences a little above this settlement.

**Bayou Manshac, or Iberville, left shore,**     15 | 888

Here the river turns short to the right.

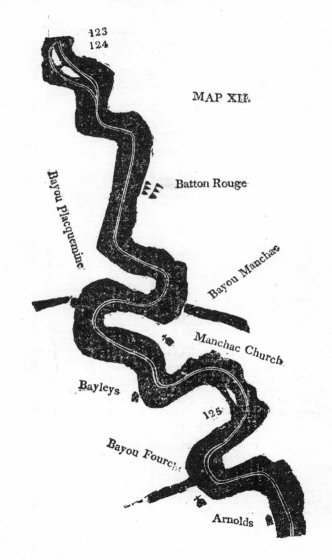

123
124

MAP XII.

Batton Rouge

Bayou Placquemine

Bayou Manchac

Manchac Church

Bayleys

125

Bayou Fourche

Arnolds

During the high waters the Bayou leaves the Mississippi in a considerable stream, and after passing the river Amitee, falls into lake Maurepas, thence into lake Pontchartrain, and communicates with the Gulf of Mexico near the mouth of Pearl or Half-way river. [o 2] This channel, which is at present much choked up, may yet become the principal communication to the coast of West Florida, which will be a much cheaper route of conveyance than by New Orleans. The island formed by this channel, and on which New Orleans stands, may be considered the Delta of the Mississippi.

| | | |
|---|---:|---:|
| Bayou Placquemine, or outlet, right side, | 8 | 896 |

Here the river winds short to the left, and from thence to New Orleans its general course is pretty near that of S. E. From this Bayou there is a water communication with the Opelousas.

| | | |
|---|---:|---:|
| Manshac Church, left bank, | 10 | 906 |
| Bayley's, a noted cotton planter, right side, | 4 | 910 |
| Island No. 126, 7 miles below Bayley's, | 7 | 917 |

Lies nearest the right shore, channel left side, it is about one mile and a half long.

| | | |
|---|---:|---:|
| Bayou la Fourche, (or the Fork) right side, | 10 | 927 |

From the Mississippi along this Bayou to the sea coast the settlement is compact.

| | | |
|---|---:|---:|
| La Fourche Church, right bank, | 1 | 928 |
| Arnold's, a sugar planter, right bank, | 4 | 932 |
| Baranges, a sugar planter, left side, | 5 | 937 |

This seat is said to be the handsomest on the river.

| | | |
|---|---:|---:|
| Contrell's Church, right bank, | 5 | 942 |
| Bona Cara Church, right bank. | 18 | 960 |
| Red Church, left bank, | 18 | 978 |
| Forteus's, a sugar planter, left bank, | 15 | 993 |
| Orange Grove, left bank, | 12 | 1005 |
| NEW ORLEANS, [p 2] | 4 | 1009 |

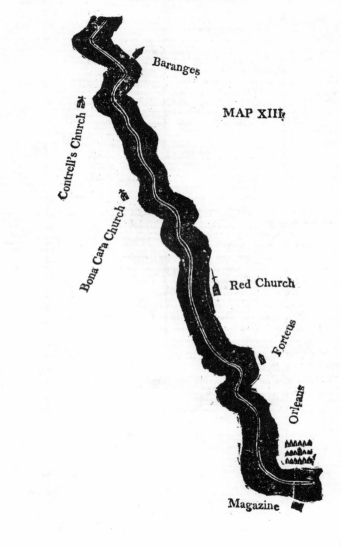

Baranges

MAP XIII.

Contrell's Church

Bona Cara Church

Red Church

Forteus

Orleans

Magazine

THE navigator having now arrived after an irksome passage of between five and six weeks, (about the time it takes to decend from Pittsburgh) at the grand mart of business, the Alexandria of America, he leaps upon shore with ecstasy, securing his boat to the bank with a careful tie, mounts the Levee, and with elated heart and joyful countenance, receives the warm and friendly hand of a fellow citizen, in whose integrity he confides, and to whom in confidence he can dispose of his cargo.—What a reverse in the situation of a trader, since the banks of the Mississippi have become the soil of the United States—since a governor of a republican people has been happily placed in the chair of not only one but many tyrants—since in fact he traffics with those to whom he looks up as friends, instead of those whose every glance was dire jealousy and suspicion; whose demeanor was bombastic pride and ostentation; whose pursuit and plan in trade was one continued system of bribery, fraud and chicanery, from the first authority in the old to the last in this their foreign government.—What a reverse in the situation of you, western Americans! What a conquest gained! a conquest equal to a second revolution! a vast and almost unlimited territory acquired without the loss of a drop of blood! Happy Columbians! prosperity smiles, must smile, on all governments equally mild, and equally just with yours!

The river opposite New Orleans is about one mile and a half in breadth, and notwithstanding the apparent velocity of the current and the distance to the sea, it " perceptibly ebbs and flows as high up as the city from 12 to 18 inches perpendicular."* It is about 108 miles to the mouth of the river from the city; to the English Bend it is 17 miles, to Fort Placquemines 48, thence to the *Passes*, where the river branches out into three parts, 24 miles, thence to the mouths of the river 19 miles. And here " the Mississippi discharges itself into a sea that may be compared to the Mediteranean, bounded on the north and south by the continents of Europe and Africa, as the Mexican sea is by the two Americas."

In a much admired and justly celebrated work,† the

* MS. Journal of Col. George Morgan.

† Jefferson's Notes on Virginia.

author of which, speaking of the convulsions that many parts of this country which he describes must have undergone in various periods of time, observes, with respect to the Gulf of Mexico, " While ruminating on these subjects, I have often been hurried away by fancy and led to imagine, that what is now the bay of Mexico, was once a champaign country ; and that from the point or cape of Florida, there was a continued range of mountains through Cuba, Hispaniola, Porto Rico, Martinique, Guadaloupe, Barbadoes, and Trinidad, till it reached the coast of America, and formed the shores which bounded the ocean, and guarded the country behind ; that by some convulsion or shock of nature, the sea had broken through these mounds, and deluged that vast plain, till it reached the foot of the Andes ; that being there heaped up by the trade winds always blowing from one quarter, it had found its way back, as it continues to do, through the gulf, between Florida and Cuba, carrying with it, the loam and sand it may have scooped from the country it had occupied, part of which it may have deposited on the shores of North America, and with part formed the banks of Newfoundland. But," says our author, "these are only the visions of fancy."

# APPENDIX.

—

## NOTES REFERRED TO IN THE DIRECTIONS FOR NAVIGATING THE RIVERS.

[a] HALF a mile from the ferry resides Mr. Tomlinson, an old and respectable inhabitant of the country. It is 40 years since he first settled at this place, on which some years ago, he laid out a town, intending it for the seat of justice for Ohio county, Virginia, but Wheeling being fixed on for that purpose, Mr. Tomlinson's town declined. He has a fine farm, level and fertile, and susceptible of great improvement. He keeps tavern for travellers, and what is a matter of curiosity to the lovers of nature, he has a fine pair of Elk, with several young ones. The grey hairs of Mr. Tomlinson bespeak the owner to have seen years to the amount of seventy, otherwise his vigor of body and healthy appearance would announce him to be a man of fifty or less. His wife, the partner of his youth, accompanies him on the venerable road of old age, equally healthy with her mate, and equally disposed to enjoy and to share with him in the advance of life, the happiness resulting from a virtuous connection in youth, and an amiable unity of minds for a period of forty years. Mr. Tomlinson is still in the spirit of bringing his place into more notice, and the last time I saw him (in 1812) he very anxiously inquired of me what a printing press would cost being quite in the humor of having one established for the good of his neighborhood. On my doubting the success of such an establishment in so thin and scattered a settlement, the old gentleman spiritedly replied, he was determined to have a press should he be obliged to buy the types and pay the whole of the expense of carrying it on himself.

[b] AN anecdote highly favorable to the population of the western country.—Mr. Charles Wells sen. resident on the Ohio river, fifty miles below Wheeling, related to me while at his house in October, 1812, the following circumstances :—That he has had by two wives (the last of which still lives, and is a hale smart young looking woman) *twenty two children*, sixteen of whom are living, healthy, and many of them married and have

already pretty large families.—That a tenant of his, a Mr. Scott, a Marylander, has also had *twenty two*, the last being now at the breast of its mother, who is yet a lively and gay Irishwoman, being Scott's second wife.—That a Mr. Gordon, an American German, formerly a neighbor of Mr. Wells, now residing on Little Muskingum, state of Ohio, has had by two wives *twenty eight children*. Mr Gordon is near eighty years old, active and hale in health. Thus, these three worthy families have had born to them *seventy two children*, a number unexampled perhaps in any other part of the world, and such as would make Buffon stare, when he ungenerously asserts, as well as several other classical writers* of Europe, that "animal life degenerates in America."

Mr. Wells further states, that a tenant of his son Charles, has a family of fifteen children.—That last year (1811) within a circuit of ten miles around him, ten women had born to them twenty children, each having had twins.—The banks of the Ohio seem peculiarly grateful to the propagation of the human species, and perhaps, stronger evidences could not be produced than the anecdotes just related. Indeed, an observation to this effect can scarcely be missed by any person descending that river, and calling frequently at the cabins on its banks. Children are the first object that strikes the stranger's eye on mounting the bank, and their healthful, playful noise, the last thing that cheers his ears after leaving the, not unfrequently ragged looking, premises.

Mr. Wells is sixty-eight years of age, and truly a hale, healthy looking man, and it is not uncommon for him to ride to Wheeling, a distance of 50 miles, in a day, and last year he says he rode to his brothers, 12 miles above Wheeling, and got there by sun down.

[c] THE largest SQUARE FORT, by some called *the town*, contains forty acres, encompassed by a wall of earth from 6 to 10 feet high, and from 25 to 36 feet in breadth at the base. On each side are three openings, at equal distances, resembling twelve gateways. The entrances at the middle are the largest, particularly that on the side next the Muskingum. From this outlet is a COVERT WAY, formed of two parellel walls of earth, 231 feet distant from each other, measuring from centre to centre. The walls at the most elevated part on the inside are 21 feet in height, and 42 in breadth at the base, but on the outside average only 5 feet high. This forms a passage of about 360 feet in length, leading by a gradual descent to the low grounds, where it probably at the time of its construction reached the margin of the river. Its walls commence at 60 feet from the ramparts of the fort, and increase in elevation as the way descends towards the river; and the bottom is crowned in the centre, in the manner of a well formed turnpike road.

* Raynal, Robertson, &c.

Within the walls of the fort, at the northwest corner, is an oblong, elevated square, 188 feet long, 132 broad, and 9 feet high; level on the summit, and nearly perpendicular at the sides. At the centre of each of the sides the earth is projected, forming gradual ascents to the top, equally regular, and about 6 feet in width.

Near the south wall is another elevated square, 150 feet by 120 and 8 feet high; similar to the other, excepting, that instead of an ascent to go up on the side next the wall, there is a hollow way 10 feet wide leading 20 feet towards the centre, and then rising with a gradual slope to the top.

At the south-east corner is a third elevated square, 108 by 54 feet, with ascents at the ends; but not so high nor perfect as the two others.

A little to the south-west of the centre of the foot is a circular mound, about 30 feet in diameter and 5 in height; near which are four small excavations at equal distances, and opposite each other.

At the south-west corner of the fort is a semicircular parapet, crowned with a mound, which guards the opening in the wall.

Towards the south-east is a SMALLER FORT, containing twenty acres, with a gate-way in the centre of each side and at each corner. These openings are defended with circular mounds.

On the outside of the smaller fort is a MOUND, in form of a sugar-loaf, of a magnitude and height which strike the beholder with astonishment. Its base is a regular circle 115 feet in diameter; and its perpendicular altitude is 30 feet. It is surrounded with a ditch 4 feet deep and 15 wide, and defended by a parapet 4 feet high, through which is an opening or gate-way towards the fort 20 feet wide.

There are other walls, mounds, and excavations, less conspicuous and entire, but exhibiting equal proofs of art and design.
*Harris's Tour.*

[d] A MILE north of New Lancaster is a singular elevation called the *Standing Rock*. It is situated in an extensive plain and on the edge of a large prairie. The south-west front shews a bare perpendicular pile of rocks of about 500 feet in height.— It may be a mile and a half around the base, and not more than about 30 by 100 yards across the top. The north-east side is tolerable easy of ascent, but I clambered up the south-west corner, and found it very difficult to ascend. In the edge of a projecting rock on the summit of this immense pile, looking to the south-west, and commanding a most extensive view of the surrounding flat country below you, is a *hole* of about four or five inches in diameter, a perfect circle, and evidently a work of arts not more probably than from 12 to 18 inches through, where it strikes the face of another rock. On approaching Lancaster from the westward across the prairie, the front and height of the "Standing Rock" has a romantic appearance, and forms a

pleasant contrast with the level country through which you have been travelling.

[e] *A floating grist mill.* AT this island, No. 42, we saw a mill of this kind in operation, grinding corn, attended by two little bareheaded boys. I should like to give the reader some idea of the novelty of this really temporary and moving machine, but one which, however, to a thinly settled country, and where regular mills are distant, is highly useful to the inhabitants on the river, since the expense is trifling, and easily constructed. It is fashioned something in this way: A flat boat of the scow kind carries the stones and running gears, which are simply constructed, and the stones small. One end of the shaft of the water-wheel is also carried by this flat, while the other end rests upon a large canoe beyond the wheel, and which lies parallel with the flat, and fastened to it by timber running across from the ends of the canoe to those of the flat, the timbers being strongly pinned down to each. This is all the labor the big canoe has to perform, to carry one end of the shaft of the ponderous water-wheel, which of course moves between it and the flat, having the cross timbers above and below. On the other side of the flat carrying the mill, is another boat which may be denominated the *tender*, having the bags and barrels of the ground and unground grain. It is also fastened along side and close to the mill boat. The two flats are covered with clapboards, the sides and ends being all open to wind and weather, with a view, perhaps, that the whole may be the less affected by the winds of the river. The canoe has no cover, nor oars, nor paddles. The whole machinery is fastened by ropes, or grape vines to a suspending tree, projecting rock or log, and thus afloat in a rapidly running current, the mill grinds night and day, as necessity compels, or inclination serves, without tax for ground-rent, mill-dam, or race.

[f] SEVENTY miles above the mouth of the Big Kenhawa and a little below the falls of that river are a number of salt works lately put into operation, and which yield an immense quantity of excellent salt. In August, 1810, there was 11 furnaces at work, each containing 60 kettles, and making at the rate of from 35 to 50 bushels of salt daily, averaging in all about 400 bushels per day  Since which (Dec. 1810) we learn that there have been five furnaces more erected, and make an equal quantity with the others; hence we may calculate the quantity made now to be about 580 bushels per day, or 174,000 bushels annually; which they can afford at the works at 70 cents, 50lbs to the bushel, and it can be freighted to Pittsburgh, 283 miles up the Ohio, for $1 50 per barrel, which will reduce it to the low price of *five dollars per barrel;* fifty, nay, in some cases, one hundred per cent. lower than we have been able to obtain Onondago salt. These salt furnaces are immediately on the beach or edge of the

river, and extend on both sides for six miles distance. In the first place they have to dig about 10 or 15 feet through sand and mud, when they come to the rock, then the boring commences with a two and a half or three inch auger, with which they bore from 60 to 90 feet through the solid rock, passing perhaps several veins of fresh water in that distance, which is kept from the salt by means of tin pipes introduced into the holes from bottom to top and tightly caulked at top where they enter the *gum*, as it is called. This gum, though made of a hollow sycamore, answers as a *coffer-dam*, within which a man works through the mud and sand, while it sinks with him to the surface of the rock, where its lower edge is tightly secured all round, admitting neither mud nor water from below and extending upwards beyond high water mark. Into this gum enters the tin pipe introducing the salt water from its hidden reservoir. Into the gum, pumps are then fixed, which are either worked by man or horse power, and the water conveyed from these in open troughs to the kettles, which are placed in a double row under a shed, and over a long hole cut in the ground, into which wood is cast for boiling them and evaporating the water. A furnace of 60 kettles when ready for operation, costs about 1500 dollars, and four hands are sufficient, when the water is pumped by hand, to keep a furnace of this kind going night and day, besides, indeed, two or three engaged in cutting and hauling wood. The salt is conveyed to the Ohio down the Kenhawa river without difficulty; the navigation, 5 or 6 short rapids, and these not worse than those of the Ohio any where above the falls, excepted, is good, having gentle and deep water all the way. The banks of this river are composed of a black loose earth; the bottoms on each side are rich and extensive, and tolerably settled, except those large tracts owned by the heirs of the late General George Washington, which are held at ten dollars per acre, a price too high it is thought for advantageous purchases.

The great strength of the water at these works surprises us into thankfulness for the bounty of Providence. From 90 to 130 gallons make a bushel of salt, while many of those of Ohio and Kentucky take from 500 to 760 and others from 700 to 900 gals. to make the same quantity. The works on Little Sandy in Kentucky, owned principally by Mr. Grayson, have the strongest water, except those of the Kenhawa, of any that I have heard of, and it takes from 250 to 300 galls. of that water to make a bushel of salt. Thus, when there is the greatest need for economy in living, owing to external distresses, arising from the world's wars of rage and madness, Providence has been kind enough to lead the ingenious hand of man through rocks as deep almost as the ocean, and as hard as adamant, where he has found in abundance the means of producing one of the most important necessaries of life at half the price hitherto paid for that article.

In some cases when the borer first entered the vein of salt water, it spouted up with great force twenty feet in height above

the surface of the rock. It would appear from this circumstance, together with the astonishing strength of the water, that
a rock of solid salt must be in the vicinity of such vein, and
that its meltings had filled the reservoir almost to bursting for
want of vent: or otherwise, that the fountain of salt is situated
among the Kenhawa mountains, through which issues a vein of
water, receiving its salt particles as it passes, and thence finds
its way among the crevices of the embowelled rocks to the
spot where it is now fallen upon. In either case it is equally
providential, equally fortunate to the citizens of the western
country and to their rising posterity. In some places below the
present works the rock has been perforated 200 feet without
finding salt water.

In the summer of 1812, salt water was dug for and found,
on Thirteen Mile creek, which empties into the great Kenhawa,
13 miles above its mouth. The water was found at the depth of
200 feet, and as strong as that at the upper works.—Furnaces
are erecting at this place, and salt making will be carried on
here also with spirit.

[g] IF the Virginians, and others who are fond of the fashion
of having whipping posts and pillories at the door of their
court houses, and as companions to their market houses, would
enclose them, that the feelings of the innocent might not be har-
rowed up at being obliged to see the scourging and sometimes
savage peltings inflicted on the poor wretched criminal, I would
have less objection to these machines of punishment. On what
principle, I ask, does society take upon itself the right of offend-
ing and injuring the innocent person, while it inflicts punishment
on the profligate and wicked. There is a pair of stocks before
the door of the house in which I write this note, and scarcely a
day or night passes, without seeing or hearing a victim of the
law, either lashed or pinioned. And more than once has my
slumber been disturbed by the rude shoutings of a felon clap-
ped in the stocks by the police after night. When a citizen
throws nuisances on the high way, street or lane, the laws call
upon him to remove them, or suffer the penalties of the law,
made and provided for in such cases. Has not that citizen an
equal right to call upon law-makers, or society, and insist on it
or them, to remove that which may be considered by the innocent a nuisance? Without a complete reciprocity between the
power that makes the law, or the law itself, and the citizen governed by it, there cannot be complete justice. On the other
hand, as it respects the criminal—Does the law inflict punishment, merely for the sake of punishing and disgracing the criminal, by public exposure; or are its judgments fulfilled for the
bettering of the person punished?—I will venture to say, a parent, master, or guardian, never discovered that a child, servant,
or apprentice was ever the better of having been punished to
public exposure. A child, punished and reasoned with in pri-

vate, softens down to repentance and a just sense of his guilt; humility and feeling attend his cries and petitions; and when the parent, guardian, or master, quits him, he quits him as having punished him not only for his past misconduct, but that his behaviour may be the better in future. If, however, on the other hand, the boy is not only punished for his crime, but *disgraced* also, by public exposure and derision, I hesitate not in saying, that the punishment is without effect, otherwise, indeed, than oblige a frequent repetition of the like punishment for redoubled crimes. The great object of the law ought to be, to make bad citizens better. And is it possible that any law-making body in their senses, could suppose for a moment, that, in order to make a bad man a good citizen, he must in the first place be *disgraced?* Where does this monstrous idea come from? Is it not completely savage? It is at all events very unchristian like—Barbarians are its authors—The deadly tyrants of Europe have practised it from the earliest periods of their histories, in order the better to alarm and enslave the world by their arts of blood and cruelty. From England, the American colonies, feeling bound to the mother country, and unable to act, think or make laws for themselves, imported the cursed principle of stocks, gibbets, gallows, witch-burning, &c. &c. After the patriots of '76, and the brave soldiers under WASHINGTON, gained independence for their country, men began to think for themselves. Gibbets, gallows, and stocks, were, in the northern and eastern states, by degrees cut down and cast away, as barbarous to the human eye, and as fit only for foolish kings and wicked tyrants. I readily admit that it is very difficult to get clear of old habits, instance the age of the practice of hanging men by the neck. The fashion is too old to be traced. We find king Pharoh waxed wroth at his chief Butler and Baker, and after keeping them in prison a while, took them out on his birth day, and ended his feast by hanging his chief Baker on a tree, as was interpreted by Joseph, when with them in prison, according to the dream of the chief Baker. *Gen.* xl. Haman was hung by king Ahasuerus on a gallows fifty cubits high, which Haman had erected by the advice of his wife Zeresh and other friends, for Mordecai the Jew. *Esther*, chap. vi. In 1108, king Henry I. of England, hung felons. The statute runs thus, "that he be hanged by the neck till dead." Before his time, felonies were punished with pecuniary fines. Since his introduction of it, the most petty larceny has been punished by death. For murder the judges of king George II, grandfather to George III, may stay the sentence, and appoint the body to be hung in chains or anatomized, but not buried, "King George III can hang a man, within benefit of clergy, for destroying trees or shrubs, in a garden or nursery, to the value of five shillings." And "without benefit of clergy, the law of England condemns a man to death, for picking a pocket to the value of twelve pence."—*Jacob's Law Dictionary, articles Execution, Felony, &c.* And political history tells us, that a poor woman was hung in London, some years since, for the crime of taking a loaf of bread out of a baker's shop. That on trial it appeared her husband had been pressed by the press gang, and that having several small children perishing with hunger, her feelings of humanity induced the act, which brought her to the ignominious death of the gallows.

Sawing asunder, beginning either at the feet or at the head, was a most cruel punishment. So it is said Isaiah was murdered by Manasseh, *Heb.* xi, 37. This terrible punishment is said to have taken its rise among the Chaldeans and Persians, and not very long ago, it was used in Morocco and Switzerland, if it is not still so. *Brown's Dictionary of the Bible, article Punishment,* where will be found a string of punishments, that would induce a belief, that man from the earliest periods of time, has wrecked his senses more in the invention of punishment for his fellow men, than any other subject of human ingenuity—David tore off the flesh of the Ammonites, by causing them to pass under saws, harrows and axes of iron, or caused them to pass through the burning brick kiln. It is also supposed he tortured to death two-thirds of the Moabites, *Judges,* viii, 16. 2 *Sam. &c.* Stocks were also an ancient mode of punishment, I thought their invention was more modern.

There is one principle of great importance to human justice, which man in all ages seems to have either lost sight of, or never considered, i. e. in making laws for his own government, he does not seem to have understood that he takes upon himself the prerogative of his God, when the penalties of these laws exceed the bounds of his own controul, as in capital punishments.

In America there are few crimes which bring man to the gallows, still there are a few, for an old fashion cannot be got rid of. The principle of *Eye for eye, tooth for tooth, hand for hand, foot for foot, &c.*\* cannot be forgotten. In Pennsylvania they hang for murder in the first degree—In Virginia, not long since, it was lawful to hang a man for stealing a horse worth thirty dollars.—Putting the stealer of an old horse into the same scale of retribution with him who takes away the life of a human being.—It would seem reasonable to conclude from the various crimes which bring men to the gallows, that the friends of this sanguinary mode of punishment, (or rather this mode of killing a man, for punishment it cannot be) are determined that men shall be hung at all events, it being the easiest and quickest way to get rid of them. The practice of other old fashions than stocks and gallows, might be mentioned, if further evidence was wanting, to prove the imbecility of the human judgment, which, it would appear, seldom begins to act on principles originally just, but which more easily falls into some beaten path, made on bad ground, and untenable but by amendments, additions, corrections and revisions.

\* Exodus, chap. xxi, verse 24.

For fear I may be misunderstood by some, and that my non-hanging principle may alarm others, who may doubt for a moment that I wish the wicked to go unpunished, and that I want to pull down one system, without giving a substitute—I observe, I am a lover of wholesome and good laws well administered—not sanguinary laws cruelly inflicted. That I am truly and sincerely a friend to the punishment of every person according to the extent of his crime, and the circumstances under which it may have been committed, without a strict scrutiny and examination into which, the infliction of the punishment must always be unjust.—That as a substitute for hanging, solitary confinement for life and hard labor proportioned to the guilt of the criminal—That for other crimes, theft, burglary, &c. &c. confinement to hard labor, also proportioned to the degree of guilt. The penitentiary system was commenced in Philadelphia, a few years ago, and has had the most beneficial effects. Improvements in the system are making daily, and there can be no doubt of its complete success, and happy tendency, contrasted with sanguinary punishments cruelly inflicted. Other states are following the example of Pennsylvania. Penitentiaries have lately been established in New York, Kentucky and Virginia, and we hope that a moral and religious sense of duty will induce every state in the union to adopt this most righteous mode of punishing the unfortunate perpetrator of crimes against the laws of the country. I am of opinion, instead of filthy and loathsome jails, a penitentiary ought to be established in every county, where men could live comfortably with industry; by earning something to support themselves on, and where the lesser crimes could be punished rationally, while the labor performed by the criminal, would go to the benefit of that society, which by his act of wickedness he had injured. Then should we get rid of whipping posts and pillories, nor longer see the human back scored and bathed in blood, nor a fellow being pinioned in the stocks, cruelly pelted, with clods and rotten eggs, and otherwise degraded below the dignity of the basest of brutes. It would seem, indeed, by tracing the cruelties of man, that the Great and Good Almighty, had created him for the wicked sport of each other, and that, as a *first principle*, he had planted in his heart, *malice*, as the inventor of the most refined and malignant modes of punishment, and *revenge* as the executioner.

[*h*] THE honest and unsuspecting French inhabitants of Galliopolis are not the first victims to the wiles of land speculators. Our country presents a most lamentable history of the misfortunes of an honest, industrious people, willing to risk their lives and every thing they possessed, to enter the forest with axes on their shoulders, to clear fields and make improvements, as a home for themselves and a patrimony for their children after them. And after having exhausted, by labor and toil, incident

to the settlement of a new country, the prime and vigor of life, what do they see enter their peaceful, and as they thought, secure doors, but *the sheriff with a writ of ejectment,* issued by a powerful land company, who, if they cannot frighten the settler off his land, frighten him into a compromise, by which he yields at least one-half his tract, and a great proportion of his labor, rather than be turned out of house and home altogether by expensive lawsuits. The north-eastern part of Pennsylvania is a grievous witness of this, and Kentucky no better, if not still worse. Galliopolis is situated in the "Ohio Company's Purchase," which was contracted for by Manasseh Cutler and Windthrop Sargeant, agents for the company, as early as 1787, and confirmed by an act of congress, passed 21st April, 1792, which granted the issuing of patents to Rufus Putnam, Manasseh Cutler, Robert Oliver and Griffin Green, for said tract, containing 1,500,000 acres, beginning a few miles above Marietta, just below the mouth of Bull creek, and following the Ohio until it reaches within a mile of the mouth of Indian Guiandot creek.— A separate tract of 100,000 acres was granted the same company, "on the express condition of becoming void, for such part thereof, as the said company shall not have, within five years from the passing of this act, conveyed in fee simple, as a bounty and free of expense, in tracts of one hundred acres, to each male person, not less than eighteen years of age, being an actual settler at the time of such conveyance."[*] The purchase of the people of Galliopolis *happened* to be within this last tract, and the Company *happening* to neglect fulfilling the condition of the grant, the land again reverted to the United States, leaving the Frenchmen *landless,* and in many cases *moneyless,* having paid the company a pretty smart price for their land in France in the first instance, and expended much on buildings and the improvements of their town. Congress, however, always willing to redress the aggrieved, listened with the ears of a father, to the petitions of this unfortunate people, and granted them by way of some indemnification for their losses, by an act passed 3d March 1795, a tract of 24,000 acres, within the state of Ohio, (then N. W. Territory) beginning one mile and a half on a straight line above the mouth of Little Sandy, thence down the river Ohio along the courses thereof eight miles when reduced to a straight line, thence at right angles from each extremity of the said line so as to include the quantity of twenty-four thousand acres." Four thousand acres of this tract was granted by Congress to John Gabriel Gervais, on condition of his personal settlement in three years, and the 20,000 acres to be equally divided among the actual settlers of Galliopolis on condition of settlement in five years after the date of their patents, otherwise, such tracts or lots not settled within that period, shall revest on the United States. *United States Laws, Vol.* iii,

---

[*] Laws of the United States, II. vol. p. 63. Folwell's edition.

*p.* 228. This last provision was afterwards repealed by Congress, and all who had obtained a patent were invested with their land in fee simple for ever. The Galliopoleans made the purchase of their land in France about the years 1788–9, at a French crown per acre, which they paid in cash at the time of purchase. They then prepared for a removal, and arrived in the United States in 1790 and 1791, crossed the mountains and descended the Ohio, and landed at their intended seat of happiness in March 1791. It is not difficult to draw a picture of the feelings of men, women, and children, when landing in a wilderness, contrasted with their late comfortable abodes in France nor hard to form an idea of their toils and privations in this their new, rude and savage situation.

[*i*] THE Big Sciota whose mouth, according to Hutchins, is in north lat. 38° 43′ 28″, is an important river of the state of Ohio. It is generally gentle in its current, bordered by rich flats, more or less subject to inundation in the spring seasons. It is navigable to Franklinton with keel boats, of 10 tons, and those of less burden go up it near 200 miles, to a portage of only four miles to Sandusky of Lake Erie, which at its mouth is large enough for sloops, and the lands on it among the best in the state. Sciota has many tributary streams, and flourishing towns and villages on its banks, and some of the best landed farms in the state. Its ancient remains, under the name of *Indian forts*, are numerous, and some of them very extensive and interesting, particularly those on Paint creek, one of which encloses 100 acres of ground ; and another on the top of a hill, six miles from Chilicothe, enclosing the summit of the hill by the appearance of an ancient stone wall, within which are the remains of a number of fire places, apparently of some kind of furnaces or ovens. The hearths, ashes, &c. and the appearance of the works generally, is worth a visit to the curious. The plains or prairies, on this river high up, are extensive and remarkably fertile, those of Pickaway particularly, on which are some fine farms, and one field containing near two hundred acres.

The principal branches of Sciota are, *Paint* creek, which empties in from the westward, about 10 miles below Chilicothe, and the villages of Bainbridge, Amsterdam, and Greenfield. *Darby* creek west side, which runs through the counties of Delaware, Franklin and Pickaway. *Big Belly* creek, and its two branches, *Walnut* and *Alum* creeks, east side, emptying in about 12 miles below Franklinton. *Whetstone* creek, east side, joins the Sciota at Franklinton, and runs nearly parallel to it, heading within four or five miles of the heads of the Sandusky ; on Whetstone is the town of Worthington, 10 miles up it ; New Baltimore further up and a little westward of the creek, and above it the village of Norton, they both being in Delaware county.

CHILICOTHE, which signifies *town* in the Indian dialect, is most beautifully situated on the banks of the Sciota, about forty five miles by land, and nearly seventy following the meanders of the river from its confluence with the Ohio, which it joins between Portsmouth and Alexandria.—In all that distance, the river has a gentle current, and unimpeded navigation for large keels, and other craft of four feet draught of water. It continues navigable for smaller boats and batteaux upwards of one hundred miles above the town towards its source to the northward, gliding gently through a naturally rich, level, and rapidly improving country. The situation of the town is on an elevated and extensive plain of nearly ten thousand acres of as fine a soil as any in America, partly in cultivation, and partly covered with its native forests. This plain is nearly surrounded by the Sciota, which turning suddenly to the N. E. from its general southerly course, leaves the town to the southward of it, and then forms a great bend to the eastward and southward.

Water street which runs about E. by N. parallel to the Sciota, is half a mile long and contains ninety houses. It is eighty-four feet wide and would be a fine street, had not the river floods caved in the bank in one place near the middle almost into the centre of it. There is now a lottery to raise money for securing the bank against any further encroachments of the river. Main street parallel to Water street, is one hundred feet wide, as is Market street, which crosses both at right angles, and in which is the market house, a neat brick building eighty feet long.—The court-house in the same street, is neatly built of free stone on an area of forty-five by forty-two feet, with a semicircular projection in the rear, in which is the bench for the judges. It has an octagonal belfry rising from the roof, painted white with green lattices, which is an ornament to the town, as is the small plain belfry of the presbyterian meeting house, a handsome brick building in Main street; in which street also is a small brick methodist meeting house. These are the only places of public worship in the town, if I except the court house which is used occasionally by the episcopalians and other sects.

The whole number of dwelling houses as I counted them in Chilicothe, is two hundred and two, besides four brick, and a few framed ones now building. I reckoned only six taverns with signs, which small proportion of houses of that description speaks volumes in favor of the place. There are fourteen stores, a post office, and two printing offices, each which issues a gazette weekly.

The scite of the town being on a gravelly soil, the streets are generally clean.—The houses are of free stone, brick, or timber clapboarded, the first of which is got in the neighborhood, is of a whitish brown color, and excellent for building. They are mostly very good, and are well painted. On the whole, I think Chilicothe is not exceeded in beauty of plan, situation, or appearance, by any town I have seen in the western part of the United States.

There is here a remarkable Indian monument in the garden of Winn Winship, esqr. fronting Paint street, in the very heart of the town. Like that at Grave creek, it is round at the base, about seventy or eighty feet diameter, but differs from it, by being round instead of flat on the top, which has an elevation of about thirty feet perpendicular from the level of the plain. It is formed of clay, and though it has been perforated by the proprietor nothing has been found to justify the common opinion of these mounts having been barrows or cemeteries. They talk of having it levelled, but I think it a pity to destroy any of the very few vestiges of aboriginal population which this country presents to the curious and inquisitive traveller.

From a steep hill about three hundred feet perpendicular height, just outside the western extremity of the town, is a most charming view of the streets immediately below, under the eye like a plan on paper; then the Sciota, from one hundred to one hundred and fifty yards wide, winding on the left, with some low hills about two miles beyond it, terminating the view to the north-east; while to the eastward and westward, as far as the eye can reach both ways, is spread a country partly flat, and partly rising in gentle swells, which if cultivation proceeds in equal proportion to what it has done since Chilicothe was first laid out about ten years ago, must, in a very short time present one of the finest landscapes imaginable.

A two story brick academy has been erected since the above was written, and is under the direction of the Rev. Mr. Wilson. A cotton manufactory was put into operation in the fall of 1810, by Messrs. Lamb and Williams. A third printing office was established here in the fall of 1809.

The town possesses a banking company, is the seat of justice for Ross county, and being on the great leading road from Pittsburgh to Kentucky, it is generally thronged by travellers and movers, from various parts of the United States. In maps there are mentioned a Chilicothe, an old Indian town on the Great Miami, which was destroyed in 1782, by a body of militia from Kentucky, and Old Chilicothe, 3 miles S. of Little Miami, also destroyed by the United States' troops in 1780. The first of these towns was supposed by General Harmar to have been the *Tawixtwi*, the English or Picque town, mentioned in Hutchins's map, situated on the N. W. bank of the Great Miami, 35 miles below the five mile portage to the Miami of lake Erie, and which was taken from the English by the French, in 1752.

*Jefferson* and *Circleville* are thriving villages, 20 miles above Chilicothe, the first in the Pickaway Plains, the other five miles above it, laid out as the seat of justice for Pickaway county, and curiously situated in an ancient fortification. The town is in the circle part of the fort, which is surrounded with two embankments, having a ditch between them and another around the outer bank. This *circle* joins and opens into a *square fort* by a gate-way of thirty or forty feet wide, out of which at each corner

and in the middle of each side is also a gate-way or opening.—
The square as well as the circular embankment, contains each
about five or six acres of ground. In the centre of the Circle is
a mound of four or five feet elevation, the banks or walls are
from four to eight feet high. I passed this place in October,
1810, and curiosity led me to ride around the whole fort, though
much of the square lay in a thick wood. Circleville had then
just been laid out, and men were engaged in digging the foundation and clearing the ground for the first buildings.

*Franklinton*, is the seat of justice for Franklin county, is pleasantly seated on the west bank of the Sciota, forty miles above
Chilicothe, and where Whetstone creek joins that river. The
town stands on high rolling ground, and the adjacent lands,
particularly westward of the town, are flat and cannot be excel-
ed for fertility and luxuriance of soil, but some of those bottoms
are subject to inundation in high floods of the river. When at
Franklinton in 1810, the landlord shewed me a large, heavy,
black lead looking lump of ore, in which he said there was a
considerable quantity of silver, a mine of which he had discovered near that place. I have heard nothing of this mine of that
precious metal since. The same gentleman had expended much
time and money, I was told, in hunting for silver banks, while
he kept the Yellow Springs on the head waters of Little Miami,
where, however, he had been unsuccessful in the search, the
shafts he sunk throwing up nothing but pieces of a gold looking
mineral affixed to the rock, which on trial proved to be pure and
rich sulphur, but even this in too small a quantity to make it an
object of pursuit. From Franklinton to Springfield, a distance
of 40 miles westward, is, with the exception of a few miles, one
continued high dry prairie, affording fine range for cattle and
sheep, pleasantly interspersed here and there with a thin growth
of low and rather scrubby oaks.—*Bixbie Settlement* is about 15
miles northerly from Franklinton. The spot lately pitched upon, and laid off by the commissioners appointed by the legislature, intended as the future seat of state government, lies on
the east side of the Sciota river opposite Franklinton, and is
finely situated on a rising ground. The ever venerable name of
*Columbus* has been given to the new town, as a presage of its
future greatness.

"Opposite the mouth of the Sciota used to stand the Lower
Shawanee town, removed from the other side, which was one of
the most noted places of English trade with the Indians."

*Hutchins.*

[*k*] LEXINGTON is about 64 miles S. W. of Maysville—It is
the largest and most flourishing town in the state of Kentucky,
though not the capital of it. It is the seat of justice for Fayette
county, and is finely situated in the heart of a well cultivated,
thickly settled, and rich country, on the north side of Town
Fork, a small stream which falls into the S. branch of Elkhorn

river—It has a court-house, jail, market-house richly supplied with the produce of the adjacent country; 4 places of public worship, a banking company, about 400 houses, many of which are handsomely built, and 2,400 inhabitants; 30 mercantile stores, several of which are large wholesale houses; a public academy, and other well regulated schools; 2 printing offices, issuing weekly gazettes, one bookstore, owned by Messrs. Maccoun, Tilford & Co. and a book bindery by Mr. Essex; a large duck manufactory, and another for manufacturing cotton and muslin: 4 large rope-walks; 2 nail factories, and many other useful manufactories carried on with spirit; all of which are duly encouraged by the body of the citizens, the only sure pledge of their success.

Lexington in fact, is a place of great business, and the inhabitants seem peculiarly and happily calculated to enjoy their situation, and the hospitality and friendship of each other. This prevailing disposition in the people, makes the place very lively, and highly agreeable to strangers—It is 22 mile. E. S. E. of Frankfort, and about 335 by land W. S. W. of Pittsburgh, lat. 38° 6′ N. long. 85° 8′ west.

Near Lexington are found curious sepulchres full of human skeletons; and the remains of two ancient fortifications, furnished with ditches and bastions, overgrown with large trees— A regularly walled well is also said to have been discovered by a person digging five or six feet beneath the surface; over the mouth of the well a large flat stone was found.

The foregoing observations were made in 1807, the improvements of Lexington since that time have been very great. It now contains acording to the census of 1810, houses and 5,230 inhabitants. It has fifteen extensive rope walks and bagging manufactories, which manufacture into ropes, rope yarn and bagging, about twelve or fourteen hundred tons of hemp annually; each bagging manufactory has from fifteen to twenty-five little black boys spinning, from ten to twenty looms, black men weavers, four or five preparing the hemp, and two or three white men overseers. The rope-walks have from ten to fifteen workmen about them; all as busy as nailers from sun to sun, winter and summer, each earning for his master, men and boys, at least one dollar per day. The quantity of hemp thus manufactured, when got into the eastern and southern markets cannot be worth much less than five hundred thousand dollars.—Lexington has now (1810) four considerable cotton manufactories, the newest and most extensive of which belongs to a Mr. Saunders, whose manufactured articles really do honor to our country, and to his industry and perseverance. Mr. Daniel Bradford has lately established a wool carding and spinning machinery, and one or two others are in operation. Levett & Smith have established the oil-cloth and oil-carpeting business, which succeed well.— Lexington has a well regulated and extensive public library, conducted by Mr. David Logan, secretary and librarian, whose steady and vigilant attention to it, gives life and credit to the institution.  A second bookstore has been recently established by Johnston and Warner of Philadelphia, and a third printing press by a French gentleman.  The town has a public theatre and a company of actors, these keep the gay part of the town lively, and sometimes raise the dull spirited.  The style of building in Lexington is handsome, the public inns, of which there are but four, are conducted on a plan and style of neatness which makes a man feel at home as soon as he enters them;  all goes on like clock work, every man to his post late and early, and the landlord the first and last in every department.  It is not uncommon to see 30 or 40 strangers sit down to a table, which is well supplied with every thing good and comfortable.  The writer of this note speaks more particularly of *Postlewait's tavern*, having lodged there, and not being acquainted with the others but from information.—The town has bath houses, warm and cold, and neatly conducted; these are a great comfort to the citizens and strangers, and a source of health and cleanliness.

Mr John Bradford sen. is about erecting a machinery for spinning ropes by the power of steam, the plan of which he is the inventor.  Mr. Bradford's mechanical genius is very considerable, and his labors in this way have been highly useful to the citizens of the town.  He established a press in Lexington about twenty-two years ago, the second in the western country, many of the types for which he carved out of wood.

The origin of the name of the town seems to have arisen thus: A number of hunters had made the spot where the town now stands a kind of encamping ground—by whom and some others, the scite of a town was laid out in the woods, and while the proprietors were seated around a fire on blankets, deer, bear and buffalo skins, consulting with each other what to name the newly laid out town, a man arrived in camp with the news of the defeat of the British at the *"Battle of Lexington."*  The circumstance gave joy to their feelings, and they unanimously agreed to call their new town in the west, "LEXINGTON."— Thus, the early history of Lexington—thus, its present prosperous situation; from whence we may calculate on its progress in manufactures, arts and sciences, its rise from infancy to manhood, and from manhood to a maturity of extent and greatness, which may not be exceeded by any inland town in the world.

[*l*]  THE village and settlement of *Columbia* is about a mile below the mouth of Little Miami, where the bottoms are extensive and amazingly fertile, but more or less subject to inundation; they are however, finely farmed.  My eyes and my appetite enjoyed here in 1810, a feast of the finest apples and peaches I think I ever saw or tasted.  The trees were bending to the earth with their loads of deliciously flavored fruits, while the ground was strewed with the dropping banquet, giving an

odor to the atmosphere, sufficient to induce a residence here of even angels themselves. But the unhappy contrast dwelleth in the house. There, what did my eyes see, and my ears hear? An infuriated husband insulting and wickedly scolding, his apparently modest and amiable wife and daughters, for the crime of going to meeting! They were attached to religion, he, perhaps, to its destruction. The presence of strangers ought, in common decorum, to have restrained his fury, especially while enjoying a well covered dinner table. But what stoppeth a madman in the ragings of his madness, or where stayeth the folly of fools.—The strong slayeth the weak without mercy, even so doth man. O drunkenness, what art thy misdeeds! are the extent of thy evils known, or are they not as the sands of the sea, numberless!

The Little Miami, (or as Hutchins calls it, Mineami,) has much fine land on its banks, a gentle current generally, but too shallow for navigation. Six miles above its mouth is the village of *Newtown*, on its east bank. Three miles further up the East branch enters, 22 miles up which is *Williamsburgh*, the capital of Clermont county, Ohio. Four miles above the East branch is the town of *Mi'ford*. Thence 15 miles to *Deerfield*; from which to *Lebanon*, the capital of Clinton county, it is four miles in a straight line. From Deerfield, pursuing the river, it is 16 miles to *Waynesville*. Thence to the *Yellow Springs* it is about 25 miles. *

Near the head waters of the Little Miami and within four miles of the falls of that river, are situated the Yellow Springs, in Green county, 60 miles east of Cincinnati, 60 west of Chilicothe, 9 from Xenia, the county town of Green county, 17 from Dayton on the Big Miami, at the mouth of Mad river, and 9 from Springfield, Champaigne county. The water of this spring is too *medicinally valuable* to remain unknown, yet such a place as the "Yellow Springs" is not known to more than perhaps one-twentieth part of the state in which they are situated. It has been a place of considerable resort for several years back, having at some seasons from one to two hundred visitants. At present, and for a twelve month back, there have been no general accommodations, hence the place is somewhat neglected – Yet the property is about to be purchased from the present priprietor, general Whiteman, by Messrs. Baum and Ferguson of Cincinnati, who seem to know the value of the spring, and are determined to put it in order for the reception of visitants. They also calculate on erecting light running mills on the water issuing from the spring, there being a sufficient quantity for this purpose, and the water can have a fall of about 70 feet in the distance of 150 yards.

The quality of the water is diuretic, bracing, and invigorating to the whole system, peculiarly beneficial to all nervous and debilitated affections; the most obstinate rheumatisms have been completely removed by them; and wonderful cures of old and new sores have been performed by applying a kind of *jelly*, as it is called, which is thrown out by the water, to the parts affected.

One case of a cancer in the temple of a woman was nearly cured, but she was hurried away too soon by her friends who lived at a considerable distance from the spring. The water is drank plentifully, and the shower bath is freely made use of, in which way it is highly strengthening and invigorating, throwing out immediately a general glow of warmth through the whole system. The color of the stones, wood, &c. over which the water runs, would seem to justify an opinion that it contains a considerable proportion of iron. The water throws out at times quantities of earth, which the people at the spring call *clay*, but which has every appearance of iron ore, except in its lightness. The mass of earth thus thrown out is immense, and it has formed a hill of 60 feet in perpendicular height, 150 yards across its widest part, where it forms the fourth of a circle, which fronts a beautiful limestone spring water rivulet passing at its base, and the two other sides come pointing to the spring in shape of a quadrant. The greater part of this mass of earth, of which there appears to be thousands of tons, makes, with burning and pulverising, an excellent *paint*, equal to any Spanish brown.

There appears to be something in the quality of this water that is at once singular and curious. It leaves the mouth of the spring in quantities sufficient to fill or pass through a hole five or six inches in diameter, and at a rapid rate, and before it gets to the base of the hill, which it seems to have formed, it entirely disappears, nor are there any appearances of water issuing out at the bottom of the hill, one or two limestone springs excepted. I examined or tried to examine into the singular operation of this water as it passed down the hill, and almost concluded that the greater part, if not the whole of it, changes its nature, and turns into a kind of moss, in the first instance, which is found all along its passage from the spring to where it disappears, and which is evidently formed by the water and the operation of the atmospheric air; this moss, which at first is as soft as down, in a more advanced state becomes gritty and more compact; and in a still further advanced state, it begins to assume the form of a petrifaction, and actually goes into a solid rock, as appears from examining the face of the hill in different places where the water has from time to time ran down, and changed its channel as it happened to be turned by chance or accident. In one place particularly in the face of the hill, is a rock thus formed of about eight feet in length and three feet broad, and not more than about six or eight inches thick, and thinner towards the edge. This rock, when broken, gives the same appearance of the fine dust, except that it is harder from having undergone a state of petrifaction. Twigs, branches of trees, leaves, &c. are found completely petrified throughout the hill.

The summit of this *Spanish Brown* hill is nicely clothed with a growth of young red cedars, which gives it a handsome and romantic appearance. The country around the spring is of second-rate white oak land, and all level, with several extensive prairies within two or three miles. There is a post office within three quarters of a mile of the spring, kept by a Mr. Miller. A Mr. Davis has resided at the spring and kept accommodations for a few visitants for the last twelve months, but is about removing. A Mr. Brodrick formerly lived there, but he moved about twelve or eighteen months ago, (now Dec. 1810) to Franklinton, on the Sciota river, 49 miles from the springs and 45 above Chilicothe, where he keeps a public house. While Mr. Brodrick resided at the spring he expended a large sum of money with others in digging for silver ore; they sunk twenty or thirty pits adjacent to the spring for this purpose, but without any other effect than the finding some sulphur adhering to spars, or a kind of flint stone.

In the bottom of a small rivulet half a mile east of the spring are two circular wells sunk in the solid rock, the one about three and the other seven or nine feet deep, and eight feet in diameter; the one is to be seen on passing by, they being on each side of the road, the other is filled up. The deepest is said to have been cleared out 10 or 15 years ago, and a *plate or ball of copper* was found among the stones and dirt thrown out.

What are called the *Cliffs* of the Little Miami, four miles east of the Yellow Spring, is a place of great natural curiosity. The rock through which the river passes for half a mile appears to have been cleft asunder by some great shock of nature, and now lets the water pass in a channel not more, in one particularly singular place, than three or four feet wide, and so deep in the lowest stage of the water that soundings have been made for fifty feet without finding bottom. From the top of the rock, to the surface of the water is a distance of about 50 or 60 feet, and so narrow at the top that it can be leapt over in one place by an active man. A gentleman from the state of Kentucky on a visit here with some ladies, had the temerity to try this leap, and had the good fortune to escape with his life, for it being broader than he calculated on, he caught on the opposite side with one leg and arm to a root or bush, and with difficulty escaped a fall of 60 or 70 feet perpendicular, among huge rocks and roaring water. On approaching this place you are at once struck with such a degree of timidity that you are glad to hold to the trees and twigs while peeping into the gulf below, and after a few minutes anxiously searching for the current of the river, winding and roaring through its narrow and rocky bed, you feel relieved in making a safe retreat from the brink of the dark and awful abyss.

On the Little Miami are a number of very curious ancient remains, forts, mounds, &c. and few streams possess better mill seats, or a greater number of mills than does it, having already 10 or 12 in the distance of 40 or 50 miles, among which is a paper mill. Its head spring adjoins the line between Champaigne and Madison counties, and below the Yellow Spring, Massie's,

Little and Big Beaver, Sugar and Cæsar creeks, are added to
the general stream as tributaries; Tortle, Obannen, and Shaw-
ney creeks enter it still further down, the last a little above Mil-
ford, but on the opposite side to it.  At its mouth the Little Miami is about 70 or 80 yards broad, and meanders a distance of
70 miles in its whole extent.  The bottoms for several miles
above the mouth are subject to an annual flooding, in consequence the fertility cannot be exceeded, but it prevents their
tillage.

  [m]  LICKING river, an important steam of Kentucky, divides itself into three principal forks.  On the middle fork is
the Lower and Upper Blue Licks, where have been made great
quantities of salt, but latterly stronger water being found in different places of Kentucky, the works at the Blue Licks have been
given up, it taking from 700 to 900 gallons of the water to make a
bushel of salt.  The hills around the Upper Blue Licks, are numerous, rocky, and much broken, wild and unproductive.  When
there in the summer of 1810, I could not help but admire,
while rambling over the hills, the very singular manner in
which the rocks were filled with appearances of animal and vegetable substances, marine shells, particularly the cockle; the
whole shape of a bird, in form like the bat; the butterfly, &c.
These appearances were not only exhibited on the surface of
the rocks and small loose sand and limestones, but on breaking
them, the whole mass appeared a growth of this mixture. This,
indeed, is a feature of the character of Kentucky.  I have never
discovered the appearance of a fish in the rocks, that I recollect
of.  This may have arisen from the quick decay of that animal
when exposed to the atmosphere, and before it could be incor-
porated in the mass which now forms these singular growths of
rocks.  This idea goes to suppose this country was once a great
sea or lake, either of fresh or salt water, and that these substances, after the great convulsion of nature which occasioned
dry land to appear, were thrown together in the struggle, and
being exposed to a different element, from animated and soft
vegetable bodies, Time, the moulder of Nature's matter, has
shaped them into massy rocks, as we now find them.
  Major John Findley, who resides at the upper Blue Licks, and
who *did* own them, but like most of the original settlers of Kentucky, has left his land, by the intervention of a *said to be* better
title, informed me that about the year 1780 when he first settled
these Licks, then a perfect wilderness, that shortly afterwards
in digging a well for salt water, at the foot of the hill on the
west side of the river, the diggers fell upon an old well, and after passing down it 19 or 20 feet, they found an *iron wedge* of
the common size of those intended to split rails.  Had not Daniel Boon made a stand in Kentucky of a previous date to the settlement of major Findley, I should have been for putting this
wedge to the account of American antiquities. But Col. Boon, the

meritorious first settler of Kentucky, says, "On the first day of January 1778, I went with a party of 30 men, to the Blue Licks, on Licking river, to make salt for the different garrisons in the country.*

The water of the Licks is drank for health; some seasons there is a considerable concourse of people at the springs, and frequent benefits received by the visitants, not more, perhaps, from the quality of the water, which contains sulphur, iron, and magnesia, than from the novelty of the romantic appearance of the place. Five or six miles above those Licks, is one of the most valuable grist mills in the state, belonging, I think, to Mr. Riddle. Twenty-five miles above these Licks a little to the south of Licking, is Mud Lick, now known by the more fashionable name of the *Olympian Springs*. At these there is generally a large concourse of people during the warm months of summer; some visit them for health's sake, others for pleasure. There are several springs here, some strongly sulphurous, others altogether chalybeate. These last issue out at the base of a curious round knob of a hill, four or five hundred feet high, a little to the north of the sulphur spring. The accommodations at these springs are good, and I will venture to say, no person who admires nature's variety, will leave them dissatisfied. The singular formation of the country, which seems to consist of the growth of a number of short, steep, high, and curiously formed hills, rising out of a flat, cold soiled plain, whose products, however, are numerous, and whose variety of vegetable growth would feast and charm the botanist and philosopher.

The columbo grows here in abundance and in great perfection, equal, if not superior, to the columbo of the island of Ceylon, sold in our shops. I have used both kinds, and prefer the American. It is a beautiful plant, especially the third year's growth, which shoots up a handsome purple colored stalk, seven or eight feet high, having but few leaves, and at top small branches issue bearing the flowers, and small leaves tinged with purple and yellow. The large leaves which spring from the root, are of a fine yellow color; these surround the stock, and operate as conductors of the rains and dews necessary for the nourishment of the plant, whose roots are found as thick as a man's rist, spreading two or three feet in length, not far from the surface of the ground, and of a fine rich yellow color. September, when the large leaves which are then very yellow, begin to fall to the ground, is a proper time to gather the roots. They are then to be washed clean, and cut into quarter inch pieces, and dried, either in a warm oven, or on strings in a warm room, and afterwards kept from the damp. Either in wine, or spirits and water, or as a tea for the common drink of the day, there are few more agreeable or better *tonics* than the Ame-

* Filson's Kentucky, published in 1784,

rican columbo root.* The first and second years the columbo, has no stalks, but leaves, in the manner of the tobacco plant, the third year it bears its seed, then the roots die, therefore it is classed among the triennial plants. There are a number of other valuable medicinal plants in this tract of country. The late captain Michael Findley, who owned and first settled the Mud Lick, but who, like his unfortunate brother John, left it, and in the same manner, by a *said to be* better title,† shewed me,

---

* This is the root of an unknown plant, which, however, is conjectured by Willdenow to be a species of bryonia. It was supposed to have its name from a city in Ceylon, from which it is sent over all India. But more recent accounts say, that it is produced in Africa, in the country of the Caffrees, and that it forms an important article of commerce with the Portuguese at Mosambique, in the province of Zanguebar. It is generally brought in transverse sections, from half an inch to three inches in diameter, rarely divided horizontally. This is evidently done to facilitate its drying, for the large pieces are all perforated with holes. The bark is wrinkled and thick, of a dark brown color on the outside, and bright yellow within. The pith in the centre is spongy, yellowish, and slightly striped. Its smell is slightly aromatic, and readily lost when not preserved in close vessels; its taste is unpleasant, bitter, and somewhat acrid; the bark has the strongest taste; the pith is almost mucilaginous. Its essential constituents are, cinchonin, and a great deal of mucilage. It is accordingly more soluble in water than in alcohol. The tincture is not precipitated by water, and does not affect the color of infusion of turnsol, or solution of red sulphate of iron.

*Medical use.*—In India it is much used in diseases attended with bilious symptoms, particularly in cholera; and it is said to be sometimes very effectual in other cases of vomiting. It often produces excellent effects in dyspepsia. Half a drachm of the powder is given repeatedly in the day. Its introduction into practice in England has been chiefly owing to the late Dr. Percival of Manchester, and it has in general been found to answer expectation: but it is to be regretted, that it is often exhibited in a very decayed state, from the want of a regular supply.

*American Dispensatory.*

---

† How hard, how peculiarly unfortunate, for a man, with his numerous family, at the eve of an honest and well spent life, to lose a home, dearly earned by the toils of a vigorous youth. " Hard, indeed, is his fate and galling his feelings," who thus gets stripped of house and land, when too far spent to renew another beginning, and when, instead of weeping, rejoicing ought to accompany his grey hairs in peace to the end of his earthly journey. The unfortunate first settlers of Kentucky have many

while riding through the woods with him in 1810, about fifty kinds of very valuable and rare plants, highly medicinal, beautiful in flower, and delicious in fragrance. He took me to what he called his *botanic garden,* four miles west from the springs, a piece of ground ten acres in extent, surrounded with woods, filled, truly filled, with the " wild flowers of nature," in such beauty and variety as seldom to be met with in any other part

tears to shed, those who ought to have gained every thing, have gained nothing. What ought Daniel Boon to have gained? something at least to support his tottering old age. He entered lands as he thought sufficient for his purpose, and after the " Bloody Ground" (a name Kentucky first went by) began to be settled, Daniel improved his farm, and raised a numerous family. After he thought all secure, and the dangers of the wilderness had subsided, how do we find him treated! His lands by decision of law, taken from him, his goods sold, and in spite of reasoning, he abandons his state, won in blood and toil, uncommon to most countries, forsakes friends and his own family, shoulders his rifle, crosses the Ohio, and ascends the Missouri, beyond the color of those, the sight of whose faces seems to have been a burden to him, and whose conduct had been cryingly ungrateful. Here then do we see, in the 80th year of his age, the heroic, the meritorious first settler of Kentucky, Daniel Boon, sitting with his gun across his knees, at the door of a meek and lowly log cabin, on the wilderness bank of the Missouri!—We see him for a moment, roused with a lively countenance by the sight a of deer leaping through the woods on the opposite side of the river, or by the cackling of turkeys on boughs of the trees overhanging his mansion—in another moment his countenance falls to dejection—again he is elated by the recollection of the nobleness of his former deeds—sad and pensive he again falls to his seat.—He shakes his head—"my limbs," says he, " these knees, once the glory of my youth, now fail me, my bones seem marrowless, my flesh shrivelled, these eyes too, (lifting his gun to his face and endeavoring to take sight at a distant object)—yes, these eyes of mine have lost their true vision, the object trembles before the muzzle of my rifle, and the more intent I look, the worse they get, they have become (rubbing them with his right hand, while his gun rested on his left arm) absolutely dim."— He again with a sigh of regret, seats himself cross legged, and resting his rifle against the logs of his cabin—In a low voice is heard, " yes, Daniel Boon, you are no longer yourself, age, trembling age, has taken place of vigorous youth—And must I die in distress," says he emphatically, " will these legs of mine not carry me to yonder point, where haunts the deer, where flounces the turkey in the tree tops ?"—We see him again make another effort, the effect of dire necessity, old age struggling with hunger and starvation.—Thus do we leave colonel Daniel Boon.

of the state. The lobelia,* a very valuable plant in medicine, particularly for the asthma, grows here in abundance, and a hundred or more of other kinds, whose names I am sorry I have forgot, not having taken a note of them at the time.

Among the curiosities of the Upper and Lower Blue Licks, are the *Buffalo Roads*, which are still to be seen all through the country on Licking. They visited the Licks in such immense droves, frequently 1000 at a time, say the old hunters, that in their hurried marches to the springs they formed great and broad roads, bearing down every thing in their way, trees excepted, and forming on the sides of hills deep paths and roads as if they had been dug.

Near the Olympian Springs are two furnaces well supplied with good and convenient ore. One is an air furnace, the other goes by water. Licking heads near Great Sandy, runs a distance of 180 miles, and enters the Ohio by a mouth 130 yards broad, it is navigable about 70 miles. Little Licking, the western branch, heads not far from Boonsborough on the Kentucky river.

[n] CINCINNATI is handsomely situated on a first and second bank of the Ohio, opposite Licking river. It is a flourishing town, has a rich, level, and well settled country around it. It contains about 400 dwellings, an elegant court house, jail, 3 market houses, a land office for the sale of congress lands, 2 printing offices issuing weekly gazettes, 30 mercantile stores, and the various branches of mechanism are carried on with spirit.—Industry of every kind being duly encouraged by the citizens, Cincinnati is likely to become a considerable manufacturing place; it is 82 miles N. by E. of Frankfort, and about 380 by land S. S. W. of Pittsburgh, N. lat. 39° 5' 54" according to Mr. Ellicott, and W. long. 85° 44'. It is the principal town in what is called Symms's purchase, and is the seat of justice for Hamilton county, Ohio.

---

* This plant grows in moist places in Virginia, and bears the winters of Great Britain. It is perennial, has an erect stalk three or four feet high, blue flowers, a milky juice and a rank smell. The root consists of white fibres about two inches long resembles tobacco in taste, which remains on the tongue, and is apt to excite vomiting.

† Dr. Barton says, that it is considerably diuretic, and Mr. Pearson found, that it generally disagreed with the stomach, and seldom failed of affecting the bowels as a strong cathartic. It certainly possesses no power of curing syphilis; even the Indians, when they have the disease, are glad of an opportunity of applying to the whites. It is said to have cured gonorrhœa.

The Cherokees use a decoction of the root of the lobelia cardinalis as an anthelmintic. And the Lobelia Inflata has been used in leucorrhœa.

*American Dispensatory.*

It has a bank issuing notes under the authority of the state, called " *The Miami Exporting Company.*"—The healthiness and salubrity of the climate; the leveness and luxuriance of the soil; the purity and excellence of the waters; added to the blessings attended on the judicious administration of mild and equitable laws; the great security in the land titles; all seem to centre in a favorable point of expectation, that Cincinnati and the country around it, must one day become rich and very populous, equal perhaps, if not superior to any other place of an interior, in the United States. The scite of Fort Washington is near the centre of the town; it was a principal frontier post—It is now laid out in town lots.

Two considerable cotton manufactories have been lately established in Cincinnati, one by Mr. Hurdus, and another by Messrs. Baum & Co. and others are about to be established by an extensive company forming for that purpose. The citizens of Cincinnati, and those of the adjacent country seem to have a large share of a public and enterprising spirit, which is bent at this time towards the establishment of domestic manufactories, and the forming of companies for the collecting and transporting to market the surplus produce of that extensive and fertile country. A company of this kind has already formed itself at Hamilton on the Big Miami, and one on the Little Miami, and another extensive company is about forming at Cincinnati for the same purpose. According to the census of 1810, Cincinnati contained 1,217 males, 1,006 females—total 2,223 souls.

There have been lately added to Cincinnati another bank, under the name of the *Farmer's and Mechanic's Bank.* It has already formed a good credit, and does business to advantage. A *steam mill* is about to be put into complete operation, of seventy horse power, erected and owned by Messrs. Ormsby and Stanley, and others. This mill is designed for grinding grain, and for moving machineries for various kinds of manufactories.— Two *Breweries* have been lately erected, and make excellent beer and porter, in quantities sufficient for home consumption and for exportation. Two *bookstores* and a *bookbindery* have been recently added to Cincinnati. Doctors and Lawyers are plenty, Cincinnati wanting as few of these if not less, than any other part of the union, the inhabitants being pretty much in the habit of doing their business in their own way, and the climate so healthful that few drugs are wanted, other than those produced by the gardens of the town and adjacent country.— Religion is not neglected here, for a fine large church has been recently erected. Schools are numerous and under tolerable regulations, public houses are well accommodated, and afford a good and cheap living. The streets, some of the walkways excepted, are unpaved, and of course very muddy in wet weather. Mud, however, is as common in the streets of the western towns as sand in New Jersey. What occasions bad roads here, rain, there it makes them good.

Major Buskirk, a respectable farmer near Louisville, inform-ed me he assisted in building a blockhouse on the spot where Cincinnati now stands, and immediately opposite Licking river, in July, 1780, it being the first attempt to settle that part of the now state of Ohio. On the 6th August following, a battle was fought between 1000 Virginia and Kentucky militia, and the In-dians, at Piqua on Mad river.

Cincinnati was laid out by judge Symms, in May, 1788, who, the same year brought out from New England and New Jersey, a number of settlers who seated themselves in the vicinity of the new town, between the two Miamies.

The blockhouse was enlarged by the United States, and kept as a frontier post; called fort Washington, until Wayne's trea-ty with the 12 nations of the northern Indians, whom he defeated, August 20, 1794. The treaty was signed at fort Greenville, on the western branch of the Great Miami, shortly after the defeat of the Indians. After this the town of Cincinnati and the coun-try around began to improve rapidly.

The district of country formerly called the "North Western Territory," was erected into a territorial government under the old Congress. After the adoption of the new and present con-stitution in 1789, Congress accepted that territory into the union as a sovereign and independent state, by act passed 3d March 1803, when it was organized under the name of the *State of O-hio.* Cincinnati was the seat of the territorial government, and the state government continued there until 1806, when it was moved to Chilicothe, thence to Zanesville, and again back to Chilicothe.

What adds to the commerce of Cincinnati is the line of barges running regularly from that place to New Orleans, descending loaded with the produce of the country, and returning with car-goes of sugar, coffee, rice, hides, wines, rums, &c. and dry goods of various kinds, and cotton from Natchez. Messrs. Baum and Perry and Mr. Riddle, have a line of barges constantly engaged, and some others are also employed in this business. These bar-ges carry about 700 barrels, and are long in proportion to their breadth, 9 men conduct them down, from 24 to 32 up stream, oars and poles are the principal dependence, they have sails al-so that are frequently useful. Cordelling, where the water is too swift to be stemmed by the force of the oars, or too deep for the poles, is the only alternative and a bad one it is. They de-scend from Cincinnati to New Orleans in about five weeks, un-less they run day and night, when half the time serves, but with much risk. An instance occurred in February 1813, when a barge descended from the falls of Ohio to Natchez in 14 days and five hours—nothing ought to induce such running but a case of life and death. They ascend in about 80 or 90 days, some-times much longer. The part the most indifferently managed about a barge, are the sails. Few of the bargemen are sailors, and without one on board, the sail had better be thrown overboard. A fine barge was upset in the river opposite Natchez in a gale of wind and hail on the 17th March 1813, owing, it is presumed, to a failure in the proper and timely management of the sails, which were all spread to drive her up stream. Four men were drowned, and a valuable cargo of groceries, &c. lost, a few bales of cotton excepted. It is with the sails of a vessel, as with the tools of a shop, it requires a master to work them to advantage. Any strong able bodied man, can soon learn to pull an oar, or heave at the pole, and if he makes a mistake with either it is of little consequence; not so with sails, the elements operate upon them, and much care and knowledge are required to manage them with safety and benefit. Owners of barges ought to see to this point, and not leave their barges to the mercy of heedless headstrong crews, who care for nothing but their wages, and whose ignorance is as liable to run them on a sand bar as to hit the main channel. By a neglect of the pattroon for five minutes in the cabin, I have seen a full loaded barge grounded on a sand bar, and detained two days.—The crew saw the bar, but it was not their business to prevent the accident !

It would, however, be well how soon the barging business, propelled by manual forces, could be got rid of, and the steam power substituted. And this would be done soon no doubt, but for the overwhelming patent of Fulton and Livingston, which secures to them *all* the navigable rivers in the United States *for fourteen years,* for all boats propelled by the steam power, NO MATTER ON WHAT PRINCIPLE THE STEAM OPERATES.

[*o*] GREAT Miami, Assaranut, or Rocky river, is a large and important river of the state of Ohio, possessing many tributary streams, fine lands, extensive settlements, towns, villages, mills, &c. It has a stony bed, rapid water, but no falls. Its principal branches, are, first, White Water river, which enters it from the west, about 10 miles above its mouth. The greater part of this branch is of the Indiana territory, having but about 10 miles of its course in the state of Ohio. Then comes in on the west side, Indian, Two-mile, Four-mile, St. Clair, Elk, Franklin, Bear and Wolf creeks : Dick's, Clear and Hale creeks, on the east side : These bring us to the forks, or three main branches, all entering together just above Dayton. The South-West Branch runs through Preble, Stark and Miami counties ; and on Greenville creek, its most westerly branch, Fort Greenville is situated, in Stark county ; and five miles south of it is Fort Jefferson, and 21 miles south of the last is Fort St. Clair, near the head of St. Clair creek, 44 miles north from Cincinnati. From fort Greenville to fort Recovery it is 12 miles N. W. by N. and 12 to fort Lorrimore N. E  The two last forts are on the Indian boundary line. From fort Lorrimore to fort Defiance at the juncture of Au Glaise river with the Miami of the lake, it is 75 miles nearly north, thence to the rapids 75 miles, in a straight line. Making a distance by this route, of 232 miles

X

from Cincinnati to the rapids of the Miami of lake Erie; allowing nothing, however, for the crooks in the road. From the rapids to Frenchtown on the river Raisin it is 40 miles; thence to Detroit 40 miles. Fort Malden is 16 miles below Detroit at the head of lake Erie on the east side.—Detroit fort and town is situated in N. lat. 42° 30', on the W. side of the river, or strait Detroit, the connecting water between lakes Erie and St. Clair, and which is about 23 miles in length, and opposite the fort half a mile in breadth, but much broader above and below it, and deep enough for vessels of great burden. The channel of the strait is gentle and wide, but incommoded by several islands, one of which is more than 7 miles long according to Mr Hutchins. In 1775, fort Detroit, then in possession of the British, was near a mile in circumference, built with stockades enclosing 100 houses, built regularly on streets crossing each other at right angles. One entire side commanded the river. Its situation is delighful, and in the centre of a pleasant fruitful country. For 8 miles below Detroit, and for the same distance above it, on both sides of the river, the country is divided into well cultivated plantations, and from the contiguity of the farmers' houses to each other, they appear as two long extended villages. The inhabitants, who are mostly French, are about 2000 in number, 500 of whom are as good marksmen and woodsmen as the native Indians themselves.

Fort Detroit was surrendered, by the American commander, brigadier general Hull, to the British and Indians under major-general Brock, on the 16th of August 1812, without firing a single gun. Two thousand brave backwoods-men, were compelled by the dastardly and unprecedented violation of military honor of their general, to surrender to an enemy of inferior force, and without having had it in their power of trying which could do the other the most harm. In rage and madness, many of the American officers on being informed of the surrender, broke their arms to pieces, while tears of regret, mixed with sorrow and vexation, sprung from the eyes of valor, for this ignoble sacrifice of their country's honor. General Hull, and between three and four hundred regulars, were taken prisoners of war to fort George; the militia and volunteers, were permitted to return home on parole, on condition of not lifting arms again during the continuance of the war. This affair was the beginning of the present war, being the *second* with the British nation. Whether it was a misfortune or not, time must determine—It was immensely mortifying, and a considerable loss of public property, and a chain of disasters, defeats, and calamities, have since happened to the American forces. There is a providence, however, which always consoles the honest and brave, and which changes calamity into prosperity, and weeping into rejoicing. The cause of the Americans is the cause of righteousness—Providence, therefore, is with them, and will as before, if they are true to themselves—bring them out with redoubled glory.

General Winchester on his road to Detroit, was defeated in a very bloody and warmly contested battle with the British and Indians, at the river *Raisin*, Jan. 22, 1813, when he and the brave fellows under him, had to surrender to superior force.

In May following 3000 British and Indians, made a terrible onset against fort Meigs, commanded by general Harrison on the river Raisin, but after five days siege, the enemy retired with considerable loss. The Americans lost some valuable officers and men on this occasion, but the defence made by the besieged was such as to gain applause for bravery, and a knowledge of military tactics. Here major Amos Stoddart fell, a valuable officer, and an experienced engineer.

The middle or main branch of the Great Miami heads within a few miles of Sandusky, a large navigable river of lake Erie, and to which there is a portage of 9 miles. On this branch are the villages of Piqua west side, Stanton and Livingston east side. *Mad* river is the easternmost branch of the Great Miami ; it is a beautiful stream, having swift and transparent water, with a fine gravelly bottom. It washes the edges of some of the prairies on your road from Springfield to Franklinton, and heads at a spring on the Indian boundary line, a few miles above Zanestown. URBANA, the capital of Champaigne county, lies four miles east of Mad river. *Springfield*, a smart village of the same county, lies 14 miles below Urbana. DAYTON, the capital of Preble county, is handsomely situated on a level tract, just below the junction of Mad river on the east side of the Miami, and 25 miles below Springfield. There is at the mouth of Mad river, a handsome saw and grist mill. The French formerly had an establishment on Mad river. *Franklin*, east side, lies 14 miles below Dayton in a straight line. *Middletown*, east side, 8 miles below Franklin. HAMILTON, east side, the capital of Butler county, 10 miles below Franklin. *Coleraine*, on the east side, and *Crosby* west side, are situated opposite to each other, 9 miles below Hamilton, and 15 from the mouth of the river.

The Great Miami is a most valuable stream for mills, it already has many valuable grist and saw mills on it. It is about 200 yards wide at its mouth, where the land is so low, that it is subject to inundation for several miles up, and on both sides, otherwise the junction of this river with the Ohio, would form a handsome site, and a very advantageous situation for a town. It is navigable to the Pickaway towns, 75 miles up, where the river is contracted to 30 yards in width, above which canoes go 50 miles further to the portage between it and Sandusky of the lake. The western branch goes within a few miles of Au Glaize river, a branch of the Miami of the lake to which there is a portage of five miles.

[p]   ANIMALS' bones of enormous size have been found here in great numbers. Some skeletons nearly complete were not long since dug up 11 feet under the surface in a stiff blue clay. These appeared to be the bones of different species of animals, but all remarkably large. Some were supposed to be those of the mammoth, others of a non-descript. Among these bones, were two horns or fenders, each weighing 150 pounds, 16 feet long, and eighteen inches in circumference at the big end; and grinders of the carnivorous kind, weighing from three to ten and an half pounds each; and others of the graminivorous species, equally large, but quite differently shaped, being flat and ridged. Ribs, joints of the backbone, and of the foot or paw, thigh and hip bones, upper jaw bone, &c. &c. were also found, amounting in the whole to about five tons weight.

Of the history of the mammoth we are much in the dark.—Of animals having once existed carrying these enormous bones, there can be no doubt. Their present existence is much doubted; and the only proof we have to the contrary, is a curious tradition of the Indians, handed down to them by their fathers, which being delivered by a principal chief of the Delaware tribe to the governor of Virginia during the American revolution, is recorded in the following words :—" That in ancient times a herd of these tremendous animals came to the Big-bone licks, and began an universal destruction of the bear, deer, elks, buffaloes, and other animals which had been created for the use of the Indians : that the Great Man above, looking down and seeing this, was so enraged, that he siezed his lightning, descended on the earth, seated himself on a neighboring mountain, on a rock of which his seat and the print of his feet are still to be seen, and hurled his bolts among them till the whole were slaughtered, except the big bull, who presenting his forehead to the shafts, shook them off as they fell; but missing one at length, it wounded him in the side; whereon, springing round, he bounded over the Ohio, over the Wabash, the Illinois, and finally over the Great lakes, where he is living at this day."

*Jefferson's Notes on Virginia.*

There are places at the Big Bone Lick, where the salt water bubbles up through the earth, that are rendered a perfect quagmire, admitting nothing heavier walking over them than geese or other light web-footed fowl. Cattle dare not venture nearer than to their edges. One of these places appears bottomless, for no soundings have ever been found; throw in a ten feet rail endwise and it buries itself; another embraces near a quarter of an acre, over which grows a very fine and short grass. May it not be reasonable to account for so many of the mammoth's bones being deposited at this place, by presuming that in their seeking the salt water, and venturing a little too far, or otherwise, that their own enormous weight pushing them forward too far for recovery, and sinking, thus were buried one after another to the number we now find their remains. The places where their bones are now found are tolerably hard from filling up by the washings of the small stream which runs through them, and from having been much dug up and the mud exposed to the sun.

Mr. Colquohoun, a Scotch gentleman, resides at, and owns this singular spot of ground, and has two extensive salt furnaces at work, which are able to make about 60 bushels per day, notwithstanding the weakness of the water. Mr. Colquohoun has been at much labor and expense in fixing his furnaces in a superior stile, particularly in the retention of the heat, and saving of fuel. His kettles are of an oblong square, coming to about half the size at bottom that they are at top; they hold about 12 or 15 gallons, and are fixed close together in a double row, having their edges covered with sheet lead lapped down closely on all sides, so as to prevent any heat from escaping; the fuel is introduced into a grated furnace whose mouth is closed by an iron door.—The kettles rise gradually from the front to the chimney, so as to occasion a sufficient draught of air. The first kettle in the furnace is round and contains about 100 gallons, and as this receives the greatest degree of heat, and evaporates the water much faster than the smaller ones, they are partly supplied from it after the water has boiled down considerably, and the back small kettles are supplied from those near the front. The kettles are filled with the salt water in the first instance from a wooden pipe running over the middle of the furnace, having spigot holes on each side; this is supplied by a pipe from the general reservoir filled from the leading troughs.

Mr. Colquohoun was engaged (Sept. 1810) in boring for salter water, and had got 150 feet through the solid rock with an inch and half auger, and was determined to bore 50 feet further. If he failed here, to try two other places, embracing the three important points of the tract where the salt water was supposed to be embowelled.

Pigeons are seen here in thousands, in the proper season, and the noisy paroquet in considerable flocks. The pigeons seemed to be crowding on trees nearest the pond of salt water, as if wishing to get at it; I saw none drinking, and am ignorant whether they give salt water the preference. It is not uncommon to find large " *Pigeon Roosts,*" in the neighborhood of Salt Licks, which distinguish themselves by the old timber being stript of its limbs and deadened, and young timber springing up in its place.—There is something interesting in the very singular manner of the pigeons crowding together in such immense flocks as to break down considerable trees, and crushing themselves to death by the breaking and falling of the limbs on which they light, and may be more spoken of hereafter.

The Big Bone Lick is in the state of Kentucky, 20 miles from Cincinnati, on the road leading from that town to the falls of Ohio. The land about it is flat and cold, with scrubby timber, and there is no cleared ground in view of the Lick, not even a garden, notwithstanding, it is worth a visit to the curious, and the superior intelligence and hospitality of its worthy proprietor makes such a visit well paid for. The back water, in the very high stages of the Ohio, has been known to inundate this place, and extend for some distance above it.

*Note for Cave in Rock, p.* 124. LITTERARY THEFT—In looking over the pages of "Fessenden's Register of Arts," published in Philadelphia, I was pleased to find in it p. 372-3, a description of this rock as taken from "Harris's Tour," and as I penned it from the mouth of a gentleman on whom I knew I could rely, and who had visited it a short time before. I was then engaged in publishing the Ohio and Mississippi Navigator, and this account of the " Cave in Rock" was inserted in the edition of that work of 1803 or 1804. The Rev. Mr. Harris purchased a copy of that edition at my bookstore in Pittsburgh, when on his route through the Ohio country, from which he inserted the description of the "Big Cave" in his "Journal or Tour," as being in his opinion, it is presumable, correct and interesting. This was well enough, but Mr. Harris, as a *divine* and as a respectable man and considerable author, ought in common justice, to have given a reference to the work from which the extract was made. In consequence of his neglecting this piece of courtesy, Mr. Fessenden gives "*Harris's Tour*" as authority for the description of this singular rock. The moral of all this is, that Mr. Fessenden was right, the rev. divine wrong, by fathering that which did not belong to him.

This, however, is among the least of the robberies committed on the Ohio Navigator. A well known and much celebrated character of Europe has taken liberties with this book, which, had he done the like to a butcher's stall, they would have brought him to the gallows long ere this. This great personage is no other than "*Thomas Ash, esq.*" author of "Travels in America," published in London, and republished in the United States in 1809. As the ingenuity of Mr. Ash is so well shewn, and so different to the common mode in like cases, his method of committing a "literary theft" is worth taking notice of.— Most literary thieves are silent and say nothing of the work from which they are extracting matter, of which they wish the world to believe them the authors. "Thomas Ash esq." takes a different road, by denying the existence of the book, while he is quoting whole pages at a time from it. His account of the Allegheny, Monongahela and Ohio rivers, the instructions for their navigation, the towns on their banks, distances from place to place, &c. is taken verbatim from a copy of the edition of the Ohio and Mississippi Navigator he purchased when in Pittsburgh in 1806. And after he gets through his account of those rivers, places, &c. as copied from the Navigator or Pilot, he observes, "*I am less particular on this subject, understanding that*" *a Pilot for the rivers*" *is now in the press at Pittsburgh, and will soon be published, and thus I am saved of much tedious detail!*"—

These may not be the exact words of Mr. Ash, quoting him from memory, but this is the amount of his expressions, and the idea he wished to convey to the public, that his "Travels in America" were of an earlier date to the Navigator, and however, the better part of his work may be founded on it, by thus denying the existence of the book, he comes out in London fair and square as an original author, and a great and wonderful traveller. Wonderful he is, to be sure, for he tells tales that are wonderful, but which are as far from the truth as the earth is from the sun's centre.

I forgive Mr. Ash for this "literary theft," as the practice has become common now a days, but I am not going to forgive him for the *bone theft* he committed on my friend Doctor Goforth, then of Cincinnati, now of the city of New Orleans, than whom a better man does not exist, and the last man in America Mr. Ash ought to have thus basely deceived and cheated, for in his house he eat of his bread, and partook of his friendship and hospitality, while a stranger and sojourner in the land. The particulars of this circumstance are briefly this : Doctor Goforth had for several years been engaged in collecting the mammoth's and other enormous bones, at the Big Bone Lick in Kentucky, and at an expense of much time, labor, and of many hundred dollars. In the year 1804 or 1805 he conveyed about five tons of these bones to Pittsburgh, with a view of transporting them to Philadelphia, and sell them to Mr. Peale, or to the American Philosophical Society. The bones however remained in Pittsburgh some time. Mr. Ash had passed through Pittsburgh, and descended to Cincinnati. There learning that Doctor Goforth had a very valuable collection of *Big Bones*, he soon ingratiated himself into the Doctor's good graces, and entered into written articles with him to become his agent for the sale of the bones, he being allowed a specified part of the clear profits of sale, and New Orleans being fixed upon as the market for their disposal. Accordingly Mr. Ash returned to Pittsburgh in 1806-7, with an order from Doctor Goforth for the bones. They had been deposited with the late Doctor Richardson, who delivered them to Mr. Ash, (or *Arvil*, the name he then went by.) The bones were boated to Cincinnati under the command of Mr. Ash, thence he proceeded to New Orleans, where he made a feint to sell them, and was offered *seven thousand dollars* for them. He observed that that sum was not one-tenth of their value, and from New Orleans shipped them to London. Where, no doubt, he has accumulated an immense fortune by exhibiting that great natural treasure of curiosities to the court of that metropolis, while their real owner here is laboring under all the difficulties of the loss of so valuable a property. Thus Mr. Ash, a poor adventurer from Ireland, who introduced himself at Pittsburgh in 1806, wishing to take up a school for the education of children, is now seen at the court of London, exhibiting Doctor Goforth's

*Mammoth Bones*, and writing books defaming America and its citizens.

The following communication, politely handed me by Doctor Goforth, will further illustrate the subject of the Big Bones.

Sir,

I beg leave to address you on the part of the American Philosophical Society, to request that you would favor the members of that institution with a description of the bones of a large animal with claws, which you procured in the western country.— The accounts which have been circulated by travellers respecting the size of the foot, have particularly attracted our attention. We have been induced (by information from the same source) to believe that some bones of the mammoth were in your collection—being possessed of all the bones of that animal, except those of the head, we will only ask you for information of that part of the mammoth—but an account of all the other unknown bones will be interesting to us.

At the same time, I beg leave to ask your opinion respecting the probability of procuring more of those bones, and your advice concerning the method of attempting it.

If your avocations will permit you to favor the society with an answer, please to address it to the President of the United States, who is President of the Society.

With great respect,
I am your friend and servant,
CASPER WISTAR, Jun.

Dr. Goforth.
*Philadelphia, Dec. 1,* 1806.

—

*Respected Sir,*

I received a letter from Casper Wistar, jun. dated 1st December 1806, on behalf of the American Philosophical Society of Philadelphia, requesting information concerning the head of the mammoth; the bones of a large animal with claws; an account of other unknown bones; and also my opinion of the probability of procuring more bones, and the method of attempting it—and I was desired to address my answer to you.

The bones I collected were unfortunately entrusted to the care of a person who descended the Mississippi with them some months since; whether he proceeded to Europe with them I am ignorant, as from accident, or some other cause, I have received no account either of him or them.—My answer cannot therefore be expected to contain accurate or exact descriptions of the bones; but such a general description as I can give from memory follows:

The part of a head which was in my possession, and which I thought to be the head of the mammoth, appeared small. I only possessed the maxilla superior and maxilla inferior, with the teeth. The maxilla superior was furnished with four large teeth, two on each side of the jaw, the two nearest the jaw were mola-res, and had two points or cones on each side of the tooth, making double processes thickly enamelled on the cones or masticating surface.

The maxilla inferior was in two parts naturally, teeth the same as in the maxilla superior, and from the appearance of both jaws I concluded they had their full complement of teeth—I judged the head to which these bones belonged was small, as I had teeth of the same kind more than five times the size of the largest in either jaw—each under jaw with the teeth weighing 48lbs.

I had a number of teeth ribbed transversely on the masticating surface, and enamelled, weighing from 1½ to 12lbs. each.

Of the teeth of the mammoth kind furnished with double coned or blunt pointed processes on the masticating surface and thickly enamelled, and generally four processes for insertion in the jaw, as many as a wagon and four horses could draw, weighing from 12 to 20lbs. each.

One small femoris, weight 31lbs. four ribs, weight and length not recollected—they appeared to be so connected with the vertebræ as to throw their edge outwards; one tusk weighing 100lbs. 21 inches in circumference in the middle, which was the thickest part ; one other tusk, weight 150lbs. 23 inches in circumference, and measuring 10 feet 6 inches in length ; its form thus J one horn 5 feet long, weight 21lbs.

The bones of one paw nearly filled a flour barrel ; it had four claws, and when the bones were regularly placed together, measured from the os calcis to the end of either middle claw 5 feet 2 inches.

The bones of this paw were similar to those of a bear's foot. Where I found these bones I found large quantities of bears' bones at the same time, and had an opportunity of arranging and comparing the bones together, and the similarity was striking in every particular except the size.

The vertebræ of the back and neck, when arranged in order with the os sacrum and coccygis, and measured nearly 60 feet, allowing for cartilages. Though I am not confident the bones all belonged to one animal, and the number of vertebræ I cannot recollect.

I had some thigh bones of incognita of a monstrous size when compared with my other bones, which I much regret I neither weighed or measured, and a number of large bones so much impaired by time it was fruitless to conjecture to what part of any animal they belonged.

As to the probability of obtaining more bones and the method of attempting it ; the best answer I can give will be a relation how and where I procured the fore mentioned : They were all procured at a place called the Big Bone Lick, about 60 miles below this place and 3 from the Ohio. From my long residence in this country I had long cherished a strong desire to make researches at Big Bone Lick, but my circumstances (having a large family and my practice as a physician, though extensive, is not profitable, owing to the poverty of the people,) would not enable me to bear the necessary expenses.  About three years ago, some persons understanding the avidity with which skeletons of this kind were sought after in Europe, and believing a complete skeleton of the mammoth might be procured, and that it would sell well in Europe.  After several exertions to obtain what might be necessary to carry my object into execution, I accordingly proceeded to Big Bone Lick, and with a few hands, such as my trifling resources would permit, commenced my researches, when the agent of David Ross of Virginia, who owns the tract of land, forbid my proceeding further.  Since which time I have endeavored by every means which my contracted situation enables me, to procure liberty to prosecute my search.

Big Bone Lick was formerly a salt marsh—Salt is made there at present—we generally dug through several layers of small bones in a stiff blue clay, such as deer, elk, buffalo and bear bones, in great numbers, many of them much broken, below which was a strata of gravel and salt water, in which we found the large bones, some nearly 11 feet deep in the ground though they were found upon the surface.

The large bones were not found regularly connected together as those of a carcase which has been consumed by time without disturbance, and I was led to form strong suspicions that the carcases of the large animals were preyed upon and the bones scattered here and there—I am so firmly persuaded that large, nay, almost any quantity of the teeth bones and tusks may be procured, that I have long entertained a sanguine hope of bettering my circumstances by procuring skeletons, provided I could obtain permission to prosecute my search, perhaps it may be in the power of your learned body, to procure me this permission, and if the society would wish collections of the bones of these non-descripts for their own use, I would undertake to superintend the collection and forward it to Philadelphia, or elsewhere, for such compensation as the Society should think proper to allow me for my trouble, and quitting my business during the time of the work.  I spent about four weeks in my former research, with 6 and sometimes 8 hands, and I think with 10 or 12 hands, who must be found with victuals and liquor, I could completely search the whole lick.  The expense would be about $1 25 each man per day, we could take provisions from this town, or take a hunter to kill for us.  I have now, respected sir, given all the information that suggests itself, and have mentioned the place were the collection is to be made, and the best method to pursue.  With sincere wishes, that the Society may prosper, and that you may long continue your labors for the benefit of your country, I am,

                    With sincere respect, your friend,
                              WILLIAM GOFORTH

THOMAS JEFFERSON, ESQ.

[q] KENTUCKY river is a large and important water of the state of the same name. It heads in the Cumberland mountains, entwining with the waters of Licking and Sandy rivers on the one hand, and Dick's river, its western branch, with those of Cumberland on the other.

FRANKFORT, the seat of government for the state of Kentucky, is situated on the east side of Kentucky river, about 60 miles from its mouth. It contains about 140 houses, three printing offices, one bookstore, a circulating library, and book bindery; 18 mercantile stores, a state bank established in the fall of 1807. The state legislature meet here annually, and sit during the winter months. The town is improving fast in buildings, manufactories, &c.

There have been a number of vessels of burden built here and freighted with the produce of the country, to New Orleans, West India islands, &c. A few miles above Frankfort, on the Kentucky river, are two considerable Vineyards, which are likely to prove successful in the manufactory of good wine.

Frankfort is seated on a flat or plain, under a considerable hill to the N. E. while the Kentucky river runs around it to the S. W. in the form of a half moon. Part of the plain to the N. W. of the town, is subject to inundation, and consequently not built on. It used to be a stagnant pond, but general Wilkinson, when stationed at Frankfort, about the year 1795–6, dug ditches through it, and drained it of its noxious effluvia; the same practice has been continued by the inhabitants, and the health of the citizens preserved. The river at Frankfort has an appearance of having left its old bed, which may have run through a pleasant valley or glen (now a fine meadow) between the hill back of Frankfort and that whose point comes to the river just below town, and obliquely opposite the hill on the S. W. side of the river, where the fracture by some great convulsion of nature may have taken place. This conjecture is formed from a slight view of the place, we leave the hypothesis for further examination by naturalists. On the S. W. side of the river, opposite the upper end of the town, is an extensive bottom, called *South Frankfort*. It is not yet built on.

The river at Frankfort is narrow, with bold banks of limestone rock admirably calculated for building, running in horizontal veins of from 6 to 12 inches thick; it has been known to rise 50 feet perpendicular in 24 hours. The bridge now erecting at Frankfort will add facility to the commerce of the town. It is building on the plan of judge Finley's *chain-bridge*; will cost about 25,000 dollars, is 334 1-2 feet span, having one pier in the middle of the river, 65 feet in height; whole length about 700 feet, and 18 broad. The two chains for this bridge were made at Pittsburgh, by Mr. Thomas Hazleton, and weigh about 12 tons, of inch and a half square bar. Much difficulty has been experienced in getting a foundation for the western abutment, arising from a kind of quick sand and water rushing in at the bottom upon the workmen as fast as they could discharge them at top, with pumps and buckets worked night and day.

Frankfort has a well conducted penitentiary, in which the criminals of the state, work at various mechanical branches, and at labor, during the term of their confinement. I saw a variety of handsome stone and marble work in the yard, among which, some elegantly wrought tombs were the most conspicuous. The marble slabs are very handsome, having variegated veins running through them, and which bear a high and beautiful polish; these are brought from a marble quarry 25 or 30 miles distance.

Messrs. Hunter & Instone, have recently got into operation in Frankfort an extensive bagging manufactory, in which about 25 hands, blackmen and boys, are busily engaged, spinning, weaving, &c. At the end of this and immediately on the bank of the river, the same gentlemen have erected a large ware house for the storage of goods, which centre here from different parts of the state, to descend the Kentucky river to the Ohio. A bagging manufactory was burnt down at Frankfort about twelve months ago, by design, it was conjectured.

An extensive rope walk was erecting (Sept. 1810) at the edge of the town, calculated to do business largely. And a steam boat, that is, a large boat to be propelled by the power of steam, was on the stocks a little above town. She is intended for the trade of the Ohio and Mississippi rivers.

The buildings of Frankfort, are principally of brick, and of a handsome style. The state house is a large three story stone building, and stands in the middle of a large yard, and like too many *public* things, appears much neglected for want of repairs and cleanliness. The new bank is a handsome brick building, and stands in range with the new bridge and the state house.

A mile below Frankfort there is a saw and grist mill in the river, which in low water does a good deal of business, but it is not uncommon to see it completely covered by the floods of the river, to withstand which it has no roof and is open on all sides, and heavily loaded down on the corners and in the middle of the frame at top, with piles of stones. The mill is owned by a Mr. Hawkins. Boats pass it through a chute, by lifting a few boards at its head, which when replaced, form a dam for the mill.

With some difficulty the Kentucky river can be navigated from Frankfort with light flat bottomed boats to the Ohio, in the lowest stages of the water, but for about eight months in the year the navigation is very good.

Two miles below Frankfort there is a bank of fine white sand thrown up by the river, said to be well calculated for the manufacture of glass. Mr. Greenup, former governor of Kentucky, has it in contemplation, it is said, to establish a glass house at or near this place; and the establishment of a brew house is talked of by the citizens of the town. Thus go on the improvements of interior America, whose inhabitants begin to feel and act like the citizens of an independent nation, possessing an extent of country capable of producing, from the luxury of its soil, and variety of climate, *every thing* which ought to make a people happy, and independent of all the venomous combinations of maddened Europe.

Boonsborough is about 80 miles above Frankfort. This town takes its name from Daniel Boon, the first settler of the state, and who first entered it, in company with John Finley, John Stewart, Joseph Holder, James Moray and William Cool, on the 7th June 1769, having set out for this purpose from North Carolina the first of the preceeding May; Boon and others began to build a fort here at a salt lick, 60 yards from the south bank of the river, on the first of April 1775, to which they gave the name of fort Boonsborough, and which occupied them to complete it until the 14th June following, having been frequently interrupted by the Indians, who began to feel jealous of this intrusion of the whites, and determined to prevent the erection of forts, and punish with death the intruders. A circumstance which enabled Boon to maintain his stand in this fort against a numerous and barbarous enemy, amidst an howling and savage wilderness, far removed from any possible succor, and which so strongly bears the mark of a kind and ever watchful Providence, that I think no reader will lament the being made acquainted with it : Shortly after the erection of this fort, Boon removed to it his family from Clinch, (where he had left it in 1773, moving from his farm on the Yodkin in North Carolina, to which he had returned for this purpose in 1772) "where," says he, "we arrived safe, my wife and daughters, being the first white women that ever stood on the banks of Kentucky river." Five families from North Carolina, and 40 men from Powel's Valley, joined Boon on his removal to Kentucky. After several bloody onsets of the savages against fort Boonsborough, in 1775-6-7, in which they were always repulsed, they formed a plan by uniting their forces, to storm the garrison, and slay every man, woman and child in it.

Boon, while making salt at the Blue Licks, in January 1778, was, with 27 of his men, taken prisoners by a party of 102 Indians, who were on their march to attack his fort. Boon himself was taken while hunting meat for his men, and capitulated with the Indians for their surrender, and on approaching the spot where they were at work, he gave them signs at a distance not to lift arms. From hence Boon and his companions were taken prisoners to Old Chilicothe, the principal Indian town on Little Miami, where they arrived 18th February. On the 10th March following, he and 10 of his men were conducted by 40 Indians to Detroit, where they arrived on the 30th same month, and were well treated by governor Hamilton, the British commander at that post, as they had also been on their march by the Indians, agreeably to the conditions of Boon's capitulation. The Indians had got attached to Boon while a prisoner, and would on no condition either sell him to the British officers, some of whom generously and humanely offered 100 pounds sterling for him, in order that he might return home at liberty, nor would they leave him a prisoner among the rest of his companions at Detroit. They took him back with them to Old Chilicothe again, where they arrived 25th April following. "Here I was adopted" says Beon "into the family of a chief as a son, which is their custom, and permitted to hunt and spend my time as I pleased. In June following they took me to Sciota salt-springs, where we continued making salt for 10 days. On our return to Old Chilicothe I was alarmed to see 450 Indians, the choicest of their warriors, painted and armed in a fearful manner, and ready, as I found out, to march against Boonsborough. I now determined to make my escape the first opportunity; there was no time to be lost. On the 16th, before sunrise, I got off in the most secret manner, and on the 20th arrived at Boonsborough, a distance of 160 miles, travelling which I had but one meal. I found our fort in a bad state, all hands were now engaged earnestly in repairing and fortifying it in the best manner possible, for the impending blow of the enemy, whose arrival we expected daily. Sometime previous to my capture a reinforcement of 45 men arrived from North Carolina, and colonel Bowman with 100 men from Virginia, and notwithstanding we had lost some in killed and others wounded, we considered ourselves pretty strong, and felt determined to brave all dangers. We were in waiting for the enemy, when we got information that they had postponed their march two weeks, in consequence of my escape from them at Old Chilicothe. In the mean time we had several skirmishes with small parties of Indians. On the 8th August, however, the ferocious Indian army arrived, 444 in number, under the command of captain Duquesne, 11 other Frenchmen, and some of their own chiefs, and marched up within view of our fort, with British and French colors flying. They halted, and despatched a summons to me, in his Britannic majesty's name, to surrender the fort. To this I returned for answer, that I wanted two days to consider on it, which was granted.

It was now a critical time with us. We were a small number in the garrison—a powerful, cruel, and savage army before our stockaded fort, whose appearance proclaimed inevitable death, and even this was preferable to captivity. It was soon unanimously determined, that we would maintain our garrison, nor yield it short of death. We immediately began to collect what of our horses and cattle we could, and bring them through the posterns into the fort. On the evening of the 9th, I returned answer, that we were determined to defend our fort while a man was living—" Now," said I to their commander, who stood attentively hearing my sentiments, " we laugh at all your formidable preparations: but thank you for giving us notice, and time to prepare; your efforts will not prevail; our gates shall ever deny you admittance." Whether this answer affected their courage or not, I cannot tell, but contrary to our expectations, they formed a scheme to deceive us, declaring it was their orders from governor Hamilton to take us captives: but if nine of us would come out and treat with them, they would immediately withdraw their forces, and return home peaceably. The sound of this proposition was grateful to our ears, and we agreed to the proposal.

We held the treaty within 60 yards of the garrison, fearing that treachery was at the bottom of this manœuvre: the articles were formally agreed to and signed; and the Indians told us it was customary with them, on such occasions, for two Indians to shake hands with every white man in the treaty, as an evidence of entire friendship; we agreed to this also, but were soon convinced they were determined to take us prisoners. They immediately grappled us: and although surrounded by hundreds of savages, we extricated ourselves from them, and got into the garrison all safe, one man excepted, who was wounded through a very heavy fire from the army. A furious attack was now made on us from all sides, and a constant heavy fire continued between us day and night for nine days, during which they attempted to undermine our fort—we began a countermine, which they discovered, and in consequence quit this project. They now began to be convinced that neither their stratagems, nor superior force was likely to overcome us, and on the 20th of August they raised the siege and departed.

During this siege, which threatened death in every form, we had 2 men killed and 4 wounded, besides a number of cattle, We killed of the enemy 37, and wounded a great number. After the battle was over, we picked up 125lbs of bullets, besides what stuck in the logs of our fort "—*Boon's Narrative*.

During Boon's captivity with the Indians, his wife, distressed, and believing her husband killed, conveyed herself and family with her goods on horses through the wilderness, beset with dangers, to her father's house in North Carolina.—After the siege against his fort was over, he went for his family a second time, and brought them back and settled them again in Boonsborough.— Thus the difficulties of settling a new and savage country, into which every step seems stained with blood, cruelty and distress. In which, however, how grateful to mark the acts of a kind and protecting Providence, ever watchful of the virtuous and brave.

*Danville* and *Stamford* are situated on Dick's river, the western branch of the Kentucky a little above the fork. *Versailles, Petersburgh* and *Harrodsburgh* are below Danville, *Georgetown* is on north Elkhorn, which empties in below Frankfort; *Madison* lies a few miles south of Boonsborough. *Franklinville* is near the head of the north-eastern branch. A *Vineyard* was established by an extensive vine company on the Kentucky river some distance above Frankfort, in the years 1798-9. It has not succeeded to expectation. The Kentucky river possesses a number of other thriving towns and villages, and many tributary streams, mills, &c. and after winding 200 miles through a most fertile country, varied by hills and vales, farms and fine settlements, running the first 60 miles nearly a west course, then turning to nearly a due north direction, enters the Ohio with a mouth 200 yards wide, in lat. 38° 40′ north. It is a crooked river, navigable for 150 miles, and has banks so curiously formed that they may be reckoned among the natural curiosities of the country. In these the astonished eye beholds from 200 to 300 feet of a solid perpendicular rock of limestone, and in other places a fine white and variegated marble, curiously chequered with strata of amazing regularity. This character of bank, accompanies Dick's river also, and they have something the appearance of deep artificial canals,, but they are not uniformly high on both sides, at Frankfort for instance, just above the town and at the road side, while the precipice on the east side is between 200 and 300 feet of a perpendicular mass of limestone, finely marked by horizontal strata of different thicknesses, that on the west is not higher than sufficient to bound the floods of the river.

[r] MISTLETOE, or Viscum in botany, a genus of plants of the class diæcia or tetrandria, and in the natural system arranged under the 48th order aggregatæ. The male calyx quadripartite ; the antheræ adhere to the calyx; the female calyx consists of four leaves ; there is no style ; the stigma is obtuse; there is no corolla ; the fruit is a berry with one seed ; there are nine species ; only one of which is a native of Britain, viz. the *album* or common mistletoe; it is a shrub growing on the branches of several trees ; the leaves are conjugate and elliptical, the stem forked, the flowers whitish in the alæ of the leaves.— This plant was reckoned sacred among the Druids.—*Encyclopedia, article Viscum.*

Darwin says of this plant,

" Oh ! stay, bright habitant of air, alight,
Ambitious VISCA, from thy angel-flight !
—Scorning the sordid soil, aloft she springs,
Shakes her white plume, and claps her golden wings;
High o'er the fields of boundless ether roves,
And seeks amid the clouds her soaring loves !"*

In a note he observes, "This plant never grows upon the ground ; the foliage is yellow, and the berries milk white; the berries are so viscous as to serve for bird-lime, and when they fall, adhere to the branches of the tree on which the plant grows, and strike root into its bark, or are carried to distant trees by birds.—*Botanic Garden, Loves of the Plants, p.* 27, 8vo.

This curious plant, this *dwarf-tree* of trees, is sometimes met with in Pennsylvania, Ohio, Kentucky, and other states of the union, but on the lower part of the river Ohio, and along the Mississippi, it becomes quite conspicuous, especially in winter, when the trees have lost their foliage, the mistletoe being an evergreen, it appears on the branches in clusters, having but a short, thick, compact bushy growth, with a strong oval formed small green leaf. The berry is a transparent white fruit, but how many seeds it contains I know not—the birds transplant the seeds from tree to tree, on domestic as well as trees of the forest. How Mr. Ellicot classes this plant with *vines*, I am at a loss to understand. He is equally under a mistake by saying the long moss, (tillandsia usneoides) is not connected, like the mistletoe, with the trees on which it hangs.* It takes root in the same manner as does the mistletoe, in the crevices or fissures of the bark on the limbs of the trees ; one root of which, however, sustains such quantities of the hanging moss, that a superficial observer might very readily be led into a mistake, and suppose, as Mr. Ellicot has done, that it had no root, no adhesion or connection with the tree on which it is suspended in loose drapery. I examined the moss myself. and found it rooted to the limbs of the trees as stated. And further discovered that it flowers annually, and bears a very delicate pod half an inch or three quarters long, full of small seeds. The mistletoe possesses valuable medicinal qualities, and is sometimes made use of for female cattle.

[s] GREEN River is a valuable water of Kentucky, has a gentle current, navigable about 150 miles, and after winding through a most fertile country 200 miles, it enters the Ohio with a mouth 200 yards wide. The country on this river is said to afford better range for cattle and hogs than any other part of Kentucky. It also produces the grape in great abundance, and of a fine flavor, such as would yield a good wine in great quantities if properly managed. Many of the inhabitants make their own wine from them, and could, if encouraged, make for exportation to other parts of the United States. Near this river there are three ponds of bitumen, forming one general reservoir, which when used in lamps answers the purpose of the best oil. Salt-petre is made on this river from the earth collected out of the caves, with which the country abounds. It is so strongly impregnated with nitric particles, that its yield of this valuable article of natural wealth and independence is immense. The whole state of Kentucky is famous for its nitric caves, and for the manufacture of salt-petre, making about 300,000lbs. annually. Green river abounds with salt licks, from some of which much salt is made every year. The principal southern branches of Green river are, first from the mouth, Muddy or Pond river, Great Barren river, whose heads entwine with the waters of Cumberland river ; Little Barren river, between which, Great Barren river, and Green river, are what is called the *Great Barrens ;* and Russel's creek a few miles above Little Barren river. Its northern branches are first, Panther creek, Rough creek, which heads at a spring called Mary's Grove ; and

* See his Journal pages 285, 288.

Nolin's creek, besides 50 other smaller streams and their branches, and finally heads within a few miles of Stamford and the
Crab Orchard or Ducks fork of Kentucky river, running generally a western course to a north-western, in which last direction
it enters the Ohio, in about 37° 47' N. lat.

[t]  THE Wabash is a beautiful river, with high and upright
banks, less subject to overflow than any other river (the Ohio
excepted) in this part of the United States.  It is about 270
yards wide at its mouth, and is navigable to Ouiatanon, 412 miles,
with keels and boats drawing about three feet water.  Above
this, in swells, boats ascend it 197 miles further to the Miami
carrying place, nine miles from the Miami village of lake Erie.
The Wabash has a gentle current to fort Ouiatanon, a few rapids excepted, some of which are considerable, both above and
below that fort.  A part of the river for three miles, and 30 below the carrying place, is so narrow that setting poles have to
be used instead of oars, when oars are applied, which is not often the case on this and similar rivers.  The land on the Wabash is remarkably fertile, with extensive natural meadows or
prairies on many parts of it, covered with long grass, affording
fine ranges for immense herds of cattle.  Almost every kind of
timber grows here in abundance, large and fine.  A silver mine
was discovered 28 miles above Ouiatanon a few years ago, and
a rich copper mine also on this river, but we have not heard any
thing more about them lately.  The Wabash abounds in salt
springs, the hills with coal, and the river with fish  Limestone,
blue, white, and yellow clays abound.  Hemp grows spontaneously on the bottoms, and grapes in great abundance, having a
black thin skin, from which an excellent red wine is made by
the inhabitants for their own consumption.  Hops and all kinds
of fruit thrive well here.  As early as the year 1775, the French
had two establishments on the Wabash, called post Vincent,
and Ouiatanon, the first 150 miles and the other 262 miles from
its mouth.  VINCENNES as we now call it, is the seat of government for Indiana Territory; considerable improvements have
been made in and about the town, but its proximity to the in-
cursions of the savages has retarded its progress much, and also the settlement of the country.  Vincennes is situated on the
east bank of the Wabash, in lat. 38° 43' north, about 8 miles east
of the line between the Indiana and Illinois territories, and is
the residence of the governor and secretary.  The country around
the town is open, pleasant, and fertile, prospect fine and extensive, and so soon as the Indians can be rendered hamless, this
will become one of the finest parts for settlement in the western country.  The land is high, fertile, and healthful, numerous limped streams and fine springs.—Mill seats and farming
grounds convenient to each other, an unbounded and excellent
range for cattle, hogs, horses, and sheep.  This particularly is

the character of what is called the *New Purchase*, which is now surveying, and lies a considerable distance above Vincennes.

The principal branches of the Wabash are first on the west side, the Little Wabash, about 20 miles from the Ohio; Fox and Umbra rivers. On the east side, are the Potoko, and White rivers, which enter within two miles of each other; and Deshe river, one of whose branches approaches close to Vincennes by a long lake or spring. At the mouth of Deshe river is the 3d rapid, the second Grand Rapid is about three miles above White river, and the Grand Chain is about 20 miles below Fox river, being the three principal rapids between the Ohio and Vincennes. The Wabash, beyond the branches mentioned, has a number of others, the Vermillion, Rock, Eel, Little, Muddy, Hill's, Brush or North branch, and Tippacanoe rivers. On this last river, and near where it joins Eel river, is the Prophet's town, now famous in the annals of our Indian wars for a desperate battle fought here by the American troops under governor Harrison, and the Indians under Tecumseh, brother to the prophet. It was scarcely a victory to the Americans, though they were enabled to keep their position and put to flight the Indians. It was however, a desperate fought battle, the Americans being rushed upon before day light by the tomahawking, scalping and treacherous enemy*, and while many of our men were yet without arms in their hands. The bravery of our troops on this occasion, and the intrepidity and generalship of their commanders, have gained them laurels of a long standing, and perhaps no one's death in that battle has been more justly lamented than that of the brave Col. Owen of Shelby, and Col Davies of Lexington, K the latter not more brilliant for his talents at the bar, than for his bravery in the field. This engagement, now known by the name of the *Tippacanoe Battle*, took place at 4 o'clock on the morning of the 7th Nov. 1811. The American troops were about 800 in number, their killed and wounded about 160. The number of the Indians were about 700, killed and wounded not known.

In 1792 Vincennes had about 1500 souls, principally French. It has less at this time. The fort stands on the same side of the river with the town, and generally has a major's command. It possesses 4 small brass pieces, beside other ordnance. Fort Harrison is about 60 miles above Vincennes, built by governor Harrison during his expedition against the Prophet's town, already mentioned. The United States have a tract of land for a fort just below the Prophet's town, and a little above fort Ouiatanon, and also at fort Wayne at the head of Little river, and

---

* The Indians had promised the preceding evening, that the next morning they would send in a white flag to governor Harrison to treat for peace, in consequence our troops were rather thrown off their guard, and the desperate attack was unexpected.

about 260 miles N. E. by N. from Vincennes. Fort Recovery is
120 miles N. E from Vincennes, on and near the head of the
Wabash, which passes a few miles into the state of Ohio, and
ends within about six miles of the Big Miami. A range of high
land begins between lakes Huron and Michigan, running nearly a S. W course, crossing the upper part of the Illinois territory diagonally, and ends at the Kaskaskia river, opposite Cahokia, on the Mississippi, forming a dividing ground between
the waters of the Illinois, and lake Michigan, from those of lake
Erie and the Wabash. The course of the Wabash is from S.
W. to a S. direction, though generally very crooked, especially
near its mouth.

The junction of the Wabash with the Ohio, forms a handsome
site for a town, and though subject more or less to inundation
in high floods, we should not be surprised that ere long, it becomes a place of business, crowded with houses, and with "the
busy hum of men." Leveeing would render it free from the waters, and perfectly safe to the inhabitants. The easy communication to the lakes, the vast and fertile country it commands,
together with the advantages of the trade of the Ohio, all tend
to corroborate the opinion here suggested.

[u] UP the Saline river about 12 miles from the Ohio, are
extensive salt works possessed by the United States, leased out
under such regulations as to enable the lessees to sell the salt
at the works for about 70 cents per bushel. The works yield
about 150,000 bushels annually, and it is thought, were they
worked to the extent of their capacity, a much greater quantity
could be produced—Major James Morrison and Mr. Charles
Wilkins, of Lexington, and others, are the present lessees.

At, and in the neighborhood of these works, is to be found
fragments of ancient pottery of an uncommon large size, large
enough it is stated, to fit the bulge of a hogshead. and thick in
proportion. On Goose creek in Kentucky, and in many other
parts, in the neighborhood of salt springs particularly, similar
fragments of ware are found. which would induce a belief that
its makers used it to boil their salt in   This is by no means
improbable, some pots of a similar composition but of a small
kind for cooking, are still found in use among many of the tribes
of American Indians, both northern and southern. The Chocktaws and Chickasaws about Natchez, are frequently seen with
pots of this composition, carrying about with them from camp
to camp, in which they boil their hommony or other victuals.
I procured a small pot of this kind from the Chocktaw Indians
a· Natchez, and by way of curiosity, when I returned to Pennsylvania in the summer of 1812, deposited it in Peale's museum
in Philadelphia, for the inspection of the curious, and that it
might be compared with the manufacture of other nations in various parts of the world, of which Mr. Peale has many sorts in
wood, stone, and the kind here spoken of. When in Kentucky

in the year 1810, I got a very ancient pot of this ware, that had been found buried in the sand of a salt-petre cave at the head of Licking river. It was of the same character in composition, shape and purpose, for which it had been made, viz. for the fire, as that got of the Chocktaws at Natchez. It being very old and tender, the composition was easily seen by crumbling pieces of it between the fingers. Pounded shells, sand, and clay, appear to be the component parts of this ware; it does not seem as if it had been turned on a laith, though nearly as regular as if it had the advantage of that operation; the manner of burning it, I was told by a white woman in habits of intimacy with the Chocktaws, is as follows: The pot when formed and sun-dried is put in the centre of a ring of fire, at such distance as at first to gently warm it throughout, and as it gets able to bear more heat, the fire is moved in gradually to the centre, and increased, and when the pot is thought sufficiently hot, it is then covered over with embers, coals and fire, and so continued baking until fit for use, the length of time it takes to burn being known only by experience and is governed by the size and thickness of the vessel. It may be asked where shells are got by the Indians for this manufacture: It is answered that vast banks of oyster shells are found in Georgia, many miles in length; and also a bank in the Mississippi territory about 150 miles from Natchez, and which is crossed on the road from that place to Nashville. The length and breadth of this bank has not perhaps been ascertained, but it is evidently very extensive. Our rivers all afford the muscle shell, and what I was a little surprised at, a considerable bed of shells was discovered in digging a hole for a saw pit a few years ago, at a boat yard at the mouth of Virginia Short creek, on the Ohio. Happening to stop at that place a few minutes in 1806, this bed of shells was thrown into my view accidently, and I picked up some of the pieces, to examine what kind they were, but could scarcely determine, not having time to dig down among them, and those on the surface being finely broken to pieces. I rather concluded, however, they were of the oyster kind. It is possible they may be the muscle shell, collected perhaps by the Indians for the purpose of making their ware.— I could wish some person would take the trouble to stop at that place, examine and determine this point, merely as it interests the natural history of our interesting country. If I mistake not, this bed of shells is just below a house above the bridge across Short creek, and immediately on the bank of the river, 8 miles above Wheeling. Even admitting the natives had no shells, there are kinds of limestone, burnt to a certain degree, and pounded, which would answer, most probably, for the manufacture of this Indian ware. Fragments of this ware is found in all parts of the United States. I recollect when a boy in New Jersey, of picking up pieces of it in old fields, together with arrow points, &c. and was then told, they were made by the Welsh.— Whether this ware is to be put to the account and genius of the people who originated and left for our admiration the remains of their fortifications, mounds, &c. or whether confined in its origin to the present aborigines of America, is a question yet to be solved by philosophers and antiquarians. The latter may have stolen the art from the former, or it may have been brought into existence by them from pure necessity. For it is highly presumable the first were a different people from the present, in manners, customs, and in the knowledge of arts, sciences, &c. and not unlikely, made totally extinct, by some law or rule of nature with which we are unacquainted, long before the present race of natives had a footing in the land, some, though well known for the correct manner in which they keep the records of their own nations for generations and even centuries, yet have no tradition by which they can inform us of the people whose ancient and very curious remains are discovered in all parts of the United States, and who most probably, were more numerous than the whole of their present population, including savage and civilized. These, however, are speculations, whose truths may be better known a century hence than at present. That which throws a shade on one side of the picture, *time,* may cast light on the other.

I have heard of the ware on Goose creek spoken of through several channels. A gentleman of Chilicothe assured me that there had been one large kettle found entire, on that creek, and which was dug up from under the roots of a large tree that had fallen by the wind. And that it was not uncommon to find them in numbers, when digging for salt at that place. The circumstance of their being found entire under ground, and large trees growing over them, is a mark of great antiquity, and of either cunning or economy of those who made use of them. Most vanquished nations either hide or destroy what they are obliged to leave behind, and it would seem this had been strictly performed with these immoveable Indian salt kettles, as they are called, not only the better to deprive the invading enemy the use of those already made, but to keep them ignorant also of the method of making others.

[w] CUMBERLAND, called by the Indians Shawanee, and by he French Shavoran, is a large winding river, partly of Kentucky and partly of Tennessee. It heads in the Cumberland mountains, not far from the head of Dick's river on the one hand, and Clinch and Powel's rivers on the other, separated from the latter rivers by the Cumberland mountains. It is navigable for large vessels to Nashville, from thence for those of a less size to Obed's river, and above this river for periogues many miles, being navigable without interruption for about 300 miles from the Ohio.

The first town as we ascend the Cumberland, is Eddyville, about 45 miles from the Ohio. It is a post town of Kentucky, and is enlivened with business by the industrious and enterprising talents of col. Mathew Lyon, who has put into operation a wool and cotton carding machine, a paper mill put into motion by oxen; he has lately erected a distillery for whiskey. Mr. Lyon built several United States' gunboats here, and is constantly building barges and other boats for the rivers. He has a barge conducted by one of his sons, running up and down to New Orleans, carrying off the produce of that river, and returning with coffee, sugar, rice, &c. &c.

Palmira, a small village 50 miles above Eddyville, is situated on the Cumberland river in Montgomery county, Ken.

Clarksville is situated at the fork where Red river joins the Cumberland, a few miles above the line between Kentucky and Tennessee.

NASHVILLE, is handsomely situated on the south side of the river, about 190 miles by water, and 140 by land from its mouth, 200 from Lexington, and 180 west from Knoxville. The town stands on a high cliff of rocks, 200 feet above the level of the river, and commands a fine view of a picturesque country around it. Nashville is in Mero district, Davidson county, is the seat of government for the state of Tennessee, and is in a flourishing state of improvement. It has a respectable banking company; a cotton manufactory by Mr. George Poyzers, and Mr. Stump and his family have a rope walk, a powder mill, and a cotton gin, all in handsome operation. William Carrol & Co. in connection with Mr. Cowan of Pittsburgh, have a nail manufactory, and an extensive ironmongery store. And the citizens generally are turning their attention to the establishment of such manufactures as will tend to render them independent and happy, in spite of wars, and the impudence, wickedness and aggressions of foreign nations, either of the English, French, Tartars, Moguls, or any other party-colored race upon earth.

Nashville contains about 200 houses, some of which are large and elegant buildings of brick; it has an academy, 2 churches, a court-house, jail, &c. The town is said to take its name from general Francis Nash, who fell at the battle of Germantown, Oct. 4, 1777.

There is a line of barges constantly running from Nashville to New Orleans, loaded down with the rich produce of Tennessee, and up with sugars, coffee, rice, hides, liquors, dry goods, &c. conducted principally by Mr. Spriggs, a very active and industrious trader, and from long habit, among the most expert conductors of a barge of any person on the river. These add facility to trade and commerce, and give employment to a number of active, hardy men. Boats conducted by the steam principle would most probably be more advantageous, and save an immense manual labor. The day is not far distant, I hope, when the citizens of Nashville will see a steam boat winding her course up the Cumberland, in all the majesty and nobleness of her internal and secreted power, without the assistance of poles, oars or sails. It wants nothing to do this but the spirit of beginning.

Nashville is in lat. 36° 25′ north, and notwithstanding the changeable nature of the winter and spring seasons, yet the citizens enjoy good health generally, cheerful spirits and independent minds, which the inhabitants of Tennessee possess to an eminent degree, being perhaps the best ingredients in this most precious of all earthly blessings. Two newspaper establishments issuing weekly papers give currency to intelligence, and create a love of inquiry, the basis of well informed minds.— Schools are numerous and under good regulations, and the children shew an ardent spirit of rivalship, a sure presage of their becoming zealous in the pursuits of life, and valuable citizens. The spot where Nashville now stands was settled by a party under James Robertson, in the year 1780.

The Cany fork, which is near 100 yards wide at its mouth, and 120 miles above Nashville, Harpeth, Stone's, Obed's and Red rivers, are the principal branches of Cumberland ; some of these are navigable for small crafts a considerable distance. There are a great number of creeks, also adding their waters to the main stream, and which afford fine mill seats, meadow and pasture grounds.

Cumberland runs nearly a W. direction through Lincoln county, as far as Price's settlement ; then S. W. to the line, passing it into Tennessee, it makes a bend enclosing Summer county, and again touches the line ; thence S. W. to Nashville, thence N. W. to Clarksville, where it again winds S. W. to Well's creek, thence N. W. by N. to the line between Kentucky and Tennessee, making nearly a half circle from where it touches the line at the western part of Summer, enclosing in this great southern bend Davidson and Tennessee counties. From the line at Martin's creek, it runs N. W. thence W. in which last direction it enters the Ohio, where it is about 250 yards broad, in lat. 36° 56′ north.

Cotton, indigo, corn, whiskey, hogs, horses, cattle, flour, gunpowder, salt-petre, poultry, bacon, lard, butter, apples, pork, coarse linen, &c. are the articles which generally constitute the loading of a boat coming out of the Cumberland river, and which are frequently shipped in boats so badly put together, that it is a matter of surprise how half of them even get to market. I got caught in the ice opposite the mouth of Tennessee, in the winter of 1811, (February) where happened to be 16 boats from Tennessee, three of which were sunk and lost, two stove and sunk, but got afloat again and repaired, five their sides drove in, but repaired before sunk, and the remainder scarcely escaped from the general wreck. To be sure, of all enemies we meet with on the Ohio, the ice is the most formidable and dangerous, but I am of opinion three-fourths of the accidents and misfortunes that happen on that river and the Mississippi, arise from the careless manner of building the common flat boats, sometimes from a bad knotty or rotten plank in the bottom, a weak gunnel of tender wood, or the want of substance and strength in the two or three first planks from the gunnel.—It is exactly with this business as with every thing else man has any thing to do with, he will not do better until sad experience compels him. After loosing half a dozen boats and their cargoes, he returns home with a determination to examine every plank in the next, and see to the building them himself, for after getting so severely whipped, like a child at school, he resolves on paying more attention to his task in future.

[x] THE Tennessee, (called also the Cherokee river, from a tribe of Indians of that name having towns and much land on it) is a long, crooked, and a very important water of Tennessee state. It has been navigated 900 miles from its mouth. The Muscle Shoals begin 250 miles from the Ohio, and here the river widens from 400 yards, its general width, to between two and three miles, and continues this breadth for 30 miles, the length of the Muscle Shoals. Here the channel is obstructed with a number of islands, formed by trees and drift wood lodged here by the floods of the river. In passing these islands, the middle of the widest intermediate water is to be navigated, as there it is the deepest. From the Ohio to the Muscle Shoals the current is moderate, and high and low lands are rich, bearing oaks, walnut, sugar trees, hickory, &c. About 180 miles above the Shoals, is the Whirl or Suck; here for three miles the river is confined to 60 yards in breadth, by the Cumberland mountain, through one of whose most southerly ridges it has broken, and now rushes in its narrow boundary with great velocity. Boats ascend it, however, by towing or cordelling. Thirty miles above the Whirl, is the Shallow Ford, where the river widens to the breadth of 1200 yards. About 100 miles above the Suck, is the Highwasee river, a S. E. branch, on which are vast bodies of fine rich land; above it the country is much broken into pine ridges, &c. 50 miles farther up is Clinch river, a N. E. branch, 150 yards wide at its mouth. From Clinch to the Tennessee river it is 20 miles; it comes in from the S. E and is 250 yards wide at its mouth. On this river are the Chata, Talasee, and Chilhowee towns of the Cherokee and Over-hill Cherokee Indians. The French Broad is 50 miles above the Tennessee, which, with the latter, are much interrupted in their navigation by rocks. Long Island, which is three miles in length, is 130 miles above the French Broad; from thence to the source of the Cherokee river, now called Holston, is 60 miles, too rocky to be navigated.

The highest point of navigation upon this river is the Tellio blockhouse, now called South West Point, at the fork formed by the junction of Clinch with the Tennessee, 900 miles, taking its meanderings, from its mouth.

_Knoxville_ is the principal town on this river, it was established by William Blount, the first governor, and was for several years the seat of government for the state of Tennessee. It is situated on a handsome spot of ground about 15 miles below the junction of the Hoiston and the French Broad, and 35 above South-West Point, in lat 35° 55' north. This part of the state is called East Tennessee, divided from West Tennessee by the Cumberland mountains, 30 miles broad. The town has barracks for 700 men, and a college called, Blount college, established by the government of the state. Knoxville is about 183 miles east from Nashville : 200 S. E. by S. from Frankfort ; 485 W. by S. of Richmond ; 728 S. westerly of Philadelphia, and is the capital of Knox county,

At the head of Lookout Mountain creek, below the Big Suck, is a Cherokee town ; Nickajack town is 30 or 40 miles below it on the Tennessee ; Crowtown 20 miles further down ; all on the south side of the river ; Creeks' Crossing Place is 15 miles still lower down

Elk river comes in from the north near the upper end of the Muscle Shoals ; a fort was established on this river about 25 years ago, a few miles above its mouth. Duck river is a considerable branch, entering from the north side, about 130 miles below the Muscle Shoals, and 120 from the Ohio.

Tombigbee or Mobile river, heads within a few miles of the Occachappo river, a south branch of the Tennessee, entering a few miles below the Muscle Shoals. The Coosee and Talapoosee rivers, branches of the Alabama, itself a part of the Mobile river, head within a few miles of Crowstown on the Tennessee, and not far from the head waters of Highwasee river, a considerable branch of the Tennessee. From the easy communication which can be had from that part of Tennessee above the Muscle Shoals, by way of these last mentioned branches of the Mobile river, to the Gulf of Mexico, and thence to any part of the world, it is not unlikely that the whole of the trade of that country may take this route in a few years in preference to the one by way of the Ohio and Mississippi, in which case a distance of not less than from 800 or 1000 miles would be saved in going to market, and probably a road less perilous than is the present. In a direct line from the town of Mobile on Mobile bay, to the Creeks' Crossing Place on the Tennessee, it is not more than 240 miles ; from the same point on the Tennessee to New Orleans by the present water route it is 1385 miles, From the Creeks' Crossing Place to a navigable part of the Coosee river, it is about 50 miles by land ; and from the head of the Muscle Shoals to a navigable part of the Mobile river, it is about 70 miles, over both of which portages a good wagon road can be made with ease. Nature herself seems to have formed the great south bend of the Tennessee in a direction best calculated for a short and easy communication to the Ocean by way of these waters, and if the people do not take advantage of her kind contrivances, they have nobody to blame but themselves. Commerce, however, finds its own level, makes its own roads, and wants nothing but time to mature system and open communications, which at present seem filled with insurmountable difficulties. Our country is so vast in its extent, possessing innumerable water courses peculiarly adapted to the easy communication of one place with another ; a soil abundantly prolific of every thing that nature and art can produce, or the sharpened appetite of man desire ; its bowels stored with mines of all the metals and earths necessary for either a simple or a refined state of society, either for a peaceful or a warring nation.—Such are the resources that Americans have within the boundaries of their own country, and which Providence has blessed them with as a people, she seems to have set apart to enjoy that natural and individual happiness, beyond every other part of the globe. So numerous, I say, are our resources, and so rapidly do they throw themselves into our view, that commerce, or even speculation itself, are scarcely able to keep pace with them, or know which to make use of first.

The Tennessee, heading in the Cumberland mountains, runs nearly W. S. W. to the mouth of Clinch ; Thence S. W. to the Creeks' Crossing Place, a short N. W. bend below the Suck excepted ; thence it winds north westerly to the mouth of Occachappo river; thence nearly due north to within 40 miles of its mouth ; thence north westerly to the Ohio, which it enters with a mouth nearly 600 yards broad, in lat 37° 11′ north. The source of the Tennessee is about the same parallel of latitude with its mouth, while the most southerly point of the Great Bend is in the latitude of 34° 18′ making a bend of 2° 53′ or 173 miles south of an E. & W. line drawn from the source to the mouth of the river.

While the Tennessee and its numerous branches furnish a variety of fine fish, its borders are not less prolific in the cackling turkey, the leaping deer, the surly bear, the drumming pheasant, and the whistling quail or partridge, all of whose flesh is as common on the table of a Tennesséean, as a potato to an Irishman, a heron to a Scotchman, pudding to an Englishman, soup-magre to a Frenchman, or rice and gumbo to a Mississippian creole. The hills abound with the most luxuriant growth of all the various kinds of timber, among which is the heavenly sugar tree in abundance, while the bottoms produce the cane, pea and grape vines, Virginia and seneca snake roots, ginseng, angelica, spice wood, plum, crab apple, sweet anise, ginger, spikenard, wild hops—the glades produce wild rye, clover, buffalo clover, strawberries and grape vines. The mountains possess mines of lead, iron, and the Indians say, silver. Caves of salt-petre are numerous, as are salt-springs, coal and sulphur have also been discovered. From these manifold blessings, far removed from the clang of war, or the turmoils of the wicked and ambitious, with a most healthful and invigorating climate, what can prevent the Tennesseeans from becoming a noble, a generous, a stout and a hardy race of men, willing to enjoy the liberty they happily possess, and ready at a moment's warning to defend it with life, whenever invaded either by a foreign or domestic enemy.

[y] THE Illinois is a most valuable river of the Illinois territory; It winds through a finely variegated and fertile country, about 450 miles, S. W. generally, receiving as tributaries many large and small streams, all uniting their waters to the Illinois, and it to the Mississippi, 18 miles above the mouth of the Missouri, and 33 above St. Louis.

The best account I can find of the Illinois is in the Journal of a Mr. Patrick Kennedy, who undertook an expedition up this river with several coureurs de bois, in the year 1773, from Kaskaskia village, in search of a copper mine. What follows is principally taken from his Journal, during the voyage, which terminated without a discovery of their object.

About 18 miles up the Illinois, on the eastern side, is a river called by the natives Macepin or White Potato river; it is 20 yards wind and navigable to the hills,* nine miles distant. The shore is low on both sides—land well timbered, with fine meadows a little distance from the river, the banks of which do not crumble away as those of the Mississippi. Between this and the mouth of the Illinois there are a number of islands, some from 9 to 12 miles in length and three in breadth.

Piorias wintering ground is about 48 miles from the Mississippi; here is a meadow on the eastern side, a quarter of a mile from the river, many miles long and six broad, in which are several small lakes communicating with each other and with the Illinois. The timber very tall oaks. There are a number of beautiful islands in this part of the river, which is generally 400 yards broad.

The Pierre island is some distance above the Piorias winter ground, near which, from a hill on the western side, the Indians procure a fleche or arrow-stone, with which they make their gun flints and point their arrows. Half a league above this island the meadows border on the river, and continue several miles—Banks of the river high—water clear—white marl and sand at the bottom—land rich, well watered with small rivulets.

Mine river comes in from the N. W. side, 120 miles from the Mississippi; it is a very rapid river, has a sandy bottom, green in some places and red in others, and is 50 yards wide at its mouth. Land low on both sides of the Illinois, but rises gradually; the prairies on the eastern side are 20 miles wide, are good for tillage or grazing, and finely watered with springs.—

* This is a chain of rocks and high hills which begin at the Piasas, about three miles above the Missouri, extend to the mouth of the Illinois, and continue on the south-eastern side of that river in an east-north-east course, up to the old Pioria fort, where they terminate on the eastern side of Illinois lake.

The Mine river is said to have an alum hill on it, and is thought to be the nearest route to the copper mine.

The river Sagamond, 135 miles from the Mississippi, is navigable for canoes 180 miles, and is 100 yards wide at its mouth.

The river Demi-Quian, 30 miles above Sagamond river, comes in from the western side, it is navigable 120 miles, and is 50 yards wide at its mouth. Here is a large savanna, called the Demi-Quian swamp. The meadows here extend further than the eye can reach, affording a delightful prospect—land on the eastern side high and thinly timbered.

Lake Demi-Quian is 200 yards west and 6 miles above the river of the same name, and 171 from the Mississippi ; it is circular, six miles across, and discharges itself by a passage four feet deep, into the Illinois—prairies or meadows increase in their extent. The general course of the Illinois varies very little, rather inclines to the eastward.

A few miles above Demi-Quian lake, the Sesemi-Quian river comes in from the western side, it is 40 yards broad and navigable 60 miles. Nine miles further up is the river De la March, on the western side also ; it is 30 yards wide and navigable only 9 or 10 miles, but is a handsomer river than the Sesemi-Quian. Here the land begins to rise gradually on the western bank.

The river Michilimackinac, comes in on the south-eastern side, above the two just mentioned, and 195 miles from the Mississippi ; it is navigable 90 miles, 50 yards wide, and has at its mouth 30 or 40 small islands, which at a distance look like a small village. Some distance up this river is a coal mine, on the banks are red and white cedar, pine, maple, walnut, &c.

Old Pioria fort and village is on the western shore of the Illinois, and at the southern end of Illinois lake, which is 19½ miles in length and three in breadth ; this lake has no rocks, shoals or perceivable current. The summit on which the fort stood, commands a fine prospect of the country to the eastward, and up the lake to the point where the river comes in at the north end ; to the westward are large meadows. Here are plenty of cherry, plum, and other fruit trees. The lake is well stored with fish, the sturgeon and picannau. On the eastern side of this lake, about the middle of it, the chain of rocks that extend from the back of Kaskaskia to Cahokia, thence to Piasa and the mouth of the Illinois river, &c. terminate. The Illinois lake is 210 miles from the Mississippi. At the time of Mr. Kennedy's visit, the stockades of the fort had been destroyed by fire, but the houses were standing.

About 30 miles above Pioria fort, is Crow-meadow river, on the eastern side ; on the west side are the meadows just mentioned. This river is 20 yards wide, and navigable 15 or 18 miles, and is 240 miles from the Mississippi. The land on both sides of the Illinois for 20 or 30 miles above the lake, is generally low and full of swamps, some for a mile wide, bordered with fine meadows, and in some places the high land comes to the river in points, or narrow necks.

Fifteen miles further up is the Rivierre de Lisle de pluge, or Rainy island river, on the south-east side; it is navigable 9 miles to the rocks, 15 yards wide and 255 miles from the Mississippi. Grass fine, thick and tall; timber birch, button and picean—river shallow and difficult of ascent.

Vermillion river is 12 miles further up, it is rocky and not navigable, 30 yards wide. A mile above the Vermillion are the Little Rocks. Here the party took land and ascended to the Forks, 61 miles above the Vermillion river and 328 from the Mississippi.

About five miles above the Vermillion river, is a coal mine on the north-western side of the Illinois, for half a mile along the bank, which is high. On the eastern side half a mile from the river and the same distance below the coal mine, are two salt ponds, 100 yards in circumference; the water is of a yellowish color; but the French and natives make good salt from it; it is salter than the saline near St. Genevieve.

It is hereabout the French settlers used to cut the mill stones; on the high lands there is abundance of red and white cedar, pine trees, &c. For 45 miles above the Vermillion river, the Illinois has a rapid current.

The Fox river is about 30 miles above the Vermillion river, which comes in on the western side; it is 25 yards wide and has five feet water in low times; it has many serpentine windings through extensive meadows or prairies.

Mr. Kennedy and his party returned to his boats at the Little Rocks a mile above Vermillion river, and in his descent attempted to ascend the Mine river, which was too low for navigation, and finding it impossible to penetrate the country to the copper mine, on account of the rocky or sand mountains, weeds, briars, &c. he concluded to give up the search, and descended the river to Kaskaskia village again, which he accomplished by the 20th August following, having been gone one month and three days.

From the Forks, the Kickapoo river, a principal head branch of the Illinois, winds to the north-westward, and in about 80 or 90 miles, taking its courses, it passes within four miles of a navigable branch of the Chicago river, which enters at the west side of the head of lake Michigan, close by the United States' fort Chicago; between these two branches is a portage of 4 miles, making a water communication, with this trifling exception, from the Mississippi to Michigan, thence down the lakes, having but 10 miles land carriage around the falls of Niagara, to the mouth of the St. Lawrence; or to the city of New York, by way of Oswego river and lake, into Wood creek, from which there is a canal of four miles into the Mohawk river, which is made navigable with several locks to Schenectada, from whence there is 16 miles (and less by way of the Cohoo falls,) of a land carriage to the city of Albany on the Hudson or North river, thence to New York 160 miles, the Hudson affords the finest schooner navigation in the world. By this extraordinary route from New York to New Orleans, there is afforded the most singular and interesting natural inland navigation, if not the greatest in the universe.

From the Forks, the Illinois river runs nearly a N. E. direction, making a bend which comes within four or five miles of San Josef river, which empties into the east side of lake Michigan at its head. There is another communication from the Illinois to Michigan by way of a small lake on the Kickapoo branch to the Kennonimie river, which enters lake Michigan at its extreme southern point; by this route there is also a portage of three or four miles.

The United States' fort Chicago, at the mouth of Chicago river, and on the bank of lake Michigan, was abandoned by the troops, with several families who had fled to it for refuge, about the time general Hull surrendered Detroit and the American troops under his command, to the British troops commanded by general Brock, August 16, 1812. The flying party from Chicago had been promised protection on their route to Detroit, by some friendly Indians, but after they had proceeded a few miles from the fort, the Indians, who had been laying in ambush, fell upon them, tomahawked and scalped, man, woman and child, in the most barbarous and brutal manner, with the exception of one man and one woman, whom they took prisoners; the man made his escape from them, the woman I believe is still a prisoner. I saw the man who had providentially escaped the tomahawk from this treacherous party of Indians, at the Falls of Ohio, in November 1812; he was if I mistake not, a young officer belonging to the garrison, active and hardy, and in his escape had undergone deprivations little short of death. His account of the massacre of his countrymen, particularly of the women and children, for brutality and savage barbarity, could not be exceeded, and was executed by them with a degree of refinement of cruelty, beyond the power of the pen to describe, or the human mind to conceive.

[a 2] FROM St. Louis to the mouth of the Missouri on the east, is a rich sandy soil, timbered with buttonwood, ash, cottonwood, hackberry, &c. The west side is highlands for a small distance above the town; then it is bordered by a small prairie, after which is bottom land with the same timber as on the east. The current is rapid, and the navigation, in low water, obstructed by sand bars.

Immediately on the peninsula formed by the confluence of the rivers Mississippi and Missouri is a small Kickapoo settlement, occupied in summer only. On the west shore a rich prairie, with small skirts of woods; and on the east shore is generally high hills, from eighty to one hundred feet, extending to the mouth of the Illinois. The current of the Mississippi above the entrance of the Missouri is quite mild, until you arrive at the mouth of the Illinois; where, owing to the large sand bars and many islands, it is rendered extremely rapid. The Illinois river is about four hundred and fifty yards wide at its mouth, and bears from the Mississippi N. 75° W. The current appears not to exceed two and a half miles per hour. The navigation and connecting streams of this river are too well known to require a description at the present day. From the Illinois to the Buffalo river the E. shore is hills, but of easy ascent. On the W. is continued the prairie, but not always bordering on the river. Timber, on both sides, generally hackberry, cotton wood, and ash. The Buffalo river comes in on the W. shore, and appears to be about 100 yards wide at its mouth It bears from the Mississippi S. 30° W. From the Illinois to this river, the navigation is by no means difficult, and the current mild.

From thence to Salt river (or Oahahah) the east shore is either immediately bounded by beautiful cedar cliffs, or the ridges may be seen at a distance. On the W. shore there is a rich low soil, and two small rivers which increase the waters of the Mississippi. The first I called Bar river, about twenty yards in width. The second is about fifteen yards. Salt river bears from the Mississippi N. 75° W. and is about 100 or 120 yards wide at its entrance, and, when I passed, appeared to be perfectly mild, with scarcely any current. About one day's sail up the river there are salt springs, which have been worked for four years; but I am not informed as to their qualities or productions. In this distance the navigation of the Mississippi is very much obstructed by bars and islands; indeed, to such a degree as to render it difficult to find (in many places) the proper channel. The shores are generally a sandy soil, timbered with sugar maple, ash, pecan, locust, and black walnut. The E. side has generally the preference as to situations for building. From this to the river Jaustioni (which is our boundary between the Sac nation and the United States, on the west side of the Mississippi) we have the hills on the W. shore, and low lands on the E. the latter of which are timbered with hickory, oak, ash, maple, pecan, &c. The former the same, with an increase of oak. The E. is a rich sandy soil, and has many very eligible situations for cultivation. About seven miles below the Jaustioni a Frenchman is settled on the W shore. He is married to a woman of the Sac nation, and lives by a little cultivation and the Indian trade. The river before mentioned is about 30 yards wide at its mouth, and bears from the Mississippi about S W. In this part of the river the navigation is good.

From this to the Wyaconda river the navigation is easy, with very few impediments; and the soil on both sides pretty good. This river pays its tribute to the Mississippi by a mouth 100 yards wide, and bears from the latter nearly due W. Just below its entrance is a small stream 15 yards wide, which discharges itself into the Mississippi. Between this river and the river de Moyen, there is one small river emptying itself into the Mississippi, on the W of about 55 yards in width, and bears S. by W. The first part of the distance is obstructed by islands, and the river expands itself to a great width, so as to render the navigation extremely difficult; but the latter part affords more water, and is less difficult. The timber is principally oak and pecan. The soil as the river below.

Above the rapid de Moyen, on the W. bank of the Mississippi, is situated the first Sac village, consisting of 13 lodges; and immediately opposite is the establishment of Mr. Ewing, the American agent at that place. From whence to a large prairie on the E. side, on which is situated the second Sac village, the E. side of the river is beautiful land, but principally prairie. The W. is in some part high land, both sides timbered with oak, ash, &c. The navigation is by no means difficult. From thence to the Iowa river the navigation is much obstructed with islands. *The Iowa river bears from the Mississippi S. W. and is 150 yards wide at its mouth. The E. shore of the Mississippi is high prairie, with yellow clay banks, and in some places red sand. On the W. shore is prairie, also, but bounded on the shore by skirts of woods. About 10 miles up the Iowa river, on its right bank, is a village of the Iowas.

From this place to Rock river,† we generally had beautiful prairies on the W. but in some places very rich land with black walnut and hickory timber, Stony river is a large river which empties into the Mississippi on the E. shore, and is about 300 yards wide at its mouth. It bears from the Mississippi almost due E. About three miles up this river, on the S bank, is situated the third town of the Sac nation, which (I was informed by a Mr. James Aird) was burnt in the year 1781 or 2, by about 300 Americans, although the Indians had assembled 700 warriors to give them battle.

A little above the rapids of Rock river, on the W. side of the Mississippi, is situated the first Reynard village: it consists of about 18 lodges. From this place to the lead mines the Mississippi evidently becomes narrower; but the navigation is thereby rendered much less difficult. The shores are generally prairie, which, if not immediately bordering on the river, can be seen

---

* In ascending Iowa river 36 miles you come to a fork, the right branch of which is called Red Cedar river (from the quantity of that wood on its banks,) which is navigable for batteaux near 300 miles, where it branches out into three forks, called the Turkey's foot. Those forks shortly after lose themselves in Rice lakes.

---

† Rock river takes its source near Green bay of Lake Michigan more than 450 miles from its mouth, and is navigable upwards of 300 miles.

through the skirts of forests which border the river. The timber is generally maple, birch and oak, and the soil very excellent. To this place we had seen only a few turkies and deer, the latter of which are pretty numerous from the river de Moyen up. From the lead mines unto Turkey river, the Mississippi continues about the same width; and the banks, soil and productions are entirely similar. The Turkey river empties in on the W. bears from the Mississippi about S. W. and is about 100 yards wide at its mouth. Half a league up this river, on the right bank is the third village of the Reynards, at which place they raise sufficient corn to supply all the permanent and transient inhabitants of the Prairie des Chiens. From thence to the Ouiscousing, the high hills are perceptible on both sides, but on the W. almost border the river the whole distance. The Ouiscousing at the entrance is nearly half a mile wide, and bears from the Mississippi nearly N. E. *This river is the grand

---

* The voyage from Michilimackinac to the Prairie des Chiens, by the Ouiscousing and Fox rivers is as follows : ——viz.

The distance between Michilimackinac and the settlement at the bottom of Green bay is calculated to be 80 leagues. On leaving Michilimackinac there is a traverse of five miles to point St. Ignace, which is the entrance into Lake Michigan. Four leagues from Michilimackinac is an island of considerable extent, named St. Helens, and may be seen from that place on a clear day. The shore from Michilimackinac to the Point du Chene, which is a league distant from the island, is rocky; and from this to the island of Epouvette, which is a very small one, and stands near the banks of the lake, is high and covered with pine—the soil very barren. From this island to the river Mino Cockien is five leagues. Two small islands on the way, and a river where boats and canoes may take shelter from a storm. The river Mino Cockien is large and deep, and takes its rise near Lake Superior. From this to Shouchoir is ten leagues. The shore is dangerous, from the number of shoals that extend a great way into the lake. This rock, called Shouchoir, is an excellent harbor for canoes, but its entrance, when the wind blows from the lake, is difficult ; but when once in, canoes and boats may lay during any storms without unlading. A custom prevails here among the voyagers for every one to have his name carved on the rocks the first time he passes, and pay something to the canoe-men. From this to the river Manistique is five leagues : it is a large river. The entrance is difficult, from a sand bank at its mouth, and the waves are very high when the wind blows from the lake. At certain seasons is found here sturgeon in great numbers. The banks of this river are high and sandy, covered with pine. It takes its rise from a large lake, and nearly communicates with Lake Superior. From this to the Detour is ten leagues. The shore is rocky, flat, and dangerous. Here begins the Traverse at the mouth of Green

source of communication between the lakes and the Mississippi, and the route by which all the traders of Michilimackinac con-

bay. The first island is distant from the main land about a league, and is called Isle au Detour, and is at least three leagues in circumference. There are generally a few Santeaux lodges of Indians on this island during the summer months. From this to Isle Brule is three leagues. There are two small islands from these to Isle Verte, and two leagues to Isle de Pou, called so from the Poutowatomies having once a village here, but now abandoned. In the months of May and June there is a fishery of trout and they are taken in great quantities by trolling. And there are also white fish in vast numbers. The ship *channel* is between this island and Isle Verte. From thence to Petit D'E-troit to the main land is three leagues, where some lodges of Ottowas and Santeaux raise small quantities of corn: but their subsistence during the summer months, chiefly depends upon the quantity of sturgeon and other fish, with which the lake here abounds. From Petit D'Etroit to the main land is three leagues, and is called the Port de Mort, from a number of Reynard ca-noes having been wrecked at this place, where every one per-ished. The shore is bold and rocky. From this is four leauges to the *Isle Racro*, which is a safe harbor, inaccessible to all winds. From this to Sturgeon bay is eight leagues. The shore is bold and rocky, and several large islands lie a few miles distant. A few Santeaux families raise corn here and reside during the summer season. Trout and sturgeon are here in great numbers. Sturgeon's bay is two miles across and about four leagues in length, and communicates by a portage with Lake Michigan, near Michilimackinac. Distant from the lake about two leagues is the Isle Vermillion. Here was a few years ago, a number of Fols Avoin inhabitants, who were accustomed to raise corn; but from what reasons they have left this place I cannot learn. From this is thirteen leagues to the entrance of the Fox river. On leaving Isle Vermillion, the woods and general appearance of the country begin to change, and have a very dif-ferent aspect from the more northern parts of this lake. A small river called Riviere Rouge falls into the lake, about half way between Isle Vermillion and La Baye. On approaching La Baye, the water of the latter assumes a whiter appearance, and becomes less deep. A channel which winds a good deal may be found for vessels of 50 and 60 tons burden; and loaded vessels of these dimensions have gone up the Fox river to the French settlements, opposite to which is the Fols Avoin village, which consists of ten or twelve bark lodges. A great number of San-teaux, and some Ottowas, come here in the spring and fall. Three leagues from La Baye is a small village of the same na-tion, and another three leagues higher at the portage of Kaka-lin. This portage is a mile long: the ground even and rocky. There is a fall of about ten feet, which obstructs the navigation

vey their goods for the trade of the Mississippi, from St. Louis to the river de Corbeau, and the confluent streams which are in

for three leagues higher, and almost continual rapids until the fall of Grand Konimee. About five feet high, above this, the river opens into a small lake, at the end of which is a strong rapid, called Puant's rapid, which issues from a lake of that name. This lake is ten leagues long, and from two to three wide. At its entrance is the first Puant village, of ten or twelve lodges. At the upper end of the lake is another Puant village, of about the same number of lodges, and at this end is a small river, which, with the interval of a few portages, communicates with Rock river. About midway between the two Puant villages is a Fols Avoin village, on the south side of the lake of 50 or 60 men. Five leagues from the entrance of the lake, on the north side, the Fox river falls in, and is about 200 yards wide. Ascending two leagues higher, is a small Fols Avoin village, where is a lake of more than two leagues long; and about a league above this lake the river de Loup joins the Fox river, near a hill called But de Mort, where the Fox nation were nearly exterminated by the French and confederate Indians. The rivers and lakes are, at certain seasons, full of wild rice. The country on the borders of this river is finely diversified with woods and prairies. Any quantity of hay may be made, and is as fine a country for raising stock as any in the same latitude through all America. From the But de Mort to the Lac a Puckway is twenty-eight leagues. Here is another Puant village of seven or eight large lodges. This lake is three leagues long: four leagues above it Lac de Bœuf begins, which is also four leagues long, and is full of wild rice, and a great many fowls in their season. From Lac de Bœuf to the forks, which is five leagues from the portage of Ouiscousing, and ten leagues above the forks, is a very small lake, called Lac *Vaseux*, and is so choked with wile rice as to render it almost impassible. The river, although very winding, becomes here more and more serpentine on approaching the portage, and the river narrows so much as almost to prevent the use of oars. The length of the portage to the Ouiscousing is two miles, and when the waters are high, canoes and boats loaded pass over. Here the waters at that time separate, the one part going to the gulph of Mexico, and the other to that of St. Lawrence. In wet seasons the portage road is very bad, the soil being of a swampy nature. There is for nearly half way a kind of natural canal, which is sometimes used, and I think a canal between the two rivers might be easily cut. The expense at present attending the transport is one third of a dollar per hundred weight; for a canoe five dollars, and for a boat eight dollars, but this is not cash, but in goods, at the rate of 200 per cent. on the sterling. There are at present two white men, who have establishments there; but they are much incommoded by the Puants of the Rock river,

those boundaries. *The village of the Prairie des Chiens is situated about one league above the mouth of the Ouiscousing river. On the E. bank of the river there is a small pond or marsh which runs parallel to the river in the rear of the town, which, in front of the marsh, consists of 18 dwelling-houses, in two streets; 16 in Front-street, and 2 in First-street. In the rear of the pond are 8 dwelling-houses; part of the houses are framed, and in place of weatherboarding, there are small logs set into mortises made in the uprights, joined close, daubed on the outside with clay, and handsomely white-washed within. The inside furniture of their houses is decent, and indeed, in those of the most wealthy, displays a degree of elegance and taste.

There are eight houses scattered round the country, at the distance of one, two, three and five miles: also, on the W side of the Mississippi, three houses, situated on a small stream called the Giard's river, making, in the village and vicinity, 37 houses, which it will not be too much to calculate at 10 persons each, the population would be 370 souls; but this calculation will not answer for the spring or autumn, as there are then, at least 5 or 600 white persons. This is owing to the concourse of traders and their engagees from Michilimackinac and other parts, who make this their last stage, previous to their launching into the savage wilderness. They again meet here in the spring, on their return from their wintering grounds, accompanied by 3 or 400 Indians, when they hold a *fair:* the one disposes of remnants of goods, and the others reserved peltries. It is astonishing there are not more murders and affrays at this place, as

who are troublesome visitors. The Ouiscousing is a large river, its bottom sandy, full of islands and sand-bars during the summer season. The navigation is difficult even for canoes, owing to the lowness of the water. From the portage to its confluence with the Mississippi is 60 leagues. The Saques and Reynards formerly lived on its banks, but were drove off by the Santeaux. They were accustomed to raise a great deal of corn and beans, the soil being excellent. Opposite to the Detour de Pin, halfway from the Portage on the south side, are lead mines, said to be the best in any part of the country, and may be wrought with great ease. Boats of more than four tons are improper for the communication between the Mississippi and Michilimackinac.

[*Dickson.*]

* The present village of the Prairie des Chiens, was first settled in the year 1783, and the first settlers were Mr. Giard, Mr. Antaya, and Mr. Dubuque. The old village is about a mile below the present one, and had existed during the time the French were possessed of the country. It derives its name from a family of Reynards who formerly lived there, distinguished by the appellation of Dogs. The present village was settled under the English government, and the ground was purchased from the Reynard Indians.

there meets such an heterogeneous mass to trade; the use of spirituous liquors being in no manner restricted, but since the American government has become known, such accidents are much less frequent than formerly. The prairie on which the village is situated is bounded in the rear by high bald hills. It is from one mile to three quarters of a mile from the river, and extends about eight miles from the Mississippi, to where it strikes the Ouiscousing at the *Petit Grey*, which bears from the village S. E. by E.

If the marsh before spoken of was drained (which might be easily done,) I am of the opinion it would render the situation of the prairie healthy, which now subjects its inhabitants to intermittent fevers in the spring and autumn.

There are a few gentlemen residing at the Prairie des Chiens, and many others claiming that appellation; but the rivalship of the Indian trade, occasions them to be guilty of acts at their wintering grounds, which they would blush to be thought guilty of in the civilized world. They possess the spirit of generosity and hospitality in an eminent degree; but this is the leading feature in the character of frontier inhabitants. Their mode of living had obliged them to have transient connexion with the Indian women; and what was at first *policy*, is now so confirmed by habit and inclination, that it is become (with a few exceptions) the ruling practice of all the traders; and, in fact, almost one half of the inhabitants under 20 years, have the blood of the aborigines in their veins. From the village to Lake Pepin we have on the W. shore, first, Yellow river, of about 20 yards wide, bearing from the Mississippi nearly due W. second, the Iowa river, about 100 yards wide, bearing from the Mississippi about N. W third, the Racine river, about 20 yards wide, bearing from the Mississippi nearly W. and navigable for canoes 60 miles; fourth, the rivers Embarra and Lean Claire, which join their waters just as they form a confluence with the Mississippi, and are about 60 yards wide, and bear nearly S. W.

On the E. shore, in the same distance, is the river de la Prairie la Cross, which empties into the Mississippi, at the head of the prairie of that name. It is about twenty yards wide, and bears N. N. W.

We then meet with the Black river, a very considerable stream, about 200 yards wide at its mouth, on which the traders frequently winter with the *Puants* and *Fols Avoins*. Next pass the river of the *Montaigne qui Trompes dans l'Eau*, a small stream in the rear of the hill of that name; and then we find the Riviere au Bœuf, of about 30 yards wide, bearing N. by W. and, at the entrance of Lake Pepin, on the E. shore joins the Santeaux river, which is at least half a mile wide, and appears to be a deep and majestic stream. It bears from the Mississippi nearly due N This river is in size and course (some distance up) scarcely to be distinguished from the Ouiscousing, and has a communication with the Montreal river by a short portage, and by this river with Lake Superior. The agents of the N. W. company supply the Fols Avoin Santeaux, who reside at the head of this river, and those of Michilimackinac, the Sioux, who hunt on its lower waters.

In this division of the Mississippi the shores are more than three-fourths prairie on both sides, or, more properly speaking, bald hills, which, instead of running parallel with the river, form a continual succession of high perpendicular cliffs and low vallies : they appear to head on the river, and to traverse the country in an angular direction. Those hills and vallies give rise to some of the most sublime and romantic views i ever saw. But this irregular scenery is sometimes interrupted by a wide extended plain, which brings to mind the verdant lawn of civilized life, and would almost induce the traveller to imagine himself in the centre of a highly cultivated plantation. The timber of this division is generally birch, elm and cottonwood, all the cliffs being bordered by cedar.

The navigation unto the Iowa river is good; but from thence to the Santeaux river is very much obstructed by islands; and in some places the Mississippi is uncommonly wide, and divided into many small channels, which, from the cliffs, appear like so many distinct rivers, winding in a parallel course through the same immense valley. But there are few sand bars in those narrow channels : the soil being rich, the water cuts through it with facility.

La Montaigne qui Trompe dans l'Eau stands in the Mississippi near the E. shore, about 50 miles below the Santeaux river, and is about two miles in circumference, with an elevation of two hundred feet, covered with timber. There is a small river which empties into the Mississippi, in the rear of the mountain, which I conceive, once bounded the mountain on the lower side, and the Mississippi on the upper, when the mountain was joined to the main by a neck of prairie low ground, which in time was worn away by the spring freshes of the Mississippi; and thus formed an island of this celebrated mountain. Lake Pepin (so called by the French,) appears to be only an expansion of the Mississippi. It commences at the entrance of the Santeaux river, and bears N. 55 W. to Point de Sable 12 miles, which is a neck of land making out about one mile into the lake, from the W. shore, and is the narrowest part of the lake. From here to the upper end the course is nearly due W. about 10 miles, making its whole length 22 miles, and from four to one and a half miles in width, the broadest part being in the bay below Point de Sable. This is a beautiful place; the contrast of the Mississippi full of islands, and the lake with not one in its whole extent, gives more force to the grandeur of the scene. The French under the government of M. Frontenac, drove the Reynards (or Ottaquamies) from the Ouiscouising, and pursued them up the Mississippi, and, as a barrier, built a stockade on Lake Pepin, on the W. shore, just below Point de Sable; and, as was generally the case with that nation, blended the military and mercantile professions, by making their fort a factory for the Sioux. The lake, at the upper end, is three fathoms deep; but this, I am informed is its shoalest part. From the Iowa river to the head of Lake Pepin, the elk are the prevailing species of wild game, with some deer, and a few bear.

From the head of Lake Pepin about 12 miles to the Cannon river, the Mississippi is branched out into many channels, and its bosom covered with numerous islands. There is a hill on the W. shore, about six miles above the lake called the Grange, from the summit of which you have one of the most delightful prospects in nature. When turning your face to the E. you have the river winding in three channels at your feet; on your right the extensive bosom of the lake, bounded by its chain of hills, in front over the Mississippi a wide extended prairie; on the left the valley of the Mississippi, open to view quite to the St. Croix, and partly in your rear, the valley through which passes the river *au Canon;* and when I viewed it, on one of the islands below, appeared the spotted lodges of the Red Wing's band of Sioux. The white tents of the traders and my soldiers, and three flags of the United States waving on the water, which gave a contrast to the still and lifeless wilderness around, and increased the pleasure of the prospect.

From the Cannon river to the St. Croix, the Mississippi evidently becomes narrower, and the navigation less obstructed by islands. The St. Croix river joins the Mississippi on the E. and bears from the latter almost due N. It is only 80 yards wide at its mouth, and 500 yards up commences Lake St. Croix, which is from one and a half to three miles wide, and 36 long. This river communicates with Lake Superior by the Burnt river, by a portage, of half a mile only, and in its whole extent has not *one fall or rapid* worthy of notice. This, with the mildness of its current, and its other advantages, render it by far the most preferable communication which can be had, with the N. W. from this part of our territories. Its upper waters are inhabited by the Fols Avoins and Santeaux, who are supplied by the agents of the North-west company; and its lower division by the Sioux and their traders.

The Mississippi from the Cannon river is bounded on the E. by high ridges, but the left is low ground. The timber is generally ash and maple, except the cedar of the cliffs. From the St. Croix to the river St. Peters the Mississippi is collected into a narrow compass (I crossed it at one place with forty strokes of my oars) and the navigation very good. The E. bank generally bounded by the river ridges, but the W. sometimes timbered bottom or prairie. The timber is generally maple, sugar-tree, and ash. About twenty miles below the entrance of the river St. Peters, on the E. shore, at a place called the Grand Morais, is situated the Petit Corbeau's village of eleven log houses. From the river St. Peters to the falls of St. Anthony, the river is contracted between high hills, and is one continual rapid or fall, the bottom being covered with rocks, which (in low water) are some feet above the surface, leaving narrow channels between them. The rapidity of the current is likewise much augmented by the numerous small rocky islands, which obstruct the navigation. The shores have many large and beautiful springs issuing forth, which form small cascades as they tumble over the cliffs into the Mississippi. The timber is generally maple. This place we noted for the great quantity of wild fowl. As I ascended the Mississippi, the falls of St. Anthony did not strike me with that majestic appearance which I had been taught to expect from the description of former travellers. On an actual survey, I find the portage to be 260 poles; but when the river is not very low, boats ascending may be put in 31 pole below, at a large cedar tree, which would reduce it to 229 poles. The hill over which the portage is made, is 69 feet ascent, with an elevation at the point of debarkation of 45°. The fall of the water between the place of debarkation and re-loading is 58 feet; the perpendicular fall of the shoot 16½ feet. The width of the river above the shoot 627 yards; below 209. In high water the appearance is much more sublime, as the great quantity of water *then* forms a spray, which in clear weather reflects from some positions the colors of the rainbow, and when the sky is o'ercast, covers the falls in gloom and chaotic majesty. From the falls of St. Anthony to Rum river, the Mississippi is almost one continual chain of rapids, with the eddies formed by winding channels. Both sides are prairie and scarcely any timber but small groves of scrub oak. Rum river is about 50 yards wide at its mouth, and takes its source in Le Mille Lac, which is but 35 miles S. of Lower Red Cedar Lake. The small Indian canoes ascend this river quite to the lake, which is considered as one of the best fur hunting grounds for some hundreds of miles, and has been long a scene of rencounters between the hunting parties of the Sioux and Santeaux. The last winter a number of the Fols Avoins and Sioux, and some Santeaux, wintered in that quarter. From Rum river to Leaf river, (called by father Hennepin and Carver, the river St. Francis, and was the extent of their travels) the prairies continue with a few interruptions. The timber scrub oak, with now and then a lonely pine. Previous to your arrival at Leaf river you pass Crow river on the W. about 30 yards wide, which bears from the Mississippi S. W. Leaf river is only a small stream of not more than 15 yards over, and bears N. by W.

The elk begin to be very plenty; some buffalo, quantities of deer, racoons, and on the prairie a few of the animals called by the French brelaws.

From thence to Sac river, a little above the Grand Rapids, both sides of the river are generally prairie, with skirts of scrub oak. The navigation still obstructed with ripples, but with some intermissions of a few miles.

At the Grand Rapids the river expands itself to about 3–4 of a mile in width, its general width not being more than 3–5 of a mile) and tumbles over an unequal bed of rocks for about two miles, through which there cannot be said to be any channel; for notwithstanding the rapidity of the current, one of my invalids, who was on the W. shore waded to the E. (where we were encamped.) The E. bank at the Rapids is a very high prairie; the W. scrubby wood land. The Sac river is a considerable stream, which comes in on the W. and bears about S. W. and is 200 yards wide at its mouth.

The quantity of game still increasing from Sac river to Pine creek, (the place where I built my stockade and left part of my party) the borders are prairie, with groves of pine on the edge of the bank; but there are some exceptions where you meet with small bottoms of oak, ash, maple, and linn. In this distance there is an intermission of rapids for about 40 miles, when they commence again, and are full as difficult as ever. There are three small creeks emptying in on the W. scarcely worthy of notice, and on the E. are two small rivers called Lake and Clear Rivers; the former quite a small one, bears N. W. and is about 15 yards wide at its mouth; about three miles from its entrance, is a beautiful small lake, around which resort immense herds of elk and buffalo. Clear river is a beautiful little stream, of about 80 yards in width, and heads in some swamps and small lakes on which the Santeaux of Lower Red Cedar Lake, and Sandy Lake frequently come to hunt. The soil of the prairies from above the falls is sandy, but would raise small grain in abundance; the bottoms rich, and fit for corn or hemp. Pine creek is a small stream which comes in on the W shore and bears nearly W. It is bordered by large groves of *white* and *red* pine. From Pine creek to the Isle De Corbeau, (or river of that name) two small rivers come in on the W. shore. The first is of little consequence; but the second called Elk river, is entitled to more consideration, from its communication with the river St. Peters. They first ascend it to a small lake, cross it, then ascend a small stream to a large lake; from which they make a portage of 4 miles W. and fall into the Santeaux river, which they descend into the river St. Peters. On the E. side is one small stream which heads towards Lower Red Cedar Lake, and is bounded by hills. The whole of this distance is remarkably difficult to navigate, being one continued succession of rapid shoals and falls; but there is *one* deserves to be more particularly noticed, viz: The place called by the French Le Shute de la Roche Peinture, which is certainly the 3d obstacle in point of navigation, which I met with in my whole route. The shore where there is not prairie, is a continued succession of pine ridges. The entrance of the river De Corbeau, is partly hid by the island of that name, and discharges its waters into the Mississippi above and below it; the lowest channel bearing from the Mississippi N. 65° W. the upper due W. This (in my opinion) should be termed the forks of the Mississippi, it being nearly of equal magnitude, and heading not far from the same source; although taking a much more direct course to their junction. This river affords the best and most approved communication with the Red river; and the navigation is as follows: You ascend the river De Corbeau 180 miles, to the entrance of the river Des Feuilles, which comes from the N. W. This you ascend 180 miles also; then make a portage of half a mile into the Otter Tail Lake, which is a principal source of Red river. The other branch of the river De Corbeau bears S. W. and approximates with the St. Peters. The whole of this river is rapid, and by no means affording so much water as the Mississippi, Their confluence is in latitude 45° 49′ 50″ N. In this division the elk, deer, and buffalo, were probably in greater quantities than in any other part of my whole voyage. From thence to Pine river the Mississippi continues to become narrower, and has but few islands. In this distance I discovered but one rapid, which the force of the frost had not entirely covered with ice. The shores in general presented a dreary prospect of high barren nobs, covered with dead and fallen pine timber. To this there were some exceptions of ridges of yellow and pitch pine; also some small bottoms of linn, elm, oak, and ash. The adjacent country is (at least two-thirds) covered with small lakes, some of which are three miles in circumference. This renders the communication impassible in summer, except in small bark canoes. In this distance we first met with a species of pine called the sap pine. It was equally unknown to myself and all my party. It scarcely ever exceeds the height of 35 feet, and is very full of projecting branches. The leaves are similar to other pines; but project out from the branches on each side in a direct line, thereby rendering the branch flat; and this formation occasions the natives and voyagers to give it the preference on all occasions to the branches of all other trees for their beds, and to cover their temporary camps; but its greatest virtue arises from its medicinal qualities. The rind is smooth, with the exception of little protuberances of about the size of a hazel nut; the top of which being cut, you squeeze out a glutinous substance of the consistence of honey. This gum or sap gives name to the tree, and is used by the natives and traders of that country as a balsam for all wounds made by sharp instruments, or on parts frozen, and almost all other external injuries which they receive. My poor fellows experienced its beneficial qualities by the application made of it to their frozen extremities in various instances. The *Pine river* bears from the Mississippi N. 30° E. although it empties in on that which has been hitherto termed the W. shore. It is 80 yards wide at its mouth, and has an island immediately at the entrance. It communicates with Lake Le Sang Sue, by the following course of navigation: In one day's sail from the confluence, you arrive at the first part of White Fish Lake, which is about 6 miles long;

and two wide. From thence you pursue the river about two miles, and come to the 2d White Fish Lake, which is about 3 miles long and 1 wide; then you have the river three miles to the 3d lake, which is 7 miles long and two in width, (which I crossed on my return from the head of the Mississippi on the      of February; and is in 46° 32′ 32″ N. latitude.) From thence you follow the river a quarter of a mile to the 4th lake, which is a circular one, of about 5 miles in circumference. From thence you pursue the river one day's sail to a small lake; from thence two days' sail to a portage, which conveys you to another lake, from whence by small portages from lake to lake, you make the voyage to Leech Lake. The whole of this course lays through ridges of pines or swamps of pinenet, sap pine, hemlock, &c. &c. From the river De Corbeau to this place the deer are very plenty, but we found no more buffalo or elk. From this place to the Red Cedar Lake, the pine ridges are interrupted by large bottoms of elm, ash, oak, and maple; the soil of which would be very proper for cultivation. From the appearance of the ice, (which was firm and equal) I conceive there can be but one ripple in this distance. Red Cedar Lake lays on the E. side of the Mississippi, at the distance of 6 miles from it, and is near equally distant from the river De Corbeau and Lake De Sable. Its form is an oblong square, and may be 10 miles in circumference. From this to Lake De Sable on the E. shore, you meet with Muddy river, which discharges itself into the Mississippi by a mouth 20 yards wide, and bears nearly N. E. We then meet with Pike river on the W about 77 miles below Sandy Lake, and bears nearly due N. up which you ascend with canoes 4 days' sail, and arrive at a wild Rice lake, which you pass through and enter a small stream, and ascend it two leagues; then cross a portage of two acres into a lake 7 leagues in circumference : then two leagues of a river into another small lake. From thence you descend the current N. E. into Leech Lake. The banks of the Mississippi are still bordered by the pines of the different species, except a few small bottoms of elm, linn and maple. The game scarce, and the Aborigines, subsist almost entirely on the beaver, with a few moose, and the wild rice or oats.

Sandy Lake river (or the discharge of said lake) is large, but is only six miles in length from the lake to its confluence with the Mississippi. Lake De Sable is about 25 miles in circumference, and has a number of small rivers running into it ; one of those is entitled to particular attention, viz : the river Savanna, which by a portage of three miles and three quarters communicates with the river St. Louis, which empties into Lake Superior at the Fond Du Lac ; and is the channel by which the N. W. company bring all their goods for the trade of the Upper Mississippi. Game is very scarce in this country. In ascending the Mississippi from Sandy lake, you first meet with Swan river on the E. which bears nearly due E. and is navigable for bark canoes, 90 miles to Swan lake. You then meet with the Meadow riv-

er, which falls in on the E. and bears nearly E. by N. and is navigable for Indian canoes, 100 miles. You then in ascending
meet with a very strong ripple, and an expansion of the river
where it forms a small lake. This is three miles below the falls
of Packegamau, and from which the noise of the shoot might be
heard. The course of the river at the falls was N. 70° W. and
just below the river is a quarter of a mile in width, but above
the shoot not more than 20 yards. The water thus collected,
runs down a flat rock, which has an elevation of about 30°. Immediately above the fall is a small island of about 50 yards in
circumference, covered with sap pine. The portage which is
on the E. (or N.) side, is not more than 200 yards; and by no
means difficult. Those falls, in point of consideration, as an
impediment to the navigation, stand next to the falls of St. Anthony, from the source of the river to the Gulf of Mexico. The
banks of the river to the Meadow river, have generally either
been timbered by the pine, pinenet, hemlock, sap pine, or the
aspen tree. From thence it winds through high grass meadows,
(or savannas) with the pine swamps, at a distance appearing to
cast a deeper gloom on the borders. From the falls in ascending, you pass the lake Packegamau on the W. celebrated for its
great productions of wild rice; and next meet with the Deer
river on the E. the extent of its navigation unknown. You next
meet with the Riviere Le Cross; on the E. side, which bears
nearly N. and has only a portage of one mile to pass from it into
the Lake Winipeque Branch of the Mississippi. We next come
to what the people of that quarter call the forks of the Mississippi. The right fork of which bears N. W. and runs eight
leagues to Lake Winipeque, which is of an oval form of about
26 miles in circumference. From Lake Winipeque the river
continues five leagues to Upper Red Cedar Lake, which may be
termed the Upper Source of the Mississippi. The Leech Lake
Branch bears (from the forks) S. W. and runs through a chain
of meadows. You pass Muddy lake which is scarcely any thing
more than an extensive marsh of 15 miles in circumference; the
river bears through it nearly N. after which it again turns W.
In many places this branch is not more than ten or fifteen yards
in width, although 15 or 20 feet deep. From this to Leech Lake,
the communication is direct, and without any impediment. This
is rather considered as the main source, although the Winipeque branch is navigable the greatest distance. To this place
the whole face of the country has an appearance of an impenetrable morass, or boundless savanna. But on the borders of the
lake is some oak and large groves of sugar maple, from which
the traders make sufficient sugar for their consumption the whole
year. Leech Lake communicates with the river De Corbeau by
seven portages, and the river Des Feuilles also, with the Red
river, by the Otter Tail Lake on the one side, and by Red Cedar
Lake and other small lakes to Red Lake on the other. Out of
these small lakes and ridges, rise the upper waters of the St.

Lawrence, Mississippi and Red river, the latter of which discharges itself into the ocean by Lake Winipie and Hudson's Bay. All those waters have their upper sources within 100 miles of each other, which I think plainly proves this to be the most elevated part of the N. E. continent of America. But we must cross (what is commonly termed) the Rocky Mountains, or a Spur of the Cordeliers, previous to our finding the waters, whose currents run westward, and pay tribute to the western ocean.

In this quarter we find moose, a very few deer and bear, but a vast variety of fur animals of all descriptions.

The first nation of Indians whom we met with in ascending the Mississippi from St. Louis, were the Sauks, who principally reside in four villages. The first at the head of the rapids De Moyen on the W. shore, consisting of 13 log lodges. The 2d on a prairie on the E. shore, about 60 miles above. The 3d on the Riviere De Roche, about 3 miles from the entrance, and the last on the river Iowa.

They hunt on the Mississippi and its confluent streams, from the Illinois to the river Des Iowa; and on the plains west of them, which border the Missouri. They are so perfectly consolidated with the Reynards, that they scarcely can be termed a distinct nation; but recently there appears to be a schism between the two nations: the latter not approving of the *insolence* and *ill-will*, which has *marked* the conduct of the former towards the United States, on many late occurrences. They have for many years past made war (under the auspices of the Sioux) on the Santeaux, Osages, and Missouries; but as recently a peace has been (through the influence of the United States) made between them and the nations of the Missouri, and by the same means between the Sioux and Santeaux, (their principal allies) it appears that it would by no means be a difficult matter to induce them to make a general peace, and pay still greater attention to the cultivation of the earth: as they now raise a considerable quantity of corn, beans, and melons. The character that they bear with their savage brethren, is, that they are much more to be dreaded for their deceit and inclination for stratagem, than for open courage.

The Reynards reside in three villages. The 1st on the W. side of the Mississippi, six miles above the rapids of the river De Roche. The 2d about 12 miles in the rear of the lead mines, and the 3d on Turkey river half a league from its entrance. They are engaged in the same wars, and have the same alliances as the Sauks, with whom they must be considered as indissoluble in war or peace. They hunt on both sides of the Mississippi from the river Iowa, (below the Prairie Des Chiens) to a river of that name above said village. They raise a great quantity of corn, beans, and melons; the former of those articles in such quantities, as to sell many hundred bushels per annum.

The Iowas reside on the rivers De Moyen and Iowa in two villages. They hunt on the west side of the Mississippi, the river De Moyen, and westward to the Missouri; their wars and alliances are the same as the Sauks and Reynards; under whose special protection they conceive themselves to be. They cultivate some corn; but not so much in proportion as the Sauks and Reynards. Their residence being on the small streams in the rear of the Mississippi, out of the high road of commerce, renders them less civilized than those nations.

The Sauks, Reynards, and Iowas, (since the treaty of the two former with the United States) claim the land from the entrance of the Jauflioni on the W. side of the Mississippi, up the latter river to the Des Iowa, above the Prairie Des Chiens and westward to the Missouri; but the limits between themselves are undefined. All the land formerly claimed by those nations E. of the Mississippi, is now ceded to the United States; but they reserved to themselves the privilege of hunting and residing on it as usual.

By killing the celebrated Sauk chief Pontiac, the Illinois, Cahokias, Kaskaskias and Piorias, kindled a war with the allied nations of Sauks and Reynards, which has been the cause of the almost entire destruction of the former nations.

The Winebagos, or Puants, are a nation who reside on the rivers Ouiscousing, De Roche, Fox and Green Bay, in seven villages, which are situated as follows, viz:

| | |
|---|---|
| 1st. At the entrance of Green Bay. | 5th. Portage of the Ouiscousing. |
| 2d. End of do. | |
| 2d. Wuckan, on the Fox river. | 6th. and 7th. Both on Roche river. |
| 4th. At Lake Puckway. | |

Those villages are so situated, that the Winebagos can embody the whole force of their nation, at any one point of their territory in four days. They hunt on the Ouiscousing, Rock river, and E. side of the Mississippi; From the Rock river to the Prairie Des Chiens; on Lake Michigan, Black river, and the country between Lakes Michigan, Huron, and Superior. From the tradition amongst them, and their speaking the same language of the Ottos of the Riviere Platte, I am confident in asserting that they are a nation who have emigrated from Mexico, to avoid the oppression of the Spaniards, and the time may be fixed at about one and a half centuries, when they were taken under the protection of the Sioux, to whom they still profess to owe faith, and *at least brotherly* attention. They have formerly been at war with the nations west of the Mississippi, but appear recently to have laid down the hatchet. They are reputed brave, but from every circumstance their neighbors distinguish their bravery as the ferocity of a tiger, rather than the deliberate resolution of a man. And recently their conduct has been such as to authorize the remark made by a chief of a neighboring nation, "That a white man never should lay down to sleep, without precaution in their villages."

The Menomene or Fols Avoins (as termed by the French) nation, reside in seven villages, situated as follows, viz. 1st. At the river Menomene, 15 leagues from Green Bay, north side of the lake. 2d. At Green Bay. 3d. At Little Kakalin. 4th. Portage of Kakalin. 5th. Stinking Lake. 6th. Entrance of a small lake on Fox river ; and 7th. Behind the Bank of the Dead. Their hunting grounds are similar to the Winebagos ; only, that owing to the very high estimation in which they are held, both by Sioux and Chipeways, they are frequently permitted to hunt near the Raven river on the Mississippi ; which may be termed the battle ground between those two great nations. The language which they speak is singular ; for no white man has ever yet been know to acquire it, but this may probably be attributed to their all understanding the Algonquin, in which they and the Winebagos transact all conferences with the whites or other nations ; and the facility with which that language is acquired, is a further reason for its prevalence.

The Fols Avoins although a small nation, are respected by all their neighbors for their bravery, and independent spirit, and esteemed by the whites as their friends and protectors. When in the country, I have heard their *chief* assert in council with the Sioux and Chipeways, " That although they were reduced " to few in number, yet they could say, we never were slaves." As they had always preferred, " that their women and children " should die by their own hands, to their being led into slavery " by their enemies " The boundary of their territory is uncertain. The Sauks, Reynards, Puants, and Menomenes, all reside (when not at their villages) in lodges in the form of an ellipsis, and some are from 30 to 40 feet in length, by 14 or 15 wide, which are sufficiently large to shelter 60 people from the storm, or for twenty to reside in. Their covering are rushes plaited into mats, and carefully tied to the poles. In the centre are the fires, immediately over which is a small vacancy in the lodge, which in fair weather is sufficient to give vent to the smoke ; but in bad weather you must lay down on the ground to prevent being considerably incommoded by it.

We next came to that powerful nation the Sioux, the dread of whom is extended over all the savage nations, from the confluence of the Mississippi and Missouri, to the Raven river on the former, and to the Snake Indians on the latter ; but in those limits are many nations whom they consider as allies ; on similar footing with the allies of ancient Rome, i. e. humble dependents. But the Chipeway nation is an exception who have maintained a long contest with them, owing to their country being intersected by numerous small lakes, water courses, impenetrable morasses, and swamps ; and have hitherto bid defiance to all the attacks of their neighbors. It is necessary to divide the Sioux nation into the different bands, as distinguished amongst themselves, in order to have a correct idea of them. Agreeably to this plan, I shall begin with the *Minowa Kantong*, (or Gens De Lac) who extend from the Prairie Des Chiens, to La Prairie du Francois, 35 miles up the St. Peters. This band is again sub-divided into four divisions, under different chiefs. The first of which, most generally reside at their village on the Upper Iowa river, above the Prairie Des Chiens, and are commanded by Wabasha, a chief, whose father was considered as the first chief of all the Sioux nation. This sub-division hunts on both sides of the Mississippi, and its confluent streams, from the Prairie Des Chiens to the riviere du Bœuf. The second sub-division resides near the head of Lake Pepin, and hunt from the riviere du Bœuf near to the river St. Croix. Their chief's name is Tentangamani, a very celebrated war chief. The third sub-division resides between the riviere au Canon and the entrance of the St. Peters, are headed by Chatewaconamani. Their principal hunting ground is on the St. Croix. They have a village at a place called the Grand Marais, 15 miles below the entrance of the St. Peters. It is situated on the east bank of the Mississippi, and consists of eleven log huts. The fourth subdivision is situated from the entrance of the St. Peters, to the Prairie Des Francois ; they are headed by a chief called Chatamutah, but a young man, Wyaganage, has recently taken the lead in all the councils and affairs of state of this sub-band. They have one village nine miles up the St. Peters, on the N. side. This band (Minowa Kantong) are reputed the bravest of all the Sioux ; and have for years been opposed to the Fols Avoin Sauteurs, who are reputed the bravest of all the numerous bands of Chipaways.

The 2d band of Sioux, are the Washpetong (or Gens Des Fieulles) who inhabit the country from the Prairie Des Francois, near to Roche Blanche, on the St. Peters. Their first chief is Wasonquianni. They hunt on the St. Peters ; also on the Mississippi, up Rum river, and sometimes follow the buffalo on the plains. Their sub-divisions I am unacquainted with.

The 3d band are the Sussitongs ; they extend from the Roche Blanche, to Lac de Gross Roche, on the river St. Peters ; they are divided into two sub-divisions. The 1st band, called the Cawrees, are headed by the chief called Wuckiew Nutch, (or the Tonnere Rouge.) The 2d, called the *Sussitongs proper*, and headed by Wacontoe, (or Esprit Blue.) Those two sub-bands hunt eastward to the Mississippi, and up that river as far as the Riviere De Corbeau.

The 4th great band are the Yanctongs, who are dispersed from the Montaignes De la Prairie, (which extends from St. Peters to the Missouri) to the river de Moyen. They are divided into two grand divisions, generally termed the Yanctongs of the north, and the Yanctongs of the south. The former are headed by a chief called Muckpeanutah ; (or Nuage Rouge) and those of the Prairie by Petessung. This band are never stationary, but with the Titongs, are the most erratic bands of all the Sioux, sometimes to be found on the borders of the Lower Red River, sometimes on the Missouri, and on those immense plains which are between the two rivers.

The 5th great band are the Titongs, who are dispersed on both sides of the Missouri—on the north, principally from the river Chienne up; and on the south, from the Mahas to the Minetares, (or Gross Ventres.) They may be divided into the Titongs of the north and south; but the immense plains over which they rove with the Yanctongs, render it impossible to point out their place of habitation.

The 6th last and smallest band of the Sioux, are the *Washpecoute,* who reside generally on the lands west of the Mississippi, between that river and the Missouri. They hunt most generally on the head of the river de Moyen. They appeared to me to be the most stupid and inactive of all the Sioux.

[*b* 2]   THE wild goose of the Mississippi and the common tame goose will herd together, and the former can be and is frequently domesticated, and breed with the common flock, but their offspring will not breed. Like the Jack and the horse, the effect of copulation of the wild and tame goose is abortive and of no avail further than the first generation. This is a clear evidence that these birds, though so much alike in appearance, and in character, are of different species. Major Buskirk of Shelby, Kentucky, informed me that he and his brother-in-law, Lewis Cray, also of Kentucky, have several half bloods of the wild and tame goose. That the egg of the female is much less than that of the common goose: that after she has laid her usual quantity, she sits on them the usual period required in other goose eggs, and with all the care and anxiety of the tame goose, does she perform and fulfil every natural and necessary duty to hatch her eggs and bring forth the young brood—and getting disappointed, shews evident marks, by her actions, of uneasiness and restlessness for some time. Such is the singular order of nature—" So far shalt thou go, and no farther." I am told, however, there is one kind of wild goose that domesticates and breeds with the tame.

[*c* 2]   NEW MADRID occupies a handsome site on the right or west bank of the Mississippi, commanding a beautiful view of the river for six miles above and ten below the town, being near the middle of a bend 25 miles in length.

The late col. George Morgan, latterly of Morganza, Washington county, Penn. and formerly of New Jersey, with a number of surveyors, carpenters, woodsmen, &c. embarked at Pittsburgh in the year 1789 or 1790, and descended to this favored spot, for the purpose of laying it out and commencing the settlement of a city, whose original plan was not to be exceeded in size and in manner by many cities in the world. It was to extend 4 miles

S. and 2 west from the river, so as to include lake St. Annis in its limits, on whose banks were to be wide streets and roads planted with trees for the health of the citizens. A street 120 feet wide on the bank of the river was also to be planted with trees. Twelve acres in the middle of the city was to be ornamented with trees and preserved for public walks ; 40 half-acre lots for other public uses, and one lot of 12 acres for the king's use.

The party that accompanied col. Morgan, after they arrived soon began to sicken. Fatigue, hunger and distress, appeared in every quarter. Some died, others scattered and made their way home as well as they could. Large Spanish grants of lands were held out to them as a recompense and a fortune for their adventure. These were never made, and col. Morgan getting himself disappointed in the encouragement he expected to receive from the Spaniards, the city was abandoned by its first projectors. Many lots, however, were sold, and a considerable town built, the inhabitants being chiefly French and Spaniards, and a few trading Americans. The town has, however, been on the decline for several years, and the terrific effects of the earthquake, which commenced Dec. 16, 1811, seems to have alarmed the inhabitants to that degree that few have had the hardihood to remain in or near the town since. There are still a few families, and a court is held here for a district of the Missouri territory. The town has two badly supplied stores, a tavern and a post office, and from the number of old shattered vacant houses, the place indeed looks like " departing greatness." But time may yet revive New Madrid, and 100 years, nay 50, make it what it was intended to be by its original projector, a great and magnificent city. Its situation possesses advantages that time alone can discover the extent of, and which can only be brought into action by a great population of the country.

The earthquake continued at New Madrid by frequent returning shocks with the most tremendous and alarming effects for two or more months, and are still slightly felt, say the inhabitants, every 24 hours.* It threw down the brick chimnies, shattered the houses, threw up the earth in some places, while it sunk in others ; water spouted up through the cracks and holes of the earth in all directions ; trees lashed their tops together, while others were split, twisted and torn from their roots ; the river itself appeared equally convulsed with the land. No wonder indeed that a people, accustomed to the quiet of a forest, and the pacific rolling of the Mississippi, should, on this occasion of one of nature's greatest concussions of matter, feel terror and alarm to a degree little short of madness. For in flight there appeared to be no safety, earth and water were equally affected ; and what rendered the distressing scene the more awful,

---

* December, 1812:

the birds and beasts seemed equally terrified as the people themselves. The winged tribe come hovering down on the houses, and lighting, I have been told, in some cases, on people's heads, and about the fires of those who had left their dwellings, and on the rocking boats in the river. The cattle sought the open ground for shelter, and it being convulsed, threw them into confusion, they ran about bellowing as in the greatest alarm and distress, seeking also the camps of the people and seemingly their protection. It has been stated that the deer, equally shocked and terrified with man, has been seen to stop suddenly, and stand as if fastened to the spot, unable for a few minutes to move. Such are thy throes, Oh God of nature! and such are their wonderful effects on animal life. Man, the proudest of earth's inhabitants, lacking but little in his own imagination, of God himself, yet, in those awful convulsions of nature, do we see him shrink into his own insignificance, mixing, as by instinct, with the fowls of the air and the beasts of the field, all equally distracted and confounded at the universal tumult of earth and water—crying for help! help!—running here, and yonder, without thought or reflection, as though he had changed his nature, and ready, as it were, for the final event of the "crush of matter, and the wreck of worlds."

The inhabitants of New Madrid say, the plot of ground the town stands on has been sunk during the shocks of the earthquake eight feet below its former level. I passed it in the spring of 1811, before the earthquake, and in the winter of 1812, after it, and from the idea I had formed of the height of the ground, it appeared evident that it had sunk several feet, probably eight; this appears further confirmed by the bank of the river about a mile below the town being considerably higher than the town itself, and looks like a natural second bank of considerable elevation above the first. The bank of the river for 10 or 15 miles above, though not as high as the bank at the town, appears to have been sunk in the same proportion with it.

Another circumstance has added inconvenience to the progress of New Madrid. The river is constantly making encroachments on it, and has, since its first commencement, swept away land to the extent of half the present breadth of the river, it being here about one mile broad. Street after street went off with the floods, keeping the citizens moving back, to their no small vexation and loss of property.

About 60 or 70 miles west of New Madrid, are the head waters of Merrimac river, between which and the town the land is high, fertile, and well calculated for farming and grazing.— Twelve or 15 miles back of New Madrid, there is already a considerable settlement, and the lake in which the Chepousa river takes its rise, about 25 miles north-westerly from the town, affords some delightful situations.

On account of a great bend in the Missouri and Mississippi, New Madrid is favorably situated in point of having a near communication with the Missouri, it being only about 150 miles by land from the town to the mouth of the Osage river, whereas by water from the latter to the former it is about 500 miles.— The head waters of the St. Francis river coming within a few miles of the head of Merrimac of the Mississippi and the Gasconade of the Missouri, will also be useful to New Madrid, as forming a convenient chain of communication from low down on the Mississippi to high up on the Missouri, which will very much facilitate trade, and the settlements hereafter to be made in this part of the Missouri territory. The St. Francis river heads within about 12 or 15 miles of the Osage river, and near G. Gravel river, a small branch of it. There are also two water courses from the Mississippi below New Madrid to the St. Francis, which, by looking at the direction they take, it is scarcely known whether they run from the latter to the former, or from the former to the latter. They however afford a communication, which, in the settlement of the country on the St. Francis, will be useful to those passing from the one river to the other.

[d 2]

*Extract of a letter from Capt. John Davis to his friend in Sweet Springs, Virginia, dated Natchez, M. T. January 5th, 1812.*

WE arrived at night on the 15th of Dec. at the 25th Island, and on the 16th at 10 minutes past 2 o'clock A. M. we were surprised by the greatest emotion that can possibly be supposed of the boat, which I could compare to nothing more picturesque than that of a team of horses running away with a wagon over the most rocky road in our part of the country. There was about 40 boats in company, and each thought their boats adrift and running over sawyers; but a man on board a boat lashed to us, hinted it to be an earthquake. An old navigator of the river just above, hailed us and said it was occasioned by the banks falling in; we were under a bluff bank which immediately cast off, and fell in about a quarter of a mile, which drew us into the current on the right side of the island which was much the shallowest where we staid till day; but in the intermediate time, we experienced about 50 partial shocks, which shook our boats with great agitation. At 12 minutes after 7, we heard a tremendous distant noise, and in a few seconds the boats, island and main land became perfectly convulsed, the trees twisted and lashed together, the earth in all quarters was sinking, and the water issued from the centre of the 25th isle just on our left, and came rushing down its side in torrents; and on our right there fell at once about 30 or 40 acres of land, some say 300 acres; but as I was till then perfectly collected, and although then much alarmed, was less so than any person in company. The shocks by this time became frequent at about every 15 minutes: the water rose from the first shock, till about 8 o'clock that day, 7 or 8 feet perpendicular, and the current ran from 7 to 8 miles per hour. As we ran from 25th island and landed on Flour island, a distance of 35 miles, in five hours and 25 minutes, and lost half an hour endeavoring to make a landing at the lower end of the 9 Mile Reach, which place and the 10 Mile Reach was in perfect commotion. The logs which had sprung up from the bottom of the river, were so thick, that it appeared almost impossible for a boat to find a passage. There were three boats sunk, two of which belonged to Mr. James Atwell, and laden from Kentucky, in value about $3000, the other a family boat; the people were all saved except one man, who belonged to the family boat. Another man had like to have been lost, from one of the boats that was stove, he jumped on the sawyer that stove the boat, and continued there about four hours, and was fortunately taken into another boat. The logs and roots we passed had the sand and mud on them which probably for many years lay in the bottom of the river, and which gave the appearance of timbered fields to the 9 and 10 Mile Reach, so that it appeared as if the order of nature was reversed. We experienced frequent shocks of earthquakes for 8 days and I have heard of no place more convulsed than where I was.————

[ e 2 ]   NO. 57 is called " *Battle Island*" from the following anecdote, viz. a battle fought on it by two boatmen belonging to a barge from the falls of Ohio; The battle was thus expressed in the captain's journal: "Two of my stoutest men having quarrelled during the day while at the oars, and having clinched, had a small round under deck; hearing the noise, I ran and parted them, and could appease them in no other way, than by granting them permission to take it out on the land. Accordingly at evening as soon as we dropped anchor, the parties having chosen their stand-by friends, set out from the barge in the jolly boat, and landed on No 57, where, after it was agreed that it should be "*rough and tumble*," and the signal for parting should be " *enough*," the combatants stripped off their jackets (the weather being cold,) and taking their distance, flew at each other most ferociously. Two rounds brought them fast clinched in each other's hug, to the ground, when the undermost, finding the thumb of his antagonist removing his eye from its socket, hollowed out vociferously to the bystanders, " *take him off !* *take him off ! he is gouging me.*" This was done immediately, and the boys got to their feet again; and discovering there was not much harm done, except a *bite* from the one, and a *gouge* from the other, they returned good naturedly to the barge again, and as usual worked friendly together during the remainder of the voyage.

Having been an eye-witness to this tiger like engagement, I no longer wonder that Schultz's story of the battle at Natchez, between two Kentucky boatmen, one calling himself *"half horse, half alligator,"* and the other *"snapping turtle,"* has obtained current belief in New York, and that the citizens of that metropolis, have got into an opinion, that if the Kentuckians are not bona fide *alligators* and *snapping turtles,* many of them, at least, are not much better, in point of good manners and civilization.

Thus, unfortunately, the character of a people gets fixed abroad, by the brutal and irregular conduct of a few of its citizens. So bad and so detestable is the character of Kentucky on the coast of the Mississippi, to the once hospitable French planters, that a traveller is liable at every place, (except the miserable taverns) to have the door shut in his face on approaching a house for a night's lodging or refreshment of any kind. Nor will any plea or circumstance alter the determined refusal of the master or mistress of the house, unless indeed, it be the uncommon genteel appearance and equipage of the traveller.

A friend of mine related the following anecdote to me : That travelling on foot from New Orleans to Natchez, and night coming on, he stept up to the door of a house and asked admission for the night. A genteel and young looking woman came to the door, and said she did not lodge strangers. In reply he observed, that it was then night, and raining hard, that he was much fatigued, and would lay in any of her out cabins, if she would permit him to remain. She said she could not let him stay any where about the premises, that it was the strict charge of her husband, who was then absent, to "lodge none of the *Kentuckians*"—My friend S. blushed for his countrymen, and said, though he had reason to think differently from her husband of the citizens of Kentucky, he was not from that state, but from Pittsburgh in Pennsylvania, many hundred miles above Kentucky. The lady, like the custom house officer at Leghorn,*

* " To illustrate the commercial habits and enterprise of the American people, he would relate an anecdote of a vessel built and cleared out at Pittsburgh for Leghorn. When she arrived at her place of destination, the master presented his papers to the custom house officer at Leghorn, who would not credit them, and who said to the master, "sir your papers are forged; there is no such place as Pittsburgh in the world ! your vessel must be confiscated !" The trembling captain laid before the officer a map of the U. S. directed him to the Gulf of Mexico ; pointed out the mouth of the Mississippi ; led him a thousand miles up it to the mouth of the Ohio, and thence another thousand up to Pittsburgh " There sir is the port whence my vessel cleared out." The astonished officer, before he saw the map, would as soon have believed that this ship had been navigated from the moon.

*Clay's Speech in Congress.*

not knowing any thing about Pennsylvania, or whether there was any such a place as Pittsburgh in America, observed in reply, "that they were in the habit of believing and taking all strangers travelling upwards, for Kentuckians, therefore they made no exception, and her husband's orders were positive."— "My good lady," replied my friend, with all his gentleness of politeness and persuasive good manners, "what shall I do! you say it is eight miles to the next house, and through, to me, a strange and dark forest, and mud and water half leg deep all the way, I assure you I am unable to go further to night, it rains hard, and I am excessively fatigued, (having on his back his bags full of dollars, besides his clothes, with which he had walked thirty-five miles that day.) Is it possible (continued he) you would turn me from your door and subject me to lodge in the woods, without cover, or other comfort, when I want nothing of you but the indulgence of an out cabin and a little fire to dry myself by?" This earnest petition, enforced by his natural modesty and good sense, got my friend admittance. The lady's heart relented, and she gave him permission to walk in out of the rain, where he had been standing all this while exposed to a severe shower. He thanked her for her kindness, and seated himself by the fire. After some little conversation, the lady's rigorous inhumanity softened down to true feminine hospitality, and my friend was as agreeably disappointed in being very kindly treated by her, as she was in the idea she had formed of the Kentuckians. An excellent supper was got, of which he partook with the lady and a younger sister, an amiable girl of much sweetness of manners.—When bed time arrived, instead of sleeping, as he expected, in an out cabin, he was shewn to an excellent bed, where he slept sound, and rose by day light next morning much refreshed. On it being made known to the lady that the gentleman wished to know "what was to pay," she smiled and ordered him a cup of warm coffee, and insisted on his staying a few minutes until it was ready, she having ordered her servant over night to have one prepared for the stranger early in the morning My friend could not but yield to her solicitation, and waited for the coffee, which was soon brought, and as gratefully drank, when he took leave of this amiable female, who at first appeared so unkind and inhospitable. My friend observed, this family had not been long from Georgia, to which place the lady's husband had returned to settle his business, leaving his worthy wife and sister, with two or three faithful slaves in charge of the premises.

How hard it is for the innocent to suffer on account of the bad deeds of the wicked. Cruel and inconsiderate is he who commits an act of mischief, whose penalty he knows will fall upon the head of his innocent countrymen, who travel the same road with himself, and who must be constantly exposed to ill-treatment and insults on his account. Malicious and desperately wicked must be that heart, and degraded below the brute creation the man, whose conduct in a strange country, is such as to disgrace the place of his nativity, and bring down upon the heads of his countrymen the character of blackguards and ruffians.

[*f* 2] SCRUB-GRASS. This grass, also called by some, rush, borders the edges of the Mississippi, and looks like fields of oats at a distance. Its lively green appearance gives cheerfulness to a winter's voyage, and forms a handsome contrast with the leafless trees and other surrounding deadened vegetation. It has a beautiful growth of the rush kind, and is very handsomely marked with whitish joints five or six inches apart, and the stalk runs up to a height of from four to six or seven feet in height, regularly and very gradually tapering from bottom to top. It has neither leaves or branches, and its surface has so keen a roughness, that it is found very useful, and is much made use of for the purpose of scrubbing pewter and wooden furniture, on account of which, it has acquired the name of *scrub-grass.*

I have seen this rush in Pennsylvania, but seldom more than eighteen inches or two feet in length, and when comparing it with that on the Mississippi, where I have picked stalks out of 8½ feet in height and with 23 joints, I could not but be charmed at the difference of the growth of the same vegetable in a different soil and climate, the effect of which indeed is wonderful, particularly in the vegetable kingdom.

[*g* 2] THE Arkansas, next to the Missouri, is the most considerable tributary of the Mississippi. In length it is nearly two thousand five hundred miles, and navigable at proper seasons nearly the whole distance. In many places its channel is broad and shallow, at least above the rapids, so as to render navigation almost impracticable. Until eight or nine hundred miles from its mouth, it receives no considerable streams, owing to the vicinity of the waters of the Missouri, of the Kansas, &c. on the one side, and those of Red river on the other. The chief rivers which fall into it, are the Verdigris, the Negracka, Canadian river, Grand river, &c. Several are remarkable for being strongly impregnated with salt; the Arkansas itself, at certain seasons is said to be brackish

The lands on this river for six or eight hundred miles up, are described as very fine and capable of affording settlements, though principally untimbered. For a long distance up, the flat lands on either side are intersected with numerous bayoux — There is a remarkable communication between the Arkansas and White river, by a channel or bayou connecting the two rivers with a current setting alternately into the one or the other, as the flood in either happens to predominate.

[*h* 2] IN this bend the *Spanish Moss or Tillandsea,* makes its first appearance on the Mississippi. This singular vegetable is

also called *Spanish Beard*, and holding this idea in mind when viewing it as it suspends itself in loose drapery from the branches of the tall majestic cypress trees, we are imperceptibly thrown into reflections bordering a certain degree of veneration, by combining with its appearance the venerable long gray-beards of former days.

This is a very singular vegetable, both in its growth and appearance, and as it is found highly useful, and I believe equal to hair, for mattresses, &c. it may be made an article of considerable trade and of exportation. It is universally used in Louisiana for all those purposes for which curled hair is applied in the northern states. Its cheapness is also an object of importance, being seldom more than from three to six cents a pound, delivered and prepared for mattresses, which is done something in this way: When gathered from the trees, which is easily performed with long hooks to tear it from the branches, it is then put under water a few days to rot the outer bark, or soft vegetable covering; when it is taken up, and after drying, it is beat with sticks, and the substance left is a fine black string or fibre, not unlike a horse hair, with the exception that it has joints from which the branches issue when growing. It is now fit for use. Mattresses made with this moss do not harden as soon as hair mattresses, but they become after some time dusty, and require to be opened, the moss taken to pieces, and beat again with sticks, and when replaced, it is better than at first, being more elastic and not so liable to acquire or make dust.

On first visiting a tree on which this substance grows, you are induced to believe that it has no root or fastening, but merely suspending from the branches, depending solely on the air for its nourishment. But on examination I found it firmly rooted in the apertures of the bark of the limbs of the trees, from which root there extended branches so numerous that it would be very difficult either to trace or count them; hence the deception, and so great, that some have said that the moss does not grow from, but is merely suspended to the branches of the trees, apparently without vegetable life. But this is a mistake; it flowers in its season, and bears a beautiful and a small pod full of seeds. The pod is about an inch long, and as thick as a stout darning needle. The flower is yellow.

[*i* 2]   STACK-ISLAND not long since was famed for a band of counterfeiters; horse thieves, robbers, murderers, &c. who made this part of the Mississippi a place of manufacture and deposit. From hence they would sally forth, stop boats, buy horses, flour, whiskey, &c. and pay for all in fine new notes of the "*first water.*" Their villanies, after many severe losses sustained by innocent, good men, unsuspecting the cheat, became notorious, and after several years search and pursuit of the civil, and in some cases the *club*-law, against this band of monsters, they have at length disappeared.

[k 2]  YAZOO. Mr. Hutchins observes the mouth of this river is upwards of 100 yards broad, and was found by Mr. Gauld to be in latitude 32° 37′ and by Mr. Purcel 32° 28′ north. The high waters of the Mississippi back up the Yazoo several miles, and cross the country and fall in again by several channels above the Walnut hills. The Yazoo takes its rise in Georgia, and running from the north-east, glides through a healthy, fertile, pleasant country, greatly resembling that about the Natchez. It is rendered famous of late years, especially in the history of American land speculation, (than which on this head no country perhaps ever groaned under heavier curses,) and from fraudulent sales of an immense track of land on it, arising out of a fraudulent act of the Georgia legislature, the transaction and the country itself are now well known by the name of the "*Yazoo Speculation.*" It has cost the United States thousands of dollars in debates on the floor of Congress, and posterity will not get clear of it short of millions in littigation. The country on the Yazoo is well watered by springs and brooks, some of the latter affording seats for mills. Twenty miles up the river the cane diminishes, and is scarcely to be seen. The Chactaws and Chickasaws have towns on the eastern and north-west branches of the Yazoo, 150 miles from the Mississippi. The navigation is practicable with large boats to the fork of those branches, which unite 50 miles from the mouth, and higher up with small crafts. There are stones near the Yazoo, well calculated for building, a circumstance favorable to this part of the country, these being seldom to be met with lower down, and Hutchins says, that "between the Petit Goufre, 31 miles above Natchez, and the Belize, there is not a stone to be seen any where near the river." This however is not strictly true, for there are considerable rocks of the granite kind at the lower landing at Natchez, seen at low water, but which appear to be of a recent growth, and probably formed since Mr. Hutchins's survey of the river. There is also a vein of rock running horizontally through the hill about half way up the bluff as you ascend from the lower landing. It is regularly formed, very hard and strong, and about one inch thick, and appears of recent formation ; the earth for an inch above and below this vein, appears to be changing from a fine sand and clay origin, and incorporating itself by the slow but regular order of nature, with the already formed vein of rock, which, in fifty or an hundred years may be strong and large enough to maintain the falling bluff.

Twelve miles from the mouth of the Yazoo, on the south side, are the Yazoo hills. There is a cliff of solid rock at the landing place, on which are seen a variety of broken and some entire sea-shells. Four miles further up is the place called the Ball Ground, near which a church, fort St. Peter, and a French settlement formerly stood. They were destroyed by the Yazoo Indians in 1729, a nation long since extinct.

The mouth of the Yazoo is the northern boundary of the Mississippi territory.

[*l* 2]   WALNUT HILLS.  As a man lost in the woods is de-
lighted to hear the crowing of the domestic cock, or the sound
of the woodman's axe, so are his senses charmed as soon as
those truely picturesque hills heave in sight.   After a dull uniformity of a flat swampy forest for six or seven hundred miles,
you now behold a bold but gradually rising ground of five or
six hundred feet in height, and near two miles in extent, covered with a fine culture of cotton and corn, whose rows are so varied in direction by the numerous hillocks and gullies on the
side of the hills, as to give great beauty and variety to the whole,
which, in the spring season ('March) look like one extensive
garden, cropped by several tenants.   There are several farms
adjoining, owned, however, by a Mr. Turnbull, from South Carolina, who resides here, and whose numerous buildings, dwelling houses, gin-house, negro quarters, &c. look like a little village.
Some few years ago, judge ———, a gentleman also from S.
Carolina, laid out the front of those hills into lots, with a view
of forming a town.   His title, however, in a suit at law with
the present proprietor, proved invalid, and he was ousted, and
the town fell through.
On the summit of these hills is still to be seen the site of
Fort M'Henry, winding up to which is also seen the old road.—
The hills take their name from the walnut tree ( juglans nigra,)
which used to grow here in great abundance.
The peach tree blooms here in the middle of February, and
other vegetation equally forward.   There is a handsome stream
of water descends from these hills into the river, but it is of a
bad quality.   From the summit of these hills you have a most
charming view of the Mississippi for many miles above and below, and of the surrounding country.

[*m* 2]   THIS river comes in on the left side of the Mississippi at the Grand Gulf, and extends 200 miles into the interior of
the Mississippi territory.   It affords good navigation in floods
for heavy flat boats 50 miles up, and small crafts go to near its
source, and within fifteen miles of a navigable branch of Pearl
river, a fine navigable stream emptying in at the Regolets, the
outlet of lake Ponchartrain.
The Big Black (or Lousa Chitto) is about 40 or 50 yards wide
at its mouth.   A mile and a half up it the high lands are close
on the right, and are much broken.   Ten miles further the lands
are near the river on the left.   Six miles further the high and
broken lands appear on both sides with springs of water.   This
land on the left was chosen by general Putnam, captain Enos,
Mr. Lyman, and other New England adventurers, as a proper
place for a town; and by order of the governor and council of

West Florida in 1773, it was reserved for the capital. The country round is very fit for settlement. Six miles above this there is rapid water, stones and gravel bottom 160 yards in length, and in one place a firm rock almost across the river, and as much of it bare, when the water is at a moderate height, as confines the stream to nearly 20 feet; and the channel is about four feet deep.

[n 2] RED RIVER takes its source in the Cordilleras, at no great distance north of Sta. Fé. In length it is about the same with the Arkansas. It is navigable six or eight hundred miles, with scarcely any obstruction. There is at that point a curious raft, formed of logs and earth, which entirely covers its channel; trees are growing upon it, and one might pass over without perceiving the river. Red river runs in a valley on an average fifteen miles wide, for at least eight hundred miles, which is every where intersected with bayoux, and large lakes. The navigation meets with the first impediment one hundred and fifty miles up. The falls or rapids are about two miles in length, the breadth of the river two hundred and fifty yards. They are occasioned by a soft rock of free stone: the greatest pitch in low water, not being more than eight or nine inches. This river might with much more justice than the Mississippi, be called the American Nile. A country lies on its borders more extensive than Egypt, and of a soil the richest perhaps in the world. Its waters, which are not potable, are very red, impregnated with some mineral. The river is remarkably narrow; it seldom spreads to the width of two hundred and fifty yards, and is more generally contracted to one hundred; it is also exceedingly crooked. The annual swell, which is early in the spring of the year, raises the water fifty or sixty feet, when it flows with great rapidity: but during the summer and season of low water, it is sunk within deep and ragged clay banks, of an unsightly appearance, and has not more than eight or ten feet of water. The outlets from this river are more numerous than even from the Mississippi, and joined by streams which flow from the uplands, or pine woods. The course of the river is constantly subject to change; many of the bayoux which at present appear inconsiderable, at no distant period constituted the bed of the principal river.

[o 2] TO give the reader an idea of the fertility of the soil and luxuriance of the productions of an island near the mouth of this river, it may not be amiss to give him the words of the celebrated American traveller and botanist, Mr. William Bartram, in his book of travels through North and South Carolina, Georgia, East and West Florida, in the years 1773 to 1778.

" THE island is six or seven miles in length, and four or five in width, including the salt marshes and plains, which invest it on every side, I believe we may only except a narrow strand at the south end of it, washed by lake Borgone at the Regullets, which is a promontory composed of banks of sea-shells and sand, cast up by the force of winds, and the surf of the lake: these shells are chiefly a small species of white clam shells, called les coquelles. Here are a few shrubs growing on these shelly heights, viz. Rhamnus frangula, Sideroxilon, Myrica, Zanthoxilon clava Herculis, Juniperus Americana, Lysium salsum; together with several new genera and species of the herbaceous and suffruticose tribes, Croton, Stillingia, &c. but particularly a species of Mimosa (Mimosa virgatia) which, in respect of the elegancy of its pinnated leaves, cannot be exceeded by any of that celebrated family. It is a perennial plant, sending up many nearly erect stems, from the root or source, these divide themselves into many ascendant slender rods like branches, which are ornamented with double pinnated leaves, of a most delicate formation. The compound flowers, are of a pale greenish yellow, collected together in a small oblong head, upon a long slender peduncle, the legumers are large, lunated and flat, placed in a spiral or contorted manner, each containing several hard compressed seed, or little beans.

The interior and by far the greatest part of the island consists of high land; the soil to appearance a heap of sea sand in some places, with an admixture of sea shells, this soil, notwithstanding its sandy and steril appearance, when divested of its natural vegetative attire, has, from what cause I know not, a continual resource of fertility within itself, the surface of the earth, after being cleared of its original vegetable productions, exposed a few seasons to the sun, winds and triturations of agriculture, appears scarcely any thing but heaps of white sand, yet it produces Corn (Zea) Indigo, Batatas, Beans, Peas, Cotton, Tobacco, and almost every sort of esculent vegetable, in a degree of luxuriancy very surprising and unexpected, year after year, incessantly, without any addition of artificial manure or compost; there is indeed a foundation of strong adhesive clay, consisting of stratas of various colours, which I discovered by examining a well, lately dug in Mr. Rumsey's yard; but its lying at a great depth under the surface, the roots of small shrubs and herbage, cannot reach near to it, or receive any benefit, unless we may suppose, that ascending fumes or exhalations, from this bed of clay, may have a vivific nutritive quality, and be received by the fibres of the roots, or being condensed in the atmosphere by nocturnal chills, fall with dews upon the leaves and twigs of these plants, and there absorbed, become nutritive or exhilerating to them.

Besides the native forest trees and shrubs already noted, manured fruit trees arrive in this island to the utmost degree of perfection, as Pears, Peaches, Figs, Grape Vines. Plumbs, &c of the last mentioned genus, there is a native species grows in this island, which produce their large oblong crimson fruit in prodigious abundance; the fruit though of a most enticing appearance, are rather too tart, yet are agreeable eating, at sultry noon, in this burning climate, they afford a most delicious and reviving marmalade, when preserved in sugar, and make excellent tarts: the tree grows about twelve feet high, the top spreading, the branches spiny and the leaves broad, nervous, serrated, and terminate with a subulated point."

As an instance of the salubrity of the atmosphere on this island, Mr. Bartram observes, "The French gentleman (proprietor of the plantation) was near eighty years old, his hair almost white with age, yet he appeared active, strong and muscular, and his mother who was present, was one hundred and five years old, active and cheerful, her eyes seemed as brisk and sparkling as youth, but of a diminutive size, not half the stature and weight of her son; it was now above fifty years since she came into America from old France.

[p 2] THE French began to build New Orleans in 1720, and two years afterwards it became the seat of government.

This city, the great mart of all the wealth of the western world, is situated on the east bank of the Mississippi, about one hundred and nine miles (following the meanders of the river) from the sea, and in twenty-nine degrees, fifty-seven minutes, twenty-seven seconds, north latitude, and ninety degrees, seventeen minutes, thirty seven seconds, west longitude. At the time it fell into our hands, it contained about one thousand houses, and eight thousand inhabitants, including blacks and people of color.

Six complete squares are embraced by the city. The fronts of these are three hundred and ninteen English feet in length, and extend north, thirty-two degrees, east and south, thirty-two degrees west, and are intersected by twelve streets at right angles. Each square is divided into twelve lots. Five of them measure sixty by one hundred and twenty feet. On the opposite side are two key lots, which measure sixty by one hundred and fifty feet. The streets are thirty-seven feet and a half in width. On the back part of the city are two narrow rows of buildings, converging to a point.

The ground plot of the city may be considered as a plain, inclining north-west two points west. It has a descent of about six feet from the bank of the river to the palisades in the rear of the buildings, and about three feet more to St. John's creek at its medium height. The lands in all the low country, gradually descend from the river, and soon terminate in lakes or swamps.

Nearly the whole of the old houses are of wood, one story high, and make an ordinary appearance. The suburbs on the upper or north end of the city, have been built since the fire in 1794, and contain about two hundred and fifteen houses, mostly composed of cypress wood, and generally covered with shingles or clapboards. Among them is one elegant brick house covered with tile. Several of them are two stories high, and two in the same quarter three stories high. One of them cost eighty thousand dollars, and the rest from fifteen to twenty thousand dollars. They are plastered on the outside with white or colored mortar; this, as frosts are seldom severe in the climate, lasts many years; it beautifies the buildings, and preserves the bricks, which, from the negligence or parsimony of the manufacturers, are usually too soft to resist the weather.

In New Orleans, as in all other parts of the low country, the houses have no cellars under ground; water is generally found within two or three feet of the surface, especially in wet seasons. The wells rarely exceed fifteen feet in depth. The water in them is clear, free from salt, but unpleasant to the taste.

The following are the public buildings : the cathedral, the town house, the prison, the barracks, the hospital, the convent and church, the charity hospital and church, the government house and stores, and some others of inferior note, which will be cursorily mentioned.

The cathedral stands at the head of a spacious open square, about four hundred feet from the river. This building is of brick, extending about ninety feet on the street, and one hundred and twenty back of it. The roof is covered with flat and hollow tile, supported by ten large brick columns, which are plastered, and afford an agreeable appearance. Each front corner has a tower considerably elevated, and the southerly one contains two small bells. This church has likewise a small organ, but on the whole is much less decorated than other catholic places of worship. It was governed by a bishop, two canons, one grand vicar, one parish priest, and four subordinate priests. Considerable funds in houses appertain to it. The bishop received an annual salary of four thousand dollars, charged on the revenues of some southern bishopric; the canons about seven hundred and twenty dollars, and the other priests about three hundred and sixty dollars each, exclusive of casual benefits arising from marriages, burials, and the like. There were likewise a few capouchins, and friars of the order of carmelites, who were paid by the crown.

The town house is rather an elegant building, two stories high, and about ninety feet long, with an arched portico, both above and below, along its whole front. The upper arches are glazed, which adds much to the beauty of the structure. The Spaniards occupied one part of the ground story as a guard house, and permitted a notary to occupy the other as an office. The upper story was appropriated to the use of the cabildo.

In the rear of the town house, and adjoining to it, is the prison. Under the Spanish government it was a wretched receptacle of vice and misery; like the grave it received many tenants, who were soon forgotten by the world : some of them perished with age and disease, and others by the hands of assassins. Criminals, under sentence of death, were often kept immured within its walls for years; owing either to the tardiness or lenity of the tribunal at the Havanna, without whose approval no sentence of death could be carried into execution.

The public barracks are situated at the lower end of the front street. They are accommodated with a spacious area, surrounded by a brick wall, as also an extensive parade ground between them and the river. The buildings are of brick, and one story high, covered with shingles, and calculated to receive about fifteen hundred men. They were built by the French, and have a spacious arcade in front and rear.

The building denominated the king's hospital, is on the same line, but higher up. It was originally intended as a receptacle for the sick and diseased belonging to the army and navy. It will accommodate about one hundred and fifty patients, and affords to the miserable a tolerable asylum.

The convent of the Ursuline nuns is situated on the upper side of the barracks, and beyond the hospital, which stands nearer the line of the street. This was likewise built by the French: It is of brick, and spacious; covered with shingles, and two stories high. An extensive garden is attached to it, extremely productive of fruit and vegetables. It will accommodate about fifty nuns, and from seventy to eighty young females, who resort to it for their education. Attached to the convent is a small house containing three rooms, divided longitudinally from each other by double gratings about six inches asunder, with apertures about two inches square, where strangers may see and converse with the nuns and boarders on particular business. Near to the main building, and on the street, stands an old school house, where the female children of the citizens appear at certain fixed hours to be gratuitously instructed in writing, reading, and arithmetic. This religious institution is possessed of considerable funds. Each nun on taking the final vow, or black veil, deposits fifteen hundred dollars, if she be able, which becomes part of the common stock, and cannot be alienated. The church belonging to the convent is small, and was the gift of a gentleman who died a few years ago at New Orleans. He was in early life a notary, and by various speculations amassed an immense property, and failed at last to leave an unspotted name behind him. He likewise built the cathedral church and charity hospital, and endeavoured by acts of beneficence near the end of his days, to atone for the errors of his youth.

The charity hospital stands on the westerly or back part of the city. Poor Spanish subjects, and sometimes strangers, (provided they paid half a dollar per day) were admitted into this asylum. Those entirely destitute were admitted gratis.— They had medicine, sustenance, and other aid, afforded them.

The government house stands on the front street, and on the fifth square, reckoning from the upper side, and one hundred feet from the river. It is an ancient building, erected by the

French, and two stories high, with galleries or arcades round
the whole of it. The lower front was formerly occupied by
the governmental secretary, and the clerks of offices. This
structure is indifferent, both as to architecture and convenience.

On the south-westerly part of the same square were the lodges and stables of the regular dragoons; which, with the gard-
en belonging to the government house, occupy about four-fifths
of the square.

On the corners of the second and third squares, lower down,
are the public stores, built of brick, extending about thirty five
feet on front street, and about two hundred feet on a cross
street   They are one story high, and were built by the French.

On the opposite, or southerly side of the stores, is the artillery yard, or ordnance depot.

Opposite to this, on the very bank of the river, is the market
house, which is usually furnished with beef, pork, some mul-
lard and veal; fish of several sorts in abundance, and cheap;
wild ducks and other game in season; tame turkies, fowls,
ducks, and geese; and vegetables of all kinds during the whole
year.

The Spaniards had the advantage of a free school, in which
boys were instructed in the rudiments of their language. The
two teachers attached to it were paid by the crown.

The grand powder magazine of the French and Spaniards, is
situated over against the government house, on the opposite side
of the river, where a guard was always stationed, and generally
relieved weekly

During the administration of the baron Carondelet, between
1791, and 1796, a ditch was extended round the city, of about
eighteen feet in width, with ramparts of earth, and palisades
nearly six feet high along the interior or inner side of them.—
Five large bastions were erected at proper distances, and likewise five intervening redoubts. The bastions were regularly
constructed. Each of them was furnished with a banquette,
rampart, parapet, ditch, covered way, and glacis. The curtains
were wholly formed of palisades, planted at a small distance
from each other, and therefore not capable of much defence
even against musket balls; they had a banquette within, and a
ditch and glacis without. A small redoubt or ravelin was placed in the centre of each bastion; and all the latter were of sufficient size to admit of sixteen embrasures, four in each face,
three in each flank, and two in the gorge facing the city.

These works of defence were badly supplied with ordnance.
Few of the bastions were furnished with more than four or five
pieces of cannon. That on the east or lower end of the city,
had its full complement; and the covered way was likewise
pretty well supplied. This arrangement or distribution of the
ordnance was rather singular; it seemed to be mounted on
those places the most invulnerable, and the least liable to be at-

tacked. An assault by way of the sea was hardly to be expected, especially as the river was well defended eighteen miles below, and as a fleet wholly unobstructed by land batteries, would find it extremely difficult to ascend against the rapidity of the current. The south west bastion, with a counterguard and traverses, and a small redoubt on the back of the river, constituted the whole defence on the upper side of the city. The first was usually supplied with ten or twelve, and the second with five pieces of cannon. Not more than ten pieces, however, could be brought to bear on any body of men descending the river. As soon as an enemy landed on the open banks, which was by no means difficult, the bastions became totally useless. A skilful officer at the head of disciplined troops, in any degree acquainted with the country, would have experienced no great trouble from these works, especially as they were mostly defended by raw militia, among whom regular duty was irksome, and considered as a grievance.

The inhabitants and others passed in and out of the city by means of four gates. The two next the river were the most considerable, and they were situated sixteen hundred and twenty yards from each other. The two in the rear, or on the back part of the city, were of much less note; one of them was placed on the road leading to lake Pontchartrain: They were defended by a breast work of no great strength or utility. All the gates were of wood, formed of palisades ten or twelve feet long. They were shut every night at nine o'clock, and after that hour no one was permitted to walk the streets without leave from the governor; those who transgressed this regulation were seized by the guards, and detained till morning. House servants, by particular indulgence, were sometimes allowed to pass the streets on business for their masters or mistresses till eleven o'clock.

Exclusive of the fire in 1794, already mentioned. New Orleans suffered by a prior one in 1788, when about nine hundred wooden buildings of all descriptions, mostly old, were reduced to ashes. Those built on their ruins have contributed to the beauty of the city.

Such in some degree were the features of New Orleans at the time it fell into the hands of the United States. Since that period it has been greatly improved; population has increased; new springs are given to commerce, property immensely augmented in value; the works repaired and strengthened, and much additional security afforded to the capital of Louisiana.

*Stoddard's Sketches.*

# ADDENDA.

———•———

A BRIEF NOTICE OF THE SPRINGS, MINES, CURIOSITIES,
&c. ON THE WESTERN WATERS, AND SOME OF THOSE
OF LOUISIANA.

A CELEBRATED AUTHOR,[*] in his observations on our western waters, has suggested an idea, that "the whole scope of country from above a range of mountains which cross the Ohio somewhere below the falls, as high up as Pittsburgh, and bordering lake Erie, was once overwhelmed with water, forming an immense lake. That the summit of those hills was sufficiently high to do this, and that by some great convulsion of nature, this barrier was rent to its base, and the waters being thus let loose, the lake above was drained, and the floods centring from all parts of the higher to the lower grounds, formed the bed of the river now called Ohio."

This great revolution of waters, our author thinks, changed the face of the country, and filled our hills with vast bodies of logs, drift wood, leaves, &c. which, through time, have formed those veins of fine stone-coal, of which we reap the benefit daily. As a corroboration of this idea of Mr. Volney, there is frequently found in our coal small pieces resembling exactly the grain of the wood, and the bark of a tree ; and it retains this appearance even after it has gone through the fire and reduced to cinder. Red pieces of cinder are also frequently discovered, resembling *crocos*, and which answers our silversmiths for the same purposes as does that substance. It also answers instead of emery, for sharpening knives, razors, &c. if it be well pounded, sifted, and mixed with sweet-oil.

Near Georgetown, about 38 miles below Pittsburgh, on the Ohio, a mine of gold has been discovered, a specimen of which having been tried by a silversmith in Pittsburgh, who declared it to be *pure virgin gold*, and without any alloy. The lump produced had the appearance of having been found in a running water.

———

[*] *Volney's View of America.*

A clay well calculated for the manufacture of delf-ware, smo-king-pipes, &c. has lately been discovered near Pittsburgh. In a creek emptying into the Allegheny a small distance above Pittsburgh, is found a stone which answers every purpose of the oil-stone made use of by carpenters, joiners, &c. On the side of the hill to the east of the Allegheny river, about two miles above Pittsburgh, is a *spring*, the waters of which have performed cures for the cholera morbis. It also cures the inflammatory sore eyes. It is called the *Allum Spring*, tasting strongly of that mineral.

On the Great Kenhawa, opposite the mouth of Cripple creek, Montgomery county, Va. are mines of lead; the metal of which is accompanied with a portion of silver, too small, however, to be worth the trouble of separation. The portion yielded is from 50 to 80lbs. pure metal from 100lbs. of washed ore. On the opposite side of the river, one mile from the ore bank, is a furnace which works about 25 tons of lead a year.

Valuable lead mines are said to abound in Cumberland, below the mouth of Red River. And in a hill between Cumberland and Tennessee rivers, is a bank of *white earth* of great extent, supposed to be good for making a fine kind of earthen ware, and a short distance from it is a bank of *red clay*, which is mixed with water and made use of for painting.

On Rock river, which empties into the Mississippi, very valuable lead mines abound, and which are said to be the most extensive on the western waters—these are very little worked.

About 60 miles N. W. of Pittsburgh, and not far from the line between the states of Ohio and Pennsylvania, is a salt spring, the water of which being weak, very little attention is paid to it as yet. There are considerable salt-works carried on within about 30 miles of Chilicothe, likewise a bank of fine yellow ochre near that place, Ohio state.

Large salt springs abound at the Blue Lick, Big Bone, Bullet's Lick, and on the north fork of Holstein; the waters of these springs yield from one to one bushel and a half of salt from 1000 gallons of water, being about 80lbs. of water to 1lb of salt; but of sea water 25lbs yield 1lb. of salt. On the Youghiogheny at Turkey foot is a salt spring; the river, however, overflows it, except in very low water—this spring is not worked.

Mr Jefferson, in his Notes, observes that " in the low grounds of the Great Kenhawa, 7 miles above the mouth of Elk river, and 67 above that of Kenhawa itself, is a hole in the earth of the capacity of 30 or 40 gallons, from which issues constantly bituminous vapor, in so strong a current, as to give to the sand about its orifice the motion which it has in a boiling spring. On presenting a lighted candle or torch within 18 inches of the hole, it flames up in a column of 18 inches in diameter, and 4 or 5 feet in height, which sometimes burns out in 20 minutes, and at other times has been known to continue 3 days, and then has been left still burning. The flame is unsteady, of the density of that of

burning spirits, and smells like burning pit-coal. Water sometimes collects in the basin, which is remarkably cold, and is kept
in ebullition by the vapor issuing through it. If the vapor be
fired in that state, the water soon becomes so warm that the
hand cannot bear it, and evaporates wholly in a short time.

"A similar one to this is on Sandy river, the flame of which
is a column of about twelve inches in diameter, and three feet
high."

Iron mines are said to have been found between the Muskingum and the Ohio, others in Kentucky, between the Cumberland
and Barren rivers, between Cumberland and Tennessee, on
Reedy creek, near the Long Island, and on Chesnut creek, a
branch of the Great Kenhawa.

On the Youghiogheny and its branches, are very valuable Iron
ore banks, and on Big Beaver creek mines of ore have been discovered.

What is called the Iron Banks on the Mississippi, are said by
competent judges to have no ore in them. And indeed what is
as yet known of that country, it seems to want iron, though rich
in other mines, of lead especially.

---

*The following description of the Hot Springs and Volcanic
appearances in the country adjoining the river Ouachitta, in Louisiana, is extracted from the New York "Medical Repository." vol. 9. p. 47.*

"DURING the summer of 1804, several persons residents of
the Missisippi Territory, visited the hot springs, and traversed
the country of the Ouachitta; some from motives of curiosity, o-
thers on account of their health : Among the latter was Major E.
a gentleman of the first respectability in this territory. To him
I am indebted for the greater part of the information contained
in the following observations.

"The Ouachitta is a river of Louisiana; it empties into the
Red River, thirty miles from the junction of the Red River and
the Mississippi, near the line of demarkation. The Ouachitta
runs nearly a south-south-east course, and can be ascended
in boats a distance of 600 miles, to where it forks. The hot springs
are 100 miles below the forks, situated between the 34th and
35th degree of north latitude, on a creek that falls into the river,
and are about ten miles distant from it.

"The lands on the Ouachitta, especially in the neighborhood
of the hot springs, are high, poor, broken, and stony. This is
the state of the Ouachitta lands generally, except near its mouth,

where, for a short distance on each side, the lands are low, level, and fertile, but for the most part subject to be overflown.

"The timber on the high lands consists of pine, black-jack, and mountain oak. Silex, or flint, with its various combinations, often in the form of granite, is the stone most commonly met with. Schistus, or slate, exists likewise in considerable quantities. Fine specimens of rock-crystal from that place have been presented to me: the form is of an hexahedral prism, terminated by pyramids of an equal number of sides.

"I have received a number of specimens of the minerals of the country. They were supposed, from their yellow and white metallic appearance, to contain the precious metals. But after a careful analysis, I could not discover any portion of gold or silver. They were composed principally of the following ores: Antimony, mineralized by sulphur, of a bluish grey metallic appearance, with a radiated crystallization, composed of slender hexahedral prisms, zinc, mineralized by sulphur, forming the ore called blende:—feldspar, of a white, inclining to a red color, granulated texture, the surface covered with crystal, of a rectangular form, and very brilliant; black schorl, with pieces of quartz intermixed.

"Volcanic productions are common. The face of the country bears strong marks of fire. A rapid decomposition of mineral bodies below the surface still appears to go on. Major E. during his stay last summer at the springs, witnessed a great explosion of one of the mountains in the vicinity, attended with the sensation of an earthquake. An immense column of flame and smoke was seen to ascend a great distance: one of his hunters was near the place at the time. He visited the mountain the day after the eruption, and observed lava still flowing in the fissure caused by the explosion.

"The hot springs are considerable in point of number. They arise from the side of a hill, at the distance of a quarter of a mile from the creek. Major E. supposed the heat during the dry season to be at the boiling point. Meat was boiled in them in a shorter space of time than could be accomplished by a culinary fire; they were made use of to prepare both tea and coffee. The temperature of these springs is influenced by the season. During the months of June and July, 1804, it was very dry, no rain fell during that time. The waters were diminished in quantity, and the degree of heat was so great, that persons could not expose themselves to the vapor, which is the usual mode adopted by those who visit them on account of their health.

"These hot springs have been, for some time, much celebrated by people settled in their neighbourhood, on the Mississippi and its branches, for their efficacy in curing or relieving chronic pains, paralytic affections, and inability to motion generally. The Indians have, time immemorial, resorted to them on account of their medicinal virtues. The ground around them is called by the aborigines, *the land of peace.* Hostile tribes, while here, remain at harmony with each other.

"Many of the white hunters, who are very liable to disease from exposure to the vicissitudes of climate and season, have been restored by the use of these springs, from a state of entire inability of motion, to complete health and activity.

"The water of the hot springs is soft and limpid, without smell. The taste is agreeable. It is drank after it becomes cool, and used for every other purpose in preference to the water of the cold springs in the vicinity.

"I received a quantity of it bottled and sealed. After a careful analysis, by evaporation and precipitation, I found that it contained less mineral impregnation than water usually does. Litmus paper, lime water, the nitrate of silver, the oxalic acid, alcohol of galls, and the prussiate of lime, indicated the presence of a small portion of carbonic acid, some of the muriate of soda, a small quantity of calcareous matter, and a scarcely perceptible portion of iron. Muriate of barytes, spirits of ammoniac, caustic pot-ash, acetate of lead, nitrate of mercury, the sulphuric and muriatic acids, with many other re-agents commonly used to detect minerals, produced no effect.

"As hot waters are usually impregnated with minerals, their heat has been accounted for by their coming in contact with pyritous substances. But the water of these springs, notwithstanding its great heat, would appear from this analysis, to be purer than spring water generally; we, therefore, cannot account for the heat, by contact with mineral bodies in a state of decomposition. These springs are similar in this respect to the water of the spring of Geyser, in Iceland, the temperature of which is 212 degrees, the boiling point; yet the celebrated Dr. Black, who analyzed the water, found it to be pure. From whence then does the heat of these springs arise, which, during a dry season are at the boiling point, and next to those of Iceland, are the hottest known? It is probable that a rapid decomposition of mineral bodies exists below the strata over which the water of these springs flows. The volcanic appearance of the country strengthens the supposition. The caloric, evolved by the decomposing minerals, may permeate the subjacent strata, and be received by the water.

"The great relief experienced by persons who have visited these springs, the healthfulness of the climate, and the security derived from the American government, will render them in time, a valuable acquisition to our citizens on the Mississippi and its branches."

---

"At about 300 miles from the village of the Great Osages, in a westerly direction, after having crossed several streams of the Arkansas, the traveller comes to a low bottom, surrounded by hills of a vast extent. This valley is about 15 leagues across.— The soil is a black sand, very fine, and so hard that horses scarcely leave any tracks on it. During the hot and dry season, vapors rise from this bottom, which condense and fall back upon the black sand, covering it with a layer of exceedingly white and fine salt about half an inch thick. The rains wash away this accumulation At about 18 miles from this bottom, he meets with mines of sal gem on the very surface of the earth — The Indians, who are perfectly acquainted with it, are obliged to make use of levers to break it up, and loosen it. At about 15 leagues distance from the last mentioned place, to the south, there is a second mine of sal gem, of the same nature with the first. They only differ in color; the former being white, and the other of a reddish hue. Further south, and still upon the streams of the Arkansas, there is a saline; which may be considered as one of the most interesting phenomena of nature.

"On the declivity of a small hill, there are five holes about a foot and an half in diameter, and two feet deep. They are always full of a very salt water, but never run over. Dip out as much as you please, there is no apparent diminution; the deficiency is instantly supplied: and about ten feet lower down the hill there issues a spring of pure and fresh water. When these regions become peopled, the transportation of this rock salt will be perfectly easy, by means of the Arkansas. Experience has proved it to be preferable to every other kind in curing provisions.

"If these remarks, made without order, but with a scrupulous regard to truth, should excite the curiosity of gentlemen who possess talents, and are capable of going to the bottom of matters which I have but superficially touched, I cannot doubt that incalculable advantages will result from them, both to the United States and to the territory of Louisiana."

*N. Y. Medical Repos.*

---

# AN ACCOUNT OF LOUISIANA,

### DISCOVERY SETTLEMENT AND TRANSFER.

THE country east and west of the Mississippi was called *Florida* by Sebastian Cabot, who visited that part of the continent by order of Henry VII. of England, about the year 1497.

John Pontio de Leon, a Spaniard, arrived on the coast, anno 1512, attempted a settlement, and erected a small fort. The subjects of Charles X, of France, seem to have made several attempts to settle this country but were still' defeated by the Spaniards, until the year 1684, when Mons. De la Sale discovered the mouth of the Mississippi, and built on the bay a fort, which he called "Fort Lewis."—The founder having been assassinated, the fort was abandoned until anno 1698, when captain Iberville penetrated up the Mississippi, and having planted a few settlers, called the country *Louisiana*. Until this time the Spaniards had a few forts on the coast, of which Pensa Cola seems to have been the principal, which is 14 leagues east of the isle of Dauphin. About the year 1720, Mons. La Sueur sailed up the St. Lewis river or Mississippi above 760 leagues from its mouth, and he observes that the river is known to flow still further up.

From this time it remained in the hands of France, whose monarchs made several grants of its trade, in particular to Mr. Crosat in 1712, and some years afterwards, with his acquiescence, to the well known company projected by Mr. Law, and which was relinquished in 1731. By a secret convention on the 31 November, 1762, the French government ceded so much of the province as lies beyond the Mississippi, as well as the island of New Orleans, to Spain, and by the treaty of peace, which followed in 1763, the whole territory of France and Spain, eastward of the middle of the Mississippi to the Iberville, thence through the middle of that river, and the lakes of Maurepas and Ponchartrain to the sea, was ceded to Great Britain. Spain having conquered the Floridas from Great Britain, during our revolutionary war, they were confirmed to her by the treaty of peace of 1783. By the treaty of St. Ildefonso, of the 1st of Oct. 1800, his Catholic majesty promises and engages on his part to cede back to the French Republic, six months after the full and entire execution of the conditions and stipulations therein contained, relative to the duke of Parma, "the colony or province of Louisiana, with the same extent that it actually has in the hands of Spain, that it had when France possessed it, and such as it ought to be after the treaties subsequently entered into between Spain and other states." This treaty was confirmed and enforced by that of Madrid, of the 21st of March, 1801.— From France it passed to us by the treaty of the 30th of April, 1803, and was taken regular possession of by our government on the 20th of December following.

### BOUNDARIES.

The precise boundaries of Louisiana, westwardly of the Mississippi, though very extensive, are at present involved in some obscurity, data are equally wanting to assign with precision its northern extent. From the source of the Mississippi, it is bounded eastwardly by the middle of the channel of that river to the 31st degree of latitude: thence, it is asserted upon very strong grounds, that according to its limits, when formerly possessed by France, it stretches to the east, as far, at least, as the river Perdido, which runs into the bay of Mexico, eastward of the river Mobile.

### DIVISIONS.

This province as held by Spain, including a part of West Florida, was laid off into the following principal divisions :— Mobile, from Balise to the city, New Orleans and the country on both sides of lake Ponchartrain, first and second German coasts, Catahanose, Fourche, Venezuela, Iberville, Galvez town, Baton-Rouge, Pointe Coupee, Atacapas, Opelousas, Ouachita, Avoyelles, Rapide, Natchitoches, Arkansas, and the Illinois.

In the Illinois there were commandants, at New Madrid, St. Genevieve, New Bourbon, St. Charles and St. Andrews, all of which were subordinate to the commandant general.

Baton-Rouge having been made a government, subsequently to the treaty of limits, &c. with Spain, the posts of Manchac and Thompson's creek, of Feliciana, were added to it.—Chapitoulas was sometimes regarded as a separate command, but was afterwards included within the jurisdiction of the city. The lower part of the river had likewise occasionally a separate commandant.

Many of the present establishments are separated from each other by immense and trackless deserts, having had no communication with each other by land, except now and then a solitary instance of its having been attempted by hunters, who had to swim rivers, expose themselves to the inclemency of the weather, and carry their provisions on their backs, for a time proportioned to the length of their journey. This was particularly the case on the west of the Mississippi, where the communication was kept up only by water, between the capital and the distant settlements; three months having been required to convey intelligence from one to the other, by the Mississippi.— The usual distance accomplished by a boat in ascending, is five leagues per day. The rapidity of the current in the spring season especially, when the waters of all the rivers are high, facilitates the descent, so that the same voyage by water, which requires three or four months to perform from the capital, may be made to it in from 12 to 16 days. The principal settlements in Louisiana are on the Mississippi, which begins to be cultivated about 10 leagues from the sea, where the plantations are yet thin, and owned by the poorest people. Ascending, you see them improve on each side, till you reach the city, which is situated on the east bank, on a bend of the river, 35 leagues from the sea.

### CHAPITOULAS, FIRST AND SECOND GERMAN COASTS.— CATAHANOSE—FOURCHE, AND IBERVILLE.

The best and most improved are above the city, and comprehend, what is there known by the Paroisse de Chapitoulas, Premier and Second Cote des Allemands, and extend sixteen leagues.

Above this begins the parish of Catahanose, **or** first Acadian settlement extending eight leagues on the river. Adjoining it, and still ascending, is the second Acadian settlement or parish of the Fourche, which extends about six leagues. The parish of Iberville then commences and is bounded on the east side by the river of the same name, which, though dry a great part of the year, yet, when the Mississippi is raised, it communicates with the lakes Maurepas and Ponchartrain, and through them with the sea, and thus forms what is called the island of New Orleans. Except on the point just below the Iberville, the country from New Orleans is settled the whole way along the river, and presents a scene of uninterrupted plantations in sight of each other, whose fronts to the Mississippi are all cleared, and occupy on that river from 5 to 25 acres with a depth of 40; so that a plantation of 5 acres in front contains 200. A few sugar plantations are formed in the parish of Catahanose, but the remainder is devoted to cotton and provisions, and the whole is an excellent soil incapable of being exhausted. The plantations are but one deep on the island of New Orleans, and on the opposite side of the river as far as the mouth of the Iberville, which is 35 leagues above New Orleans.

### BAYOU DE LA FOURCHE—ATACAPAS, AND OPELOUSAS.

ABOUT twenty five leagues from the last mentioned place, on the west side of the Mississippi, the creek or bayou of the Fourche, called in old maps La Riviere des Chitamaches, flows from the Mississippi, and communicates with the sea to the west of the Balise. The entrance of the Mississippi is navigable only at high water, but will then admit of craft of from 60 to 70 tons burthen. On both banks of this creek are settlements, one plantation deep, for near fifteen leagues, and they are divided into two parishes. The settlers are numerous, though poor, and the culture is universally cotton. On all creeks making from the Mississippi, the soil is the same as on the bank of the river, and the border is the highest part of it, from whence it descends gradually to the swamp. In no place on the low lands is there depth more than suffices for one plantation, before you come to the low grounds incapable of cultivation. This creek affords one of the communications to the two populous and rich settlements of Atacapas and Opelousas, formed on and near the small rivers Teche and Vermillion, which flow into the bay of Mexico. But the principal and swiftest communication is by the bayou or creek of Placquemines, whose entrance into the Mississippi is seven leagues higher up on the same side, and thirty-two above New Orleans. These settlements abound in cattle and horses, have a large quantity of good land in their vicinity, and may be made of great importance. A part of their produce is sent by sea to New Orleans, but the greater part is carried in batteaux by the creeks above mentioned.

## BATON ROUGE AND ITS DEPENDENCIES.

IMMEDIATELY above the Iberville, on both sides of the Mississippi lies the parish of Manchac, which extends four leagues on the river, and is well cultivated. Above it commences the settlement of Baton Rouge, extending about 9 leagues. It is remarkable as being the first place where the high land is contiguous to the river, and here it forms a bluff from thirty to forty feet above the greatest rise of the river. Here the settlements extend a considerable way back on the east side; and this parish has that of Thomson's creek and bayou Sara subordinate to it. The mouth of the first of these creeks is about 49 leagues from New Orleans, and that of the latter two or three leagues higher up. They run from the north-east to the south-west, and their head waters are north of the 31st degree of latitude. Their banks have the best soil, and the greatest number of good cotton plantations of any part of Louisiana, and are allowed to be the garden of it.

## POINT COUPEE AND FAUSSE RIVIERE.

ABOVE Baton Rouge, at the distance of fifty leagues from New Orleans, and on the west side of the Mississippi is Point Coupee, a populous and rich settlement extending 8 leagues along the river. Its produce is cotton. Behind it, on an old bed of the river, now a lake, whose outlets are closed up, is the settlement of Fausse riviere, which is well cultivated.

In the space now described from the sea as high as, and including, the last mentioned settlement, is contained three-fourths of the population, and seven-eighths of the riches of Louisiana.

From the settlement of Point Coupee on the Mississippi to Cape Girardeau above the mouth of the Ohio, there is no land on the west side, that is not overflowed in the spring to the distance of eight or ten leagues from the river with from two to twelve feet water, except a small spot near New Madrid; so that in the whole extent there is no possibility of forming a considerable settlement contiguous to the river on that side. The eastern bank has in this respect a decided advantage over the western, as there are on it many situations which effectually command the river.

*Account of a journey up the Washita ( or Ouachita ) river, in Louisiana, performed by William Dunbar, esq. and Dr. Hunter.*—Extract from the New York Medical Repository.

THESE gentlemen were employed by Mr. Jefferson, president of the United States, pursuant to a provision of congress, for exploring Louisiana, as related at large in our Hex. ii. vol. i. p. 407. They set out from St. Catharine's Landing, on the Mississippi, on the 16th of October, 1804, and proceeded to the mouth of the *Red river*. This is so called from the reddish appearance of the water, caused by some earthy impregnation tinged probably with iron. At a little more than twenty-three miles from the Mississippi they entered the *Black river*, so called from the clearness of its water, looking dark when contrasted with the muddy hue of the *Red river*. They proceeded slowly upwards, passing the place where the river Tensa enters from the east, and the Catahoola from the west, and visiting the station called Fort Miro, about two hundred miles from the entrance below, and which is out of the United States in that quarter. As far up as the junction of the three rivers just mentioned, the country is alluvial and flat, the water sluggish, and the current scarcely perceptible. Immediately above, the high land and permanent strata of soil begin. The latitude of Fort Miro is about 30° 30'. After visiting various settlements, and encountering many difficulties, amidst shoals and rapids in the upper country, they arrived at length at the Hot Springs, situated towards the source of the river, in lat. 34° 31.

In prosecuting this expedition, it was discovered that frequent salines or salt licks existed there. They learned that in the surrounding country, and in the spaces lying far towards the north and west, the rivers Washita, Arkansa, and the Red river, were too brackish to be potable in dry seasons. Salt springs, and plains incrusted with salt are reported to be interspersed through those regions. On the Washita they saw swans and alligators. About the lat. 38° the line of demarkation between Orleans and Lousiana, the long moss or tillandsia almost suddenly ceases, being found no further to the northward; and about the same place the osiers, which grow on the banks of the river, cease, and show themselves further on to the southward.

The party proceeded no further than the Hot Springs. These are six in number. They are situated about six miles from the main stream to the north-west, as it there runs, and a little above the great rapids. Their heat is too great for the hand to bear; the highest temperature is about 150°. The water, on cooling, is palatable, and very good to drink, having but little foreign impregnation. The body of the mountain from which it issues is silicious, partly flint and partly free-stone; but the superficial parts, which have been overflowed by the effusions from the springs, are incrusted with a stratum of calcareous matter, that, in the course of time, has been deposited from their water. A trifling portion of iron is contained in it too, and precipitated with the lime. In the hot water of these springs a green plant vegetated, which seemed to be a species of the *conferva* growing in such situations; probably the *fontinalis*. But what is more remarkable, a bivalve testaceous animal adhered to the plant, and lived in such a high temperature too. Here they discovered a kind of wild cabbage, which they cooked, and found to be mild and good for food. Between the Hot Springs and the place where the voyagers landed, are several licks and oozings of salt water. They relate their surprise at beholding plants, shrubs, and trees at the outlet of the springs, absolutely growing and appearing healthy, while their roots were exposed to a heat of 130°.

The coldness of the weather was very remarkable. On the 30th of Dec. the quicksilver sunk to 9°; on the 2d of Jan. 1805 to 6°. On this latter occasion, when the temperature of the atmosphere was 6°, and of the river water 32°, a condensed vapor floated over its surface, as is usual in such cases. On January 11th, the mercury in the air was at 11°, and in the Washita water at 39°. On the 12th, the atmosphere was at 20°, and the river at 40°. In those cases of unequal temperatures much watery vapor hovered over the stream. The observers relate, that although 20° of difference are more than enough to make this exhalation appear visible, yet that 13° of variation are not enough for the purpose. Approximating thereby to Dr. Mitchell's experiments made at New York in December, 1801, and published in Med. Rep. Hexade i. vol. iv. p. 309.

Above the alluvial country, the rocks were chiefly of a sort of schistus, some of it aluminous, and all of it unfit for covering houses; a kind of silicious composition, resembling oil-stone, or turkey-stone, but too brittle for gun flints; and a sort of sandy aggregate, which seemed as if it might be employed for grindstones. The mineralized and carbonated wood was found in several places. There were no certain indications of the proper fossil coal: nor did they meet with any strata of gypsum. And, notwithstanding the heat of the springs, they met with no lava, pumice, or other volcanic matter.

Having in the course of the voyage, collected in addition to what has been related, considerable information about the Caddaux, the Osages, and the other nations of Indians which sometimes frequent the Washita and the *little* Missouri, which runs into it; having acquired a good deal of knowledge about the immense prairies, which are compared to Paridises, lying towards the sources of the Red river and the Arkansas, and having made many astronomical, geological, and meteorological observations from day to day, the adventurers, with their crew of soldiers, got back to Natchez near the end of January, 1805.

From the journal of survey which they kept with all possible correctness, a map of Washita has been compiled at Washington, by Mr. Nicholas King, and engraved in Philadelphia, by Mr. William Kneass. This is a substantial addition to American geography.

This country was colonized early by the French. They projected and began extensive settlements on the Washita; but the general massacre planned and executed in part by the Indians against the French, and the consequent massacre of the Natchez tribe by the French, put an end to these undertakings, and they were never resumed under the French government.

"The *prairies* of this region are described as plains or savannas, without timber, generally very fertile, producing an exuberance of strong, thick, and coarse herbage. When a piece of ground is once got into this state in an Indian country, it can have no opportunity of reproducing timber; it being an invariable rule to fire the dry grass in the fall or winter, to obtain the advantage of attracting game when the young tender grass begins to spring. Thus the young timber is destroyed; and annually the *prairie* encroaches upon the woodland. It is probable that the immense plains known to exist in America may owe their origin to this practice. The plains of the Washita lie chiefly on the east side, and being generally formed like those of the Mississippi, sloping from the banks of the river towards the great river, they are more or less liable to the influence of inundation in the rear. This has been known to advance so far in certain great floods, as to be ready to pour over the margin into the Washita. Such an occurrence has however become very rare, and it may be generally estimated that from one-fourth of a mile to a whole mile in depth, will remain exempt from inundation during the high floods."

Fishes are not plentiful in the Washita. In the year 1799, the waters of the Mississippi, during an inundation, dammed up the Washita by regurgitation, to such a degree, that they swelled considerably above Fort Miro. The stagnation and corruption of the water from this cause, destroyed all the fishes in that part of the river; and they have been scarce ever since. The bois d'arc (bow-wood,) or yellow dye wood, is sometimes seen near the Washita. It bears a gold coloured fruit as large as the egg of the ostrich; its deep green foliage resembles that of the orange tree; and no forest-tree can compare with it for ornamental grandeur.

About three hundred miles above Nachitoches on the Red river, the navigation is opposed by a very serious obstacle. This is the raft, or natural covering which conceals the whole river for about seventeen leagues, and, is continually augmenting by the drift-wood brought down with every considerable freshet.— This bridge, which was for a time nothing but floating trees, &c. supports at this time a growth of every thing growing in the neighboring forest, not excepting trees of a considerable size. And the river may be frequently passed without any knowledge

of its existence, so perfectly is it concealed by the superincum-
bent mass of materials. It is reported that the water is working for itself a new passage through the neighboring low
grounds.

## CONCORD—ARKANSAS—ST. CHARLES—ST. ANDREW, &c.

THERE is no other settlement on the Mississippi, except the
small one called Concord, opposite to the Natchez, till you come
to the Arkansas river, whose mouth is two hundred and fifty
leagues above New Orleans.

Here there are but a few families, who are more attached to
the Indian trade (by which chiefly they live) than to cultivation.
There is no settlement from this place to New Madrid, which is
itself inconsiderable. Ascending the river you come to Cape
Girardeau, St. Genevieve and St. Louis, where, though the inhabitants are numerous, they raise little for exportation, and
content themselves with trading with the Indians, and working
a few lead mines. This country is very fertile, especially on
the banks of the Missouri, where there have been formed two
settlements, called St. Charles and St. Andrew, mostly by emigrants from Kentucky. The peltry procured on the Illinois is
the best sent to the Atlantic market: and the quantity is very
considerable. Lead is to be had with ease, and in such quantities as to supply all Europe, if the population were sufficient to
work the numerous mines to be found within two or three feet
from the surface in various parts of the country. The settlements about the Illinois were first made by the Canadians, and
their inhabitants still resemble them in their aversion to labor,
and love of a wandering life. They contain but few negroes,
compared to the number of whites; and it may be taken for a general rule, that in proportion to the distance from the capital,
the number of blacks diminish below that of the whites; the former abounding most on the rich plantations in its vicinity.

## GENERAL DESCRIPTION OF UPPER LOUISIANA.

WHEN compared with the Indiana territory, the face of the
country in Upper Louisiana is rather more broken, though the
soil is equally fertile. It is a fact not to be contested, that the
west side of the river possesses some advantages, not generally
incident to those regions. It is elevated and healthy, and well
watered with a variety of large rapid streams, calculated for
mills and other water works  From Cape Girardeau, above the
mouth of the Ohio, to the Missouri, the land on the east side of
the Mississippi is low and flat, and occasionally exposed to inundations; that on the Louisiana side, contiguous to the river,
is generally much higher, and in many places very rocky on the
shore. Some of the heights exhibit a scene truly picturesque.

They raise to a height of at least three hundred feet faced with perpendicular *lime and free-stone*, carved into various shapes and figures by the hand of nature, and afford the appearance of a multitude of antique towers. From the tops of these elevations, the land gradually slopes back from the river, without gravel or rock, and is covered with valuable timber. It may be said with truth that, for fertility of soil, no part of the world exceeds the borders of the Mississippi ; the land yields an abundance of all the necessaries of life, and almost spontaneously ; very little labor being required in the cultivation of the earth. That part of Upper Louisiana, which borders on North Mexico, is one immense *prairie ;* it produces nothing but grass ; it is filled with buffalo, deer, and other kinds of game; the land is represented as too rich for the growth of forest trees.

It is pretended that Upper Louisiana contains in its bowels many silver and copper mines, and various specimens of both are exhibited. Several trials have been made to ascertain the fact; but the want of skill in the artists has hitherto left the business undecided.

The salt works are also pretty numerous : some belong to individuals; others to the public. They already yield an abundant supply for the consumption of the country ; and if properly managed, might become an article of more general exportation. The usual price per bushel is 150 cents in *cash* at the works. This price will be still lower as soon as the manufacture of the salt is assumed by government, or patronised by men who have large capitals to employ in the business. One extraordinary fact relative to salt must not be omitted. There exists about 1000 miles up the Missouri, and not far from that river, *a Salt Mountain !* The existence of such a mountain might well be questioned, were it not for the testimony of several respectable and enterprising traders, who have visited it, and who have exhibited several bushels of the salt to the curiosity of the people of St. Louis, where some of it still remains. A specimen of the same salt has been sent to Marietta. This mountain is said to be 180 miles long, and 45 in width, composed of solid rock salt, without any trees, or even shrubs on it. Salt springs are very numerous beneath the surface of this mountain, and they flow through the fissures and cavities of it. Caves of saltpetre are found in Upper Louisiana, though at some distance from the settlements. Four men on a trading voyage, lately discovered one several hundred miles up the Missouri.— They spent five or six weeks in the manufacturing of this article, and returned to St. Louis with 400 weight of it. It proved to be good and they sold it for a high price.

The Geography of the Mississippi and Missouri, and their contiguity for a great length of way, are but little known. The traders assert, that 100 miles above their junction, a man may walk from one to the other in a day: and it is also asserted, that 700 miles still higher up, the portage may be crossed in four or five days. This portage is frequented by traders, who carry on a considerable trade with some of the Missouri Indians. Their general route is through Green Bay, which is an arm of lake Michigan; they then pass into a small lake connected with it, and which communicates with the Fox river; they then cross over a short portage into the Ouisconsing river, which unites with the Mississippi some distance below the falls of St. Anthony. It is also said, that the traders communicate with the Mississippi above these falls, through lake Superior—but their trade in that quarter is much less considerable.

## CANAL OF CARONDELET.

BEHIND New Orleans is a canal about $1\frac{1}{2}$ mile long, which communicates with a creek called the Bayou St. Jean, flowing into lake Ponchartrain. At the mouth of it, about $2\frac{1}{2}$ leagues from the city, is a small fort called St. Jean, which commands the entrance from the lake. By this creek the communication is kept up through the lake and the rivulets to Mobile and the settlements in West Florida Craft drawing from 6 to 8 feet water can navigate the mouth of the creek, but except in particular swells of the lake cannot pass the bar without being lightened.

## ST BERNARDO.

ON the east side of the Mississippi, about five leagues below New Orleans, and at the head of the English Bend, is a settlement known by the names of the Poblacion de St. Bernardo, or the Terre aux Bœuf, extending on both sides of a creek or drain whose head is contiguous to the Mississippi, and which flowing eastward, after a course of 18 leagues, and dividing itself into two branches, falls into the sea, and lake Borgne. This settlement consists of two parishes; almost all the inhabitants of which are Spaniards from the Canaries, who content themselves with raising fowls, corn and garden stuff for the market at New Orleans. The lands cannot be cultivated to any great distance from the banks of the creek, on account of the vicinity of the marsh behind them, but the place is susceptible of great improvement, and of affording another communication to small craft of from eight to ten feet draught between the sea and the Mississippi.

## SETTLEMENTS BELOW THE ENGLISH TURN.

AT the distance of 15 leagues below New Orleans, the settlements on both banks of the river are of but small account. Between these and the fort of Placquemines, the country is overflowed in the spring, and in many places is incapable of cultivation at any time, being a morass almost impassable for man and beast. This small tongue of land extends considerably into the sea, which is visible on both sides of the Mississippi from a ship's mast.

## COUNTRY FROM PLACQUEMINES TO THE SEA, AND EF-
## FECT OF THE HURRICANES.

Placquemines to the sea is 12 or 13 leagues. The country is low and swampy, chiefly covered with reeds, having little or no timber, and no settlement whatever. It may be necessary to mention here that the whole lower part of the country from the English Turn, downwards, is subject to overflowing in hurricanes, either by the recoiling of the river, or reflux from the sea on each side, and on more than one occasion it has been covered from the depth of from 2 to 10 feet, according to the descent of the river, whereby many lives were lost, horses and cattle swept away, and a scene of destruction laid. The last calamity of this kind happened in 1794, but fortunately they are not frequent.—In the preceding year the engineer who superintended the erection of the fort, Placquemines, was drowned in his own house near the fort, and the workmen and garrison escaped only by taking refuge on an elevated spot in the fort, on which there were, notwithstanding, 2 or 3 feet water.—These hurricanes have generally been felt in the month of August : their greatest, lasts for about 12 hours. They commence in the south-east, veer about to all point of the compass, are felt most severely below, and seldom extend more than a few leagues above New Orleans. In their whole course they are marked with desolation. Until that of 1795, there had been none felt from the year 1780.

## PASSES, OR MOUTHS OF THE MISSISSIPPI.

About 8 leagues below Placquemines, the Mississippi divides itself into three channels which are called the Passes of the river, viz. the East, South and West Passes. Their course is from five to six leagues to the sea. The space between is a marsh with little or no timber on it ; but from its situation, it may hereafter be rendered of importance. The East pass, which is on the left hand going down the river, is divided into two branches about two leagues below, viz. the pass a la Louvre and that known to mariners by the name of the Belize, at which there is a small block house and some huts of the pilots who reside only here. The first of these secondary channels contains at present but 8 feet water ; the latter from 14 to 16, according to the seasons.— The South pass, which is directly in front of the Mississippi, has always been considered as entirely choked up, but has 10 feet water. The S. W pass, which is on the right, is the longest and narrowest of all the passes, and a few years ago had 18 feet water, and was that by which the large ships entered and sailed from the Mississippi. It has now but 8 feet water, and will probably remain so for some time. In speaking of the quantity of water in the passes, it must be understood of what is on the bar of each pass; for immediately after passing the bar, which is very narrow, there are from 5 to 7 fathoms at all seasons.

### COUNTRY EAST OF LAKE PONCHARTRAIN.

The country on the east side of lake Ponchartrain to Mobile, and including the whole extent between the American line, the Mississippi above New Orleans, and the lakes, (with the exception of a tract of about thirty miles on the Mississippi, and as much square, contiguous to the line and comprehending the waters of Thompson's creek, Bayou Sara and Amet) is a poor thin soil, overgrown with pine, and contains no good land whatever, unless on the banks of a few small rivers. It would however afford abundant supplies of pitch, tar, and pine lumber, and would feed large herds of cattle.

### CULTIVATION OF SUGAR.

The sugar cane may be cultivated between the river Iberville and the city on both sides of the river, and as far back as the swamps. Below the city however the lands decline so rapidly that beyond 15 miles the land is not well adapted to it. Above the Iberville the cane would be affected by the cold and its produce therefore be uncertain. Within these limits the best planters admit that one quarter of the cultivated land of any considerable plantation may be planted in cane, one quarter left in pasture, and the remainig half employed for provisions, &c. and a reserve for a change of crops. One Pausin Arpent of 180 feet square may be expected to produce on an average 1200 weight of sugar, and 50 gallons of rum.

From the above data, admitting both sides the river are planted for 90 miles in extent, and about ¾ of a mile in depth, it will result that the annual product may amount in round numbers to 25,000 hogsheads of sugar, with 12,000 puncheons of rum. Enterprising young planters say that one-third, or even one half of the arable land might be planted in cane. It may also be remarked that a regular supply of provisions from above at a moderate price would enable the planter to give his attention to a greater body of land cultivated with cane. The whole of these lands, as may be supposed, are granted; but in the Atacapas country there is undoubtedly a portion, parallel to the sea-coast, fit for the culture of the sugar cane. These vacant lands are to be found, but the portion is at present unknown

In the above remarks the lands at Terre aux Bœuf, on the Fourche, Bayou, St. Jean, and other inlets of the Mississippi, south of the latitude supposed to divide those which are fit, from those which are unfit, for the cultivation of the cane, have been entirely kept out of view. Including these, and taking one-third instead of one-fourth of the lands fit for sugar, the product of of the whole would be fifty thousand, instead of twenty-five thousand hogsheads of sugar.

## SUGARS EXPORTED.

The following quantities of sugar, brown, clayed and refined, have been imported into the United States from Louisiana and the Floridas, viz.

| In | 1799 | . | . | 773,542lbs. |
|----|------|---|---|-------------|
|    | 1800 | . | . | 1,560,865   |
|    | 1801 | . | . | 967,619     |
|    | 1802 | . | . | 1,576,933   |

## IMPORTS AND EXPORTS.

The productions of Louisiana are—sugar, cotton, indigo, rice furs and peltry; lumber, tar, pitch, lead, flour, horses, and cattle. Population alone is wanting to multiply them to an astonishing degree. The soil is fertile, the climate salubrious, and the of communication between most parts of the province certain, and by water.

| | | |
|---|---|---|
| 20,000 bales of cotton, 3 cwt. each, at 20 cts. per lb. | $ 1,344,000 | Increasing. |
| 45,000 casks sugars, 10 cwt. each, at 6 cts. per lb. | $ 302,400 | do. |
| 800 do. molasses, 1000 gallons each. | $ 32,000 | do. |
| Indigo, | $ 100,000 | Diminishing rapidly |
| Peltry, | $ 200,000 | |
| Lumber, | $ 80,000 | |
| Lead, corn, horses, cattle, | uncertain | |
| All other articles suppose | $ 100,000 | |
| Total | $ 2,158,000 | |

According to the official returns in the treasury of the United States, there were imported into our territory from Louisiana and the Floridas, merchandise to the following amounts, in the several years prefixed :

| In | 1799 to the value of | $ 507,132 |
|----|----------------------|-----------|
|    | 1800                 | 904,322   |
|    | 1801                 | 956'635   |
|    | 1802                 | 1,006,214 |

*Descriptive Observations on certain parts of the Country in Louisiana; by Anthony Soulard, esq. Surveyor-general of Upper Louisiana, in a letter to J. A. Chevallié, esq. of Richmond. Translated from the French Manuscript by Dr. Mitchill.*

Med. Rep.

THE Missouri, whose sources are still unkown, is, however, already classed amongst the largest rivers. It is an object of astonishment to every body. The uninstructed man admires the rapidity of its stream, its extraordinary length, the salubrity of its waters, and their uncommon color. The experienced traveller is astonished at the riches seattered along its banks, and, looking into futurity, beholds this rival of the Nile passing through countries as fruitful, as populous, and more extensive than those of Egypt.

The best informed observer can give but an imperfect idea of the riches accumulated on its shores. This note can only point out some of the principal.—Happily for our own time, an expedition is now going on under the auspices of an enlightened government, to explore this river to its sources. What gratitude is due from the whole world to those persons who expose themselves to the greatest fatigues, and even to the greatest dangers, to enlarge the circle of human knowledge in thus bringing, as it were, a new world to our view.

The Missouri unites with the Mississippi about five leagues above the town of St. Louis, in about the 40th degree of N. lat. And it must be remembered that after this junction, it runs about 1200 miles before it falls into the gulf of Mexico. But as this part of its course is well known, I shall confine myself to the Missouri alone.

I have ascended this river about 600 leagues, without perceiving any diminution of its breadth or velocity.

The principal streams which fall into the Missouri, as you ascend it are the Gasconade, the Osage, the two Charatons, the Grand river, the river of the Plains, the Nichinan, the Batoney, the Great and Little Nimahas, the Platte, the Sioux, the Running Water, and others.

For 25 leagues above its junction with the Mississippi, there are different settlements of American familes, especially at Bonhomme, Femmeosage, &c. beyond these the banks are inhabited by savages only. The great and Little Osages, settled at 120 leagues on the waters called by their respective names, the the Cams, the Otto's, the Panis, the Loups, or Panis Mahas, Mahas, the Pincas, the Ricaras, the Mandans, and the Sioux.— The latter tribe has no fixed habitation on the Missouri, but visit it regularly for the purpose of hunting.

The borders of the Missouri are alternately forests and prairies or cleared plains. The higher we go up this river, the more common are the prairies; and they seem to enlarge every year, in consequence of the fires which overrun them in autumn. These fires are kindled by the Indians or the white hunters, sometimes by accident, and at others for the purpose of favoring their hunting.

The water of the Missouri is turbid, and deposits a sediment of very fine sand, which readily falls to the bottom. This admixture, which renders it unpleasant to the sight, diminishes not in the least its wholesomeness. Experience has proved it to be more salubrious than that of the Ohio and the upper Mississippi.

The rivers and streams that empty into the Missouri below the Platte, are clear and limpid; but above that river they are as turbid as the Missouri itself. This muddiness is caused by the sandy banks or hills of white earth through which they run. The bed of the Missouri is interrupted by shoals, sometimes of sand, and sometimes of gravel, which frequently change place, and consequently always render the navigation uncertain. Its general course is north, a quarter north-west.

To give a precise idea of the incalculable riches scattered along the sides of the Missouri, would require unlimited knowledge. The low bottoms are covered with huge trees, especially the poplar and cotton trees, large enough for first rate canoes; the sugar maple; the red and black walnut, so useful to joiners; the red and white elm; the three-thorned acacia, of which impenetrable hedges may be made; the osier; the red and black mulberry; the lime-tree, and the horse-chesnut; all of which are very plentiful. Red and white oak, fit for vessels, and all other sorts of timber, pine, and on the Stony mountains, cedar, are common productions.

I find it impossible to enumerate all the trees which are yet unknown in other countries, and with whose uses and qualities we are as yet unacquainted. The smaller plants are still more numerous; I, however, touch that article superficially for want of sufficient botanical information. The Indians know the virtues of many of them. Some are used to heal wounds, others to poison arrows; some again for dyeing colors; and they employ certain vegetable simples to cure radically and promptly the venereal disease. They conceal from us, with great care, a plant which renders them for some instants insensible of the most vehement fire. I have seen them take hold of red hot irons and burning coals without suffering any inconvenience.

The lands in the neighborhood of the Missouri are excellent, and when cultivated are capable of yielding all the productions of the temperate climates, and even some of the hot ones; such as wheat, maize, and every kind of grain; common and sweet potatoes; hemp, which seems to be an indigenous vegetable; even cotton succeeds there, though not so well as further south;

and the raising of it answers a good purpose for the families already settled on the river, for from a field of about two acres of this they can obtain a crop sufficient to clothe a family.—— The natural prairies are a great resource for them. These afford excellent pasture, and require but little labor to clear them. After one year's exertion, a man may enjoy his fields duly prepared for crops. Brick and potter's earths are very common, and the true Chinese Kaolin is reported, by good judges, to be there, that substance to which porcelain owes its peculiar fineness. And there exists on the borders of this grand river, salt springs enough to furnish salt for the country when it shall be inhabited, and a great deal to spare.

Saltpetre is found very abundantly in numberless caverns near the Missouri. The rocks are generally calcareous; though there is one which is peculiar to this river. It is of a blood-red color, compact, yielding to a tool, hardening in the air, and receiving the neatest polish. The natives make their pipes of it. The strata are so extensive that there is any quantity that may be wanted for other purposes. There are also quarries of marble, but we know as yet little more than its color, which is veined red. It is said there is a body of gypsum there; and this would not be difficult to explore. Volcanic productions are also found there, evincing the existence of burning mountains in former times, or in situations now unknown.

The short stay as usually made among the savage nations has hitherto been unfavorable to the acquirement of correct information concerning the mines and ores near the Missouri; we know with certainty of none other than those of iron, lead and coal: but from the accounts given by the Indians, there can be no doubt that tin, copper, and silver, are found in those parts; and particles of gold are said to have been picked up on the surface of the earth, and in the bottom of brooks.

The productions of the Missouri at this time are received from the Indians and the hunters, in exchange for goods and merchandise, and may be exhibited in the following table.

## MISSOURI PRODUCE.

| | | | | |
|---|---|---|---|---|
| Beaver . . . . . | 12,281lbs. at | $ 1 20 | $ | 14,737 00 |
| Fox skins . . . . | 802 | .. 0 50 | .. | 401 00 |
| Bear skins, black, grey, yellow and brown | 2,541 | .. 2 00 | .. | 5,082 00 |
| Cow skins . . . . | 189 | .. 1 50 | .. | 283 50 |
| Deer skins in the hair | 6.381 | .. 0 50 | .. | 3,190 50 |
| Bears' grease . . . | 2,310 galls. | 1 20 | .. | 2,572 00 |
| Otter skins . . . . | 1,267 lbs. | 4 00 | .. | 5,068 00 |
| Raccoon skins . . . | 4,248 | .. 0 25 | .. | 1,062 00 |
| Bison hides or robes . | 1,714 | .. 3 00 | .. | 5,142 00 |
| Dressed deer skins . | 96,926 | .. 0 40 | .. | 38,770 40 |
| Tallow and fat . . . | 8,313 | .. 0 20 | .. | 1,662 60 |

$ 77,971 00

This table, which is made as correct as possible on an average of fifteen years, thus gives an amount of 77,971 dollars, without mentioning musquashes and martins. Calculating at the same rate, the value of goods carried up the Missouri, and exchanged for this peltry, would be 61,250 dollars, reckoning the charges to amount to a quarter part of the worth of the articles. From this it follows, that the trade affords an annual profit of 16,721 dollars, or about a profit of 27 per cent.

If the Missouri trade, badly regulated, and without encouragement, gives annually such a profit, there can be no doubt of its increase, if encouraged by government. It must be observed, that the price fixed in the preceding table is that current at the Illinois. If the London price was taken, deducting freight and charges, the profit would appear much greater. If the Missouri, left to the savages, and having but a single branch of trade, affords such great returns, in proportion to the capital employed in it, what might we not expect from individuals or companies with large funds, aided by a numerous population, and devoting themselves to other sorts of traffic. Some of these, I am bold to say, may be undertaken with a certainty of success, when we consider the riches afforded by its banks, and of which, in this note, I have endeavoured to sketch an outline.

*Dated at St. Louis, of the Illinois, March 1805.*

---

## ABRIDGEMENT OF LEWIS AND CLARK'S EXPEDITION.

BEFORE the cession of Louisiana to the United States, this was the region of fable. Fancy peopled it, and a thousand miraculous tales were related. The mammoth, that wonder of the creation, it was thought, might be there, and Welsh Indians, with remnants of the Jewish tribes. The ancient maps represented the Missouri as an inconsiderable river, rising at no great distance from the Mississippi, and running nearly parallel with that river, until it discharges itself: and a country extending to the west for a distance unknown. The British establishments on the lakes, in a short time after their commencement, ascertained that this was not the case; they frequently went across to the Missouri at its north bend, but found themselves a long way from its source. No one had ever ventured far beyond the Mandan villages. By the voyage of M'Kensie it was satisfactorily ascertained that the Missouri took its rise in the great Rocky mountains.

All the tract claimed by the United States, between the Mississippi and the Pacific ocean, remained unknown. We were unacquainted with its animal and vegetable productions. Shortly after the cession, it was of course deemed necessary by an active and enterprising government, that these regions should be explored. Accordingly captains Merriwether Lewis and William Clark, with a chosen band, were despatched across the continent, by the way of the Missouri; and lieutenant Pike, first to find the source of the Mississippi, and afterwards to explore the Arkansas and Red rivers, and the southern part of this immense tract. Journals of the travels and voyages of these gentlemen have been promised to the world; and they have been long expected with impatience.* Their discoveries have been highly important both as to the geography, and the natural history of America; and in a political point of view of considerable moment.

I will endeavor to give a brief narrative of the expedition of Lewis and Clark, as far as I am able to collect from the best information.

They began to ascend the Missouri on the 14th May, 1804.— The whole party was forty-three in number, persons in every respect adapted to the occasion. Every thing necessary for their security and comfort, as well as whatever was believed conducive to the assistance or advantage of the enterprise, had been provided with great care and caution. They proceeded on their voyage up a part of the river that was considerably frequented, and was not unknown The French and some American traders had ascended to trade with the Osages, and a number of other nations higher up, as far as the Sioux, and some even as far as the Mandans. Without meeting with any occurrence of importance, the party after passing through a fine country, arrived on the 27th July at the mouth of the Platte or Shallow river, which comes in from the south, and is three quarters of a mile wide at its mouth. Hunters were sent out at this place to announce the change of government to several tribes of Indians who inhabit this river, the Panis, the Otto's and the Loups. Not being able at this time to find any of the natives, they continued their voyage a few days, to a place in lat. 41° 17', where the hunters brought in some Indians. A council was held, and the place called Council Bluffs. The Indians were pleased with the change of government, and still more with the trinkets that were given them. Three Otto's and the same number of Missouri's were made chiefs by giving them a medal,† suspended to a riband. The next Indians they met in

---

* Both of these have appeared since this sketch was made from Gass's Journal. That of Lewis and Clark is one of the most interesting ever published in America. Since this, H. M. Brackenridge, esq. has published his Journal of a Voyage up the Missouri, as far as the Mandans.

† In imitation, perhaps, of the star and garter, of some barbarians in Europe. The taste of uncivilized nations must be con-

the course of their voyage, were about sixty in number of the
Sioux nation. Five of these were presented with medals, and
their chief persuaded to go to the Federal city. When they arrived at the main body of this party, consisting of about eighty
lodges, and eight hundred or a thousand souls, they were received with much kindness. Captains Lewis and Clark were by
turns, carried by them to their council lodge, in buffalo robes.
They killed a dog, according to the Indian custom, to feast on;
and entertained their guests by their dance and song. Although
they manifested considerable friendship, some disagreeable occurrence took place. Many of them appeared disposed to pil-
fer. At one time when capt. Clark was about returning to the
boat, they surrounded and attempted to detain him. With
presence of mind taking advantage of their superstitious fears,
he told them that there was more medicine‡ on board his boat
than would kill twenty such nations, upon which they desisted.
This was, however, before their arrival at the lodges; and the
Indians who made this attempt, alledged by way of excuse, that
they only wished them to stop there, that their women and children might get a sight of the boat. When about to push off,
several of them attempted to detain the boat by taking hold of
the cable, notwithstanding some of the chiefs were on board.—
Capt. Lewis was near ordering his men to fire; this act
might have put an end to the expedition. Some of the chiefs
went on shore, talked to them, and they finally agreed for a little tobacco to be civil. These were part of a wandering tribe,
on whom little faith could be placed; they had been in the habit of attempting to detain the traders amongst them by force;
and it was only by assailing their fears that safety could be expected. The party continued their voyage, through a country
of a different appearance from that which they had left; vast
prairies stretched forth on either side of the river, with hardly
a stick of timber, excepting the willow and the cotton wood, on
the bottoms. Sometimes the river washed the base of high
bluffs or banks of a dark color, composed of earth, crumbling
like sugar. It is remarkable, that on the tops of these, many
singular petrifactions were found of vegetable and animal kinds,
while none were to be seen in the plains. The skeleton of an
enormous fish 45 feet in length, was found, upon the top of one

---

sulted. Whether we had a right to make constitutions and or-
dain these chiefs, I will not say. If we are the true successors
of the Pope, then there can be no doubt. But policy certainly
required that every measure should be taken to conciliate the
good will of these people. The method was harmless to say
the most of it; and indeed, the medals were generally given to
the chiefs of the nations when they could be found. This was
no more than recognizing their authority.

‡ Some drug, supposed to have magic power.

of these hills. In other places, trees completely stone were seen, and many other curiosities. But nature seemed disposed to make amends for the steril appearance of the country. It was stored with vast quantities of game; the buffalo, the deer, and the elk, and many animals not common elsewhere; such as the goat or antelope, in flocks of sixty or an hundred; the blaireaux or badgers; the prairie dog, a singular quadruped, resembling a common domestic dog of a small size, and living in towns or burrows.

After traversing the territory of the Sioux, who occupy nearly eight hundred miles on the Missouri, the party arrived at the villages of the Ricara's. A stationary people, who have considerable agriculture, and raise for their sustenance and trade, Indian corn, beans, peas, pumpkins, simlins and tobacco. They were treated with much kindness, and liberally presented with these articles. Leaving these people they continued their voyage, and on the 27th September arrived at the Mandan villages, more than 1600 miles from the mouth of the Missouri. The season being advanced, the party concluded to winter here.— This nation has the character of being the most civil on the Missouri. They resemble the Ricara's in being stationary and agricultural; but in some traits they differ from most of the Indian nations. Their skin is whiter, and we are informed that fair hair is not unusual amongst them. Their manners are like those of other Indians, with but little variation. There is this affinity in all the Indian nations of North America, perhaps of all savages, superstition is the predominate quality; the invariable attendant of ignorance. In their treatment of the dead they differ from others; instead of burial, they are wrapped in buffalo robes, and placed upon a scaffold. A similar method was formerly practised amongst the nations of the Mississippi, but it has for some time been disused. On this scaffold are placed the offerings of those who wish to manifest their respect or friendship to the deceased; which is estimated according to the value of the article offered. Some have been known to fasten a horse to this scaffold, and permit the poor animal to remain until it perished; in order that the deceased might be able to pursue the buffalo in the other world on horse back.

Our adventurers sat off again in the spring, having sent back their batteaux, loaded with various articles, and many curiosities which had been procured in the course of the expedition.— They proceeded two hundred and seventy-eight miles, to the Yellow stone river. The country from the Mandans was not so level. Some hills rose to a vast height; and it was ascertained beyond any doubt, that many of them were volcanic. The pumice stone was strewed around in great abundance, the smell of sulphur in places still strong, and smoke was seen issuing from the earth. Many of the hills were even washed bare of soil and herbage by the rains, and looked like vast heaps of clay. This must contribute to the muddiness of the Missouri. A curious reflection that the soil on which New Orleans is built, may have been brought two thousand miles down this river! In the neighborhood of the Yellow-stone river, the lands are exceedingly fine. On the Missouri there are frequently rich bottoms, but with great scarcity of timber. The party had now got into a region, which no whiteman that we know of, had passed through. After passing this river, they found a country steril and barren, and procured with difficulty a sufficiency of wood to cook with. Game however was abundant. The mountain sheep, an animal that is probably a non-descript, was now first seen. It is called the ibex, from the affinity which it is said to have to that animal. The white bear, a fierce and enormous beast of prey, began to be frequent. The size is at least twice that of the common brown bear: and instead of flying from man will openly attack him. The Indians declare that many of their best warriors have fallen victims to his fury. They are said to thirst for human blood; the men were frequently pursued by them, and several times narrowly escaped. It was now remarked that the waters of the Missouri became more clear; a number of very considerable rivers emptying in from the south had been passed, and which were all observed to be of the same turbid color of the Missouri. At the junction of a considerable stream with the Missouri, called the Maria river, the party was at a stand which to take. After examining both, the northern one was chosen. At the mouth of the Maria, they concealed their large periogue, and the greater part of the baggage. On the 16th June they arrived at the falls of the Missouri. With much difficulty and labor they transported their canoes and baggage over a portage of eighteen miles. These falls in the course of seventeen miles have a descent of 362 feet; the first great pitch is 98 feet, the second 19, the third 47, the fourth 26, besides several smaller ones. This is the first great interruption in the navigation of this astonishing river, for two thousand five hundred miles. Sand bars, sawyers and rapidity of current opposed considerable difficulties; but in spite of these they were able to ascend on an average fifteen or twenty miles per day. But it must be observed that the channel of this river is in general amazingly crooked. In many places, after ascending for twenty or thirty miles, they found themselves within sight of a former encampment. The iron boat invented for this occasion was now unpacked; buffalo skins were procured to cover it. It was launched into the water, and called the Experiment. But the Experiment would not do, it leaked so much in spite of every exertion, that it was thought adviseable to leave it behind.

Above this place the Missouri was found more smooth and gentle, and beautified by many handsome islands. The country became mountainous. Immense peaks of solid rock of a dark brown color, rose to the hight of a thousand or twelve hundred feet. Mountain sheep were seen on the very tops of them, though their sides were almost perpendicular. As they advanc-

ed, these mountains in some degree subsided, and were well
timbered with pine, cedar and fir; but nothing grew in the val-
leys except short grass and some willows. This was probably
a spur of the great Rocky mountains. About the latter end of
July the party arrived at the three forks of the Missouri. Here
they encamped some time, and having explored for a considerable distance the three branches, they resolved to pursue the
northern, and which was called Jefferson river, as the west was
called Gallatin and the southern Maddison. After proceeding
through a desolate, barren and mountainous country, and ascending with great difficulty a shallow and rapid stream, they
were met on the 17th August by capt. Lewis, accompanied by
about twenty of the Snake Indians, with horses. The capt. had
crossed the mountains, to the waters of the Columbia, about
forty miles distant. It was resolved to leave the canoes at this
place, and horses being procured from the Indians they continued their course up the north branch of Jefferson river, and in
about twenty-five miles, arrived at the very head or source of
this river and of the Missouri. The same day they crossed the
dividing ridge, little more than a mile to one of the sources of
the Columbia. Here they were met by two Indians apparently
much rejoiced to see them. These people instead of shaking
hands as a token of friendship, have a singular custom of throwing their arms round the neck of the person whom they salute.
Pursuing their journey across the mountains, they came to a
village of the Snake Indians on a branch of the Columbia. Having procured some horses here, proceeded down the south side
of the stream, but soon found it impracticable from the vast
precipices that every where presented themselves, and were
compelled to turn back. By the advice of the Indians they
crossed to the north side, and again pursued their journey.—
During two or three weeks they continued to clamber over precipices, and travel across snow topt mountains, worse if possible than the Alps, until they became almost exhausted with
fatigue and hunger; their provisions were exhausted and game
was extremely scarce. The portable soup was thought of, and
accordingly issued to the men as provisions. But it had the
same effect as Don Quixot's balsam. The men preferred killing
one or two of their horses, and subsisting on that flesh. At
length, however, with much joy, they reached the termination
of these vast mountains; and arrived at a considerable branch
of the Columbia, called the Koos-koos-ke. Here they found Indians of the Flat-head nation, they appeared an inoffensive,
harmless people, like the Snake Indians, and lived miserably;
a few roots and berries manufactured into a kind of bread, and
the fish caught in these rivers, which are in the season in great
abundance, particularly the salmon, constitute their usual diet.
This nation had beads and other articles which they said were
procured from white people at the mouth of the river. They
frequently cross the mountains to hunt the buffalo, there being

no game on their side of any account. It is a singular circumstance, there was found in their possession several fleeces of the common sheep, or at least resembling it very much. Whether the animal from which this was taken, can be found in that quarter or not, is uncertain. The fleeces might have been brought from New Spain. After presenting medals to some of the chiefs of this nation, the party provided themselves with canoes, and once more consigned themselves to the water.

For several hundred miles they passed through a country of high prairie land, with scarcely any timber, and but little game ; the chief dependence for provisions was on the natives, whose lodges were to be seen every ten or twelve miles on the river, and who were always inoffensive and obliging. After entering the Columbia they proceeded until they came to the rapids, where the face of the country began to change and become more mountainous. It is the first range from the sea shore, and which confines the river for several hundred miles, between it and the Rocky mountains, preventing the Columbia from discharging itself into the sea. After passing this range, a better timbered country was found, and a soil of a better kind, though by no means of an excellent quality. The timber was chiefly fir, pine and spruce ; on the bottoms. cotton wood, maple and ash : a great proportion of the country, however, is prairie. There were several different nations, generally of a more hostile and thievish disposition than those the party had left.

On the 15th Nov. 1805, our adventurers, with much satisfaction, entered the bay into which the Columbia discharges itself, and at length, in 46° 19′ N. lat. came in sight of the Pacific ocean.

The enterprise having been thus far satisfactorily completed, the party wintered at this place, subsisting principally upon the elk, which abounded and was almost the only kind of game to be found. In the spring the party measured back their steps to the Rocky mountains, encountering more difficulties and hardships, if possible, than at first. On ascending the Columbia, a large river of 500 yards wide, which on their descending had been hid by an island, was discovered making in from the south. Having all passed the mountains in safety, they separated at the head of the Missouri, in order to explore that part of the country. Captain Lewis had a skirmish with an Indian nation, in which he killed one of them, and another was killed by one of his men : he therefore found it necessary to hasten to the place of rendezvous, sooner than it was intended. Having united the parties, they descended the river to the Mandan nation, and here prevailed on one of the principal chiefs, She-he-keh and his family, to accompany them. After an absence of two years and four months, they arrived on the 26th of Sept. 1806, at St. Louis, to the great satisfaction of their fellow citizens, who had begun to entertain serious apprehensions for their safety.

## A GEOGRAPHICAL AND STATISTICAL SKETCH OF THE
### DISTRICT OF MOBILE.

## SITUATION.

That tract of country which we have denominated the District of Mobile, is situated in the eastern part of the Mississippi territory, and comprehends the county of Washington on the Mobile* and its tributary streams and the new county of Madison in the great bend of the Tennessee.

The District of Mobile, as laid off for the purpose of collecting duties on imports and tonnage, comprehends the shores, waters and inlets of the bay and river Mobile and others emptying into the gulph of Mexico west of the Mobile to the Pascagola inclusive. That tract of country which we have here denominated the district of Mobile lies between the 31st and 35th degrees of North latitude, and according to the maps, between about the 7th and 12th degrees of longitude west from the city of Washington.

## BOUNDARIES.

This district is bounded on the North by the Tennessee state line, on the west by the Pearl river, and a line† running due north from its source to the Tennessee line; on the south by the boundary line between the United States and Florida, and on the east by the Chatahouchee river, as far as the mouth of the Uchee, and from thence by a direct line to Nickajack on the Tennessee river, and by that river itself, from Nickajack, up as far as the southern boundary of the state of Tennessee.

## EXTENT.

From Mr. Ellicott's survey of the national boundary at the 31st degree of north latitude, it appears that Pearl river the western limits of this district, is 106 miles from the Mississippi, and that from Pearl river to the Mobile river it is 100 miles, and from thence to the Chatahouchee the western limit of Georgia 175 miles—making the whole extent of the district on the boundary line 275 miles. It appears in like manner from a map lodged in the war office by captain E. P. Gaines, that from the upper end of the Muscle Shoals to the Tennessee river due south to the national boundary it is 262½ miles, which after adding the

---

* So called by the French, probably on account of the uncertainty of its freshes. Mobille instead of Mobile, is a name very lately introduced, probably from inadvertency.

† The proclamation establishing the county of Washington, made the territorial boundaries upon North, East and South, and Pearl river on the West, the limits of that country. The northern territorial boundary at that time crossed Pearl river: but the territory has since been extended so as to throw its northern limit above the source of Pearl river.

distance from the Muscle Shoals to the Tennessee state line, will make the whole length of the district of Mobile about 280 miles.

So that this district, the existence of which is scarcely known to the American people, probably contains a greater number of square miles, than the important states of Pennsylvania or New York. However as a great proportion of it is claimed by the Indians, that part to which the Indian title has been extinguished, and which is partially settled by the citizens of the U. States, approaches nearer to the extent of Maryland, New Jersey or Connecticut.

The United States have the absolute right of soil and jurisdiction from the Pearl river to the Creek line, but a few miles east of the eastern channel of the Mobile. The northern boundary between the land of the United States in this district, and the Choctaws, is where it crosses Pearl river, 52 miles north of the national boundary, but the eastern termination, on the dividing ridge, between the waters of Tombigby and Alabama, will probably be found (for the commissioners are now engaged in running it) to be considerably farther north from the Spanish line.

## SOIL.

The Soil of this district varies considerably in different parts of it. For the first 40 miles above the national boundary, the good land is, generally speaking, confined to the low grounds, of the larger water courses. The swamps, as they are called, of Pearl river, of the Estobacha and Chichasawhae, forks of the Pascagola, of the Mobile river, and of the Tombigby and Alabama, forks of the Mobile, are extensive, rich, and productive. The higher parts of the swamps are thickly covered with amazingly large and lofty cane, and the growth of timber, is cotton wood, gum, oak, bay, laurel and magnolia. The lower swamp lands have no cane, but a magnificent growth of cypress is intermixed with other timber. The highest part of the swamp, is generally nearest the river. There are no levees or embankments, as on the Mississippi, and the floods which occur in a greater or a less degree every year evidently increase the fertility of the land.— The breadth of our river bottoms or swamps, varies very considerably. Probably they are for the most part from 1 mile to 3 miles wide, but more frequently less than 2 miles than more than that width.

Below the division, indeed, of the Mobile river, between Fort Stoddard and the line, the whole of the river swamps, including that of its three channels, is from eight to ten miles wide; and the same may be said of the land lying in the forks of the Alabama and Tombigby, for the space of a few miles above their junction.

The other lands through this large extent of country, are generally open pine woods, affording good range for cattle, immense supplies of lumber, pitch, tar, and turpentine, but whilst unmanured, affording no encouragement to tillage.

The same general observations which are here made, as to the country forty miles above the national boundary line, will apply to the country below the line; except that where you approach within 20 or 25 miles of the sea shore, the pine lands, instead of being deversified by hill and dale, as they are above, become a dead uninteresting flat, a great part of which is in the rainy season covered with water, so as to render it unpleasant, though not impracticable to travel through it.

At a greater distance than 40 miles from the national boundary, as you proceed northward, the face of the country and the natural soil considerably changes. Large bodies of fertile land, are then found at a considerable distance from the Tombigby river, and instead of the long-leafed pine alone, you behold a diversified and luxuriant growth of white oak, black oak, gum, magnolia, hickory, walnut, cherry, and poplar. And the same observations hold good, not only as to the land west of the Tombigby, but likewise with regard to the land lying on the forks of that river and of the Alabama. Not, however, that in either place there are compact bodies of such rich lands, extending over a country of a great many miles in circuit, as in Kentucky and the state of Ohio; but there are several parcels of such land sufficiently large to support respectable settlements.

As to that part of the district which lies in the great bend of Tennessee, and forms the new county of Madison, the writer of this article can speak with no precision about it. The country however, in the Great Bend, has been uniformly represented, as containing a fine body of land of excellent quality, and the rapid formation of an extensive settlement there, as soon as the Indian title was extinguished, established the truth of this representation. The land is said to be rich, but very broken.—The water courses all afford good land: and so indeed do the hills, but they are frequently too steep to admit of cultivation.

## PRODUCE.

The actual produce of this country consists principally of Indian corn, and cotton. The river low lands, where not too wet, are probably as well adapted to the cultivation of those articles, as any land in America; and it is a circumstance very favorable to the opinion that the Sea-island cotton would flourish well in the lower part of this country, that the green-seed cotton has a perpetual tendency to change into the smooth black-seed cotton, whereas in situations not favorable to the cultivation of the latter, it is said that it regularly degenerates into the former.— The pine lands also, with the assistance of manure, provided the soil be sufficiently tenacious to hold it, will afford tolerable crops of corn and cotton; but no such assistance is necessary in the oak and hickory lands above, and much less on those rich bodies of land, which in a state of nature produce walnut, poplar and cherry. Some wheat, rye and oats for family consumption, are likewise raised in the good uplands; but wheat is by no means a certain or important crop. Small quantities of rice are cultivated in the river swamps; and there can be no doubt, but that there are many thousands of acres, very advantageously situated as to tide water, and at present useless, which might be profitably devoted to the production of that article.

Indigo, it is probable, would likewise be worthy of attention. Whether sugar cane would answer in the lower part of the district, has not yet been subjected to experiment.

It is said not to admit of cultivation in so high a latitude of the Mississippi; but it is probable that the influence which the nearer position of the sea has upon the climate of the country on the Mobile, would justify the cultivation of the sugar cane on that river, in a latitude in which, on the Mississippi, it would be attended with no advantage.

Tar, pitch, turpentine and lumber, will no doubt become objects of great magnitude in this country, when a deliverance from Spanish oppression shall give free scope to the exertions of its inhabitants. The pine timber which grows here is remarkably magnificent, and it is esteemed to be the best kind of pitch pine. It is so abundant, and stands so close on the ground, that in the space of 3 or 4 acres you will frequently find straight logs of 70 to 80 feet in length, sufficient in number to build a large log house. Saw mills, therefore, will become a valuable article of property, and there is no country probably in which the streams of water are more permanent. We have no meadows, no artificial pastures, no timothy, no blue grass, no clover; we have but little fruit; apples are scarcely known; peaches are scarce, and yet both appear to flourish well, where attention has been paid to the cultivation.

## CLIMATE.

The climate of the Mobile country is unquestionably highly favorable. The winters are mild, and the summers, though longer, not materially hotter than they are several degrees further to the northward. The direct heat of the sun is no doubt very great in the summer, and very unpleasant to strangers; but those who are accustomed to it, whether negroes or white men, appear to work under its powerful influence, without any material inconvenience; the heat is seldom oppressive within doors, and the nights are more comfortable than they are even in Virginia. We have but little ice and rarely any snow. A few flakes fell, but none in the lower part of the settlement made any appearance on the ground during the last winter. The cattle, so far from wanting any winter supplies, from the industry of summer, will not in general eat either hay or corn; nor do they require any salt. Indian corn may frequently be planted with success early in March; but it will come to maturity though not planted till the middle of July. In the spring,

water of this country near the 31st deg. Fahrenheit's thermometer, stands at 69 deg. which agrees with the mean annual temperature in the same latitude as ascertained by the ingenious Mr. Kirwan. He sets it down for the standard situation, the Atlantic ocean, at 69 deg. 9 min. The following extracts from a thermometrical register, kept in the years 1807 and 1808, near Fort Stoddard, will give the most accurate idea of the vicissitudes of our seasons. Those observations shall be selected which were made in the warmest time of the day, and at 10 or 11 o'clock at night; and the hottest and coldest days in every month shall be noticed. The thermometer being completely in the shade, unless the contrary be particularly mentioned.

On the 15th April, 1807, being the hottest day in the m nth, the thermometer stood early in the afternoon at 82 deg, and at 71 deg at night.

On the 2d April, being the coldest day. at 52 deg. at two o'clock.

On the 17th May, the hottest day, it stood at 90 and 80 deg. On the 2d May, the coldest day, it stood at 66 and 61 deg. On the 6th June, the hottest day, it stood at 90 and 82 deg. On the 28th June, the coldest day, it stood at 82 and 69 deg. On the 10th July, the hottest day, it stood at 94 and 78 deg. On the 29th July, the coldest day, it stood at 74 and 65 deg.

The result of twenty-three observations in this month, taken in the hottest part of so many days, gives 86 deg. as the mean heat.

The only observation made in August was on the 2d, when the thermometer was at 88 deg. at 4 in the afternoon.

On the 5th of Sept. the hottest day in the month, it stood at 95 and 80 deg.

On the 8th, the coldest day, (36 hours of rain having intervened since the 5th) it stood at 74 deg. only at 3 in the afternoon.

The mean temperature of this month in the hottest part of the day, calculated from 22 observations, was 84 deg.

In Jan. 1808, (for the register of the intermediate months is mislaid) it was at 55 deg. on the 8th at noon, at 61 deg. on the 9th, at 3 in the afternoon, at 56 deg. on the 21st at 2 P. M. and at 60 deg. at 10 P M rain having intervened

On the 24th it was at 34 deg. at 8 A. M. at 52 deg. at 2 P. M. and at 76 deg. in the sun, and at 34 at 10 P M.

On the 12th Feb. the warmest day in the month, it stood at 79 and 62 deg.

On the 8th, the coldest day, at 56 and 43 deg

On the 29th in the sun, at 2 P M. it stood at 99 deg it was then 71 in the shade.

On the 28th day of March, the warmest day in the month, it stood at 86 deg. at 3 P M.

On the 21st, the coldest day, it stood at 63 and 55 deg.

To the bulk of readers these details will afford no satisfaction; but to others they will be highly interesting, and will communicate a much more accurate idea of the climate than the more amusing descriptions which might be written under the dictate of corporal sensation. The progress of the spring may probably be gathered from the following memorandum: April 2d, the trees in the swamps in leaf; peach blossoms gone; green peas just in bloom. April 12th, peas (planted in Feb.) in pod; peaches the size of a hazel nut. Fig trees in leaf. May 2d, green pease at table, which were planted in February. Strawberries ripe. May 16, mulberries, blackberries, dewberries and whortle berries ripe. May 13, cucumbers large and in perfection. We have no glasses or hot beds to force vegetation.—June 29th, roasting ears at table. Lettuces and cabbage, though the latter do not head well, stand out very well all the winter.

In point of health, this climate is favorable, or otherwise, according to local circumstances. The prevailing diseases, are those of the class of cachexy, and the fevers usually termed bilious. Where our powerful southern sun brings the swamp miasmata into action, diseases seem to follow of course, and none but negroes well accustomed to the climate, can safely take up their residence in the low ground, on the banks of our rivers. That grade of fevers however, which is termed the yellow fever, does not seem to have made its appearance here; the high lands are probably as healthful as any so far to the south, and it is usual for those who cultivate the swamps, to have their residence in the pine woods, at some distance from their plantations.

## STOCK.

Almost the only stock of the country on the Mobile and its waters, are horned cattle, hogs and horses. The stocks of horned cattle are numerous. Many of the inhabitants have from 500 to 1000 head. The only expense attending them, is that of keeping them together, driving them off to a distance from the settlements in the fall, visiting them occasionally in the winter, to prevent the depredations of the Indians, and collecting them in the spring at their respective cow-pens. The cows, however, do not generally have calves more than once in two years, and the milk they give, is far less in quantity than is given by cows in more northern countries. This is owing probably in part to the heat of the climate, and partly to the persecutions of the numerous swarms of flies, that perpetually torment them. They are rarely milked in the winter, as they are then kept at a distance from the habitations of their owners. The usual price of a cow and calf is 12 dollars, and of beef, from 3 to 3½ per hundred weight. Hogs are easily raised—In favorable seasons they fatten in the woods; but if they are not fed occasionally, they are very prone to go wild. The price of pork is generally 6 dollars per hundred weight. The enemies of the hogs and calves are the wolf and panther, and pigs are frequently destroyed by the wild cat and the alligator. Horses are not numerous. There is a sufficient quantity to answer the purpose of the inhabitants—but they are seldom raised for sale. A small breed of Indian horses seem the most hardy and best adapted to the climate—but the fine horses imported from the northern states, appear peculiarly liable to be affected by diseases similar to those which most frequently attack the human species. Sheep are scarcely known. There are not probably one hundred head among all the settlers in the county of Washington. The few, however, which are kept, are healthy and thriving; but the wool is generally coarse, and some of them have a tendency to be hairy.

## POPULATION.

The number of inhabitants in the county of Washington, amounts to about 5,000. The population of the county did not probably exceed 2,000—but the emigrations from Georgia and other states have recently been very considerable as to numbers, though not as to wealth. In the county of Madison it is said there are several thousands.

## STATE OF SOCIETY AND IMPROVEMENTS.

The people are considerably dispersed, and have enjoyed but few opportunities for mental improvement. We have no colleges—no permanent schools—no regular places of worship—no literary institutions—no towns; no good houses, and but few comfortable ones.

Not many of our plantations exhibit any appearance of neatness, and the greatest part of our cotton is raised in open fields, in the river swamps, without even a fence to protect it. There are no manufactures carried on, except some small ones of cotton in the household way. There are few mechanics, and scarcely any professional men but lawyers. This disheartening prospect originated partly, perhaps, in the negligence of the inhabitants, but still more probably in other causes. The country long languished under the Spanish government. After the Americans obtained possession of it, the titles to land were for some years unsettled. But what has more than all retarded the prosperity of the district, is its insulated situation, and its political connexion with the Mississippi territory. Our neighbors on every side are Indians or Spaniards. We naturally catch the spirit and manners. We have heretofore been too small to form a distinct political community : and our being hung on to a territory, the seat of whose government and population is so remote from us, augmented the contemptibleness of our natural situation; and discouraged the approach of men, whose wealth and energies are necessary to make a country thrive. The rivers of this country, not extending as the Mississippi does, through populous settlements of civilized men, bring no visitants to our district, and the attention of emigrants by land, who have any money to spend, is naturally fixed on that part of the southern country which has some political consideration, which is more likely than ours to engross the care and the power of the local government, and to enjoy a representation in the national legislature. Hence this country, from its first settlement, has received but a small accession of agricultural or domestic improvement, of learning, or of taste.

## TRADE.

The people of this district usually dispose of their beef, pork, and corn, to the Spanish subjects in Mobile and Pensacola.—Corn usually sells at a dollar per Spanish barrel, which is at the rate of 66 cents per bushel. The cotton commonly goes to Orleans, but is compelled to stop at Mobile and pay a duty of 12 per centum ad valorem. As our population increases, our trade will assume a more respectable character. We are close to the Havanna. Thither, and to the West Indies generally, will go our provisions, our tar, pitch, turpentine and lumber. Our cotton will be transmitted direct to Europe; for vessels not drawing more then 13 or 14 feet of water, can come more easily to Fort Stoddard, six miles above the line, than they can go to New Orleans. Nor indeed will they meet with any obstruction in proceeding 40 miles farther to St. Stephens, which may be regarded as the head of our navigation for sea vessels, and at the same time the centre of our population. Above that, there is an excellent boat navigation almost to the heads of the Tombigby, the depth of water in the shallowest places, where there is a tolerable fresh, being 4 feet. Both forks of the Alabama are likewise navigable; and it is much to be lamented, that the first adventure down that stream, with the produce of Eastern Tennessee has, it is said, been stopped by a band of worthless Creek Indians, to whom the want of a super-intendant of Indian affairs in this country has long given a latitude of behaviour and a confidence in villainy, to which a speedy check is demanded by the honor of the United States, and the interests of this settlement.

## ON THE NAVIGATION OF THE OHIO.

—

*[The following just and judicious observations were addressed to the earl of Hillsborough, in the year* 1770, *when Secretary of State for the North American department.]*— Harris's Journal.

" NO part of North America will require less encouragement for the production of naval stores, and raw materials for manufacturies in Europe, and for supplying the West India islands with lumber, provisions, &c. than the country of the Ohio; and for the following reasons :

" 1st. The lands are excellent, the climate temperate ; the native grapes, silk-worms, and mulberry trees, abound every where; hemp, hops, and rye, grow spontaneously in the vallies and low lands ; lead and iron are plenty in the hills ; salt springs are innumerable ; and no soil is better adapted to the culture of tobacco, flax, and cotton, than that of the Ohio.

" 2nd. The country is well watered by several navigable rivers, communicating with each other ;—by which, and a short land carriage, the produce of the lands of the Ohio can, even now (in the year 1772,) be sent cheaper to the sea port town of Alexandria, on the Potomac river in Virginia (where the troops of General Braddock landed,) than any kind of merchandise is sent from Northampton to London.

" 3d. The river Ohio is, at all seasons of the year, navigable with large boats, like the west-country barges, rowed only by four or five men ; and from the month of February to April large ships may be built on the Ohio, and sent to sea, laden with hemp, iron, flax, silk, tobacco, cotton, pot-ash, &c.

" 4th. Flour, corn, beef, ship plank, and other useful articles, can be sent down the stream of the Ohio to West Florida, and from thence to the West-India islands, much cheaper and in better order, than from New York or Philadelphia to those islands.

" 5th. Hemp, tobacco, iron, and such bulky articles, may also be sent down the stream of the Ohio to the sea, at least 50 per cent. cheaper than these articles were ever carried by land carriage, of only sixty miles, in Pennsylvania ; where wagonnage is cheaper than in any other part of North America.

" 6th. The expense of transporting European manufactures from the sea to the Ohio, will not be so much as is now paid, and must ever be paid, to a great part of the countries of Pennsylvania, Virginia, and Maryland. Whenever the farmers or merchants of the Ohio, shall properly understand the business of transportation, they will build schooners, sloops, &c. on the Ohio, suitable for the West India or European markets : or by having black walnut, cherry tree, oak, &c. properly sawed for foreign markets, and formed into rafts in the manner that is now done by the settlers near the upper parts of the Delaware in Pennsylvania, and thereon stow their hemp, iron, tobacco, &c. and proceed with them to New Orleans.

" It may not perhaps, be amiss to observe, that large quantities of flour are made in the distant (western) counties of Pennsylvania, and sent by an expensive land carriage to the city of Philadelphia, and from thence shipped to South Carolina, and to East and West Florida, there being little or no wheat raised in those provinces.

"The river Ohio seems kindly designed by nature, as the channel through which the two Floridas may be supplied with flour ; not only for their common consumption, but also for the carrying on an extensive commerce with Jamaica, and the Spanish settlements on the bay of Mexico. Millstones in abundance are to be obtained in the hills near the Ohio ; and the country is every where well watered with large and constant springs and streams for grist and other mills.

" The passage from Philadelphia to Pensacola is seldom made in less than a month, and sixty shillings per ton, freight, (consisting of sixteen barrels,) is usually paid for flour, &c. thither. Boats carrying 800 or 1000 barrels of flour may go in about the same time from Pittsburgh as from Philadelphia to Pensacola, and for half the above freight ; the Ohio merchants would be able to deliver flour, &c. there in much better order than from Philadelphia, and without incurring the damage and delay of the sea, aud charges of insurance, &c. as from thence to Pensacola.

" This is not mere speculation ; for it is a fact, that about the year 1746, there was a great scarcity of provisions at New Orleans ; and the French settlements at the Illinois, small as they then were, sent thither in one winter upwards of eight hundred thousand weight of flour."

———

The list of road presented here was received from Mr. Seelye and recommended by him as the best and nearest route for the trader returning by land.

| | | | |
|---|---|---|---|
| Wharton's to Marlow's | 15 | Smith's | 14 |
| Brumfield's | 5 | Riser's | 10 |
| Spel's | 20 | Zadok Beshoe's | 15 |
| Bond's | 10 | Roads's | 17 |
| Basling's | 10 | Westly Frayhorn's | 7 |
| M'Grain's | 4 | Fisher's | 6 |
| Taylor's | 4 | Boshier's | |
| Norman's | 3 | where Natchez road intersects with this | 12 |
| Partman's | 4 | | |
| Bristoe's | 3 | | 159 |

## COMMERCE OF THE OHIO.

—

*We have been obligingly favoured with a transcript from the books of Messrs. Nelson, Wade, and Greatsinger, for two months, viz. Nov. 24, 1810, to Jan. 24, 1811, 197 flat, and 14 keel boats, descended the falls of Ohio.*

| | |
|---|---|
| 18,611 bls. flour | 59 do. soap |
| 520 do. pork | 300 do. feathers |
| 2,373 do. whiskey | 400 do. hemp |
| 3,759 do. apples | 1,484 do. thread |
| 1,085 do. cider | 154,000 do. rope yarn |
| 721 do. do. royal | 681,900 do. pork in bulk |
| 43 do. do. wine | 20,784 do. bale rope |
| 323 do. peach brandy | 27,700 yds. bagging |
| 46 do. cherry bounce | 4,619 do. tow cloth |
| 17 do. vinegar | 479 coils tarred rope |
| 143 do. porter | 500 bushels oats |
| 62 do. beans | 1,700 do. corn |
| 67 do. onions | 216 do. potatoes |
| 20 do. ginseng | 817 hams venison |
| 200 gross bottled porter | 4,609 do. bacon |
| 260 galls. Seneca oil | 14,390 tame fowls |
| 15,216 lbs. butter | 155 horses |
| 180 do. tallow | 286 slaves |
| 64,750 do. lard | 18,000 feet cherry plank |
| 6,300 do. beef | 279,300 do. pine do. |
| 4,433 do. cheese | |

### ALSO,

A large quantity of potter's ware, ironmongery, cabinet work, shoes, boots, and saddlery—The amount of which could not be correctly ascertained.

☞ Taken from the Pilot's books, at Louisville, Ken. this 8th Feb. 1811. By JAS. M'CRUM.

*FINIS.*